CONSTRUCTING LIVES AT MISSION SAN FRANCISCO

Constructing Lives at Mission San Francisco

NATIVE CALIFORNIANS AND
HISPANIC COLONISTS, 1776–1821

QUINCY D. NEWELL

UNIVERSITY OF NEW MEXICO PRESS ⚜ ALBUQUERQUE

© 2009 by the University of New Mexico Press
All rights reserved. Published 2009
Printed in the United States of America

First paperbound printing, 2011
Paperbound ISBN: 978-0-8263-4707-7

15 14 13 12 11   1 2 3 4 5

Library of Congress Cataloging-in-Publication Data

Newell, Quincy D., 1975–
Constructing lives at Mission San Francisco : native Californians and Hispanic colonists, 1776–1821 / Quincy D. Newell.
    p. cm.
Includes bibliographical references and index.
ISBN 978-0-8263-4706-0 (cloth : alk. paper)
1. San Francisco de Asís Mission (San Francisco, Calif.)—History.
2. Indians of North America—Missions—California—San Francisco Bay Area.
3. Indians of North America—Cultural assimilation—California—San Francisco Bay Area.
4. Indians of North America—California—San Francisco Bay Area—Social life and customs.
5. Indians of North America—California—San Francisco Bay Area—Religion.
6. Franciscans—California—San Francisco Bay Area—History.
I. Title.
E78.C15N44 2009
979.4'6—dc22
                    2009017761

DESIGN AND LAYOUT: MELISSA TANDYSH
Composed in 10/14 ScalaOT Regular
Display type is ScalaOT Regular

*In loving memory of John "Jake" Waddell Brownlie III,
October 23, 1945–January 9, 2007*

CONTENTS

Illustrations	viii
Acknowledgments	ix
INTRODUCTION	1
CHAPTER 1: Going to Church	21
CHAPTER 2: Building Faith	49
CHAPTER 3: Forming Families	82
CHAPTER 4: Love and Marriage	109
CHAPTER 5: Ties That Bind	125
CHAPTER 6: The Varieties of Religious Experience at Mission San Francisco	151
CONCLUSION: Uichase's Story	177
Notes	191
Bibliography	229
Index	253

ILLUSTRATIONS

MAPS

1. The Franciscan missions, Spanish military presidios, and civilian settlements of Alta California	8
2. Linguistic regions of the San Francisco Bay Area	13
3. Tribal communities and villages of the San Francisco Bay Area	171

FIGURES

1. Pismote's family	22
2. Keqecég's family	84
3. Huetlícs's family	134
4. Guonis's and Alajuta's family	138
5. Uichase's and Ygnacia Barbara's family	140
6. Lachi's family	174
7. Uichase's family	178

ILLUSTRATIONS

1. Louis Choris, *Jeu des habitans de Californie*	29
2. Georg H. von Langsdorff, *Gegenstände von New-Californien und Norfolk-Sound*	35
3. Mission San Francisco church interior	36
4. Edward S. Curtis, *Baskets in the Painted Cave—Yokuts*	63
5. Mission San Francisco church wall	64
6. Mission San Miguel Arcángel reredos	159

ACKNOWLEDGMENTS

☙ Many people have contributed to the genesis and completion of this book. I cannot thank all of them here, but I can at least acknowledge some of them. Matt Stewart kept me in my first Religious Studies class, helping me connect with my first mentor, David Wills. My graduate school classmates—especially Nora Rubel, Katie Lofton, and Jill DeTemple—made the experience both challenging and rewarding. Laurie F. Maffly-Kipp guided this project from its very beginning, and Mike Green added invaluable advice and insight. Peter Kaufman and Roberto Lint Sagarena read the text critically and provided immense encouragement. Jill DeTemple, Miranda Hassett, Celeste Gagnon, and Marsha Michie were perhaps my most careful and generous readers, kick-starting stalled chapters and sharing plenty of laughter along the way.

In Laramie, Val Pexton, Andromeda Hartwick, and Kris DeForest read and responded to several portions of the manuscript—and they became good friends as well. Emily Hind provided valuable assistance with difficult translation questions. Melissa Thompson made sure I ate well and got outside; Elizabeth Traver was (and remains) a good friend and indefatigable source of encouragement. Erin Emme answered random questions about Catholicism and provided endless entertainment by e-mail, all the while cheering the book on to completion.

Several colleagues at other institutions proved themselves invaluable conversation partners, adding a crucial tidbit of information here and a useful reaction there. Barb Voss was especially generous with her time, knowledge, and support; Eric Blind, Bob Senkewicz, Rose Marie Beebe, and Randall Dean were also quite helpful. Randall Milliken shared his database constructed from the San Francisco mission registers. Theda Perdue helped me navigate the world of academic publishing.

This book received significant institutional support as well. The University of North Carolina's Religious Studies Department provided a travel grant that allowed me to conduct the initial research at the Santa Barbara Mission Archive Library; Amherst College granted me a fellowship that gave me a full year to work on the manuscript; and the University of Wyoming provided a Basic Research Grant that allowed me to go to the Archivo General de la Nación in Mexico City. The staffs of all of these archives, as well as of the Bancroft Library, Davis and Wilson Libraries at the University of North Carolina at Chapel Hill, Charles von der Ahe Library at Loyola Marymount University, Peabody Library at Johns Hopkins University, and Coe Library at the University of Wyoming, were immensely helpful. Mina Suk made me welcome in Baltimore; Skip and Judy McGinty gave me a place to stay while researching at the Bancroft Library; Gerardo and Paula Gurza helped me feel at home in Mexico City. Brother Guire Cleary, the curator of Mission Dolores when I started this project, gave me a thorough tour of the old church and its grounds. He graciously shared his knowledge of and love for the mission with me. Andy Galvan, who succeeded Brother Guire, continued that support, answering questions promptly and thoroughly.

Chapter 6 of this book was originally published in somewhat different form as "The Varieties of Religious Experience: Baptized Indians at Mission San Francisco de Asís, 1776–1821" in the *American Indian Quarterly* 32, no. 4 (Fall 2008). I thank the University of Nebraska Press for permission to use this material.

Through all the ups and downs of this project, my family has supported me unfailingly. John and Cheryl Dawson and Kara Newell read an early draft of the manuscript; although I did not respond to all of their comments and questions, I greatly appreciated their careful readings. My parents, Robert and Melinda Newell, in addition to doing all the wonderful and necessary things that good parents do, read and responded to multiple drafts; my brother, Eli Newell, made sure that I laughed from time to time.

Introduction

༄ **17 March 1786.** Keqecég, the leader of a Ssalson Indian village south of Mission San Francisco, and Attiom, his junior wife, stand in the church, waiting to be married by the priest. They have already married each other before, outside the mission, but if they go through this ceremony, they will be allowed to live together at the mission. Keqecég has just been baptized; with a few exceptions, the rest of his family has already undergone the ceremony. Kegecég's senior wife, Sappím, has not been baptized; she was not pleased when Keqecég told her of his decision to send the family to be baptized at the mission.

Father Pedro Benito Cambón notes the marriage in the mission register, using the couple's baptismal names:

> 117   Marcial and Candida   Indians
> *In this Mission of Our Father Saint Francis on the seventeenth of March, 1786, having just been baptized in the Church, Marcial, Adult Indian number 517, and Candida baptized number 515, who in their Gentile state had been his second wife. The first did not wish to be baptized, and ceded the right that she could have had, with the assurance*

that because her husband had become a Christian, she did not want to cohabit anymore with him. ([Marcial] married Candida in front of me.) Diego Olvera, Luis, Eustachio, and others who attended the ceremony were witnesses; and on the following day 18 [March], they were veiled, and I blessed them with the ceremonies, and Holy Mass, etc.[1]

3 January 1799. Father Ramón Abella hands the two-day-old infant to Malany'eum, the godmother. The baby, whom Abella has just named Macario, is still wet from the baptismal font. The child's father, Alajuta, watches the proceedings. He is married to Malany'eum's sister, Guonis. If Guonis should die now, Macario will still have his aunt to care for him, just as if Alajuta had married both sisters.

Later, Father Abella records the event:

1976 Macario Child
The third day of January, 1799, in the Church of this Mission of Our Father Saint Francis, I solemnly baptized a Boy, who was born on the first day of January of said year, the legitimate son of the Neophytes Guillermo and Sinforosa; I gave him the name Macario. His Godmother was the Neophyte Micaelina, whom I informed of the spiritual relationship [created], and the other obligations.[2]

7 November 1813. Juniqueme and his wife Guallec return to Mission San Francisco from visiting their home village. Guallec's hair has been cut short, and her face is smeared with pitch and ashes. Their son Ynocencio, born three summers ago on another journey to the village, has died.

In the mission's death register, Father Juan Sainz de Lucio makes a note of the child's passing:

3396 Ynocencio Child
We have been informed with certainty that the following have passed away in the woods. . . . Ynocencio, child, baptismal entry 4409. His parents were traveling.[3]

These scenes are partially the result of reading between the lines of Mission San Francisco's marriage, baptism, and burial registers and partially the product of extrapolation from anthropological and historical data. The mission registers were written by Spanish priests who were unfamiliar with San Francisco Bay Area Indian cultures and often unable to speak the languages of the people to whom they attempted to minister. However, read carefully, the mission registers reveal the resourcefulness and flexibility that Bay Area Indians displayed as they responded to the Franciscans' missionary efforts and constructed their lives in and around the missions, adapting to the transformations that Spanish colonialism wrought in Alta California's physical and social environment.[4]

The baptismal, marriage, and death registers from which these scenes come are three of six books that the priests were required to keep at Mission San Francisco. They also kept a register of confirmations; a book called the *padrón*, in which all of the baptized Indians were listed; and a *libro de patentes*, in which the missionaries transcribed royal decrees, pastoral letters, and the circular letters they received from their superiors.[5] In addition, the priests kept an account book, in which they tracked the mission's income and expenditures. Most of these records are extant, though they are not all complete. The baptism, marriage, and death registers, however, are almost entirely complete for the years 1776–1821, the period I discuss in this book.[6]

These handwritten registers are now kept in a safe at Mission San Francisco de Asís (or, as it is now more commonly known, Mission Dolores). They are large, leather-bound books with tattered pages, an occasional ink stain blotting out the priest's writing, and periodic entries recording their inspection by the *padre presidente*, the head of the mission system. These registers and their counterparts from other missions have long been used as sources for demographic analysis of the mission era.[7] More recently, scholars have begun to mine the individual and family stories concealed between the covers.[8]

These individual stories are relatively easy to recover because of the way the priests structured the registers. In all three books, the priests numbered each individual entry. They used these numbers for cross-referencing between entries. For example, when Keqecég and Attiom married, the priest identified them in the marriage record by both their baptismal names, Marcial and Candida, and their baptismal numbers, 517 and 515. When Attiom died, her death entry again included her baptismal number, linking the records together. The number assigned to an individual's baptismal entry thus became an identification number, and it enables us to track the lives of individual Indians at Mission San Francisco. The priests' record keeping was far from flawless, but the vast majority of the baptism, marriage, and death entries contain enough information that scholars have been able to find and correct the priests' clerical errors.[9]

Each time an Indian accepted baptism at Mission San Francisco, the officiating priest recorded her or his new Spanish baptismal name. In many cases, the priest also wrote down her or his Indian name. Wherever possible, I use these Indian names to refer to individual Indians. To aid the reader, I also provide the person's baptismal name in the endnotes. The priests' records occasionally refer to Indians using both their Indian and their baptismal names. For example, the priest who baptized Jobócate and her little sister in 1800 listed the girls' parents as "Demetrio Juniase" and "Atanasia Uyumate," almost as if the adults' Indian names were surnames.[10] These double names suggest that baptized Indians continued using their Indian names, to the extent that even the priests learned and used those names. When the priests did not record a baptismal candidate's Indian name (as was often the case during mass baptisms and in the baptisms of infants and young children, who frequently had not yet received names), I use the baptismal name only. The names I use here—personal names as well as names of villages and tribal communities—are the priests' approximations of Indian pronunciations, and thus already a few steps removed from what the Bay Area Indians called themselves, their villages, and their polities. Nevertheless, they are closer to those Indians' identities than are the names that the Franciscans imposed on them.

The registers contain far more than simply names and numbers: a typical baptismal entry includes the person's Indian and Christian names; baptism number; names, or at least baptismal numbers, of any relatives who had already been baptized; village or tribal community affiliation; approximate age; parents' names and baptismal status; godparents' names; and any other unusual information, such as physical disabilities like blindness or status markers like relation to a village headman. When Father Francisco Palóu baptized Liloté, for example, he penned the following entry:

> On the ninth of July of 1777 in the Church of this Mission of Our Seraphic Father Saint Francis I solemnly Baptized a girl of about eleven years of age, Sister of Francisco Moraga the first Gentile who was baptized, known among the Gentiles by the Name of Liloté; Daughter of a Deceased Gentile Father, and of a Mother also Gentile called Huitpote who lives; I gave her the name Maria Francisca; her godmother was Francisca Xaviera Balanzuela, wife

of Sr. Gabriel Peralta, captain of the Guard of this Mission, whom I notified of the relationship and the obligation contracted, in witness whereof I sign, on stated day, month, and year.[11]

With entries like these, the registers offer the possibility of tracing life histories, family trees, and social hierarchies.

The familial and social relationships recorded in the mission registers, and individual stories traced over the entire Spanish colonial period, show that despite their move into Mission San Francisco, Bay Area Indians were able to preserve key elements of their cultures. Although the priests intended to create a completely Catholic environment at Mission San Francisco, they achieved only partial control over the baptized Indians' lives. Bay Area Indians who accepted baptism retained the ability to make crucial choices about key moments in their lives, and they combined Catholicism and indigenous religions in ways that suited their needs. While some baptized Indians adopted Catholicism wholeheartedly, many Bay Area Indians bent Catholic rituals to traditional ends, and some accepted baptism but later opted out of the beliefs and practices the priests advocated.

Franciscans began founding missions in the area the Spanish called *Alta California* (Upper California) in 1769, with Mission San Diego. The missions were part of the Spanish governmental effort to discourage Russian encroachment from the north and generally to establish a buffer zone against the advancement of other European colonial powers. As Herbert Bolton pointed out in his seminal essay, the missions were, in this sense, "frontier institutions," doing double duty as agents of both church and state.[12] The Franciscan order had dominated missionary efforts in the northern reaches of Spain's American colonies since the 1500s. In Florida, New Mexico, and Arizona, and later in Texas and California, Franciscan priests accompanied and sometimes preceded the advances of Spanish military personnel. In many of these locations the Franciscans found indigenous populations already living in towns and villages, but where they found nomadic groups, the priests attempted to persuade the Indians to become sedentary agriculturalists.[13] Even as they tried to make Indians act more like Hispanic people, however, the Franciscans attempted to shield them from actual Europeans or their descendants. The priests feared that their compatriots would exercise a baleful influence on the Indians, whom they viewed as innocent and childlike. By restricting contact between the two groups, the Franciscans hoped to preserve the Indians' purity, which seemed to guarantee the Indians' entrance into heaven.

The Alta California mission system began under the direction of Junípero Serra, a diminutive Franciscan known for his heartrending preaching abilities, his ardent and self-abnegating piety, and his missionary zeal. Serra had taught philosophy and theology in Mallorca—where he was born and raised—before coming to Mexico to serve as a missionary in 1749. He served as president of the mission system until his death in 1784, presiding over the foundations of nine missions in the region, including Mission San Francisco.[14] It is almost a commonplace among scholars to say Junípero Serra had a medieval intellectual and theological outlook, while the military officials with whom he worked were shaped by the Enlightenment.[15] The medieval Franciscans, who had evangelized much of Mexico along with other mendicant orders, were millennialists—they expected the imminent end of the world as they knew it. One prominent Franciscan writer, Gerónimo de Mendieta, saw the Indians of the New World as having been saved for evangelization until the "eleventh hour" of the world's history. Mendieta saw the Indians as the spiritual, if not the literal, descendants of the Jews and believed they were free of the Old World's corruption. Along with members of mendicant religious orders, he thought the Indians would populate the City of God when it was realized in the New World.[16] Later generations of Franciscans appear to have been less ardently millenarian—as were many of Mendieta's colleagues. Centuries of mixed success, as well as a shift away from the teachings of twelfth-century millenarian prophet Joachim of Fiore, tempered the Franciscans' millennial expectations. Nevertheless, they retained their devotion to Mary, whom they saw as both the mother of Jesus and the Lady of the Apocalypse, and they continued to view the Indians as fundamentally good until tainted by the corruption of Hispanic society.[17] The Franciscans emphasized Marian devotion in the missions, teaching baptized Indians and catechumens to sing the Salve Regina and the Alabado, both hymns that include praise directed to the Virgin.[18]

After Serra's death, his former student and later missionary companion Francisco Palóu became the acting president of the Alta California missions. Like Serra, Palóu had come from Mallorca in 1749 and served as a missionary in both the Sierra Gorda and in Baja California before the Alta California mission enterprise began in 1769. He functioned in many ways as Serra's assistant, serving as interim president of the mission system in Serra's absence, inviting individual Franciscans to work in Alta California, and sometimes assigning priests to missions. Palóu's interim presidency of the mission system that had begun with Serra's death ended with the appointment of Fermín Francisco de Lasuén to that position in 1785. During his eighteen years in the post, Lasuén presided over the founding of nine more missions. That brought the total number of missions to eighteen by 1798, where it stood at Lasuén's death in 1803. The following year saw the foundation of Mission Santa Inés; no other missions were founded until 1817, when Mission San Rafael Arcángel was created. The last mission in the chain of twenty-one that stretched along the Alta California coast, Mission San Francisco Solano, was founded in 1823, after the Spanish had lost control over the region.[19]

Mission San Francisco de Asís, named for the founder of the Franciscan order, Saint Francis of Assisi, was the sixth mission founded in the Alta California system. It was placed at the tip of the San Francisco peninsula, in the heart of what is now the Mission District of San Francisco. Several factors went into the selection of the site: the soil seemed fertile; a nearby stream provided a ready supply of fresh water; and apparently friendly Indians populated the surrounding area.[20] Fathers Francisco Palóu and Pedro Benito Cambón officially founded the mission in October 1776, though they had been in the area since June of that year.

The mission was only a few miles from the San Francisco Presidio, a Spanish military installation founded at about the same time. The presidio buildings included a chapel, where the priests stationed at Mission San Francisco said Mass for the presidio residents' benefit on holy days of obligation. In addition to attending to the religious needs of the presidio, the missionaries supplied presidio residents with food and other goods produced by Indian labor. Mixing the sacred and the secular, church and state, in this way, Mission San Francisco fit perfectly into Herbert Bolton's definition of a frontier institution.[21]

As the missionaries saw it, though, the mission's primary role was to convert the Indians in the San Francisco Bay Area. Though the mission was founded in 1776, Bay Area Indians did not begin accepting baptism until the summer of the following year. Over the next four decades, the number of Indians baptized grew steadily, eventually exceeding six thousand in 1821, when Spain lost its control over Mexico, including Alta California. The mortality rate at the mission was very high, however, so

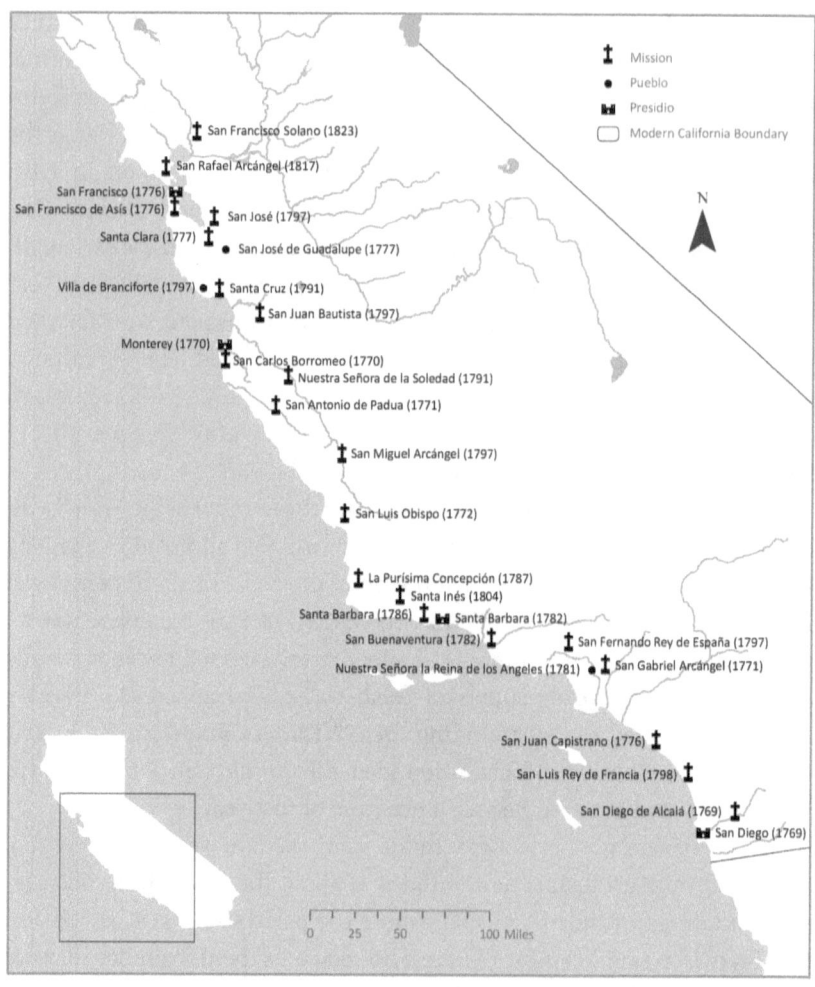

MAP 1. The Franciscan missions, Spanish military presidios, and civilian settlements of Alta California, with founding dates. Wyoming Geographic Information Science Center, 2009.

the number of baptized Indians alive at any given time was much lower: in the Spanish colonial period the population reached its largest size, 1,801, in 1821. Throughout the Spanish colonial period, deaths exceeded births among Indians baptized at the mission, so the baptized Indian population never became self-sustaining. Instead, the missionaries depended on new recruitment to perpetuate the Indian population at the mission.[22]

Each Alta California mission was supposed to be staffed by two Franciscan missionaries, together with a small detachment of Spanish soldiers and a few mission servants. At Mission San Francisco, the number of priests varied from a minimum of one to a maximum of four. Some priests stayed at the mission only a few months; others stayed fifteen to twenty years. With one exception, all of the priests had been born and raised in Spain.[23] The soldiers and mission servants, in contrast, hailed primarily from various regions of New Spain. Although most of these people referred to themselves as *gente de razón* ("people of reason") or even *españoles* (Spaniards), I use the term *Hispanic* to refer to the colonists and soldiers who settled in Alta California at the encouragement of the Spanish government. In so doing, I seek to acknowledge the fact that few, if any, of these people were born in Spain or descended solely from peninsular Spaniards. Some of the mission servants were indigenous Mexicans; most of the soldiers were of mixed European and Mexican descent. Most probably had more Mexican Indian ancestors than Spanish forebears.[24] *Hispanic* thus refers broadly to the cultural heritage and orientation of these colonists and soldiers. I use the term *Spanish* with reference to the soldiers in Alta California simply to mean that these men were in the employ of the Spanish government.

That government granted the Franciscan missionaries broad authority to act on behalf of the Indians they evangelized. In their capacity as guardians, the missionaries claimed lands around the mission, holding them in trust for the baptized Indians. Since the missionaries' land claims were never put to the test, it is unclear exactly how much land they controlled, but each mission generally received more than one hundred thousand acres.[25] At Mission San Francisco, the Franciscans used the vast tracts of land they claimed to establish several outstations for farming and ranching during the Spanish colonial period, some of them many miles from the mission itself.[26]

According to Spanish law, each mission was to exist for only ten years— just long enough to convert and Hispanicize the Indians. After that, the mission was to be "secularized": the mission church was to become a parish church staffed by secular clergy (priests not in a religious order) and the mission lands and other assets were to be distributed to the Indians, who would become ordinary tax-paying subjects of the Spanish crown. The law, which was based on Spanish missionaries' experience with dense, sedentary populations of indigenous Mexicans during the early colonial period, was ill-suited to Spain's northern frontier. In fact, none of the

Alta California missions were secularized during the Spanish colonial period. Instead, they remained Franciscan missions well into the Mexican period, only gradually succumbing to pressure from anticlerical elements in the Mexican government until the missions were finally secularized in the early 1830s. The mission lands ended up in the hands of Mexican and American ranchers, land speculators, and others, quickly turning the Indians who had lived at the missions, as well as their descendants, into landless laborers. When the United States took control of California after invading Mexico in 1846–48, relations between whites and Indians deteriorated. While white colonists had viewed California Indians as "primitive" but economically "useful" during the Spanish and Mexican periods, Anglo-American miners came to see Indians as economic competitors during the Gold Rush, leading to violent confrontations between the two groups.[27] The informal policy of "extermination" that many Anglo-American colonists advocated exacerbated the Indian population's decline due to illness and led to the murder of more than four thousand California Indians.[28] Only in the 1870s, after whites ceased to perceive California Indians as an "obstacle," did hostilities between the two groups subside.[29]

Before Spain began colonizing the area, California's resource-rich environments had supported a dense human population. According to one estimate, the Indian population of California dropped by a third—from three hundred thousand to two hundred thousand—between 1769, when the first mission was founded in Alta California, and 1821, when the Spanish government lost control of the region. The population decline in California's coastal region, where Spanish colonization was concentrated, was even more dramatic: in 1769, an estimated sixty thousand Indians lived in the area. By 1800 that number had fallen to just thirty-five thousand.[30] The San Francisco Bay Area was relatively thinly populated in comparison to other parts of California, ranging from under two to as many as six people per square mile. Even this density is high, however, for nonagricultural populations, and it attests to the wealth of food resources in the region.[31]

The San Francisco Bay Area was home to numerous small groups of Indians that anthropologists of Native California long called "tribelets." Anthropologist Alfred Kroeber coined this term to denote "groups of small size, definitely owning a restricted territory, nameless except for their tract or its best known spot, speaking usually a dialect identical with that of several of their neighbors, but wholly autonomous" and to replace the terms *village* and *village community*, which Kroeber found too vague to be useful.[32] Many descendants of colonial-era Native Californians have rejected this term as demeaning and politically detrimental, because it has been used to imply that these native groups are ineligible for federal recognition.[33] In this book, therefore, I use the term *tribal community* to refer to groups that occupied multiple villages. Each village or tribal community controlled an area of approximately ten square miles where its members fished, hunted, and gathered plant foods. Groups traded with one another for goods not available in their home territories, socialized at seasonal festivals, went to war with and against one another, and intermarried to create and reinforce intergroup alliances.[34]

Religious beliefs and practices varied from group to group, but the peoples of the San Francisco Bay Area shared a basic cosmological framework and associated assumptions about humans' position in and relationship to the natural and supernatural worlds. Origin myths featured the collaborative creation of the world and its human population by such culture heroes as Coyote and Eagle, who also imparted crucial survival skills to the first humans. The oral narratives of each group were tailored specifically to that group's land and, as one ethnohistorian has written, "served as a charter that established the group's origins and rights of ownership to a particular territory."[35] Some of these narratives identified locations and objects that held extraordinary spiritual power and therefore had to be treated with special care. Failing to ritually honor these places and objects could induce illness.[36] A variety of animals were also treated with particular respect, because they were thought to be particularly powerful. Most important among these was Eagle, who was often seen as the creator of the world, closely followed by Coyote, who was often a trickster figure. Other animals were the namesakes of lineages and may have been thought of as the mythical ancestor of those lineages: deer, bear, and other animals occupied these positions.

Religious traditions in the San Francisco Bay Area, as in the rest of Native California, grew out of shamanic traditions.[37] In the Bay Area, both men and women could become shamans. Shamans might receive their call to the profession in dreams, which functioned as a way of connecting to the supernatural world and receiving power, or through other extraordinary experiences. The shamans' main function was to conduct the rituals that maintained harmony between their people and the natural and supernatural worlds they inhabited.[38] While many of these rituals focused on the collective good, shamans also helped individuals as healers. They used various healing techniques, including singing, dancing, sucking foreign objects out of their patients' bodies, and herbal remedies.[39] Like village headmen, shamans usually wielded significant influence in their communities, in part because their spiritual power could be used for both good and evil. People therefore viewed them as a necessary but dangerous element of society. The supernatural power that shamans held, however, was available to everyone; shamans were different only because they had a greater quantity of power and a wider range of techniques for acquiring and managing it.[40]

Some groups to the north and west of the San Francisco Bay practiced a set of religions that anthropologists have come to call the Kuksu cult. Kuksu religions, according to two anthropologists, shared few activities in common and were distinguished instead by their "complexity and formalized organization."[41] Most groups that practiced Kuksu religions had at least one secret society, membership in which distinguished elites from commoners. These secret societies organized yearly ritual cycles, including the most sacred Kuksu dances: the Coyote, Condor, and Hawk dances. In these rituals, members of the secret societies appeared in elaborate costumes to represent supernatural figures and ghosts.[42] Even in societies that did not practice the Kuksu cult, communal dances were the main religious rituals. These dances followed a yearly ceremonial cycle and often functioned as a way of maintaining or restoring harmonious relations with neighboring villages and tribal communities, who were invited to join in the dancing.[43]

The Indians baptized at Mission San Francisco spoke several different languages that anthropologists and ethnohistorians have identified as dialects of at least five main languages, now known as Costanoan, Bay Miwok, Coast Miwok, Yokuts, and Patwin. Although variations in language did not necessarily correspond with variations in other cultural traits in the San Francisco Bay Area, some scholars have used linguistic groups as cultural designations. However, this method of distinguishing between Indians is misleading. Villages and tribal communities probably differed culturally according to their environment far more than their language. Thus, a Costanoan-speaking village living along the San Francisco Bay might have much more in common with a Bay Miwok-speaking village in a similar environment than it would have with another Costanoan-speaking group living further south on the Pacific coast.[44] Nevertheless, linguistic

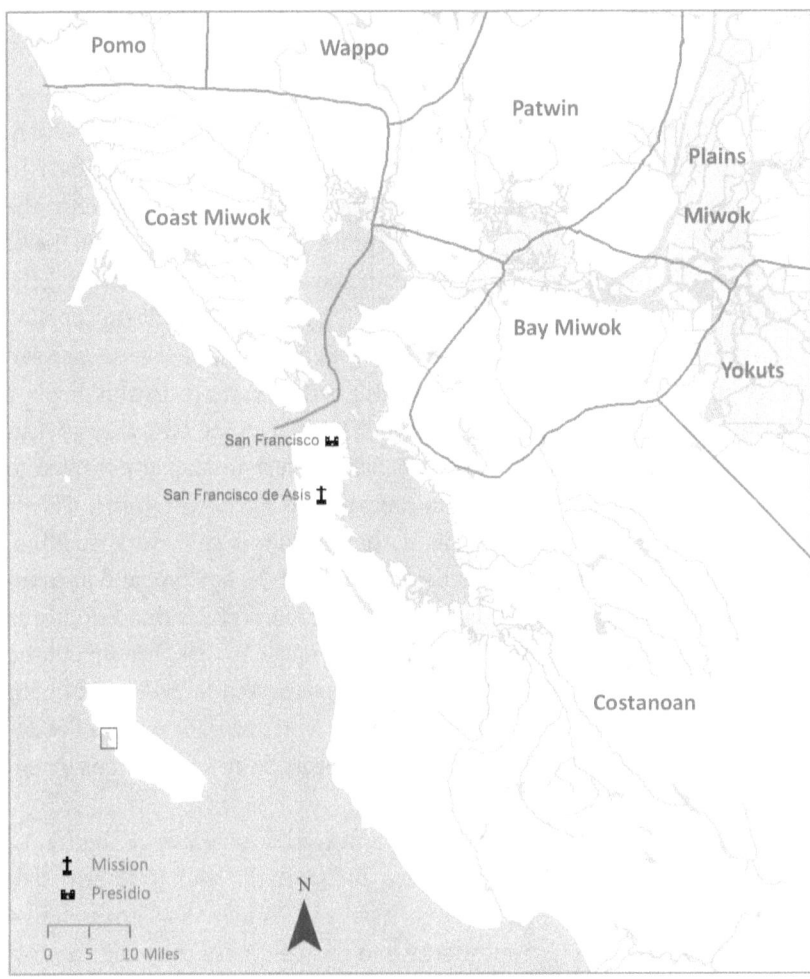

MAP 2. Linguistic regions of the San Francisco Bay Area, with Mission San Francisco and the San Francisco Presidio. The majority of Indians who accepted baptism at Mission San Francisco during the Spanish colonial period were Costanoan speakers. Wyoming Geographic Information Science Center, 2009.

commonalities may have contributed to the formation of coalitions among baptized Indians concentrated at Mission San Francisco. Costanoan speakers dominated the population of Indians baptized at Mission San Francisco for the first quarter-century of its existence. Between 1801 and 1803, an influx of Coast Miwok speakers altered this balance, making Costanoan (spoken by 43 percent of the population) and Coast Miwok (spoken by 42 percent of the population) codominant at the mission.[45]

The term *Costanoan* comes from the Spanish word *costeño*, meaning "person from the coast." The term is a misnomer: many Costanoan-speaking villages and tribal communities were not coastal residents. In recent years, descendants of Costanoan-speakers have come to prefer the term *Ohlone* over Costanoan. "Ohlone" probably comes from the name of the Oljon Indians, one group of Costanoan-speakers who lived on the Pacific Coast, west of the Santa Clara Valley.[46] This name was mistakenly applied to Costanoan-speakers generally by some European and Euro-American observers, who also changed the spelling of the name.[47] In this book, I use the term *Costanoan* instead of *Ohlone* to refer to the language spoken by this group, because although both names were mistakenly applied to the Costanoan/Ohlone people by Europeans and Euro-Americans, *Ohlone* hides that colonialist history in its authentic sound and exotic spelling, while *Costanoan* lays bare its colonial roots in both its spelling and pronunciation. *Costanoan* thus reminds the reader more forcefully that Europeans and Euro-Americans have held the power to impose names throughout the history of contact between Indians and Europeans and Euro-Americans in the San Francisco Bay Area. When I discuss Costanoan-speaking individuals or groups, I use specific village or tribal community designations whenever possible.

In a similar vein, the terms *Indian* and *Native American* are both ultimately the creations of colonial powers: *Indian* harks back to Columbus's mistaken belief that he had sailed to Asia, and *Native American* contains within itself the name Europeans gave to the landmass they had "discovered." Though *Native American* is a more recent coinage meant to acknowledge the precedence of indigenous peoples on this continent, neither term escapes the colonialism that arrived with Columbus and those who came after him. Many descendants of those first peoples today prefer the term *Indian*, and that word is the most exact translation of *indio*, the term that Hispanic colonists used to refer to the people they found in Alta California. Therefore, I use the word *Indian* to refer to these people.

༄

Indians' experiences at Mission San Francisco would be far easier to analyze had the Bay Area Indians left written documents attesting to their thoughts, attitudes, and activities, but they did not. In fact, only three Indian accounts of life in the Spanish missions survive, and all three are about Southern California missions. Pablo Tac, who wrote about life in Mission San Luis Rey de Francia, is the only Native Californian known to have written his own account of life in the missions. He composed his narrative as a twelve- or thirteen-year-old while training for the priesthood in Rome.⁴⁸ Two other California Indians, Lorenzo Asisara and Fernando Librado, gave oral accounts of mission life to researchers, well after the mission period, drawing on their own early childhood memories and stories handed down by their grandparents.⁴⁹ Meanwhile, observers of European descent left copious documentation. Spanish priests and governmental officials kept extensive records; colonists wrote personal letters and memoirs; and European and Euro-American visitors to Alta California, including such illustrious figures as British captain George Vancouver and Russian count Nikolai Rezanov, published accounts of their travels.

These European sources, often shot through with racism and ethnocentrism, are a poor substitute for the Indians' own accounts. Nevertheless, they are useful and, read with a critical eye, may be more revealing than their authors intended. As ethnohistorian James Sandos points out, drawing on the work of anthropologist James Scott, there exist within the public, European records of the Spanish colonization of Alta California "hidden transcripts" in which the California Indians contradict the Hispanic colonists' narrative of dominance.⁵⁰ Scholars of American Indian history have sought to bring those "hidden transcripts" to light by reinterpreting historical evidence in light of anthropological and archaeological data.

Scholars of marginalized groups, including the California Indians, have made extraordinary strides in recent decades by reexamining the assumptions that undergird our interpretations of contact situations and insisting that the assumptions be the same for both sides of the contact experience. In other words, if we assume that Hispanic colonists brought Hispanic cultural forms with them to California, then it is logical to assume also that Bay Area Indians brought Bay Area Indian cultural forms with them into the missions. James Sandos articulates this principle in an article on the Chumash of Southern California. Writing about polygyny inside and outside the missions, he asks, "If concurrent marriage for chiefs prevailed outside the mission, why should we think that ipso facto it disappeared when chiefs were baptized?"⁵¹ In the absence of compelling evidence to the contrary, we should assume that cultural forms persisted. By making the best use possible of European sources to write the history of colonized American Indians, and by bringing the same assumptions to our interpretations of Indian experiences as we do to our understanding of European and Euro-American experiences, we can ensure that American Indians do not remain "historyless" peoples, as European and Euro-American colonizers often portrayed them.[52]

In the chapters that follow, I examine various aspects of life in and around Mission San Francisco to show that Indians at the mission exercised a great deal of agency over important parts of their lives even after accepting baptism. I begin in chapter 1 by discussing the experience of going to church at Mission San Francisco. The Franciscan missionaries knew that a great deal of information could be conveyed nonverbally through images, textures, smells, tastes, and sounds. The opulence of the Mass at Mission San Francisco, employing incense; fine garments for the priests; gleaming instruments of gold, silver, and crystal; esoteric European language and Western musical cadences; and occasionally the taste of European wine and bread, was designed to be impressive. The Franciscans taught their brand of Catholicism to Bay Area Indians daily, both by reciting the catechism with them and by performing the Mass in a church full of images that depicted concepts and stories central to the religion. However, the priests could not prevent Bay Area Indians from interpreting these images in indigenous ways. In this chapter, I explore some of the lessons—intended and unintended—that Indians learned at church at Mission San Francisco.

In the second chapter, I examine labor at Mission San Francisco. The mission depended for its survival on Indian labor, and the Franciscan priests also believed that both the Hispanicization and the salvation of the Indians depended on their learning to work in Hispanic ways. That dependence on Indian labor, though, forced the priests to compromise: Indian laborers at Mission San Francisco employed a combination of indigenous and Hispanic techniques and aesthetics, and they sometimes prioritized traditional tasks like acorn harvesting over mission work. The priests used a social hierarchy that they had put in place at the mission to help organize labor there: *alcaldes*, the top-ranking Indian officials at the mission, were in charge of delegating tasks and ensuring they were accomplished. While at some missions priests chose the alcaldes from among existing Indian leaders, at Mission San Francisco they appear to have created a hierarchy that competed with, rather than overlapped with, existing indigenous leadership structures. Some Indians also chose to work at the San Francisco

Presidio. Mission priests augmented Mission San Francisco's coffers by hiring gangs of day laborers out to the military for construction projects, as well as more skilled laborers for fixed terms of employment. However, Indians who worked on their own initiative, and for their own benefit, escaped this priestly control.

Leadership structures and labor practices were not the only ways in which the Franciscan missionaries intended to change Bay Area Indian cultures. In the third chapter, I discuss the ways in which the priests tried to alter family structures among Indians in the California missions and the far-reaching consequences of the changes they imposed. Examining changes in Indian family structures is one way to track the ways missionization disrupted the lives of Bay Area Indians. The chapter begins with an overview of family structures in Bay Area and Hispanic societies. I discuss how families were constituted in each culture, the roles that men and women played in their families and in their societies more broadly, and how status and authority were acquired and exercised. After considering Indian and Hispanic models of family, I turn to the California missions. I examine how Franciscan priests imposed their own authority as spiritual "fathers" to baptized Indians, overriding the authority normally exercised by men and women in Bay Area Indian societies. Finally, I explore ways in which the priests encouraged the transformation of Indian patrilineages into Hispanicized nuclear families through the structuring of time and space, the distribution of resources, and the enforcement of Catholic kinship rules. I focus particularly on the control priests exercised over marriage at Mission San Francisco and the multiple ways in which the imposition of Catholic rules modified this traditional means of creating familial, social, political, and economic alliances.

While the imposition of priestly authority and a nuclear family model would seem to have wreaked havoc on Bay Area Indian societies by disrupting traditional family patterns and networks of relationships, I show in the following chapters that Indians used Catholic rituals and relationships to maintain of those very networks. In chapter 4, I explore the performance and uses of marriage among baptized Indians at Mission San Francisco. I begin by describing the ways Hispanic Catholics understood marriage in both theological and social terms, and the rituals that surrounded the institution. I then discuss marriage as it was understood and practiced in Bay Area Indian societies. Though the Franciscan priests focused on the differences that separated Indian marriage from Catholic marriage as they understood it, the broad similarities between Indian and Hispanic marriage allowed the Indians baptized at Mission San Francisco to add the Catholic wedding ceremony to the complex of rituals surrounding marriage while retaining traditional rituals and understandings of marriage. Indians in the San Francisco Bay Area had long used marriage as a means of creating and reinforcing networks of familial, social, political, and economic alliances between lineages, villages, and tribal communities, and baptized Indians continued to do so at Mission San Francisco. I focus on this use of marriage as a way of creating alliances to show that baptized Indians maintained their positions in the networks that connected people in the San Francisco Bay Area, and I suggest that marriages between Indian women and Hispanic men at Mission San Francisco may have represented an effort to weave the newcomers into that web of relationships.

In the fifth chapter I consider godparenting at Mission San Francisco, a phenomenon that has yet to be studied in the Alta California mission system. With few exceptions, each Indian received at least one, and sometimes two, godparents when she or he was baptized. Catholic theologians in the eighteenth century agreed that godparents were responsible for the Christian education of their godchildren. However, the priests at Mission San Francisco assumed this responsibility in the godparents' place. Therefore, to the many soldiers, colonists, and others of European descent who acted as godparents to Indians at the mission, godparenting was little more than a ceremonial function, creating no lasting relationship between godparent and godchild. For Indians, however, godparenting seems to have been invested with other significances. Many Indians acted as godparents to other Indians at the mission, and in these cases, godparenting frequently created a relationship between godparent and godchild, between godparent and biological parents, or between godparent and the godchild's village or tribal community that created, repaired, or reinforced networks of relationships among Bay Area Indians.

In the face of a demographic collapse initiated by Spanish colonization of the Bay Area, Indians there adopted godparenthood as one element of a salvage strategy, using the spiritual kinship ties it created to forge, strengthen, and repair networks of social, political, and economic relationships, as well as to strengthen bonds of kinship. Although the numbers of baptized Indians at Mission San Francisco grew more or less steadily throughout the Spanish colonial period, this increase was due largely to the recruitment of unbaptized Indians rather than to natural reproduction.

Death rates consistently exceeded birth rates in the mission because of poor living conditions, cultural stress, and diseases introduced by the colonists. Mortality was higher for women and young children than it was for men, skewing the gender and age distributions of the mission population and further exacerbating the demographic collapse.[53] In this situation of devastating population loss, godparenthood became a way for Indians at Mission San Francisco to fill the holes left by deaths in their political, social, economic, and familial networks. Thus, just as Indians baptized at Mission San Francisco used marriage in the mission to make alliances between families, villages, and tribal communities, they also adopted baptism and used the godparenting relationship it entailed in similar alliance-building ways.

The networks Indians created through marriage and godparenting often provided them with places to go when they left Mission San Francisco, which they did on a regular basis. While some Indians left the mission on errands, and others left without permission, a large number spent time outside the mission with the priests' permission on what the missionaries referred to as *paseos*. These journeys took Indians away from Mission San Francisco, often back to their original villages, in order to visit friends and family, gather food, or simply relax.[54] In chapter 6, I examine these movements out of the mission and show that many Indians baptized at Mission San Francisco arranged to be away from the mission when they gave birth or when they died. In so doing, these Indians underscored their attachments to their home communities and to the traditional rituals that surrounded birth and death in Bay Area villages and tribal communities, even after they had accepted baptism and begun to participate in Catholic rituals as well.

This ambivalence was one way in which Bay Area Indians responded to the Catholicism that the Franciscan missionaries preached, but it was not the only way. Some Indians appear to have embraced the new religion wholeheartedly, earning nicknames like *monja*, or "nun," or inspiring the priests to bury them in the Franciscan habit when they died. Others responded very differently: although they accepted baptism, these Indians chose to forgo the Catholic sacraments intended to help the believer die well. This choice suggests a fundamental rejection of the religion the missionaries preached, or at least a lack of confidence in the rituals of penitence and extreme unction. The variety of these responses emphasizes the ability that Indians baptized at Mission San Francisco had to make choices regarding the most important moments of their lives, and to act on those choices.

The story of Uichase, an Indian baptized at Mission San Francisco, and his family brings this book to a close. Using Uichase's story as a focal point, I bring together the themes discussed in all six chapters to consider what they tell us about Indians' experience at Mission San Francisco de Asís and about the Catholic missionary effort in Alta California more broadly.

By examining the ways in which Indians participated in Catholic life at Mission San Francisco, as well as the ways in which they refused to participate, I highlight the control Indians had over their own lives, even after accepting baptism at the mission. Without question, Indians had to confront the facts of Spanish colonization, Catholic missionization, and a demographic decline that bordered on collapse. However, multiple means of dealing with those circumstances were available, and accepting baptism at Mission San Francisco did not lock Indians into a life of subservience to Franciscan missionaries and Hispanic colonists.

1

Going to Church

༺ Father Francisco Palóu baptized Pismote, an Indian woman about eighteen years old, on the twenty-third of December, 1782, in the Mission San Francisco church.[1] According to her baptismal record, Pismote claimed to be single, and in the eyes of the Catholic Church, she was: her former husband, Puyeles, had been baptized about two weeks earlier, and had solemnized his marriage with Au-luté, Pismote's older sister and former co-wife.[2] According to ecclesiastical law, that act had nullified Puyeles's marriages to Au-luté's two younger sisters, Nayomi and Pismote.[3]

Because she was an adult, Pismote had to demonstrate a rudimentary knowledge of the Catholic faith in order to receive the sacrament of baptism. Father Palóu had quizzed her outside the church that day and again as she stood before the baptismal font. To prepare for those questions, Pismote had probably attended the recitals of Christian doctrine that the priests held every morning and evening in front of the big wooden doors of the mission church for at least a week, and possibly as long as a month.[4]

These recitals must have been easy for the missionaries: Father Palóu and his companion, Father Pedro Benito Cambón, the priests assigned to Mission San Francisco at the time, had a total of sixty-seven years of

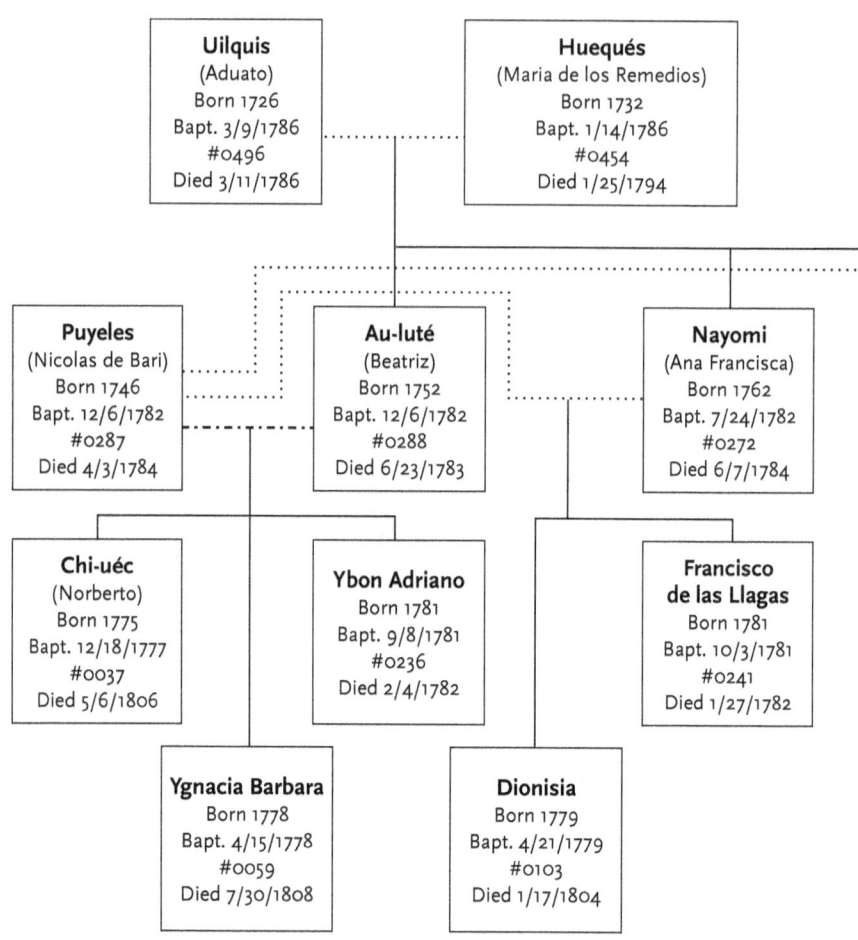

FIGURE 1. Pismote's family. Pismote was one of three sisters married to Puyeles before accepting baptism at Mission San Francisco. Sororal polygyny, in which one man marries multiple sisters, was a common form of polygamy in the San Francisco Bay Area. When Puyeles chose to solemnize his marriage to Au-luté, Pismote was left without an ecclesiastically sanctioned husband. Pismote eventually married Ssuíle, another Indian baptized at Mission San Francisco.

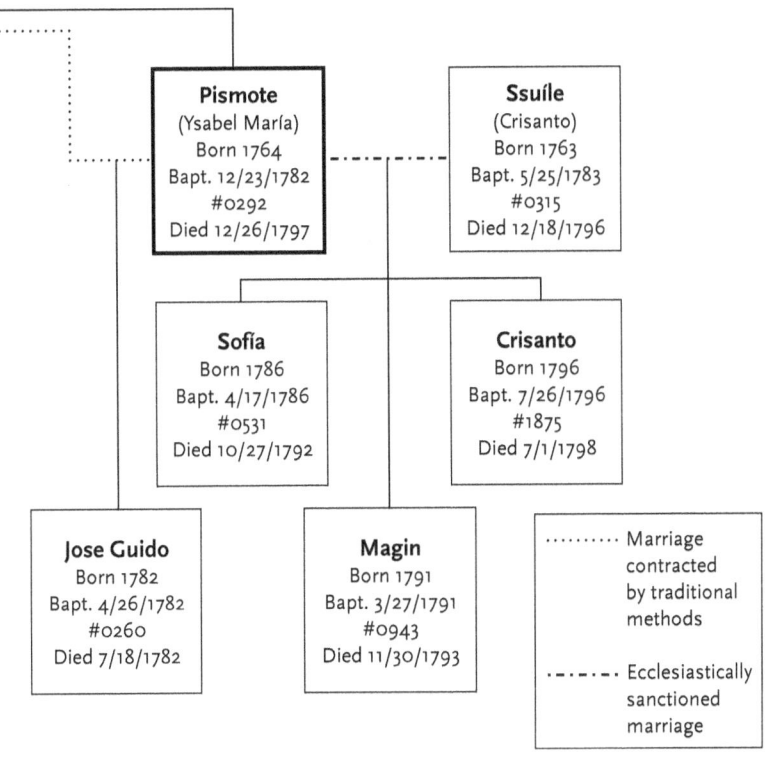

experience as priests between them and had been teaching doctrine to new converts for at least half that time.⁵ The catechism they used was Bartolomé Castaño's *Catecismo breve*, a summary of Catholic doctrine in question-and-answer format that bore the subtitle "Short catechism of precisely what a Christian must know."⁶ This choice of catechism suggests that Palóu and Cambón harbored no extravagant ambitions for their converts; if the Indians learned the basics of the faith, that would be enough. In five small pages, the *Catecismo breve* delivered the bare bones of the Catholic faith. It focused on the nature of God; Jesus's sacrifice; the nature of the church; the Eucharist; and the requirements for salvation.⁷ The question-and-answer format probably aided the priests' memories, and chances are that it appealed to the children who attended these recitals and understood Spanish. Adult Indians, however, were less likely to speak the new language. In their 1814 response to a questionnaire that had been sent to all the missions, inquiring about the California Indians and mission life, Fathers Abella and Sainz de Lucio remarked that at Mission San Francisco, "the people who come at the age of thirty years and above never learn another language than their own."⁸ For these Indians, the questions and answers of Castaño's catechism may have seemed little more than nonsense syllables.⁹

The missionaries' own fluency in native languages was almost certainly no better. A 250-year-old law, still in effect, mandated that "[w]here it is possible schools for learning the Castilian [Spanish] language are to be established in order that the Indians might learn it,"¹⁰ creating a disincentive for missionaries to learn native languages. Adding to the enormity of the task was the multiplicity of languages: "in passing a Swamp or a Mountain Range there is another Language, and in this Mission there are five Languages as distinct from one another as Castilian is from Mexican [Nahuatl]," Abella and Sainz de Lucio complained.¹¹ Visitors to Mission San Francisco noted the missionaries' ignorance of the local languages. Otto von Kotzebue, for example, visited Mission San Francisco in 1816. "The missionaries," he charged, "do not trouble themselves to learn the language of the Indians."¹² While Kotzebue's opinion may have been somewhat harsh, the scientist who accompanied his voyage concurred that the missionaries lacked facility in the native languages. "The pious Franciscans, who hold the missions in New California," wrote Adelbert von Chamisso, "are not skilled . . . in any of the languages spoken by the nations to whom they are sent."¹³ English captain Frederick Beechey found that the situation had not changed significantly a decade later. Recalling his visit to San Francisco in

1826, he remarked that "Many of the Indians surpass their pastors . . . and can speak the Spanish language, while scarcely one of the padres can make themselves understood by the Indians."[14] Alonso de la Peña Montenegro, a Jesuit moral theologian whose work was widely read by the Franciscan missionaries in Alta California, argued that missionaries must learn the local languages. Recognizing that this goal was not always feasible, however, he also allowed for the training and use of Indian interpreters.[15] Since the priests at Mission San Francisco never mastered the local Indian languages, they made extensive use of the alternative that Montenegro provided, routinely employing interpreters to render their words into one or more of the many Indian dialects represented at the mission.[16]

While translating the questions and answers of the catechism into indigenous languages would have been a difficult task in any case, the problems of translation were likely far more extensive than the catechism's simple language might initially suggest. Before the arrival of the Spanish, many basic Christian concepts were unknown in California. Asked about Indian ideas regarding the afterlife, Ramón Abella and Juan Sainz de Lucio responded that "the most that those of this area say, is that they go to the sea, and that there are many; but they do not examine in detail what they do, and if asked about it, they respond, who knows; and they do not know more about the ultimate end of Man, and this is the most that they know in their Gentile state, some do not even know this."[17] While Bay Area Indians may have simply been stonewalling the priests, unwilling to reveal this information, Abella and Sainz de Lucio's comments may also indicate that the afterlife was of little concern to Bay Area Californians, and therefore the concept was not well developed in their religious thought.[18] It is also possible—indeed, probable—that Bay Area religious concepts had no equivalents in Western Catholic traditions and that the Indians were therefore unable to communicate their more complex religious ideas to the priests, even if they wanted to do so. For the Franciscan missionaries, then, translating concepts like "heaven" and "hell," let alone "Trinity" or "salvation," into native languages was an inexact science at best.

In earlier missionary experiences with indigenous groups further south, the Franciscans had adopted Indian terms to express Catholic concepts without fully grasping the consequences of this decision. In Central Mexico, sixteenth-century Franciscans equated the Christian concepts of good and evil with the Nahua concepts of order and disorder. In Nahua thought, however, order and disorder were not moral absolutes, nor were

Going to Church

they polar opposites. Instead, order arose from the fertile energy found in chaos: the two depended on each other, and neither was completely desirable nor completely undesirable. By equating good and evil with order and disorder, Louise Burkhart has shown, Franciscans "[made] their value judgments meaningful to the Nahuas, yet . . . effectively 'Nahuatized' what they were trying to say,"[19] changing the meanings of the concepts they were trying to communicate. Franciscans in Alta California two centuries later almost certainly faced similar dilemmas in their attempts to find terms to communicate European Catholic concepts foreign to the California Indian cultures and languages. It is impossible to know how distorted Catholic doctrine became when local Indians translated it into Costanoan, Miwok, or other Bay Area languages, but doing so surely muddied the clarity of the priests' catechism. While Pismote understood the words when the interpreter translated the catechism lesson into the Costanoan language, she may not have grasped the meaning the priests intended to convey.

We do not know when Pismote began living at Mission San Francisco, if she ever did. She may have moved to the mission when Puyeles solemnized his marriage with Au-luté, effectively leaving Pismote without a husband or, in this patrilocal culture, a home. Alternatively, when Puyeles entered the mission, Pismote may have gone back to the Ssalson Indians, a tribal community near the mission to which her father, and therefore she, belonged. From there, she could easily have traveled regularly to the mission for prebaptismal instruction. If she had not already relocated to the mission, the priests probably pressured her to do so as the date of her baptism neared. As the spiritual fathers of the baptized Indians, the priests felt themselves responsible to civil, military, and ecclesiastical authorities, as well as to God, for the behavior of the new converts. Missionaries were particularly concerned with protecting and controlling the sexuality of their charges, especially the women. Like other Indian women, Pismote would be far easier to supervise if she lived at the mission.

The day after her baptism, then, Pismote probably woke up in the *monjerío*, a large women's dormitory on the mission grounds. According to Palóu's 1782 description of the mission, this room probably stood opposite the church, across the mission quadrangle on the north side of the complex. It was next to the kitchen and a little over eight feet high.[20] In 1778, that room, along with many of the others at the mission, had been roofed with tule reeds, a building material in common use among the Indians of the Bay Area. Because the only entrance to the mission quadrangle, and therefore to the monjerío, was through the priests' quarters, the missionaries were able to keep a close eye on the women's comings and goings and control men's access to the area and its residents. In their annual report for 1789, Fathers Diego García and Faustino de Solá also reported another dormitory, about thirty-three feet long and half as wide, for single men.[21] This dormitory was situated adjacent to the main quadrangle of the mission, rather than inside it, so access to it was unrestricted. When he got old enough, Puyeles's and Au-luté's son Chi-uéc would move into this dormitory.[22]

In 1782, though, Puyeles, Au-luté, and their son and daughter, Chi-uéc and Ygnacia Barbara, if they moved to the mission, were housed together.[23] Indian families—which in the missionaries' definition included only one husband, one wife, and any children they might have—lived in what amounted to an Indian village adjacent to the mission. At first homes followed indigenous architectural patterns: Francisco Palóu described them in 1782 as a "village made up of thatch huts."[24] A decade later English naturalist Archibald Menzies visited Mission San Francisco and provided a detailed description of the Indians' homes:

> Their Habitations or Wigwams were aptly compared to a crouded [sic] cluster of Bee-hives each of which was of a hemispherical form about nine feet high & nearly the same in diameter & consisted of slender sticks or rods stuck in the ground & lashd [sic] together with thongs into the above form & afterwards/closely thatchd [sic] all round with Bulrushes, excepting a small hole left on one side just sufficient to creep in at.[25]

The following year, the priests began replacing these houses with "houses of walls of adobe." Nineteen such houses were built in 1793.[26] Twenty more were added in 1796, and by 1797 Fathers Martín de Landaeta and José de la Cruz reported that "the houses of the Indians have been finished,"[27] though many Indians continued to live in homes of thatch rather than adobe.

Leaving the monjerío, Pismote walked with the other women and girls across the mission quadrangle and out of the mission to the main doors of the church for the morning recital of doctrine. The air was probably chilly and damp that morning—a Tuesday, the day before Christmas—so perhaps Pismote found herself shivering. The mission gave each mission resident clothing so that the Indians would conform to Hispanic standards of decency. For women that meant a blanket, a work shirt, and a skirt; for men, a blanket, a work shirt, and a loincloth. In his 1784 report, though, Father Palóu expressed concern about the adequacy of these garments. He noted that the Indians used cards and looms imported from Mexico to spin and weave the mission's wool. With the cloth, he wrote, they made garments "to help dress themselves, and defend against the great cold here." These garments supplemented those made with cloth imported from Mexico, but even then Palóu was concerned that they were not enough: the mission spent the largest part of its budget each year, he complained, on clothing the Indians "in order to cover their nakedness, so that they appear in the Church with some decency, and so they see the improvement that they gained in corporeal matters by becoming Christians."[28] Despite the priests' efforts, Pismote may not have considered these garments much of an improvement over the grass skirts and fur cloaks she had worn before her baptism. As she left for the morning lesson, perhaps she took an extra blanket with her from the monjerío to ward off the chill.

In 1782, almost exactly one-third of Mission San Francisco's budget went to clothing the baptized Indians, but the priests held out hope that the mission would one day be self-sufficient. The Indian women's production of cloth out of the wool Indian men sheared from the mission sheep was a means to that end. A decade later, Vancouver would remark on the quality of the that cloth. "I saw some of the cloth," he wrote, "which was by no means despicable; and, had it received the advantage of fulling, would have been a very decent sort of clothing."[29] As Pismote looked around, she might have been able to identify the women who had manufactured the nubby cloth that now covered her body. She may even have had a hand in producing it herself; the spinning of wool and weaving of cloth was a task reserved for the women of the mission.[30] Together, these women wove as much as they could to help clothe the 181 men, women, and children for whom the priests considered themselves responsible by Christmas Eve, 1782.[31]

After the recital of doctrine was over, the priest excused himself to prepare for Mass, and the sacristan went to ring the church bells, calling everyone else to the service. The sound of bells was new in this part of California: before the priests had arrived in 1776, their ringing tones literally were unheard in the Bay Area, with the possible exception of the occasional ship's bell. Since the foundation of the mission and presidio on the

ILLUSTRATION 1. Louis Choris, *Jeu des habitans de Californie*. Choris's drawing of California Indians playing what may be a gambling game provides a nice illustration of the fabric that women like Pismote produced at Mission San Francisco to clothe the baptized Indians. Library of Congress Rare Books and Special Collections Division, LC-DIG-ppmsca-02900.

San Francisco Bay, however, bells had become a pervasive element in the Bay Area soundscape, infiltrating the acoustic ambience like a European weed in California's fertile soil. Their jangling rang out several times a day, calling people to Mass, to meals, and to other gatherings. The bells rang to celebrate events that occurred half a world away: the birth of a new member in the royal family, the coronation of a king, a military victory for the Empire. They rang, too, to mark tragic occasions: the passing of a ruler or a padre presidente or a pope—and to signal danger: fire, the approach of a hostile military force, Indian rebellion. The sound of the bells was not as ubiquitous in California as it became in some European towns, where the ringing rarely ceased.[32] Nevertheless, the bells played the same role in the Bay Area as in these European towns, serving as "an acoustic delineation of a sphere of authority"[33]—in this case, the authority of the Franciscan missionaries. Drawing on centuries-old formulae, Fathers Francisco Palóu and Pedro Benito Cambón would write at the close of 1782 that "all the

Going to Church

Indians mentioned in this [1782 annual] report live in this Mission under the bell." Throughout the mission period, Franciscans stationed at Mission San Francisco would use the same formula, demarcating the boundaries of the mission by the reach of the bells.[34]

Amid their cacophony, the bells introduced a new sense of time to Indians who had previously relied on the natural rhythms of the days and seasons, but they did not fully replace this more intuitive sense of time. Although European monasteries, desiring a more precise way of determining the hours of prayer, had figured prominently in the invention of more accurate measurements of clock time,[35] Mission San Francisco did not run wholly according to this artificial system. Instead, the priests blended clock time with earlier ways of measuring time, dividing the day according to the movements of the sun and the activities to be performed. Therefore, Indians at Mission San Francisco rose not at a set hour, but at dawn, which shifted throughout the year; they finished working on most days shortly before dusk, rather than at a predetermined hour. In 1814, asked about how the Indians measured time, Fathers Ramón Abella and Juan Sainz de Lucio admitted that not much had changed. Bay Area Indians still distinguished the seasons of the year according to the cycles of nature: the blooming of flowers, the ripening of seeds and later acorns, the return of geese and ducks, and the arrival of rains marked the passage of the Indians' year, the priests reported. Further, they continued, "They do not have, nor have they had, Calendars. Customarily they divide the day in three parts, morning, midday, and afternoon, and this anyone can know according to the rise or fall of the sun in the East."[36] Though the bells provided additional information, signaling specific events and smaller divisions of the day, Indians continued to reckon time much as they had before the Hispanic colonists arrived.[37]

Pismote heard the sacristan call people to Mass by ringing the two large bells that the mission owned. They were part of the goods that the Spanish king, through his representatives, had donated to the mission for its foundation. One was "medium," and one was "small,"[38] producing two distinct tones that pealed across the peninsula, proclaiming the mission's presence in the ears of Indians and Hispanic colonists alike. Soldiers and servants at the San Francisco Presidio surely heard the bells as clearly as did Indians in nearby villages, though it is unlikely that the Hispanic colonists at that military installation would attend Mass that morning. Presidio inhabitants did frequent the mission church for special occasions like baptisms and weddings, as well as feast days and sometimes Sunday masses. A Tuesday morning Mass, though, was unlikely to draw many Hispanic colonists: the mission was too far away, and the presidio residents had work to do.

⁓

When she entered the church, Pismote would have genuflected toward the altar, as she had been taught to do. The elaborately carved and decorated tabernacle immediately above the altar contained wafers that the priest would use to celebrate the Eucharist. Pismote had probably learned that once consecrated, the host was literally the body of Christ, according to Catholic belief. As such, it deserved the elaborate reverence with which it was treated. The host at Mission San Francisco was housed in beautiful containers like the tabernacle that glinted in the candlelight, and the priests taught the Indians that, as the body of Christ, the host also merited the physical expression of reverence enacted in the genuflection.[39] Kneeling so that her right knee touched the earthen floor, Pismote made the sign of the cross. Rising, she walked to the right-hand side of the church—the Epistle side—where the women and girls stood during Mass. The women may have arranged themselves by age, as Indians at other missions are reported to have done. If so, Pismote probably stood toward the back of the church. At eighteen years old, she was among the oldest 20 percent of living baptized women at the mission.[40]

The altarpiece with the tabernacle probably caught Pismote's eye first when she walked into the church that morning. This was the main altar straight ahead of her, at the other end of the almost twenty-three-yard-long church. A description dated December 31, 1782, recorded that the altar at the front of the church was mounted on a sturdy base. On the altar were a set of steplike graduated platforms called gradines that held six candleholders painted with gold and other colors. Along with the natural light coming from the doors and any windows that may have been built into the church walls, the candles illuminated the altarpiece that rose behind the altar table.[41] If the morning was overcast, as it often was, the candlelight would have seemed to shine more brightly, bringing a gleam to the gold leaf and making the crystal sparkle inside the dim building.

The largest figure in the altarpiece was a statue of Saint Francis of Assisi, the founder of the Franciscan order and the patron saint of the church. According to the priests' inventory, the statue was about five and a half feet tall.⁴² Saint Francis's image occupied the paramount niche of the altarpiece, directly above the tabernacle and elevated above the other images as well. This niche was the only one in the altarpiece that was decorated with an arc of mirrors. They caught the flickering light of the candles on the altar and reflected it onto the statue, further enhancing the image's prominence in the assemblage.

Although the priests did not describe the statue, it is likely that it depicted Francis in his monk's tunic, with a rope tied around his waist, carrying a crucifix or a skull.⁴³ Pismote would probably have recognized Francis as a priest, because the missionaries wore a similar outfit every day. Francis probably wore a brown robe, but Pismote had seen Fathers Palóu and Cambón in gray tunics of the same style. The missionaries, though, did not have the wounds that this statue probably displayed. The most noticeable and, to a non-European observer like Pismote, least explicable feature of the statue might have been the stigmata Francis was believed to have received, bloody holes in his hands, feet, and side, which became one of the primary identifying attributes of the saint.

Below Saint Francis, immediately above the gradines of the altar itself, was another niche that held both the tabernacle and a carved image of Our Lady of Sorrows that priests described as "very beautiful." Traditionally, this manifestation of the Virgin Mary was dressed in black, with at least one, and as many as seven, daggers piercing her heart and giving concrete form to her sorrows. While the priests do not mention the color of clothing the image at Mission San Francisco wore, they do describe one silver dagger that presumably pierced the image's heart. The priests also made note of the image's "radiance," most likely carved rays of wood emanating from behind the figure and painted to resemble a blaze of light.⁴⁴

Images of the Virgin Mary resonated with Indians further south in California, because they already had a powerful female deity with whom to identify her. When missionaries in Kumi·vit territory unveiled a painting of the Virgin Mary as a prelude to the founding of Mission San Gabriel, Junípero Serra recorded, the local Indians demonstrated great devotion to the image. "As soon as the fathers showed [the Indian women] a beautiful image of Most Blessed Mary ... which [the priests] had brought, and placed in the church," reported Serra, "[the women] were so enraptured, that they did not know how to remove themselves from its presence. They would go to their houses and return loaded with their seeds and foods which they offered to the holy image, leaving them before the altar."⁴⁵ While Serra and other missionaries interpreted this reaction as a sign of nascent Catholicism in the local population, historian Edward Castillo explains that it is far more likely that the Kumi·vit interpreted the painting as a representation of the female spirit Chukit who, according to Kumi·vit belief, had been impregnated by lightning and bore a child known as "the Son of God."[46] Less clear is how Californians further north, like Pismote, perceived Hispanic Catholic devotion to Mary, particularly because women appear to have played a less prominent role in traditional Bay Area Californian religious life than they did in Southern California.[47] Bay Area Indian women like Pismote may have seen Marian devotion as an expression of the importance of women, potentially signaling an increase in women's religious status.[48] Marian devotion may therefore have been part of the reason that women accepted baptism at consistently higher rates than men throughout the Spanish colonial period at Mission San Francisco.[49]

To either side of the statue of the Virgin and the tabernacle were niches constructed of cedar, each with a painting nearly three and a half feet tall. The priests did not record the subjects of these paintings, but they surely depicted other saints that the Franciscans held dear. Together with the Virgin of Sorrows and the statue of Saint Francis, these images comprised the main altar.

Two side altars complemented the images contained in the main altar. These altars appear to have been relatively simple in 1782: Father Francisco Palóu described them simply as "niches of cedar."[50] One niche, probably on the Gospel side to Pismote's left, held a painting of the Archangel Michael.[51] Michael is typically depicted killing the devil, represented as a dragon or serpent, and this image likely followed that tradition; certainly later images of Michael acquired by the mission depict him in this manner.[52] The other niche, probably on the Epistle side where Pismote stood, held a print of Our Lady of Remedies behind the glass of a hammered silver frame. This image of the Virgin Mary was about two feet tall. Our Lady of Remedies is often depicted holding out a bag of money in one hand with the Christ child in her other arm. For Pismote, these images might have reinforced the Hispanic gender roles the priests promoted at the mission: women were the primary caregivers for children, while men were responsible for the protection of their families.[53]

Perhaps Pismote's attention wandered during the Mass. If she looked away from the priest at the main altar to the walls of the church, she would still find plenty of spiritual material to ponder. Wherever Pismote had chosen to stand, the walls were not far away: the church was under seventeen feet wide. The side walls were probably decorated with a combination of Indian designs painted by local artists and European images imported from Mexico, though we only have descriptions of the latter. A new church building at Mission San Francisco, consecrated in 1791, was extensively decorated by indigenous artists using apparently abstract geometric designs on the side walls. Even the beams of the ceiling were painted in chevrons of red, ochre, and blue.[54] It is reasonable to believe that earlier church buildings were similarly decorated, though evidence does not exist to test that hypothesis. If indigenous artists decorated the walls, the designs they used may have reminded Pismote of the figures she wove into the baskets her mother taught her to make.[55]

These simple, repetitive designs almost certainly seemed out of place next to the images the priests had ordered from Mexico and hung on the walls. In 1782 the priests enumerated a number of paintings that adorned the side walls of the church: there were four canvases, each about five and a half feet high, depicting various devotional subjects. Among these were probably three the mission reported acquiring in 1778. One depicted Our Lady of Sorrows; another, the Patronage of Saint Joseph; and the third, Saint Francis receiving the stigmata.[56] By 1782, the church also held four smaller canvases—two about three feet high, and two half that size—with similar images. Prints of the fourteen stations of the cross, with fourteen small crosses accompanying them, hung at intervals around the sides and back of the church.

These images, like the images in the main altarpiece, served a variety of functions other than decoration. For centuries European priests had used images as visual aids in their efforts to educate a largely illiterate public. The priests at Mission San Francisco probably employed the images that filled the church in just this way. Some pictures in the mission church told stories: the stations of the cross, for example, illustrated a central narrative of the Catholic faith, walking viewers through Jesus's suffering and ultimate crucifixion. The statue of Saint Michael the Archangel killing the beast at his feet would also have provided illustration for a thrilling tale. Other images were less narrative, providing instead a representation of a Christian hero as a role model and a fitting object of contemplation. The statues of Saint Francis and the Virgin Mary probably fell in this category. Still other images, like the Patronage of Saint Joseph, illustrated important Christian concepts.

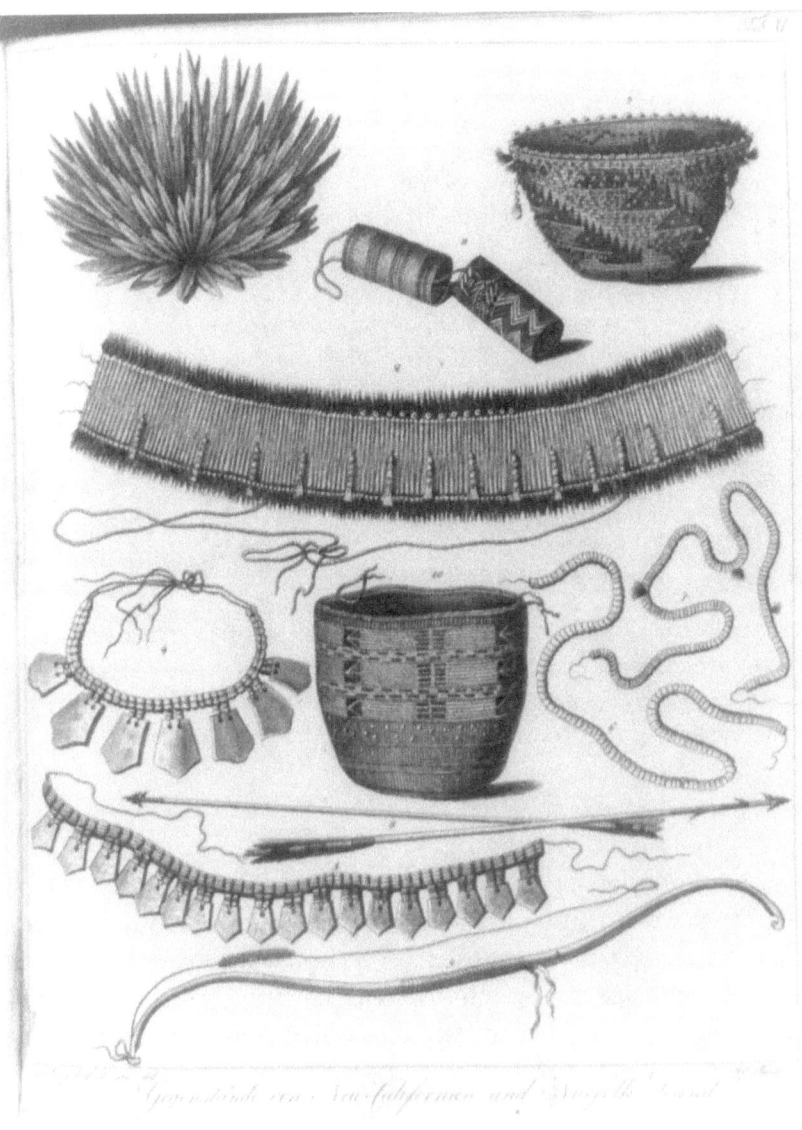

ILLUSTRATION 2. Georg H. von Langsdorff, *Gegenstände von New-Californien und Norfolk-Sound*. This engraving from Langsdorff's account of his voyage around the world shows the geometric designs that California Indians used to decorate baskets and other objects. Library of Congress Rare Books and Special Collections Division, LC-USZ62–8108.

ILLUSTRATION 3. This 1936 photo of Mission San Francisco's interior shows the geometric designs that California Indians painted on the ceiling, recalling traditional basketry designs. Photo by Robert W. Kerrigan. Library of Congress, Prints and Photographs Division, Historic American Buildings Survey, HABS CAL, 38-SANFRA, 1–22.

The painting of the Patronage of Saint Joseph that Pismote might have contemplated that Tuesday morning in 1782 no longer survives. However, a later painting of the same subject, which may have supplemented or replaced the image displayed in the San Francisco church in 1782, still exists. This image, painted in Mexico no earlier than 1788, shows Joseph floating amid clouds and attended by cherubim. In his left hand he holds lilies, symbolic of his chastity; in his right arm, he supports the Christ child, who rests his right hand on an orb. In the European iconographic tradition, the infant Jesus's gesture symbolized his dominion over the world. Joseph, dressed in a tunic of sumptuous brocade and an elaborately decorated cape, gazes directly at the viewer while the Christ child looks off to the viewer's right. In the foreground, a number of modern personages appear, all kneeling in adoration. Chief among these figures are King Carlos IV and Pope Pius IV. The king gazes upward, encouraging the viewer to do the same by gesturing with his left hand toward Saint Joseph, hovering above.

Pope Pius IV, on the other hand, looks directly at the viewer, his hands crossed on his chest, modeling an attitude of reverence. His gaze suggests an admonition that the viewer follow his lead.[57]

Saint Joseph was ubiquitous in the California missions, with sculpture and paintings representing him at every establishment. Joseph's popularity among the Franciscans was probably due, at least in part, to the role he played in Jesus's life. As Jesus's "foster father," Catholics believed, Joseph took a paternal role in the life of a boy to whom he was not biologically related. Franciscans saw their relationship to baptized Indians in analogous terms and likely used the Patronage of Saint Joseph as a way of visualizing this relationship. Saint Joseph's status as "a special patron of the converted Indians" in Mexico probably encouraged Franciscans to make this link.[58] However, the painting at Mission San Francisco illustrated more than the relationship between Joseph and Jesus, or even the ideal relationship between the Franciscans and the Indians. With its inclusion of both King Carlos IV and Pope Pius IV, this painting illustrated the close relationship between church and state in the eighteenth-century Spanish empire. At Mission San Francisco that relationship was enacted every day in the cooperation between the Franciscans and the Spanish military, which posted a guard at the mission. Pismote had only to look around the church to see soldiers representing the Spanish king.

The relationships to which the Patronage of Saint Joseph abstractly alluded, between Franciscans and Indians or church and state, may not have mattered much to Pismote or other Indians who viewed the painting. For them, the array of figures depicted in the Patronage of Saint Joseph painting may have seemed somewhat incongruous: while Indian fathers normally took part in the child-rearing process, this child's mother was nowhere to be found. Joseph was clearly a powerful man, as his luxurious dress and the adoration of kings and popes indicated. For such a powerful figure not to have even one co-wife to help raise the child must also have seemed strange. Nevertheless, perhaps Pismote recognized the demographic situation of the mission in this incongruity: parents of both sexes at the mission frequently were left to raise children on their own as Hispanic colonists looked on passively. When Au-luté died in June of 1783, Pismote may have seen a parallel between Saint Joseph, alone with the Christ child, and her own former husband Puyeles, left alone to raise the children he had with his senior wife.[59]

As she stood in church that day before Christmas, then, Pismote was surrounded by images of humanity and divinity. These images illustrated stories central to the Catholic religion and invited Pismote to enter the world of those stories by emulating the heroes of the faith. That world was a dangerous one, though: most of the images in the church were united by an underlying theme of violence. The Virgin of Sorrows and Saint Francis, each depicted at least twice in the church, bore physical evidence of supernaturally inflicted wounds—the dagger in the heart and the stigmata piercing hands, feet, and side—while Saint Michael fought against the terrifying beast that writhed at his feet. Meanwhile, the Stations of the Cross depicted the painful injuries and eventual death that Jesus suffered at human hands. Pismote may not have grasped the cosmological significance of the crucifixion; she may not have been able to identify the monster against which Michael struggled; she may not have connected Mary's stylized western symbol of a heart with the organ that beat inside her body; and she may not have been able to divine the source of Francis's wounds. The language of violence, though—daggers, spears, and blood—would surely have translated. The altarpiece and other church decorations told Pismote of a world fraught with violence inflicted by both natural and supernatural beings.

Perhaps, then, the Mass made sense to Indians like Pismote as a ritual meant to appease a violent deity. Indeed, Mass is explained in catechisms of the time as a sacrifice. Gerónimo Ripalda's catechism, which was popular among Hispanic colonists in Alta California, includes several questions and answers on the topic: "Q. With regard to hearing Mass, tell me: What is Mass? A. A sacrifice that is made of Christ, and a representation of his life and death. Q. To whom is this divine sacrifice made? A. To the eternal Father. Q. For what? A. For three ends: to give him thanks, to satisfy him, and to ask blessings of him."[60] Pismote may not have believed that sacrificing God's son was the best way to gain divine favor, but the logic of sacrifice—of ritually giving gifts to a powerful spirit to ensure good fortune—had parallels in traditional Bay Area religion.

The closest parallel might have been Bay Area Californians' relationship to the sun, which they regarded as one of the most powerful beings in the universe. Before her baptism, and perhaps also after it, Pismote joined other Indians in greeting the sun each morning with cheers and shouts of encouragement for its rising. Likewise, each winter solstice, traditional Bay Area Californian societies held ceremonies offering food, trade goods, and tobacco smoke to the sun.[61] The Catholics' daily sacrifice in the Mass, then, performed just after sunrise at the mission, and the Catholics' Christmas celebration—special ceremonies held near the winter solstice—may have seemed quite familiar to Pismote and other Indians.

The Mass also worked as spectacle, seducing Pismote's senses: the opulence of the altarpiece adorned with gold, silver, mirrors, and glass was heightened by the flickering candlelight inside the dim building. Objects of shining metals and sparkling crystal lay on the altar, further focusing spectators' attention. Among other objects, the 1782 inventory listed a monstrance—used to display the consecrated host for adoration—made of silver and gold; a silver cross for the altar; and sets of tin, silver, and crystal eucharistic dishes.[62] The only people authorized to approach the altar and handle these objects were the priests, who did so in sumptuous ceremonial garments that changed with the church season. That Tuesday before Christmas in 1782 fell during the Advent season, so the priests wore vestments of purple damask, decorated with gold and silver trim. Soon they would change to white, for Christmas, and then green for ordinary time. Lent, Easter, and Pentecost would bring vestments of purple, white, and red, respectively, with black interspersed for Good Friday and for the many burials of adults that the priests officiated.[63] The day before, when Pismote was baptized, Father Palóu wore vestments of white with a purple stole.[64] These changes of color, many of which bore little relation to the seasonal cycles that dictated traditional Californian lifeways, may have seemed arbitrary to Pismote and other Indians. The rich fabrics and detailed decoration of the garments, though, set the priests apart from the laity and the Mass apart from the rest of the day.

Pismote's attention, wherever it wandered, was called back to the front of the church at the climax of the Mass, when the altar server rang a small silver bell to mark the elevation of the host. Along with her fellow congregants, she knelt. The priests had probably told her that this was the most important moment of the Mass, the moment when the bread turned into the body of the Christ. By accepting baptism, Pismote had become eligible to receive the Eucharist. She had crossed the line, in the priests' vocabulary, from "gentile" to "Christian." However, though the priest would break the wafer and eat it that day, it is unlikely that any of the Indians in the congregation would take communion. Few Indians received the Eucharist at Mission San Francisco: between 1808 and 1821, the priests reported an average of between eight and nine communicants each year.[65] Indians were not alone in keeping their distance from the altar: in fact, they resembled

Catholics elsewhere in Latin America and in Europe in this practice. While its name came from the Greek for "thanksgiving," the Eucharist presented grave dangers. Scripture warned believers of the hazards of partaking unworthily, so many Catholics worldwide chose not to partake at all, except at Easter and in preparation for death.[66] Most Indians at Mission San Francisco, like their fellow Catholics elsewhere, partook visually, letting the priest run the risks of actually eating and drinking the body and blood of Christ.[67] While a cautious approach to the Eucharist made good sense from a lay Catholic's point of view, it was reinforced by the priests in California, who were wary of serving the elements to Indians who, though baptized, may not have understood the full import of the sacrament.[68] In 1813 Father Vicente Francisco de Sarría, the newly elected president of the mission system, advised priests against allowing Indians with little knowledge of the faith to receive communion.[69]

Throughout the Mass, Pismote's senses of smell, taste, and touch were seduced along with her sight and hearing. Incense wafting through the church invited her sense of smell to pay attention. Candles, oil, wine, and bread must also have emitted novel aromas, though they were more subtle than the incense. Pismote tasted the food of Europe on the rare occasions that she took communion, taking the host on her tongue and the wine in her mouth. She had tasted salt at her baptism the day before—not an unfamiliar flavor, of course, but perhaps a new sensation in its granular form. Throughout, she touched, or imagined the touch of, new sorts of surfaces: silk and linen, bread and wine, shining metal and sparkling crystal. The decorations of the church—the images, drapery, and other ornaments—spoke to Indians and colonists alike of the power and wealth of the Spanish empire and the Catholic Church. Though the rest of the mission may have seemed poor and ordinary, the church was richly furnished.

In the following years, the priests consistently sought to make the mission church both bigger and better. In 1783, the year after Pismote's baptism, the priests decided to move the mission about 367 yards to the west, apparently because the mission sat atop a parcel of prime agricultural land.[70] The entire mission was rebuilt on substantially the same plan that year, though the church was slightly enlarged, perhaps to accommodate—or in optimistic anticipation of—a growing number of converts.[71] When Pismote entered the church to be married, in May of 1784,[72] she had to walk a little further to reach the front of the church, which was now a little more than twenty-seven yards long but, at not quite seven yards wide, still relatively narrow.[73]

The priests also continued adding images and objects to the church, multiplying the sensory information available to congregants. By the time of Pismote's marriage, two new small cedar niches that had arrived the year before adorned the church walls. One held a small statue of Saint Francis, just about eleven inches high; the other, a marble statue of the Virgin Mary approximately the same size. As Pismote and her intended, Ssuíle, knelt in front of the altar, they had an opportunity to examine up close some of the statues of the crucified Christ that had arrived in the same 1783 shipment. Five of these statues had been imported from Mexico: two large ones, each about two feet high, one with its own canopy and curtain; and three small ones made of metal. The large statues probably occupied space in the main altarpiece or a side altarpiece, while the small statues were intended, according to the priests' report, "for the altars."[74]

Yet another statue of Saint Francis arrived by boat sometime in the months following Pismote's wedding. This one was not quite three feet high, and the priests described it as "very devout." Pismote's mother, Huequés, may have had an opportunity to contemplate it in 1786 when she was baptized.[75] Huequés would have seen in Francis's hands a crucifix and a golden diadem, symbols of faith and power. Affixed to his chest was a cross of the Holy Office made from Chinese porcelain.[76] Like the painting of the Patronage of Saint Joseph, then, this statue brought together the temporal and the spiritual, the religious and the economic—though Huequés may not have made all those connections.

By 1786 the priests had replaced the baptismal font that they had used when Pismote joined the Church: Huequés received the waters of baptism from a copper font plated with tin, which the missionaries had ordered from Mexico. The old font, and perhaps also its canopy and curtain, were moved to a satellite mission known as San Pedro y San Pablo, where Ssuíle's and Pismote's daughter Sofía would be born a few months later.[77] Whether or not Huequés had a chance to examine the latest image of Saint Francis during her baptism, she could hardly have missed the painting of John the Baptist baptizing Jesus that hung in the baptistry.[78] This painting, acquired from Mexico in 1784, depicted a subject common in the iconography of the California missions. If the painting sent to Mission San Francisco was like one sent to Mission San Antonio two years later, it showed Jesus standing in the Jordan River, a shallow stream that rose only slightly higher than Jesus's ankles. Standing on the bank of the river, John the Baptist used a shell to pour water over Jesus's head. Above the two figures, a white dove representing the Holy Spirit hovered in the sky. Like John the Baptist, Father Giribet used a silver shell to pour water over Hueques's head, cementing the link between the picture and the ritual.

∽

Though baptism was the means by which Hueques, Pismote, and other Indians crossed the line from, in the language of the Hispanic colonists, *Indios gentiles* to *Indios cristianos*, they remained *Indios*. Hispanic colonists recognized the divisions that separated California Indian villages and tribal communities from one another, but they treated the Indians as one large, homogeneous group defined in contrast to the *gente de razón* (people of reason), the group to which the colonists assigned themselves. By the late eighteenth century, these distinctions had taken on the character of racial classifications, allowing the Hispanic colonists to think of the quest for dominance in California as essentially a struggle against the racialized Indian "other."[79] Indians, in contrast, had long thought of themselves as members of one local group or another, rather than as members of a large racial group. Evidence suggests that many Indians saw the Hispanic invaders as one more tribal community, a potential trade partner, ally, or enemy in war, but not a group that was different in any essential way from any other group in the area. The Mass, and its concomitant erasure of distinctions among Indians, taught Pismote and other California Indians to see themselves in these racial terms. Daily, Pismote and Indians from myriad other villages and tribal communities went to church, where they acted as an undifferentiated group in response to the priests' commands. On the day of her baptism, Pismote likely thought of herself as a Ssalson woman, and it is impossible to tell whether her self-understanding ever changed. However, some evidence suggests that Indians began to think of themselves as a single group defined against the Hispanic "other." Besides rebellions at some missions, supported by members of various tribal communities,[80] an Indian version of the Stations of the Cross also suggests a growing "racial" consciousness among Indians.

When the mission system began, it is unlikely that skin color was a salient marker, but some evidence suggests that during the mission period at least some Indians began to see skin color as a social locator: the Stations of the Cross, painted by an Indian artist at Mission San Fernando Rey de España sometime late in the mission period, depict many of the auxiliary figures in the scenes with markedly darker skin than Jesus, who appears as a light-skinned European.[81] Some scholars have suggested that the soldiers bear the likenesses of hated Indian overseers, and that these paintings therefore represent a covert rebellion against a cruel Indian elite.[82] Just as plausible is that, since the Indian-faced Romans are shown inflicting pain on a European-skinned Jesus, these paintings represent a more generalized resistance against European domination. Whether either or both of these interpretations is correct, it does seem clear that skin color had emerged as a meaningful marker by the time the stations were painted.

In the Mass, this racial ordering of Hispanics and Indians found physical expression. While Pismote and the other Indians may have known their parts well, their presence was ultimately unnecessary. The priests, however, were indispensable to the sacrifice of the Mass. Without them, the show quite literally could not go on. Thus, even though the Catholics' Marianism may have seemed to promise greater status to women like Pismote, that gain in status was insignificant in light of the vast gulf that separated Pismote and other Indians from the priests. The Mass reduced all of the Indians, not just the women, to the same incidental status. Headmen and commoners alike kneeled, stood, spoke, and were silent according to the priests' cues, regardless of tribal community affiliation, lineage, religious power, or social or political status. Reactions to this leveling probably differed: Indians who were accustomed to commanding others probably chafed at their sudden lowliness, while commoners may have relished their equality with the high and mighty. Some may have experienced the collective movements of the Mass as a sense of community; others may have disliked the anonymity and interchangeability that these implied.

The division, and ranking, of racial groups was not the only element of social structure that the Mass introduced and, through daily repetition, reinforced. Perhaps even more noticeable was the strong division between men and women that the Indians enacted every day. Men stood on the Gospel side, and women on the Epistle side, of the church. This gender division was not in itself remarkable to Pismote and the other baptized Indians: Bay Area Indians routinely segregated the sexes for social, economic, and religious activities and they prescribed a strict separation of men and women at certain spiritually important times. However, in the Mission San Francisco church the division of the sexes was linked to an implicit hierarchy that elevated men over women. The Gospel side was the side of the church from which the priest proclaimed the words and deeds of

Jesus and delivered the homily. It was to the right hand—the more honorable position in Hispanic culture—of Saint Francis and the other figures who gazed out on the congregation from the main altar. The physical layout of the church thus reinforced the gendered messages that Pismote received from the church's iconography, subtly communicating Hispanic notions about the subordinate status of women in society. The liturgy strengthened messages about the subordination of women by privileging the voices of men. The only individual voices Pismote was likely to hear in the Mass on a regular basis were those of the male priests. Her own voice was always submerged, along with the other women's voices, into the collective voice of the congregation. Males also occupied any leadership roles that might be performed in the Mass. Singers, sacristans, acolytes, and altar servers were all men and boys. Thus, even when Pismote heard an individual Indian voice, it was still a male voice.

Perhaps Pismote thought about that disparity as she and her husband Ssuíle brought their daughter to be baptized in 1786. Two boys—Telempis, age eight, and Mequeig, age six—were baptized along with Pismote's infant daughter Sofía and a seven-year-old girl, Heytém.[83] As she watched the proceedings that officially inducted her daughter into the Catholic community, Pismote may have reflected on how the opportunities open to the boys differed from those available to her daughter and Heytém. Telempis and Mequeig might sing in the mission choir within a few years, and later—if they lived—they might act as interpreters or sacristans. For Heytém and Sofía, no such future existed. Outside the mission, if either girl had the right lineage and the requisite leadership skills, it was conceivable (though not likely) that she might one day lead her village. Certainly, if one of them had the gift, she could become a shaman or medicine woman.[84] Even ordinary women were highly valued for their knowledge of local plant resources and their skilled labor in basketry and food gathering, preparation, and storage. In the mission, these skills were not valued, nor even taught. The best these girls could hope for was a good marriage.

In its privileging of men, the mission hierarchy reinforced and strengthened the patriarchal structures that prevailed in most Bay Area Indian societies. However, the mission hierarchy also reversed existing social structures in some ways. Men like Puyeles, who accepted baptism as mature adults, were unlikely to receive a position in the mission. Baptized at the age of approximately thirty-six, Puyeles probably struggled with Spanish, gaining a rudimentary knowledge of the language at best. Younger men like

Telempis and Mequeig, those baptized as teenagers or even as boys, were far more likely to pick up the language. Since the Indians that priests selected for leadership positions at Mission San Francisco acted as go-betweens for the priests and the Indian populace, a good knowledge of the colonists' language was essential. Thus, younger men—particularly those who had been baptized for a long time—were more likely to occupy respected positions like that of interpreter. Indeed, of the six interpreters who can be identified in Mission San Francisco records, five were baptized before the age of nine.[85] Instead of following their elders, these young men led them.

It is likely that the children led their elders in less formal ways, as well. Pismote may have noticed that the voices of the children sounded loudest in the Mass during the congregational responses: the beneficiaries of an extra catechism lesson on many afternoons, the children probably spoke with more confidence and less hesitation than the adults. The children might also have been more comfortable than the adults with the kinesthetic experience of the Mass, because they had learned the movements of the ritual from a young age. For those Indians baptized as adults, the movements of the Mass were new, at least in the particular order in which they were arranged for the ritual. Though the Mass may have borne some resemblance to a traditional dance in its purpose, in that specific movements corresponded to particular moments, and in the esoteric language that accompanied the ritual, in other ways the Mass was very different. Pismote and her fellow congregants shaped their mouths to new forms, repeating words and responding to cues in Latin and Spanish. They adopted new postures of submission and respect, kneeling and standing as the occasion required. They learned to make the sign of the cross, marking themselves as members of a new community. In the Mass, Indians learned to move differently in the world. It is impossible to say how foreign these new movements may have felt to Pismote and her fellow congregants, but perhaps she surreptitiously sought a place near the back of the church where she could follow the movements of her niece and nephew, Ygnacia Barbara and Chi-uéc, and their peers, using the children's words and actions as her guide through the Mass.

Many boys took an active part in leading the congregation by providing music during the Mass. The missionaries took great pride in having taught some of the baptized Indians to sing and play in European harmonies and rhythms, and they put those skills to use in performances and church services. "In the Mission we teach some boys to play the Violin, the Viol, the

Drum, and other Instruments that are used in the Churches," Ramón Abella and Juan Sainz de Lucio reported in 1814.[86] Otto von Kotzebue and Louis Choris, the artist who accompanied him, both noted the indigenous musicians' contributions to Masses performed at the mission when they visited in 1816. "The orchestra consisted of a violoncello, a violin, and two flutes," wrote Kotzebue, adding with typical disdain, "these instruments were played by little half-naked Indians, and were very often out of tune."[87] Choris was more charitable. Children "assist [the priest] during the service which they also accompany with the sound of musical instruments," he wrote. "These are chiefly drums, trumpets, tambours, and other instruments of the same class. It is by means of their noise that they endeavour to stir the imagination of the Indians and to make men of these savages."[88] Musicians enjoyed a certain status at the mission: the adults among them were given distinctive clothing and choice work assignments.[89] Becoming a musician, then, was one way for Indian men and boys to improve their lives at the mission. Like many other positions, that of musician was only open to males at the mission, a restriction that would not have seemed unusual to Pismote: men dominated musical production outside the mission as well.[90]

⌒

The sun set at about five o'clock on Christmas Eve.[91] As the light faded, Pismote and the other Indians gathered once again in front of the church doors for a recital of doctrine and prayers. The missionaries alternated between Spanish and native languages for these lessons, hoping in this way to encourage the Indians to learn Spanish without completely shutting out those who struggled with the language.[92] For priests who spoke little of the local languages to begin with, the procedure varied little from morning to evening; the only difference was that for native language sessions, interpreters rendered the missionaries' Spanish words into the indigenous languages. For Indians like Pismote and Puyeles, though, who likely spoke little Spanish, responding in their mother tongues must have been a relief. Even so, Pismote may have been bored and perhaps resentful of the hours the priests required her and others to spend at prayer. The evening recital of doctrine and prayers was dropped from the daily schedule sometime in the late eighteenth or early nineteenth century. By 1807, Father Martín de Landaeta was complaining about that decision: it should not have been made, he said, because any attempt to reintroduce evening lessons would be met with considerable resistance from the Indians—a remark suggesting that Indian participation in these lessons was less than enthusiastic.[93]

After about an hour of instruction and prayer, the Indians retired to their dwellings for an evening meal. This night was unlike other nights at the mission because at midnight they would gather for a special Mass. Instead of returning to their sleeping quarters after dinner, then, perhaps the Indians stayed out in the darkness or gathered in one of the larger dwellings in the Indian village. This evening might have been the perfect opportunity to observe the traditional rituals associated with the winter solstice, which had occurred a few days earlier. That night, and the following day, Indians may well have performed traditional dances, made offerings to the sun, and performed other ceremonies. Evidence shows that Indians at Mission San Francisco continued to perform traditional dances after their baptisms. In fact, some observers suggested that these dances were regular occurrences. Louis Choris, an artist who visited the mission in 1816, saw Indians dancing after Mass on Sundays. In addition to producing visual depictions of these dances, Choris described them:

> Half of the men adorn themselves with feathers and with girdles ornamented with feathers and with bits of shell that pass for money among them, or they paint their bodies with regular lines of black, red, and white. Some have half their bodies (from the head downward) daubed with black, the other half red, and the whole crossed with white lines. Others sift the down from birds on their hair. The men commonly dance six or eight together, all making the same movements and all armed with spears. Their music consists of clapping the hands, singing, and the sound made by striking split sticks together which has a charm for their ears; this is finally followed by a horrible yell that greatly resembles the sound of a cough accompanied by a whistling noise. The women dance among themselves, but without making violent movements.[94]

It may be that Choris was mistaken about the regularity of traditional dances at Mission San Francisco. Nevertheless, his description suggests that dances did occur at least occasionally, perhaps allowing baptized Indians to meet the minimal requirements of their traditional religions.

Pismote and other unmarried women may not have been able to join in the festivities that Christmas Eve. Because the priests were concerned, in particular, with preserving the sexual purity of female baptized Indians, it is unlikely that Pismote and other monjerío residents were allowed to wander the mission grounds freely after dark. Indeed, Jean-François de Galaup de la Pérouse observed that at Mission San Carlos Borromeo, "the religious take care to lock up one hour after supper the women whose husbands are away as well as all girls over the age of 9."[95] Confined to the monjerío, Pismote and the other women may have whiled away the hours playing traditional games, gambling, telling stories, or just talking.

Called once more by the bells, the Indians returned to the church at midnight to find it, and the priests, arrayed in white to mark the arrival of Christmas. After another Mass, this one probably augmented by special music from the choir and certainly enhanced by the use of incense, they would retire to their beds until the sun rose again the next morning. Christmas Day would no doubt bring prayers and celebrations; Otto von Kotzebue observed that on holidays "the Indians did no work, but, divided into groups, amused themselves with various pastimes." He went on to describe a gambling game on which Indians staked "little white shells, which serve instead of money."[96] (See Illustration 1.) Work would resume the following day, along with the regular regimen of prayers, Mass, and recital of doctrine.

For Pismote and the other Indians baptized at Mission San Francisco, the Mass provided a novel sensory experience while subtly instructing them in the norms of Hispanic culture. Surrounded by images of saints and supernatural figures, observing richly attired priests handling precious objects, and listening to the male voices that filled the air, Pismote learned her subordinate place—as a woman and as an Indian—in the society of the Hispanic colonists. As she genuflected, stood, knelt, sang, spoke, and kept silent, Pismote enacted that position. Even as she did so, however, Pismote probably also made sense of this new life in terms of her own cultural experience, drawing parallels between traditional Bay Area practices and Catholic actions and interpreting Catholic ideas according to an Indian intellectual framework. Told of her subordination, Pismote had only to look at her clothing or taste her food to remind herself of the valuable services she and other women contributed to the mission; reminded of her superfluousness in the Mass, she had only to reflect that without her and other Indians, the mission itself would not exist. Not only were the Indians the reason for the mission's existence but their labor was also crucial to its survival.

2

Building Faith

ᴄᴏ "No one is more concerned or more interested than the missionaries that the Indian should continue in his native ignorance of horsemanship," wrote Fermín Francisco de Lasuén to Pedro Fages in August of 1787. Fages, then the governor of Alta California, had complained to Lasuén about a number of problems he perceived in the mission system, including his belief that too many Indians were allowed to ride horses. Mounted Indians moved faster, and could do more damage, than Indians afoot, so keeping Indians dismounted was, in effect, a security measure.[1] As president of the Alta California mission system, Lasuén answered Fages's complaints as diplomatically as he could. However, there was a problem: "Your Lordship is well aware," Lasuén continued, "of the cattle and horses which, with the King's pleasure, every one of the missions possesses, and that horsemen are needed to look after them. And these have to be Indians, for there are no others."[2]

Not satisfied with this response, Fages took his complaint to his superiors, and a few months later Lasuén found himself defending the missions in a lengthy letter to Don Jacobo Ugarte y Loyola, the commander in chief of the Interior Provinces of New Spain. Summarizing his previous exchange with Fages, Lasuén wrote that

I satisfied His Lordship with the very scarce number of saddles and cowhands that each mission maintains for that purpose, and with the vigilance of the missionaries, who are more interested than anyone else that the Indian does not become adept in the use and management of the horse. . . . It is known to Your Lordship that without some mounted men, who here of necessity must be Indians, the missions would lack an indispensable means of caring for, and making use of, all of the resources of their lands.[3]

Mounted cowhands were certainly necessary at Mission San Francisco, where cattle herds multiplied year after year. In 1787, the year of Fages's complaint, Fathers Pedro Benito Cambón and Diego García reported that the mission had more than one thousand head of cattle. To patrol the mission herds, including not only the cattle but also hundreds of sheep and goats, the mission owned twenty-three horses.[4] Those horses were ridden primarily by Indians. Massea, one of the earliest Indians to accept baptism, apparently became a cowhand at the mission; in 1797 another Indian claimed that he had left Mission San Francisco because "the vaquero Salvador [Massea's baptismal name] sinned with his wife."[5] This accusation, in which occupation precedes baptismal name in identifying the alleged wrongdoer, suggests the extent to which Massea was identified with his work. His occupation was not without its risks: over the course of the Spanish colonial period, a small number of Indians died on the job, falling off horses or being gored by bulls. Perhaps most tragic was Gualamuc, a twelve-year-old boy, who died "from a pair of kicks." According to the surprised and somewhat mystified Father Ramón Abella, the young cowhand in training had restrained a horse himself, put a halter on it, and led it down the hill, all in the presence of the priest and two other baptized Indians, before receiving the death blows from the horse's hooves.[6]

Despite the dangers posed by aggressive horses and angry bulls, and despite the complaints and threats of Alta California's military authorities, selected Indians baptized at Mission San Francisco were allowed to ride horses, because prohibiting them from doing so would effectively bring the work of the mission to a halt. As many scholars have recognized, the Spanish colonial enterprise in California, and with it, Catholic mission activities, depended on Indian labor. In the Bay Area, Indians—many, but not all, baptized—did the work Spanish soldiers refused to do: they built buildings, dug ditches, herded animals, and farmed crops; they wove cloth, made meals, washed clothing, and waited tables. Soldiers in the Spanish military saw themselves primarily as a fighting force and complained vociferously about the construction work required to build and maintain the California presidios. Though they tolerated some of this work, the soldiers forced their superiors to delegate much of the building work to local Indians.[7] Yet priests and presidio commanders alike complained about Indians' laziness.[8] In 1814 Fathers Ramón Abella and Juan Sainz de Lucio, the priests then stationed at Mission San Francisco de Asís, complained that making baptized Indians work was "like making water flow uphill."[9] Nevertheless, it was crucial to the existence of the mission and the ongoing evangelization of surrounding Bay Area Indians that the baptized Indians do the work of the mission.

Indian labor was necessary to the survival of the mission system, but it was also an integral part of the priests' attempt to Hispanicize Indians. Indeed, labor was one of the main characteristics that distinguished unbaptized "gentile" Indians from baptized "neophytes" in the eyes of the San Francisco priests. In the same 1814 document in which they complained about the Indians' laziness, Abella and Sainz de Lucio explained that

> the Gentiles do not sow, they are like the Birds of the Field who neither work nor have granaries. The Neophytes in the Mission sow when the Missionary Fathers determine to do so, in Community— as children of a family on Lands belonging to the Mission: That the Plows and Teams, and everything necessary, are ready, falls to the Fathers; and it is advisable to make them fond of this because they, to maintain themselves in the Woods and Beaches, would not need to sow.[10]

Teaching Indians to labor like Hispanic peasants, then, was a way of sustaining the colonial enterprise and also a way of teaching the Indians their place in the new colonial order. As laborers, Indians learned to be the children of the Church and vassals of the Spanish king.

This view of labor was hardly exclusive to the California missions. A theology of labor had been developing in the Catholic Church for centuries before the first California mission was founded. This "gospel of work"[11] was carried far and wide, propagated in the sermons of itinerant Catholic preachers. Seventeenth-century French Jesuit Louis Bourdaloue, for example, proclaimed that "each of us . . . is sanctified in the state to which he has been named by God."¹² In other words, salvation was contingent upon one's satisfactory fulfillment of one's role in life—a role that had a great deal to do with work. Other preachers agreed. In the last question of his *Catecismo breve*, Bartolomé Castaño made fulfilling one's role a condition of salvation. Priests at Mission San Francisco taught Indians to respond to the question "And to be saved, what must we do?" with the answer "Keep the commands of the law of God and those of the holy church and the obligations of our estate."¹³ Father Pedro de Calatayud y Florencia, a Spanish Jesuit who traveled his country preaching retreats in the mid-eighteenth century, shortly before the first Alta California mission was founded, declared that all people, "as sons of Adam, were born to work."¹⁴ In describing humans as "sons of Adam," Calatayud alluded to the Catholic doctrine of original sin and the view of work as penance for sins. Work thus became a distinctly human act, integral to humans' salvation. The same theology of work, casting labor as a result of original sin and a necessity for salvation, found expression in manuals of piety, pastoral letters, and other ecclesiastical writing in the eighteenth century.¹⁵

The Catholic theology of work received a boost from secular governmental agencies in the eighteenth century when the Bourbon monarchs determined to transform the Spanish empire's poor and idle into an economically productive segment of society. Secular social commentators joined churchmen in conceiving of idleness as damaging to the body politic.¹⁶ Quite apart from its spiritual consequences, secular writers saw idleness as a problem because it decreased the economic production of the empire. The Spanish empire depended on that production, so those Spanish subjects who did not work increased the burden borne by those who did. In the words of one commentator, this freeloading constituted "continuous robbery at the expense of the nation."¹⁷ Not only was it selfish of the idle to refuse to work and therefore not contribute to the nation's welfare but it was also actually harmful to civilization. "The country that has loafers in greatest abundance," warned Nicolas de Arriquibar, "comes closest to barbarity, and it is a republic of caribs, who eat each other in various ways."¹⁸ By putting people to work, then, the Spanish government both enhanced its economic potential and suppressed the possibility that its citizens would become no better than the cannibalistic barbarians that Spaniards imagined living on tropical islands half a world away.

The Franciscans at the California missions absorbed and reflected this understanding of labor and its relation to civilization and salvation. In 1802

Father Fermín Francisco de Lasuén argued against a proposed policy of allowing Indians to stay in their villages, or rancherías, after accepting baptism, because they would not work: "They do not have any industry nor any application of those conducive to the rational, social, and civil life, which they have learned from their elders," he protested.

> Everything is taught to them by the Missionaries; and their observance of it depends on the vigilance and incessant care of these; since if it is not only this mode of living, but principally the Christian one that the King Our Lord wants to be imposed on the Indians, how will this Royal and Catholic will be achieved by leaving them in liberty and in their rancherías after they are baptized?[19]

In Lasuén's mind, the Indians' acquisition of "industry" was inextricably linked with their adoption of Christianity and opposed to the idle "liberty" in which the Franciscans believed unconverted Indians lived: without work, there could be no salvation. Priests at Mission San Francisco drew the same connection just over a decade later, using the performance of agricultural activity to distinguish between baptized and unbaptized Indians.[20]

To the Franciscans in California, then, teaching Indians to labor was an integral part of the evangelization campaign. "Your Lordship knows," Father Lasuén wrote to Brigadier Jacobo Ugarte y Loyola, "that we are dealing with peoples whom we are teaching that they are men; and with men, whom the King looks at now as sons, while we complete the obligation His Majesty has placed upon us of shaping them, so that he can later rule them as Vassals."[21] By teaching the Indians to forgo their hunting and gathering in favor of Hispanic-style work such as farming, the Franciscans believed that they could transform the Indians from Arriquibar's "republic of caribs" into civilized human beings, Christians, and fit subjects for the Spanish crown.

The Franciscans were thus forced into a paradox: they were certain the Indians had to work in order to be saved, and the mission needed Indian labor to succeed. However, to obtain Indian labor, the missionaries had to let the Indians labor in Indian ways, rather than enforcing Hispanic custom. The effect of the work, then—the civilizing, Christianizing, Hispanicizing influence it was supposed to exert—was counteracted by the priests' dependence on the performance of that very labor. This need for the Indians to work, both to sustain the colonial enterprise and to accomplish its goal of Hispanicizing the Indians, opened a space for Indian agency within the colonial system. Baptized Indians, like their unbaptized counterparts, were able to exercise some control over the nature and quantity of labor that they performed. The priests were forced to accept compromises in labor practices and techniques, schedules, and products, despite their desire to create model Hispanic peasants by teaching the Indians to labor in Hispanic ways. We see these compromises most clearly in the areas of foodways, specifically food preparation and consumption, and what we might call "buildingways"—building design, construction, and decoration.

In every society, the selection, preparation, and consumption of food are important ways of marking group identity.[22] At Mission San Francisco, baptized Indians created hybrid foodways, preparing new foods in traditional ways and supplementing Hispanic-introduced foods with traditional food items.

Women prepared much of the food at Mission San Francisco. Each day, they received grain to roast, which Georg H. von Langsdorff observed them doing, using bark baskets: "Corn and pulse are put in [baskets]," he wrote, "and the Indians, by turning them quickly and dexterously over a slow charcoal fire, get every grain thoroughly browned without the basket being scorched in the least."[23] French explorer Jean-François de Galaup de la Pérouse provided a similar description of the process at Mission San Carlos, observing that the roasting took place because of heated rocks placed in the baskets.[24] This technique was the same one women had used before the Spanish arrived to roast acorns; instead of adopting new, Hispanic techniques to cook these new grains, Bay Area Indian women assimilated the new grains into their existing repertoire of cooking methods.[25] These roasted grains became the base for *atole*, a sort of porridge served for the morning and evening meals at Mission San Francisco. La Pérouse described atole as "porridge . . . of which [the Indians] are very fond, . . . [it] is seasoned with neither butter nor salt, and would taste very insipid to our palates."[26] Although it differed in flavor, most Indians at Mission San Francisco probably found atole reminiscent of the acorn mush that was a staple of indigenous Bay Area diets. The switch to wheat and corn may have been nutritionally beneficial. Robert Heizer determined that wheat flour and cornmeal contain more protein and carbohydrates, and less fat, than acorn meal.[27] Nevertheless, the techniques used to prepare these new grains and the manner in which they were most often served suggest that Indians' food preparation and consumption did not change drastically when they accepted baptism at Mission San Francisco.

The techniques used to roast grain may not have mattered much to the priests, so long as the task got done. When it came to meat, though, the priests seem to have been more particular. Archaeological evidence from both Mission Santa Cruz and Mission San Antonio de Padua indicates that baptized Indians adopted Hispanic butchering practices. Instead of cutting up cows as they would other large game, Indians used metal blades provided by the colonists and divided the carcass according to Hispanic notions about appropriate cuts of meat. Archaeologist Rebecca Allen concludes that baptized Indians at Mission Santa Cruz "apparently adopted Hispanic methods of butchering animals" instead of adapting the techniques they used for large game like deer.[28] Archaeologists Paul E. Langenwalter and Larry W. McKee found similar patterns at Mission San Antonio, but they argue that these changes represent limited acculturation, at most, on the Indians' part. Several features of the butchering that took place at Mission San Antonio during the mission period—"dismemberment at joints by cutting tendons and ligaments, stripping of meat from the skeleton, and fracturing of limb bones for marrow extractions"—are elements typical of Spanish butchering, but they are also "all attributes common to aboriginal butchering processes as described in California," write Langenwalter and McKee. "The main differences [between traditional California Indian butchering and that found at Mission San Antonio] are the use of steel tools and the production of spare rib cuts."[29] It is likely that Bay Area Indians baptized at Mission San Francisco also butchered Hispanic livestock—mostly cattle, along with some sheep and the occasional pig—in a similar manner, combining the priests' tools and techniques with the methods they had used before accepting baptism.

The beef that the missionaries considered a staple was a novel taste for Indians at the mission. Before Indians moved to the mission, their meat came from a variety of sources: fish and shellfish, deer, antelope, rabbits, birds, and rodents all contributed to a traditional Bay Area diet. Men were responsible for capturing and killing this game, which the women then prepared for consumption. At the mission, the men almost certainly were still responsible for killing the animals, but slaughtering a domestic animal—even one as large as a cow—was very different. No hunt was required, so the spiritual preparation for the kill was probably abbreviated, at best. Outside the mission, men preparing for a hunt abstained from sexual relations, spent most of their time in the sweathouse, and waited for propitious dreams or other omens. They worked to get in touch with their spiritual allies, who would help them with the hunt, and to propitiate the spirit of the animal they hoped to kill.[30] At the mission, though, men slaughtered livestock on the priests' orders, probably with little or no spiritual preparation.

Although they butchered animals according to Hispanic norms, Indians at Mission San Francisco did not adopt a fully Hispanic diet. Instead, they ate a combination of traditional and Hispanic foodstuffs, as did Indians at other Franciscan missions in Alta California. Archaeological remains show that Indians at Mission San Francisco ate beef, mutton, and domesticated grains and pulses, but supplemented these foodstuffs with shellfish and fish. Archaeologist Richard Ambro writes that these remains "reflect continued exploitation of traditional shoreline resources."[31] The Mission San Francisco burial register shows that Indians baptized there continued to hunt, fish, and gather wild foods after accepting baptism. In 1784 Puyeles—the husband of Pismote and her sisters before his baptism—died while hunting ducks. "The neophyte Indians of this mission brought the news that the widower Nicolas de Bari had drowned in the estuary," wrote Father Francisco Palóu in the death register for the mission. "Nobody saw him fall, nor could his body be found, but because . . . in the evening they left him on the shore of the estuary hunting ducks and at dawn they did not find anything but his clothing on the shore of the estuary near the fire, the net set with a duck tangled in it[,] they judged it certain that the current of the estuary had taken him."[32] The importance of wild game in the Indians' diet may have diminished once they accepted baptism, and Indians may have abbreviated, or even forgone, the spiritual preparation for the hunt. However, as Puyeles's death shows, the priests did not eliminate hunting altogether.

Whether the priests were able to eliminate the ritual preparations that preceded hunting among Bay Area Indians is impossible to tell. Puyeles and other baptized Indian men at Mission San Francisco may have continued to observe the customary spiritual preparations as they made ready for hunts. Though the mission had no sweathouse, Adelbert von Chamisso wrote after visiting in 1816 that "the usual bath of the Indians, like that of most of the northern nations, is the following: at the entrance of a cave on the sea-shore, in which the bathers are, a great fire is made; they suffer it to go out, when they have perspired sufficiently, and then leap over it, and plunge into the sea."[33] This practice may have provided an acceptable substitute for sweathouse baths, allowing men to embark on hunts in a spiritually appropriate state. When hunters returned, they shared their game according to traditional rules governing the distribution of game. "The ones who know best how to Fish and Hunt . . . serve the others because they give [to the others] out of their Catch and Kill," Ramón Abella and Juan Sainz de Lucio observed in 1814.[34] Outside the mission, a hunter ate little to nothing of the game he killed. Instead, he distributed the meat, repaying others' generosity and showing respect to community leaders. To keep the meat for himself would be antisocial as well as "dangerous in regard to the spirit world."[35] While not conclusive, these Europeans' observations about sweat baths and the sharing of game suggest that those who accepted baptism at Mission San Francisco continued to think of hunting as an activity with spiritual aspects.

Death reports confirm the Indians' ongoing exploitation of other traditional food resources as well. In 1811 a young woman named Pispispuquel and seven other Indians who had gone on paseo were reported dead as a result of eating bad clams. "These eight died within hours, the travelers assured me, due to a clam, which was damaged," wrote the priest who recorded the deaths.[36] Shellfish, including clams, had been a staple of Bay Area Indian diets before the Hispanic colonists arrived. It may be that Pispispuquel and her companions were unable to recognize the bad clams because they were less experienced in gathering shellfish, having fewer occasions on which to do so. Most shellfish gathering expeditions, though, did not result in illness or death, suggesting that older generations of Indians passed on sufficient traditional knowledge to younger generations that baptized Indians could continue to exploit such traditional resources as the abundance of clams and other shellfish in the Bay Area.

Indians also continued to gather acorns, formerly a staple of their diets. Two separate death records document this activity. In 1787 seven-year-old Se'pente died in the mountains while accompanying her mother and stepfather on an acorn-gathering expedition.[37] Over thirty years later, in 1820, Nopete and his wife Tuglum went to the mountains in search of acorns. Tuglum returned alone; Nopete, she said, had died in the mountains.[38] Although the priests at Mission San Francisco intended to Hispanicize the baptized Indians, Indians maintained their traditional identities through their foodways.

To do so, Indians continued to pay attention to traditional seasonal cycles—the acorn harvest, shellfish season, annual duck migrations—and in fact, Indians at Mission San Francisco may have privileged these traditional seasonal cycles over the new seasons introduced by the Hispanic colonists. This was certainly true elsewhere; Mission San Carlos lost more than three hundred *fanegas* of corn in 1799 because the baptized Indians at the mission had laid the harvested corn out in the mission square to dry and then left the mission on paseo. While they were gone, rains ruined the corn.[39] Despite this devastating loss, the priests were unable to prevent the Indians from leaving the mission, sometimes in large numbers and for sustained periods.[40]

However, priests frequently allowed and even encouraged Indians to gather traditional foods. In 1798 Captain José Arguello wrote to his superior, Governor Diego de Borica, that "the Father Ministers usually give them permission in the season of their seeds for one week to harvest them in their lands."[41] Indians' control over their movements implies an associated ability to prioritize mission labor among other activities. Given the amount of labor that Indians performed at the mission, it seems unlikely that most Indians felt completely free to refuse to do the mission's work at any time or for any reason. However, it appears that they could decide not to work in order to lay in a store of acorns, or go hunting, when the occasion demanded.[42] These priorities, worked out by baptized Indians who may have been trying to keep a foot in their traditional culture while learning the Hispanic Catholic culture of the newcomers, were negotiated with priests as well. The priests had good reason to compromise: if they tried to make the Indians work too hard, they might lose their labor force altogether. Thus, although not completely independent, Indians baptized at Mission San Francisco did exercise some control over their labor in food production and preparation. This control over their own labor also allowed Indians some control over the extent to which their foodways changed once they accepted baptism.

⌒

The ways in which Indians combined traditional Indian and Hispanic forms were not limited to foodways: construction techniques, architectural styles, and decorative aesthetics were another arena of fusion. Indian recruits built the majority of Mission San Francisco. The Franciscans cared deeply about how the mission's buildings were built, where they were placed in relation to one another, and what they looked like.[43] In fact the perdurability of the buildings mattered greatly to the priests because it set Hispanic forms apart from—and above, in their minds—Indian ones. Writing of the Mission San Francisco church's construction in 1788, Fathers Pedro Benito Cambón and Diego García remarked that "the masons and peons are some neophytes, who in their gentile state never made a wall, nor did they see one made, because all their buildings are reduced to chaff without a grain of permanence."[44] The priests, on the other hand, intended to create an enduring institution, and so put Indians to work at the mission and its outstations "for the permanence of this Mission."[45] Nevertheless, as with food, the priests' dependence on Indian labor led to compromises and accommodations in the design, construction, and decoration of the "permanent" buildings erected at Mission San Francisco.

The mission ranchería is a good example. The housing of baptized Indian families was primarily in the ranchería, or village, immediately outside the mission quadrangle. If priests had had their way, this village would have been a cluster of adobe apartments, arranged in neat, parallel rows. However, over the life of the mission most of the apartments were traditional Bay Area Indian huts, circular buildings constructed of reeds and other readily available materials. In 1792 English captain George Vancouver visited Mission San Francisco and provided a detailed description of the Indians' homes. "Their houses," he wrote,

> were of a conical form, about six or seven feet in diameter at their base (which is the ground) and are constructed by a number of stakes, chiefly of the willow tribe, which are driven erect into the earth in a circular manner, the upper ends of which being small and pliable are brought nearly to join at the top, in the centre of the circle; and these being securely fastened, give the upper part or roof somewhat of a flattish appearance. Thinner twigs of the like species are horizontally interwoven between the uprights, forming a piece of basket work about ten or twelve feet high; at the top a small aperture is left, which allows the smoke of the fire made in the centre of the hut to escape, and admits most of the light they receive: the entrance is by a small hole close to the ground,

through which with difficulty one person at a time can gain admittance. The whole is covered over with a thick thatch of dried grass and rushes.

Although Vancouver found these dwellings to be "miserable habitations," he did note that they "were erected with some degree of uniformity, about three or four feet asunder, in straight rows, leaving lanes or passages at right angles between them."[46] We see here a concession, then, to the priests' aesthetic preferences: though Indians built the houses in the traditional manner, they arranged them in a grid, following Hispanic standards for city building.[47]

Vancouver's comment that the huts were "miserable" exemplifies the attitude of most European and Hispanic observers, clearly indicating a preference for upper-class European-style architecture and building techniques.[48] However, La Pérouse contended that even after their baptisms, Bay Area Indians preferred their traditional architectural forms. "This architecture," he wrote, "widespread in the two Californias, has never been changed, in spite of the missionaries' endeavors."[49] According to La Pérouse, this holdover was due to Indians' preference for the open air and for the ease of construction and destruction inherent in the circular dwellings. While Eurocentrism permeates La Pérouse's comments, a preference for the traditional architecture may partly explain the slow progress in replacing these houses with adobe buildings at Mission San Francisco. The adobe apartments were probably also a low priority on the priests' building wish list, despite their desire to do away with the traditional thatch dwellings. While the baptized Indians at Mission San Francisco were able to tear down the mission complex—then built of palisade—and raise it again within about a year, from 1782 to 1783, apartments arose in small numbers over the course of years.[50] The first nineteen adobe apartments were built in 1793.[51] Indians built twenty more in 1796, and the building continued, sporadically, for several more years. Though Fathers Martín de Landaeta and José de la Cruz declared these apartments complete in their 1797 report, the priests never were able to do away with the traditional circular houses entirely.[52] Despite that inability, the priests continued to impose Hispanic organization on Indian dwellings. Martín de Landaeta wrote to Father Tomás de la Peña in 1801 that a new "Indian village [at Mission San Francisco] is being built where the tannery was, not with a square like the other, but rather with streets and a corral in front of each house."[53] Though this ranchería departed from the most traditional Hispanic urban model, in which the city centered on a plaza bordered by religious and government buildings—the "square" to which Landaeta referred—Landaeta's description indicates that the geometric grid continued to be the organizing principle for Indian villages built under priestly supervision.[54]

The adobe apartments may have represented the triumph of Hispanic urban organization and architectural forms, but it is most likely that baptized Indians continued to utilize the space these apartments enclosed in traditional ways. Rebecca Allen has pointed out that the transition to adobe apartments, with their rectangular dimensions, required baptized Indians to do more than move their belongings from one shelter to another; the move from circular to rectangular space necessitated something of a mental reorientation, a rearrangement of activities and movements within that space.[55] Franciscan priests attempted to influence these activities: Father Lasuén noted in 1801 that "the houses of the Indians of San Francisco and Santa Clara are fitted out, many of them, with grinding-stones, pans, pots, stew-pots, and even small ovens for baking bread."[56] Despite the priests' attempts to Hispanicize the interiors of baptized Indians' dwellings, Allen's archaeological study of Mission Santa Cruz suggests that baptized Indians continued to arrange the space inside their adobe dwellings in ways based on traditional norms. For example, the cooking fire in traditional dwellings was located in the center of the circular space, with smoke rising through a smoke hole directly above the fire. In the adobe apartments, Indians continued to build their fire in the center of the room, despite the lack of a smoke hole in the ceiling.[57] Excavations at Mission San Antonio reveal a similar pattern.[58] It is reasonable to suppose that Indians at Mission San Francisco did the same.

The Franciscans were far more particular about the architecture of the mission church than they were about Indian families' apartments. Nevertheless, even this most important of buildings demonstrates a fusion of traditional Bay Area Indian and Hispanic forms. At Mission San Carlos, La Pérouse remarked that "the parish church is very clean, although thatched."[59] The same was true at Mission San Francisco for nearly two decades after its founding: the mission church, built in European style, was covered by a thatch roof, just like a traditional Indian dwelling.[60] Thatch was, of course, a familiar building material in Europe as well, but one associated with peasants and thus connoting an impoverished establishment.[61]

That impression may have been correct; nevertheless, it is clear that La Pérouse and other observers found it inappropriate.

More important, thatch was a traditional building material for the California Indians as well. This is an instance, then, of what James Lockhart, historian of Latin America, terms "Double Mistaken Identity," wherein "each side of the cultural exchange presumes that a given form or concept is functioning in the way familiar within its own tradition and is unaware of or unimpressed by the other side's interpretation."[62] Priests and Indians both familiar with the use of thatch for roofing likely both saw this architectural feature as emerging from their own cultural backgrounds, not as a technique borrowed from the other.

The decoration of the 1791 church also followed Hispanic convention. Even the original altarpiece, a mural painted by baptized Indians, was, according to Norman Neuerburg, "very freely done by someone not particularly well-trained but at least well-acquainted with the late baroque style in Mexico."[63] However, some decorations escape European conventions. In particular, the red, blue, and ochre chevrons on the ceiling of the church and the geometric designs on the walls recall traditional basketry designs, and almost certainly emerged from traditional Bay Area aesthetics.[64]

Basketry was the highest aesthetic expression in indigenous California, and it was reserved almost exclusively for women.[65] Just as men prepared spiritually for hunting, women readied themselves for basket weaving by fasting and seeking propitious dreams. They sometimes received basketry designs in these dreams.[66] Therefore, unbeknownst to the priests, the walls of Mission San Francisco's church may have borne the imprint of the traditional Bay Area spirit world in the seemingly innocuous triangles and circles that Indian artists painted. These geometric patterns were not necessarily off-limits to male artists. In fact, ethnohistorian James Bennyhoff found that among the Plains Miwok, men routinely carved bone ear tubes for women with "delicate geometric designs resembling but not identical to basketry motifs."[67] In some areas, Bennyhoff wrote, these designs included "an emphasis on cross-hatched bands and complex chevron and diamond designs."[68] Indians who attended Mass at Mission San Francisco may very well have seen the resemblance between the decorations on the church walls and the designs in traditional basketry and women's jewelry, and therefore may have experienced the building as a markedly feminine site.[69]

Although priests intended to Hispanicize the Indians through their labor and its products, it was not possible to do so fully. The Franciscans

ILLUSTRATION 4. Edward S. Curtis, Baskets in the Painted Cave—Yokuts. These Yokuts baskets demonstrate some of the geometric designs frequently used in the San Francisco Bay Area. Library of Congress, Prints and Photographs Division, Edward S. Curtis Collection, LC-USZ62–118769.

ILLUSTRATION 5. These geometric patterns on the wall of Mission San Francisco were painted by California Indian artists. They probably reminded the baptized Indians who attended Mass in the church of their traditional basketry designs. Photo by Robert D. Newell.

and other colonists in the San Francisco Bay Area depended on Indian labor for the survival of the colonial enterprise. This dependence forced them to accept less-than-fully-Hispanic labor techniques, products, work schedules, and aesthetics, to let the Indians do things "their way" from time to time. Indians' food selection, preparation, and consumption and building techniques, styles, and aesthetics all demonstrate Indians' desire and ability to retain elements of traditional Indian cultures, fusing them in some cases with Hispanic forms, despite priests' objections.[70] Thus, labor was one arena at Mission San Francisco in which Indians were able to exercise some autonomy. Though limited, the agency they exercised was significant enough to affect both the nature and the quantity of Indian labor at Mission San Francisco.

Most descriptions of the workday in the California missions suggest that Indians' labor was not unduly strenuous. According to Richard Street, field hands "seldom if ever worked more than eight hours in a single day, or more than forty hours per week. . . . Additionally, field hands [and all mission residents] did not work on the twenty-four annual 'saints' days. . . . In total, field hands enjoyed ninety-two holidays from work every year."[71] Contemporary observers commented more often on the length of the work day. La Pérouse, describing Mission San Carlos in 1786, wrote that "there are 7 hrs of work a day, 2 hrs of prayers and 4 or 5 on Sundays or feast days which are days of complete rest and divine services."[72] About thirteen years later, Captain José Arguello described a somewhat less demanding regimen at Missions San Francisco, Santa Clara, San José, and Santa Cruz, the northernmost missions at the time. "In the winter," he informed Governor Diego de Borica, baptized Indians "work scarcely three hours in the morning, and some more in the afternoon, in the summer something like four hours the one and the other, leaving to the pregnant women, to the nursing women, to the old people and the children, the trivial tasks and those of less weight."[73] All told, Indians at Mission San Francisco were probably left with a fair amount of free time—time that the priests could fill only partially with prayers, catechism, and Masses.

Arguello's description of the workday at the northern missions clearly indicates that gender and age were determining factors in the assignment of tasks at Mission San Francisco. However, these factors could be ignored when the situation demanded. Fathers Pedro Benito Cambón and Diego García reported in 1788 that "throughout the summer, and part of the winter, no work was done in the workshops, because even the women were employed in transporting adobes, mud, rock, and other necessities for the new Church, in order to be able to roof it before the rains came."[74] Women and children likewise helped in harvesting and other time-specific tasks that required mobilizing large amounts of labor for limited periods of time. This practice of employing all able-bodied workers, regardless of gender or age, in order to complete urgent and labor-intensive tasks was similar to traditional labor practices outside the mission, in which men helped with the acorn harvest during the few weeks when work was heaviest and women aided in salmon fishing during seasonal salmon runs.[75]

In normal day-to-day labor, men performed the mission's agricultural, ranching, and construction work while women worked in the workshops, weaving, grinding flour, and performing other domestic tasks. George

Vancouver observed during his 1792 visit to Mission San Francisco that unmarried women and girls prepared, spun, and wove the mission's wool, and that "besides manufacturing the wool, they are also instructed in a variety of necessary, useful, and beneficial employments."[76] According to Hispanic gender norms, such domestic tasks were more appropriate for women than were the food gathering activities that Bay Area Indian women had traditionally performed, because they lent themselves to supervision by the watchful priests and their deputies.[77] The priests' culturally determined labor assignments turned the Indians' traditional division of labor on its head in many ways. Outside the mission, women were responsible for the care and harvest of plants and plant products, while men produced most of the clothing worn by both sexes.[78]

Indians' work appears to have been routine enough for Franciscans to have used it as a way of identifying individual people. Thus, Junípero Serra could write from Mission San Carlos that many Indians had left the mission, including "the people who are most necessary, such as the blacksmith, carpenters and day workmen."[79] That Serra could identify Indians not only by skilled trades but also as "day workmen" suggests that labor was a strong defining characteristic in the priests' minds. It also seems to have figured in Indians' identifications and estimations of one another. One Indian man, for example, identified the man who cuckolded him as "the vaquero Salvador," naming the man's occupation even before giving his baptismal name.[80] Labor contributed to the formation of a social hierarchy among the baptized Indians at Mission San Francisco, the contours of which are barely visible in the extant records.

Just as the priests depended on Indians' labor for the mission's survival, some Indians found in the mission labor system a new way of shaping an identity and acquiring status. They depended on the labor opportunities at the mission to establish and maintain their social positions. One avenue to increased status seems to have begun with serving as a page to a Hispanic colonist. Mission San Francisco's sacramental registers identify thirteen pages, all of whom were boys. One, Litel, "was raised as a page in the house of Lieutenant Don Manuel Gomez," according to his burial record.[81] Another unnamed boy served a man identified in the mission's account book only as "Don Luis," who was most likely Lieutenant Luis Arguello. Don Luis purchased "a blanket and work shirt for his page" in 1814 and another new set of garments the following year.[82] While some pages, like Litel and the boy who worked for Don Luis, served military officers at the

San Francisco Presidio, most probably served the Franciscan missionaries themselves. Of the thirteen pages identified in the sacramental registers, at least two went on to hold other important positions at Mission San Francisco. Cullniq, a Yelamu man baptized in 1778, served first as a page and later as a sacristan.[83] Jacinto, a Huimen man baptized as an infant in 1790, became an interpreter at the mission.[84] As sacristan and interpreter, Cullniq and Jacinto both enjoyed enhanced access to the Franciscan missionaries and the resources of the mission. They probably also acquired greater status among the Indians baptized at Mission San Francisco as a result of their positions. The priests depended on such men to ensure the mission ran smoothly.

Interpreters and sacristans were not the only Indians who may have enjoyed elevated status at Mission San Francisco. Like all the other California missions, San Francisco de Asís had Indian leaders known as *alcaldes*. In 1796, Hermenegildo Sal, the commander of the San Francisco Presidio, wrote to Governor Diego de Borica that "In the Mission of San Francisco Valeriano and Juan are Alcaldes in addition to another who is Luis, they call him the *fiscal*, the first two were named last year, and continue this year, the last has exercised his functions for more than five years."[85] The offices of alcalde and fiscal had a long history in Spanish municipal government. Alcaldes, who functioned as judges in Spanish and Spanish American towns, normally served one-year terms as ex officio members of town councils.[86] In the missions of Alta California, alcaldes served as leaders of the baptized Indian community and as the missionaries' assistants.[87] In Spain, the fiscal was a high-ranking legal advisor,[88] but in Spanish America this office took a different shape. Indian town councils in central Mexico usually included a religious official known as the fiscal who "managed local church finances, rang bells for Mass, and gathered parishioners for religious celebrations. At a minimum, fiscales were 'church constables' who punished villagers for violating Catholic teachings."[89] In the Alta California mission system, the office of fiscal underwent further transformation: Luis, the fiscal of whom Hermenegildo Sal wrote at Mission San Francisco, was probably only responsible for making sure that the baptized Indians at the mission attended worship services.[90]

According to Hermenegildo Sal, missionaries appointed Valeriano, Juan, and Luis, as well as the Indian officials at Missions Santa Clara and Santa Cruz. Sal continued, "I know that in the missions of San Francisco and Santa Clara, the Indians themselves used to name [the officials], this has ended, I cannot explain to your Lordship the motives because I do not know them."[91] The selection, and even the existence, of Indian officials in the California missions was a point of contention between the Franciscan missionaries and the civilian authorities in Alta California. Ordered in 1778 by the governor of California, Felipe de Neve, to conduct elections in accordance with the *Recopilación de leyes de los reynos de Indias*, the 1681 laws governing Indian communities in Spanish America, the priests first disputed the law's applicability to the missions. They argued that since the laws required elections to be supervised by parish priests, and since the Franciscans were not parish priests but apostolic missionaries, there could be no elections.[92]

When this strategy failed to relieve governmental pressure, the Franciscans began to hold elections in the missions, but they sought to maintain as much control over the outcomes as possible. By handpicking the candidates and limiting the franchise to those who had held office (a common practice in colonial Spain), the priests ensured that alcaldes and other elected officials in the missions would be more or less cooperative.[93] For the first five years of their existence, missions were exempted from the requirement that they elect alcaldes and other officials, so while some missions began to comply with Neve's order in the 1770s, missionaries at San Francisco put off elections until the 1780s. By 1783 Governor Pedro Fages had ordered the priests at Mission San Francisco, as well as at other missions that had been founded later, to hold elections in compliance with Neve's previous order.[94]

One strategy for selecting Indian officials was to choose men who were already community leaders. This was the course of action Junípero Serra, the first president of the Alta California mission system, recommended. Advising Father Fermín Francisco de Lasuén on choosing councilmen at Mission San Diego de Alcalá, Serra wrote, "whether or not [the councilman] is captain of his village does not matter, though it will be more proper if he is; that way the matter will be settled without raising any uproar."[95] The same pattern governed the initial official selections at Mission San Carlos Borromeo.[96]

Steven W. Hackel conducted the most intensive study of Indian officials in the Spanish missions of Alta California, using the unusually complete records of Mission San Carlos Borromeo. He found that Indian officials at Mission San Carlos shared a number of characteristics. Alcaldes and councilmen were generally born outside the mission and had usually accepted baptism earlier than most of their fellow village members. By the time they held office, they were at least married, if they had not already been widowed, and they tended to be older than other men from their villages.[97] An important prerequisite for officeholding was serving as a marriage witness. "Nearly all Indian officials at Mission San Carlos seem to have served as marriage witnesses sometime before their election as officials," Hackel writes. "To the extent that there was a ladder of leadership at the mission, serving as a marriage witness seems to have been an important rung."[98] Finally, and perhaps most importantly, Indian officials during the first several decades of Mission San Carlos's existence tended to be village captains, their relatives by blood or marriage, or their close associates. While Mission San Carlos went through a transition in the early 1790s, moving from leadership composed primarily of village captains to "a cadre of men who spoke Spanish and were familiar with the Franciscan regime," these connections to regional power brokers remained important into the 1820s.[99]

At Mission San Francisco only five alcaldes can be identified during the Spanish colonial period, all of whom served during the 1790s.[100] While these officials fit some of the patterns Hackel identified at Mission San Carlos, other patterns do not hold for Mission San Francisco. Like the officials at Mission San Carlos, the alcaldes at Mission San Francisco were all born outside the mission and all had married and served as marriage witnesses by the time they took office. Four of the five accepted baptism earlier than most in their villages or tribal communities; perhaps more importantly, however, by the time each served as alcalde, he was among the longest-baptized men from his village or tribal community. For example, Uilmoxsi was an alcalde from the Yelamu community. By 1795, the first year documentary evidence indicates that Uilmoxsi served as an alcalde, only six Yelamu men who had been baptized longer than Uilmoxsi were still living.[101] Like Uilmoxsi, the other alcaldes also had a sort of seniority among their village or tribal community members, having accumulated more experience with the Franciscan missionaries than most men from their communities.

That seniority of experience did not translate into absolute seniority, however: while Indian officials at Mission San Carlos tended to be older than other men from their villages, the average difference in age between the Mission San Francisco alcaldes and other men from their villages and tribal communities was less than three years. Since the ages that priests recorded were approximate, this difference is well within the margin of error. Two alcaldes, Monózse and Jojuis, were measurably older than the average age of men from their tribal community and village, by more than seven and ten years, respectively.[102] When the Yelamu man Huetlícs began serving as an alcalde in 1797, however, he was just over six years younger than the average age of the other baptized Yelamu men.[103]

Huetlícs's familial connections may have counterbalanced his relative youth: he appears to have come from, and married into, high-status families. Tacsinte also had good connections; he was born into a high-status family and his first wife was the daughter of a village headman. Strikingly, however, the other three alcaldes appear to have come from, and married into, undistinguished families. Whereas most of the Indian officials at Mission San Carlos had "blood ties to former village captains" or were "related to other leading Indians,"[104] that does not appear to have been the case at Mission San Francisco. This apparent discontinuity may be due to the dearth of information on alcaldes at Mission San Francisco; perhaps the officials whose identities were not recorded were mostly village captains and their relatives, or perhaps priests simply did not record information about relationships between the Mission San Francisco alcaldes and regional power brokers. Alternatively, it may be that priests at Mission San Francisco decided to follow a different strategy than the one in place at Mission San Carlos, setting up a leadership hierarchy in the mission that would compete with, rather than overlap with, existing regional power structures.

As alcaldes, Valeriano and Juan were responsible for assigning tasks every morning to the residents of Mission San Francisco, who gathered in the mission square. As those who enforced the Franciscans' labor regime, alcaldes also became the target of baptized Indians' resentment and even anger, sometimes with very good reason. Ssojorois, for example, testified to military investigators that he had left Mission San Francisco "because the alcalde Valeriano was constantly beating him with a stick, and when he was ill the same Valeriano made him go out to work." Sumipocsé gave similar reasons for leaving: "the alcalde Valeriano caned him for having gone to look for clams at the beach" even though Sumipocsé had permission to do so. Guecusia, another baptized Indian who left Mission San Francisco, also testified that he had been physically abused by an alcalde, in his case Luis: "when [Guecusia] was feeling very poorly the Alcalde Luis went to get him out, and whipped him." The violence that alcaldes inflicted was not always direct: Llucal complained that "when he was hungry, he was put in the stocks by order of the alcalde."[105] The violence that Ssojorois, Sumipocsé, Guecusia, and Llucal described is consistent with what Indian officials at other missions inflicted on their fellow baptized Indians and testifies to the pressures alcaldes felt to keep Indians at the mission in line.[106]

Alcaldes acquiesced to pressure from the baptized Indian population as well. In 1814 Fathers Ramón Abella and Juan Sainz de Lucio complained that "those who have been Alcaldes, by order of the Fathers go to direct some job with some men and not a few times all of them together get to playing, and it is put off for another day, and that even when it is urgent."[107] Pressed on one side to enforce discipline and heighten productivity, and on the other to relax requirements and ease the workload, alcaldes walked a fine line as mediators between the Franciscan missionaries and the baptized Indians, fully satisfying neither side. In return for taking on this balancing act, alcaldes received certain privileges, including greater access to the missionaries' ears, a larger share of the mission's resources, and, according to the memory of one Indian baptized at Mission San Luis Rey, license to ride on horseback.[108]

Though much of the work that Valeriano, Juan, and other Indian officials doled out at Mission San Francisco was assigned to large groups of Indians and completed in cooperation, the missionaries also employed a piecework system to organize and accomplish a great deal of labor at the mission. In this system, Indians' labor was organized around a task or quota: those who completed their task early were either given free time or they were paid in goods for any extra production.[109] According to Father Fermin Francisco Lasuén, this was "the more common way of working at the missions."[110] It was also efficient: by giving Indians incentives to finish the assigned task, the priests found they could motivate faster work. "Many [baptized Indians] could finish in a morning the work of a whole day; and in three or four days they could do that of a whole week, and be entirely on their own for the balance," wrote Lasuén.[111] The piecework system was particularly suited to the work of skilled workers like Tapuissé, who was baptized at Mission San Francisco and trained as a blacksmith.[112] His daily tasks most likely included the production and repair of horseshoes, knives, cooking implements, agricultural tools, and any other metal items around the mission. If Tapuissé finished his work for the week early, he most likely had the rest of the week off to do with as he pleased.[113]

Tapuissé acquired his training as a blacksmith because of the colonial government's effort to make Alta California economically viable. In order to do so, the government decided to provide incentives for skilled artisans to live in the territory for a number of years and teach their skills to baptized Indians. This initiative was not meant solely for the Indians' uplift: Miguel Costansó, in a 1794 letter about strengthening the Alta California presidios and the colonization effort in general, recommended having the settlers teach trades to the Indians.[114] The economic viability of the region was, in his mind, a security issue: a productive Alta California would be a secure Alta California, and that productivity required the labor of both settlers and Indians. Accordingly, artisans were sent to the colonies, and Indians learned to be potters, blacksmiths, furniture builders, weavers, tailors, and other skilled workers.

Though artisans were originally intended to live at the California missions, the plan was soon changed so that artisans would live at the California presidios and Indians would be sent to the presidios to learn their trades. This change displeased mission president Father Lasuén, who opposed sending Indians to the presidio because of the bad habits he believed they would acquire there. Nevertheless, a master blacksmith and a master carpenter lived at the San Francisco Presidio at least briefly and taught their trades to Indians from the northern missions, including several baptized at Mission San Francisco.[115] Of the three carpenters and two blacksmiths baptized at Mission San Francisco and identified in the sacramental registers, three ended up at Mission San Rafael, founded in 1817, and one ended up at Mission San Francisco Solano, founded in 1823.[116] This mobility was probably due to the desirability of metalworking and carpentry skills at these newly founded missions.

Occasionally the presidio also tried to take advantage of the skilled craftsmen in the Indian population. In February 1807 Father Martín de Landaeta complained to José Viñals, then the Alta California mission president, that the San Francisco Presidio commander wanted to let an Indian enlist in the presidial company. "I found out about it in time and I went to said Commander," recounted Landaeta breathlessly, "pointing out to him that the fellow to whom he wanted to give a term was an Indian, son of an Indian from the other shore who had been a servant of the mission and of a female neophyte of this mission, when his Parents died he was still an infant, that the mission having raised him and had him as a son and a Neophyte, it did not seem proper to me that he be signed up as a soldier, on top of which he was the only carpenter . . . of the mission." Unimpressed with Landaeta's argument, the commander nevertheless gave in, "only because of the repugnance that I demonstrated and the desire he had to maintain harmony," reported the priest. The result worried Landaeta: the missions remained "exposed," he worried, to the ever-present danger "that whenever they have a notion to, they may deprive us of the most useful . . . Indians of the Mission."[117]

Some commentators have likened the mission labor system to chattel slavery, but this comparison—meant to highlight the race-based inequality between Indians and priests, the allegedly involuntary nature of Indians' labor at the missions, and the cruelty of the coercive means supposedly used to extract that labor—obscures more than it illumines.[118] It is true that Indians occupied the bottom of the labor hierarchy in colonial California, that they did the jobs that Hispanics did not want to do, and that the missionaries and the military used coercive measures to obtain the Indians' labor. By the time colonists arrived in Alta California, Hispanics had amassed centuries of experience in coercing labor from Indians and the poor, using overlapping systems of slavery, *encomienda, repartimiento*, debt peonage, and free wage labor.[119] Despite the oppression of these systems, historians have shown that workers frequently maintained a good deal of control over the conditions in which they lived and worked.[120]

The labor system that evolved at Mission San Francisco and the other Alta California missions bears perhaps the closest resemblance to the "great estate," as Latin American historian James Lockhart describes it. Lockhart argues that the great estate was the common functional thread that connected the legal institutions of the encomienda, repartimiento, and hacienda.[121] The owners of these estates attempted to achieve an ideal of self-sufficiency, a goal that the Franciscan missionaries shared.[122] The paternalism of estate owners toward Indian workers is also similar to the Franciscans' attitude toward baptized Indians at the mission, and it is this paternalism that perhaps best explains the labor system at the mission.[123] Priests at Mission San Francisco clearly conceived of the mission community in terms of an extended family, an analogy that structured their understanding of labor at the mission. "The Neophytes in the Mission sow when the Missionary Fathers determine to do so, in Community—as children of a family on Lands belonging to the Mission," wrote Ramón Abella and Juan Sainz de Lucio in 1814. "In a Word we all live as a Father with his family."[124] This familial conception of the relationship between individual Indians and the mission community as a whole explains why the Franciscans felt entitled to hire Indians out to the presidio and have the Indians' wages credited to the Mission's account: the mission community, as an extended family, was entitled to benefit from the labor of each of its members.

Although the Franciscans thought of Mission San Francisco as an extended family, it was also a "frontier institution" in the classic sense defined by historian Herbert Bolton, an institution doing double duty as agent of both church and state.[125] The economic production of the Alta California missions, made possible by the labor of baptized Indians, was crucial to the survival of other Spanish institutions in the territory. Missions sold food, building supplies, and other manufactured goods as well as labor to civilians living in California pueblos and to the four presidios along California's coast. In 1815, Father Miguel Lull, the guardian at the College of San Fernando, wrote to the syndic Don Estevan Velez Escalante about the scarcity of supplies in Alta California since 1810. "The missionary Fathers have aided the troops until now insofar as it has been possible for them, even with preference to their neophytes, first because of the indigence in which they saw [the soldiers], and second to avoid revolutionary movements that could occasion the loss of that interesting Province harassed by scarcity and shortages," Lull wrote. However, supply ships had all but stopped going to Alta California after 1810, rendering the situation untenable. The missionaries "cannot do it anymore," Lull continued, "not even to provide them with food, for which it is necessary to work the fields which the missionaries cannot do without agricultural tools, and lacking these the missions and the troops, who in that area depend on the missions, will perish."[126] Lull's alarmist prediction did not come true, at least not as rapidly as his tone suggested: a similar set of ideas appeared in another letter about supplying Alta California missions and presidios a decade later, after Mexico had gained its independence from Spain.[127]

Though Lull was concerned primarily with food supplies, the missions and presidios owed their survival in part to the production of nonfood surpluses at the missions. In addition to food, Mission San Francisco supplied the San Francisco Presidio with building supplies, including tiles and hides for reroofing several buildings, as well as ceramic objects and other goods.[128] Mission San Francisco also manufactured hide and tallow, taking advantage of its seemingly endless supply of cattle. In 1813 priests at Mission San Francisco signed a contract to produce nearly fourteen thousand pounds of tallow over the following three years. The mission's cattle herds, which peaked at more than eleven thousand head between 1809 and 1811, decreased steadily in the following decades as the mission increased its hide and tallow production.[129] The hide and tallow trade, as it became known, gained increasing importance at many Alta California missions when the San Blas supply ships stopped arriving after 1810, though the trade did not fully develop until the 1820s and 1830s. Franciscan missionaries at Mission San Francisco and elsewhere used hide and tallow, as well as lard, otter pelts, and other goods, to trade legally with Spanish boats that arrived from Lima during the second decade of the nineteenth century and illegally with English, American, and Russian ships.[130]

One of Mission San Francisco's earliest and most important surplus products was Indian labor itself. The mission frequently hired gangs of Indians out to the presidio to complete major construction projects. In 1787, Father Fermín Francisco de Lasuén, then president of the mission system in Alta California, wrote to Pedro Fages, assuring Fages that he would "instruct the missionary Fathers of San Francisco and Santa Clara, if it should be possible and no notable inconvenience should result, to make available either from one or from both of these missions six or eight Indian volunteers to assist in the building of the warehouses and the construction of the defense works in the Royal Presidio of San Francisco."[131] To persuade the priests at Missions San Francisco and Santa Clara to comply, Lasuén continued, he would "inform them of the grave urgency of these works, the good treatment Your Lordship offers to the workmen, the daily wages of one and a half reales, and the satisfying meals of which meat forms a part."[132]

The San Francisco Presidio stood in dire need of manual laborers that year: not only was the construction of the presidio's physical plant an ongoing process but in January 1787 the area had also been hit by what one priest described as a "hurricane" of wind.[133] The storm brought down the Mission San Francisco church as well as several of the mission buildings. The kitchen, forge, granaries, storerooms, and carpentry workshop were all ruined. The presidio's structures were also severely damaged, leading the military to hire Indian workers from Mission San Francisco "because of the urgent necessity, and ruin, that threatened its storehouses." The presidio paid Mission San Francisco just under forty-eight pesos for the Indians' labor, in addition to providing food for the workers.[134]

The daily wages and the "meals with meat" that Lasuén mentioned were standard compensation for baptized Indian workers at the San Francisco Presidio and did not vary over the course of the Spanish colonial period. Only the meals benefitted the Indian workers directly; the money was paid to the mission rather than to the workers. Like other Alta California missions, Mission San Francisco did not receive cash for the Indians' work. Instead, the wages were credited to the mission's account with the presidio, a sum that was eventually communicated to the *habilitado general* in Mexico City. The Franciscans used this credit to purchase goods from Mexico that could not be produced at the mission.[135] In Alta California's cash-poor economy, this system made sense, but it also reduced the value of the Indians' wages: freight charges for shipping goods from San Blas to the San Francisco Bay varied from year to year, from as low as about 10 percent to at least as high as 27.5 percent.[136] In 1788 the government fixed freight charges for all the California missions at one and a half pesos per arroba, or the equivalent of eight days' wages for an unskilled Indian worker per every twenty-five pounds of freight.[137] As the placatory tone of Lasuén's letter to Fages suggests, however, the Indians' wages were not the only benefit the missions reaped from sending Indians to work at the presidios: the goodwill of the Spanish military was also worth a great deal to the priests.

A decade later in 1797, Indians at Mission San Francisco played a prominent role in constructing batteries outside the San Francisco Presidio walls. Receipts show that the military paid for a total of 1,214 workdays put in by baptized Indians from Mission San Francisco from the beginning of June through the end of August, and another 1,279 workdays from September until the end of that year. Indians from Mission San Francisco also helped gather the building supplies necessary for constructing the batteries: the presidio paid for approximately fifty deliveries of wood over the course of the year at four pesos each "for the roof of the house of the Palisade that was constructed in the new battery of Yerbabuena."[138] In addition to crediting the Indians' daily wages to the mission, the presidio supplied the Indian workers with about a quart of wheat daily and slaughtered approximately one steer a month to feed the Indian workers.[139]

As the presidio shifted from construction to maintenance of its physical plant, it continued to rely on Indian workers from Mission San Francisco, as well as the other local missions, to supply its labor needs. Presidio official Raymundo Carillo minimized the Indians' role in these projects, complaining in July 1801 that they were "occupied in trivial jobs carting around dirt, moving stone, unloading sand, which is abundant, and the continual winds move it from one place to another."[140] That same year, though, eight parties of baptized Indians from Mission San Francisco worked a total of 921 days cutting hay and using it to roof a presidio officer's house. Between wages and rations—this time of corn, rather than wheat—the presidio spent just over 213 pesos on the project, as well as six pesos for 250 roof tiles.[141]

Carillo's comments conveyed the impression that Indians only performed unskilled day labor, but Indians baptized at Mission San Francisco actually filled a number of occupational niches at the presidio. In December 1797 Mission San Francisco's account showed a credit of seventy-two pesos for the "salary of the Indian tortilla maker that the Artillery employed for eighteen months until the end of December." Indians were also employed as servants and temporary laborers: the Mission San Francisco account book contains repeated entries noting that Indians worked for individual soldiers and officers, sometimes for a few days and other times for extended periods. The priests frequently labeled the hired laborers as *rancheros*, or ranchers, suggesting that the Indians would be employed in general husbandry and field labor.[142] However, the tasks these Indians performed frequently went unspecified: "On the 19th of October Ju[an] Jose Yguera took one Indian for a month and a half," the priests recorded in 1805. Later they noted that "On the fifth of January [1806] Juan Jose Yguera's Indian went to the House of Sepulveda," apparently for another term of employment.[143]

The priests occasionally refused to hire Indians out to the presidio: in 1815 the priests turned down a request from the presidio for twenty Indians to serve as oarsmen. Workers were in short supply, they explained, and they were afraid the Indians would drown as a result of their lack of expertise with the oars.[144] When presidio officials could not get baptized Indians to work on presidio projects—and, sometimes, even when they could—they turned to unbaptized Indians. Civilian settlers followed suit. Unbaptized Indians were paid directly for their work, in contrast to baptized Indians whose wages went straight to the missions. Both baptized and unbaptized Indians received food while on the job, but unbaptized Indians received their wages in the form of blankets, clothing, and other goods that were relatively cheap. This difference made the hiring of unbaptized Indians a far less expensive prospect for settlers and the military, probably resulting in a preference for the labor of unbaptized Indians.[145]

The common practice of employing unbaptized Indians, complained Father Isidro Alonso Salazar, exacerbated the indolence of settlers in Alta California. "They think more of playing, and strumming the guitar, than indoctrinating their children, and attending to their work," he wrote to the Marqués of Branciforte. To make matters worse, "the Gentile [unbaptized

Indian] is the Farm Hand, he is the Cowhand, and irrigator, and in a word he does everything, such that at the time of the harvest he takes half, and must be given a blanket, and a tunic, so that he goes about better than a Christian, and these never convert because they get along better than in the Mission."[146] Far from demonstrating or rewarding the virtues of hard work and Christian faith, the settlers made it clear that labor and religion were separable and that Indians who wanted access to the material culture of the Hispanic colonists need not necessarily accept baptism. This example, worried Salazar, might seriously compromise the missions' ability to attract Indians, upon whose labor they depended.

Contractual arrangements did not govern all Indian labor at the San Francisco Presidio. In September 1799 Brevet Captain José Arguello summarized the state of the Spanish forces at the presidio, including a note that "There is an imprisoned Indian who is occupied in the chores of this Presidio."[147] Arguello included no clue to the Indian's identity or the reason for his imprisonment, but capturing and holding Indians at the presidio for periods of time was not unusual for the Spanish military. While prisoners, those Indians were made to work around the presidio. The Franciscan missionaries took for granted the military's right to put its prisoners to work. Indeed, the Spanish government had used convict labor to complete public works projects and to subsidize private enterprise for centuries, and presidios around the world housed captive labor forces composed primarily of convicts.[148] However, the missionaries complained that the soldiers at the San Francisco Presidio exploited this right, imprisoning Indians for the sole purpose of creating a captive workforce. Father Lasuén complained bluntly to Pedro Fages in 1787 that "at the present time they are carrying off Indians to the presidio on any pretext of guilt in order to have peons to work for nothing, perhaps in the orchard of His Lordship."[149] More diplomatically, he wrote to Jacobo Ugarte y Loyola about six weeks later that "It has happened very frequently that Indians are carried off to the presidios because they have killed some beast or animal, or simply because they ran away from the mission. There they are held technically as prisoners, but in reality as peons. . . . some provision is needed against such a mode of procedure because it is due to a greedy desire to obtain free labor."[150] Though the military paid for the upkeep of these laborers, no wage or other compensation was paid to the mission or directly to the Indian worker. Thus, Lasuén was right: the presidio saved money while gaining an able, if unwilling, worker.

Imprisoned Indians were not the only ones who worked at the presidio without a contractual arrangement between the military and the church. Perhaps most tantalizing are the hints in the historical record of informal labor agreements between individual Indians and presidio residents. These arrangements, by their nature, are difficult to document. However, both Indian men and Indian women appear to have entered into informal labor arrangements with presidio residents. According to the presidio residents, Indians were grateful for any scrap of informal employment they could find at the presidio.[151] Raymundo Carillo, by then the quartermaster of the presidio and the ensign of the presidio company, testified in 1796 that Indians were treated harshly at the mission, but at the presidio they were treated well, and "they achieve the benefit that by bringing a bit of water or firewood to the inhabitants [of the presidio, in return for which the inhabitants] take away the hunger which moves [the Indians] to do this light chore."[152] The degree of gratitude that Carillo and others imputed to Indians is unlikely, but one advantage of these labor arrangements was that Indians who worked under the table for individual soldiers at the presidio got to keep all that they earned. The benefits of Indians' labor thus accrued directly to them, rather than being diverted to the mission.

While many—probably most—of the Indians who labored at the presidio did so on a temporary basis, a few made themselves a permanent part of the presidio workforce. The case of Tujulalis is a good example.[153] We know more about Tujulalis than about many California Indians because in 1805 he was accused and eventually convicted of raping and murdering eight-year-old María Guadalupe Galindo, the daughter of a presidio soldier.[154] Tujulalis confessed to the crimes, though the veracity of his statements is certainly open to question. The value of Tujulalis's case for historians today lies primarily in the other information it reveals about life at the presidio and Tujulalis's position therein. Witnesses in Tujulalis's case testified that they knew him by sight and by his baptismal name, Aurelio; some even mentioned that he was a stutterer, suggesting that they had conversed with him enough to learn that he had a speech impediment, or at least some difficulty speaking Spanish. Tujulalis worked as a cowhand for the military, a year-round job that he had apparently held for some time. According to the investigation, Tujulalis had been baptized at Mission San Francisco when he was "a little Gentile."[155] How long Tujulalis had lived at the presidio is unclear, but soldier Ramón Linares testified that he had known Tujulalis "since he was young, and everyone else in the Presidio may be presumed to know him well."[156] Soldier José Galindo echoed Linares's testimony, asserting "that in the Presidio most know him, and they have dealt with him because said Aurelio has resided for some time in this Presidio."[157] The statements of both these soldiers suggested that Tujulalis had long since removed himself from Mission San Francisco.

We cannot now know why Tujulalis chose to move to the presidio and work for the Spanish military. As a free agent working at the presidio, Tujulalis would have been directly compensated for his labor. Perhaps this material reward was his goal: as Father Salazar suggested, the material gains that came from working for the Hispanic colonists could be a powerful draw. As the investigation of his case indicates, Tujulalis became a part of the presidio community, though he remained on the margins of that society.

Other Indians seem to have followed suit, making lives for themselves in and around the presidio. On September 9, 1816, Franciscan Juan Amoros wrote from San Francisco to the governor of Alta California, Pablo Vicente de Solá, to complain about the behavior of three such Indians. "Last night at about eight three Presidio Indians were found in one of the ranchería houses," he wrote. "One Yndalecio, one Martin, and another who for many years has wandered all over the place, a Gentile." Amoros sent Yndalecio to be punished, explaining, "for many days he has been tangled up with a young woman from Carmel, in whose house he was found; . . . it has been many years that I have been asking for justice for this Yndalesio [sic], and he continually visits the Mission, but not the Church."[158] Amoros's complaint reveals the existence of a category, by the middle of the second decade of the nineteenth century, known as "Presidio Indians," some of whom were baptized while others were not. All of these Indians appear to be free agents, working and living on their own account in and around the Spanish presidios.

In fact, this category seems to have come into existence by at least a quarter century before Yndalecio and Martin started causing trouble. The 1790 report for the San Francisco Bay Area shows sixteen Indians living at the San Francisco Presidio and eight in the San José de Guadalupe pueblo. In the presidio, Indian men outnumbered women eleven to five; in the pueblo, the Indian population was composed of five women and three men.[159] While some of these Indians were likely indigenous Mexicans, others were almost certainly California Indians like Tujulalis, who chose to make a life among the Hispanic newcomers. Like unbaptized Indians, these individuals were directly compensated for their work, but unlike those who worked temporarily at the presidio or in the pueblo, they appear to have become a more or less permanent part of the Hispanic community. Relegated to the lowest rungs of the social and economic ladder, these individuals represent, in some ways, what the priests were working toward at Mission San Francisco and throughout the California mission system: a breakdown of tribal communities and the economic integration of individual Indians into the lowest levels of Hispanic society.[160]

This goal was tempered by the priests' desire to maintain control over, and reap the benefits of, Indians' labor. Mission San Francisco's dependence on Indian labor obliged priests to accept compromises about the nature and quantity of work that Indians performed in and around the mission. While priests intended to teach Indians their place in Hispanic society by teaching them to labor in Hispanic ways, they found themselves forced to allow Indians to leave the mission to exploit traditional food resources, to accept the construction of traditional Indian dwellings in the mission village, and to permit the persistence of traditional Bay Area labor techniques such as roasting grains in baskets and roofing buildings with thatch. Thus, even in the labor most vital to the mission's survival, Indians exercised agency, blending traditional Bay Area techniques and aesthetics with Hispanic ones instead of choosing between them. Indians' ability to combine aspects of Indian and Hispanic cultures diluted the Hispanicizing and Christianizing influence the priests intended to exert through labor at the mission. Although the reasons that Tujulalis, Yndalecio, Martin, and others chose to become "Presidio Indians" are lost to us, the fact remains that this decision was, at some level, a choice—and it did not preclude their continuing practice of traditional Bay Area customs in important areas of life. While Presidio Indians remained on the margins of Hispanic society, they did not necessarily surrender their commitments to indigenous Bay Area cultures and communities, just as Indians baptized at Mission San Francisco manipulated their labor conditions so as to keep one foot in traditional Bay Area cultures while also adopting, and adapting, some Hispanic cultural practices.

3

Forming Families

୵∞ Keqecég was an influential Ssalson Indian man in the San Francisco Bay Area when the Spanish arrived in 1776. He was the headman of his village, Uturpe, known to the Spanish as San Matheo. Keqecég's political influence reached beyond his village, extending even to other tribal communities on the San Francisco peninsula. He cemented political, social, and economic alliances with other lineages, villages, and tribal communities by creating marriage bonds with them. The San Francisco mission registers record that Keqecég was married to at least one Ssalson woman, probably from an important lineage in Uturpe or from another Ssalson village. The registers also show that he was married to at least one woman from the Puichon tribal community, which lived to the south of the Ssalsons. Keqecég's marriage to this woman created an alliance between the two groups that facilitated the flow of foodstuffs and trade goods and provided both communities with important military allies in the event of armed conflict. In addition, Keqecég used his children's marriages to create alliances. Two of his daughters, for example, married a Ssalson man named Jaluntis, the head of another important lineage in Keqecég's village. These marriages ensured the support of Jaluntis and his lineage for Keqecég's leadership in the village.[1]

When Spanish Franciscans founded Mission San Francisco in 1776, some ten miles north of Uturpe, Keqecég may have seen it as an opportunity to forge another alliance, this time with the powerful Spanish newcomers.[2] One by one, Keqecég, his children and grandchildren, and his wives accepted baptism and entered the mission. At Mission San Francisco, the Spanish priests attempted to make Keqecég's family and other Indian families conform to a Hispanic Catholic model. As they imposed Hispanic Catholic family structures, the Franciscans limited Keqecég's ability to create alliances, dissolved many of the alliances he had already made, and weakened the authority he and his wives exercised within their own family. As a result, while Keqecég's association with the Spanish may have increased his political status among residents of the Bay Area, it also limited his ability to gain and exercise authority by traditional means. Just as the Franciscans tried to reshape the Bay Area Indians' economic lives, changing the modes of production and integrating individual Indians into the lowest levels of the colonial economy, so also they tried to alter family structures in the Bay Area, replacing lineages with nuclear families and imposing their own paternal authority. If they succeeded, these changes would unravel the fabric of Indian societies in the Bay Area, leaving Indians no choice but to weave themselves into the margins of colonial society.

The basic organizing unit in California Indian societies was the lineage. Most Bay Area Indian groups reckoned kinship patrilineally, so families were constituted primarily by a relationship of descent from, or marriage to, the male head of the lineage. Members of Keqecég's lineage, for example, belonged to the family by virtue of their relationship to Keqecég. While women retained basic rights in their natal lineages, marriage removed them from the families in which they were reared and made them members of their husbands' lineages instead.[3] When Keqecég's daughters Guasnete and Najam married Jaluntis, the head of another important lineage in their village, they left Keqecég's home to live with Jaluntis's family.[4] The children that Guasnete and Najam bore to Jaluntis were members of his lineage, not of Keqecég's. Cross-cousin marriage appears to have been a common practice among some Costanoan-speaking groups, and Guasnete may have considered the possibility that her son Samisi might one day marry the daughter of one of her brothers.[5] Some Costanoan-speaking groups also practiced wife's-brother's-daughter marriage, so it is also possible that Jaluntis contemplated strengthening his ties to Keqecég's lineage by marrying the daughter of one of Guasnete's brothers.[6]

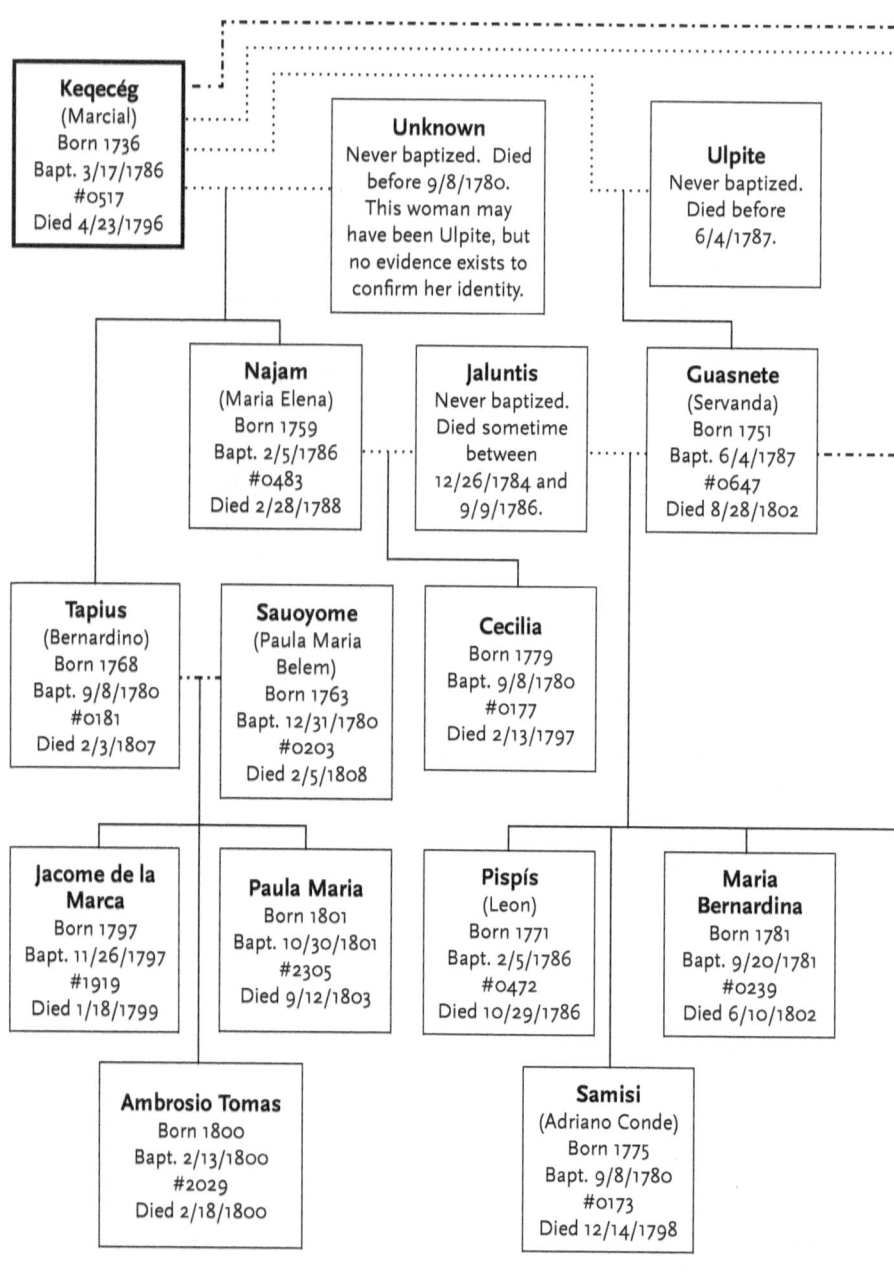

FIGURE 2. Keqecég's family. Only marriages that produced children are shown. Keqecég was a powerful figure in the San Francisco Bay Area and used his children's marriages to create and reinforce alliances with other villages and tribal communities. Once his children accepted baptism, however, Keqecég no longer had much influence in selecting their spouses.

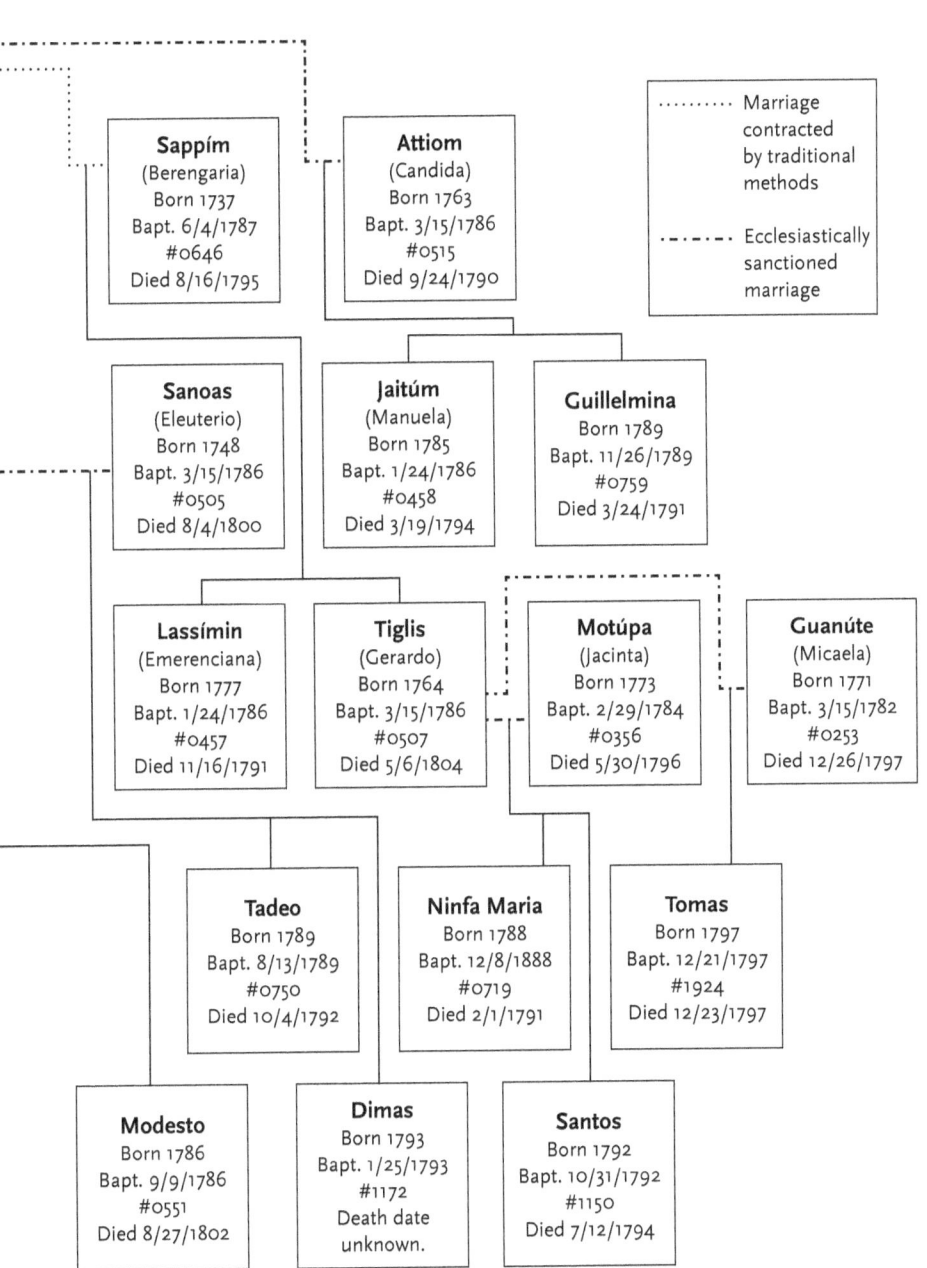

Forming Families

Polygyny, the marriage of one man to multiple women, was widely accepted in indigenous California, but it was not widespread; the practice was generally reserved for important men such as village headmen and shamans, who could support additional wives and who required the help those women could provide. Keqecég's multiple wives therefore serve as a clue to his high status. Monogamy is so normative in twenty-first-century American society that polygyny is almost invariably depicted as a debased, exploitative system that caters to men's excessive sexual desires. For eighteenth-century California Indians, however, nothing could have been further from the truth. Rather than exploiting women and harming families, polygyny gave wives female companionship and extra hands to complete the tasks of daily life. In addition, it provided for more comprehensive childcare, since more mothers were available, and, in the event of a woman's death, it ensured that her children would not be without maternal care.

Keqecég's stature allowed, and may even have required, that he have multiple wives: the San Francisco Mission registers indicate that before his baptism Keqecég had at least three, and possibly four, wives.[7] He also may have married other women whose relationships with him were never recorded. Sororal polygyny, the marriage of multiple sisters to one man, appears to have been a common form of polygyny among the Costanoan Indians. Pismote's family is one example: Pismote and her two sisters were all married to one man, Puyeles. Keqecég's daughters Guasnete and Najam, who married Jaluntis, are another example. Sororal polygyny may have been preferred among Costanoan speakers for a variety of reasons: it strengthened the alliances made through marriage, ensuring that if one woman died, the alliance would continue through her sister's marriage. It may also have created more tightly knit polygynous families. Women related by blood, who had grown up together, may have been more likely to get along because of both their greater familiarity and their closer kinship.

Because California Indians commonly used marriage as a means of creating alliances between lineages, villages, and tribal communities, selecting a marriage partner was far too important a decision to leave up to individuals. Instead, parents like Keqecég and his wives usually arranged marriages for their children, keeping the lineage's interests in mind. Status—social, political, and economic—was an important consideration in selecting a marriage partner, and a good match could benefit the families of both partners. The alliance created by the marriages between Jaluntis and Keqecég's daughters Guasnete and Najam, for example, brought political and economic advantages to both lineages, while contributing to political stability in Uturpe. Like most children, Guasnete and Najam probably agreed to the marriages their parents arranged: as they grew up, they learned to value the same things as their parents in a husband and to think of marriage as a way of creating social, political, and economic bonds. Just like their parents, Guasnete and Najam would have seen Jaluntis's social status as a strong argument in favor of marriage.[8]

The pool of potential marriage partners was limited by the moiety system in indigenous Bay Area societies. *Moiety*, a term that comes from the French word meaning "half," is the word anthropologists use when a society is divided into two groups: each of these groups is a moiety, and every member of the society belongs to one moiety or the other. Among Bay Area Indians, moieties were exogamous—that is, people were not allowed to marry within their own moiety. Therefore, every married couple consisted of one person from each moiety. By dividing the community into two opposing but mutually dependent groups, the moiety system paradoxically demonstrated the unity of the group.[9] In the San Francisco Bay Area, a child automatically belonged to her or his father's moiety, though in some groups a father could choose to "give" a child to his wife's moiety instead.[10]

Moiety membership conferred certain rights and responsibilities with regard to members of the opposite moiety, primarily having to do with important life-cycle events such as birth, the onset of puberty, and death. Among Bay Miwok speakers and other Bay Area groups, moiety members cared for the dead of the opposite moiety. For example, Olavú and his wife Esupame, two Bay Miwok-speaking Chupcan Indians, accepted baptism and solemnized their marriage at Mission San Francisco on the same day in 1804.[11] Their two daughters, Eyume and Mayunucse, had been baptized about a month earlier.[12] When Esupame died the following year, Olavú and his daughters may have helped prepare her corpse for burial and care for members of Esupame's patrilineage as they grieved her death. As members of the opposite moiety, it was their duty to do so. When Olavú died in 1815, however, his daughters would have been the beneficiaries of this care, extended by members of their late mother's moiety.[13]

Bay Area Indian communities were also divided along gendered lines, with men and women bearing distinct and complementary responsibilities in the life of the group. Because men and women were in charge of different types of labor, parents taught the children of their own gender. Women like Ulpite, Sappím, and Attiom, Keqecég's wives, taught their daughters to recognize, gather, and prepare important food and medicinal plants. They also instructed their daughters in the art of basket weaving, one of the most important crafts in Californian life. Keqecég and other Bay Area Indian men taught their sons to hunt and fish and showed them how to make the tools they needed for both activities.

Keqecég also taught at least one of his sons the skills he would need to be village headman. These probably included esoteric ceremonial knowledge as well as leadership skills and fighting techniques. While the position of village headman in the Bay Area was an inherited position, passing from father to son, a headman also had to earn his political status by proving his ability to lead. The headman was confirmed by consensus in the village. Village headmen led more by example and persuasion than by fiat, and Keqecég's son would need a thorough understanding of diplomacy to be a good leader. Although in rare cases village leadership could pass to the daughter of a headman, Keqecég had at least two sons among his children. His daughters therefore probably never considered the prospect of leading their village.[14]

These markedly distinct gender roles were typical in Native Californian societies. In Pomo communities to the north of the Bay Area, as well as in Yokuts, Miwok, and Mono societies to the south and east, women bore the primary responsibility for harvesting and processing acorns for their families, just as they did in the Bay Area and elsewhere in California.[15] Women also produced the baskets that made these and other tasks possible. Yokuts, Miwok, and Mono women, for example, made baskets for harvesting and transporting acorns, for storing acorns for months or years, and for sifting acorn flour. Since acorns were a staple of Native Californians' diet, the baskets that made their large-scale harvesting, processing, and storage possible were crucial for survival. Basketry was not limited to use with acorns, or even plant foods; women made baskets that were used to transport infants, as accessories for gambling and other games, as gifts and trade goods, and as ritual objects, grave markers, and burial goods.[16] In addition to basket making, Californian women also developed other specializations. Among the Pomos, for example, both women and men produced clamshell-bead money, became healers, and hired themselves out as ceremonial dancers and singers.[17] Yokuts, Miwok, and Mono women could become "'chief,' 'sub-chief,' healer, messenger . . . mid-wife, ceremonial singer, dancer, clown, and undertaker."[18] While the specific contours of gender roles among Bay Area societies are less well known, it is reasonable to believe that these groups resembled their neighbors. Ulpite, Sappím, and

Attiom, then, were valued members of their families and communities in their own right, quite apart from their status as Keqecég's wives.

Whereas a relationship of kinship constituted families and lineages among California Indians, a relationship of authority constituted families among Hispanic colonists. The 1732 *Diccionario de la lengua castellana* defined *padre de familia* (father of family) as "the lord of the house, even though he may not have any children. He is so-called," the definition's author went on, "because of his obligation to exercise the role of father for everyone that lives under his dominion." *Hijo de familia* (son, or child, of family) found meaning in the same volume as a person "who has not taken the state [of marriage] and remains under the father's authority."[19] Thus, the family unit was based less on kinship than on the authority of the father, and it included servants, slaves, and any others under the authority of the padre de familia. Marriage was the constitutive event that removed a child from the father's authority and formed a new family unit.

Spaniards, like other Europeans, reckoned kinship bilaterally—that is, a child was considered equally related to the families of its mother and father. In Hispanic society, this bilateral kinship system and other Catholic regulations restricted the pool of potential marriage partners: marriage between people related within five degrees by blood (consanguinity) or marriage (affinity) was prohibited without a papal dispensation. The Catholic Church also prohibited divorce and polygamy. Even if a couple received priestly permission to separate, remarriage was only permitted after the death of one of the spouses or the annulment of the marriage. These restrictions did not prevent many Hispanic Catholics from cohabiting and even going through marriage ceremonies with multiple partners without obtaining annulments of their marriages to their original, still-living spouses.[20] In theory, however, Catholic marriages were to be monogamous and lifelong.

As in California Indian societies, status was an important consideration in the selection of marriage partners in Hispanic society. Though the criteria for measuring status varied somewhat according to class, race, ethnicity, and region, status in colonial Mexico was determined in large part by what scholars have termed the "honor-shame complex," a set of cultural values and ideals that Spanish colonists imported from Europe.[21] The honor-shame complex included both ascribed and achieved elements. Ascriptive honor depended on such variables as ancestry, race, ethnicity, occupation, and land ownership. These variables, which determined social rank, were not set in stone, but individuals had limited control over them.

Achieved honor served to rank individuals within their social classes. In theory, individuals were able to control this kind of honor by adhering to gender-specific behavior rules.[22]

Scholars generally agree that these rules described Spanish ideals of femininity and masculinity, ideals that remained remarkably stable throughout the sixteenth, seventeenth, and eighteenth centuries in Spain's American colonies.[23] Feminine honor was inextricably bound up with women's sexual reputations, which could only be protected through strict enclosure within the home and church. According to colonial Spanish understandings of femininity, women were ruled by passion rather than reason and thus lacked the self-control necessary to avoid sexual sin.[24] By enforcing women's enclosure within the home or church, men protected the sexual virtue of women too weak to protect themselves. A woman who failed to remain enclosed, or who was not properly escorted when she ventured beyond the protective confines of home or church, allowed her sexual reputation to come under suspicion. She thus threatened both her own honor and that of the male head of household who was responsible for her supervision. *Recogimiento*, or enclosure, came to be understood as a measure of women's respectability in Spain and Latin America: women described as *recogidas* were more virtuous, or came closer to prescribed standards of behavior and character for women than those who could not claim that description.[25] These standards were, of course, intertwined with class: women of higher socioeconomic status were more able to conform to the feminine ideal of the honor-shame complex.[26] Nevertheless, the ideal of recogimiento pervaded Hispanic society.

For men, on the other hand, historian Antonia I. Castañeda writes that "honor and ideal conduct centered on their conquest and domination of others, including women, as well as on protection, which included protecting the honor (sexual reputation) of females in the family."[27] This linkage of a man's honor with the sexual behavior of the women in his family and with his conquest of others meant that by seducing or raping a woman, a man might dishonor both her and the men in her family while increasing his own honor.[28] However, the primary arena for a man to act out his "conquest and domination of others" was his own family. The behavior of the members of a man's family reflected the authority he wielded within his home as the padre de familia. The honor-shame complex justified a Hispanic man in disciplining members of his family for contravening social norms, because their transgressions adversely affected his own reputation.

Priests occupied an anomalous position in the honor-shame complex. Literate and often much better educated than the populations they served, priests acted on God's behalf. Their profession thus conferred a measure of prestige. However, the vows of poverty, chastity, and obedience that a Franciscan took when he entered the order changed the way he participated in the honor-shame complex. The vow of poverty prevented him from accumulating significant personal wealth, though by becoming a priest he gained access to the resources of the Catholic Church. The vow of obedience meant that, having left his father's authority, he was now subject to the intrusive authority of his religious superior in every aspect of life. As a priest, however, he also exercised considerable authority over laypeople.

Perhaps most significant, priestly vows of chastity limited priests' ability to participate in the sexual side of the honor-shame complex so prevalent in Hispanic culture. A sexual relationship between a priest and a woman was not only fornication or adultery, depending on the woman's marital status, but also sacrilege, because it violated the priest's sacred vow of chastity. Any children produced in such a union could never be legitimated through their parents' marriage; the only chance these children ever had to rehabilitate their honor was through the purchase of *gracias al sacar*, certificates attesting to their racial and religious purity.[29] Despite their vows, historian William Taylor has found that priests' "heterosexual activity and fathering children were not, in themselves, regarded as particularly scandalous or worth prosecuting" by parishioners and ecclesiastical courts in colonial Mexico. In fact, Taylor writes, "heterosexual relations were common among parish priests," and monogamous long-term relationships were especially common among priests in "second- and third-class parishes."[30]

In the Alta California mission system, a small number of Franciscan priests were accused of breaking their vows of chastity, including one, Father Luis Gil y Taboada, who had been stationed at Mission San Francisco from 1801 to 1802 and again from 1804 to 1806. Lorenzo Asisara, a California Indian born to baptized Indian parents at Mission Santa Cruz in 1820, told a historian in 1877 that Taboada had "hugged and kissed the Indian women [at Mission Santa Cruz, where Taboada was stationed from 1820 to 1827] and he had contact with them until he had syphilis and skin eruptions broke out."[31] Asisara's account is problematic on several levels. First, given the length of time intervening between Taboada's misconduct and Asisara's accusations, and Asisara's young age during the period that Taboada worked at Mission Santa Cruz, the accuracy of Asisara's memory is open to question. Asisara names a corroborating witness: "Don José Maria Amador affirmed [Taboada's diagnosis and its cause], and since they were good friends, [Amador] gave him medicines to cure him."[32] However, Amador provided no independent account of Taboada's behavior. Asisara also undermines his account by asserting that despite the priest's apparently predatory behavior, "Taboada came to be very well liked by all the Indians."[33] Virginia Marie Bouvier argues that Asisara's "comments rendered virtually invisible the separate female experience of sexual vulnerability."[34] It may also be, however, that Asisara exaggerated or even fabricated Taboada's sexual predations. Nevertheless, William Taylor points out that sexual misconduct by parish priests in colonial Mexico was underreported, and it is reasonable to believe that the same behavior by Franciscans in Alta California likewise did not always enter the written record.[35]

In the California missions, priests asserted a fatherly authority over the Indians they baptized, creating spiritual families in place of biological ones. Father Francisco Palóu told of one Indian he encountered while journeying to San Francisco Bay in 1774 who, "whenever he came [to visit the exploratory party] he approached me, and raising my mantle, he covered himself with it, saying, 'Me apam,' 'Thou art my father.'"[36] The priests did nothing to discourage this notion; in fact, they encouraged the California Indians to see them as spiritual fathers. The idea that priests should have a paternal relationship with the laity they served was not new: as early as 1565, the Roman Catholic Church's Second Provincial Council described the priest first and foremost as a "Father, . . . [who] ought to look out for his children."[37] Throughout the Spanish colonial period, seminaries, church officials, and professional manuals all encouraged priests to play this paternal role, taking on the tasks of teaching, protecting, and judging their flocks.

The Franciscans in California took their spiritual fatherhood seriously. In 1814, Father Ramón Abella sat down to answer a questionnaire that had been sent to all of the California missions in 1812. To one question asking about educating Indian children, Abella responded,

> The Indians do not give any education to their children, at the most they teach [their sons] to Fish and Hunt, and their daughters to gather the seeds that the country naturally produces, and to distinguish

the grasses on which they maintain themselves for some time during the year. They do not know Agriculture nor Mechanical Arts; this they leave to the care of the Missionary Fathers.[38]

Missionaries elsewhere in California answered similarly. They reported that they had assumed responsibility for the education of all of the Indians in the missions, teaching them, one missionary wrote, "to feed and clothe themselves as do the civilized people." Another remarked that

> the missionary father has to educate [adult Indians] even with regard to the smallest things such as commanding them to sweep, wash, to sleep off the ground and eat with cleanliness. . . . Hence it is that both parents and children are being educated by the missionary fathers not only in spiritual matters but in temporal things. . . . Behold how these poor Indians, fathers of families, if not entirely, at least in part, are held excused before both God and man.[39]

These comments indicate clearly that, in the missionaries' eyes, Indian men were not fulfilling their paternal duties, as those duties were defined in Hispanic society. Thus, the priests were "forced" to step in to establish "proper" order (again, as defined by Hispanic culture) in the lives of Indian families. "In a word," wrote Abella at San Francisco, "we all live as a Father with his family."[40] The missionaries cast themselves as padres de familias, making the decisions that kept the mission running; by following the missionaries' directions, the baptized Indians at Mission San Francisco played the role of hijos de familias.

The missionaries' educational responsibilities extended beyond "Agriculture and the Mechanical Arts" to other aspects of life in Hispanic society as well. Children in the mission learned Spanish from the missionaries so that the priests could catechize them more easily. The priests also taught some of the boys to read, hoping that this skill would enable them to understand Christian doctrine more thoroughly and make them better singers in the mission choir.[41] The priests saw children as the key to changing Indian cultures and pursued what Virginia Marie Bouvier has called a "child-focused strategy,"[42] in that they expended the most energy in attracting the interest of, and teaching, children.

The priests encouraged Indian children to reject the beliefs their elders taught them through stories. Traditional customs and beliefs were difficult to eliminate from the mission: Abella wrote that, among baptized Indians who interacted with unbaptized Indians, "something [of the Indians' customs and beliefs] sticks to them, and much more to those who inherit it from their Parents."[43] Nevertheless, the priests remained optimistic that they would, eventually, replace traditional beliefs with Catholicism. "It seems to me that there is no formal Idolatry, some Old peoples' tales only, and most times not even those who tell the stories believe them, this with the Help of God and with time, will be taken away," Abella opined.[44] Thus, by stepping in to fulfill what they saw as the father's proper role, the Franciscans competed with the transmission of traditional skills and knowledge from elders to children.

Spanish law reinforced the Franciscans' self-identification as the Indians' "fathers," transferring authority over baptized Indians and their material resources to the priests. The Franciscans were the legal guardians of baptized Indians, who were defined as wards of the Spanish crown. Spanish law had defined indigenous Americans as minors almost as long as the Spanish had been in the Americas. The designation was meant, in part, to protect the Indians from prosecution by the Inquisition. Once the Indians were sufficiently Hispanicized to function as subjects of the Spanish crown, however, their status as minors was supposed to expire. By the eighteenth century, Spanish law provided for Catholic missions to the Indians, including the missions in Alta California, to last no longer than ten years, a term the government considered adequate for Hispanicizing any indigenous population. After that time, the mission church was to be turned over to secular clergy and the mission lands divided among the missionized people. Most California missions lasted far longer than their allotted ten years, because they continued to receive new groups of Indians. This continuing influx of new recruits bolstered the Franciscans' argument that the California Indians were not adequately prepared to function as ordinary subjects of the Spanish crown, and that the ten-year time limit on the missions should therefore be extended. As long as the missions remained in existence—and they did until the 1830s—the Indians remained minors in the eyes of the law and the Franciscans retained their claim to legal authority over them.[45]

As the Indians' guardians, the missionaries also administered the Indians' material resources, including the vast tracts of land surrounding the mission. Theoretically, Indians retained title to this land; however, as the Franciscans' legal wards, they lacked standing to administer it.[46]

The missionaries' control over the land entailed the administration of the resources the land produced as well. Before they accepted baptism, Bay Area Indians turned to lineage heads and community leaders to decide when they would harvest acorns, gather seeds, collect shellfish, and hunt game. At Mission San Francisco, the priests decided what crops would be grown on mission lands and when they would be harvested; how many head of livestock would be raised, where they would graze, and when they would be slaughtered; and how the foodstuffs produced on these lands would be distributed among Indians at the mission as well as among Hispanic colonists who depended on the missionaries' willingness to sell some of the mission's produce. Although Indians retained a great deal of control over their labor, the priests' control of mission lands profoundly affected the nature and products of the work Indians did.

As guardians of the Indians, the missionaries also claimed the right to discipline their charges. Father Junípero Serra, the first president of the mission system in Alta California, requested in a letter to the viceroy of New Spain, Antonio María de Bucareli y Ursúa, "that the officer and soldiers understand that the management, command, punishment and upbringing of the baptized Indians, and those that are baptized hereafter, belong strictly to the missionary fathers (except the crimes of blood) and so [the military] cannot punish or mistreat any of [the Indians], without the consent of said missionary fathers."[47] Serra's request hints at the ways in which the missionaries' appropriation of patriarchal authority over the Indians placed them at odds with the military. The priests extended their control over the California Indians in part by assuming responsibility for the Indians' physical well-being, which the soldiers threatened.

Spanish soldiers were notorious throughout Alta California for sexually abusing Indian women and physically harming Indian men who tried to prevent that abuse. A few weeks earlier, Serra had lamented the behavior of the Spanish soldiers assigned to protect Mission San Diego in another letter to the viceroy.

> Six or more soldiers used to go out together in the morning, with or without the license of their corporal, on horseback; they went to the villages, though they were many leagues distant; and when men and women, upon discovering them, began to run, they took advantage . . . of the ability that they have of lassoing a cow or a mule, and so they lassoed the female Indians, for the nourishment

Forming Families

of their unbridled lust; and they killed with gunshots several male Indians when they tried to defend the women.[48]

Serra and other missionaries in California documented numerous instances of similar behavior. Historian Antonia Castañeda writes that "under conditions of war or conquest, rape is a form of national terrorism, subjugation, and humiliation, wherein the sexual violation of women represents both the physical domination of women and the symbolic castration of the men of the conquered group."[49] Within Spanish gender codes, in which ideals of femininity and masculinity were intertwined with women's sexual purity, this effect was magnified: the rape of Indian women dishonored both the women and the Indian men while increasing the honor of the rapists. The murder of the women's would-be protectors reinforced the effect by revealing the Indians' physical vulnerability to Spanish force and emphasizing their inability to protect the sexual purity, or even the physical well-being, of Indian women.

When threatened in similar ways by Indian men, Spanish soldiers responded forcefully. As he recalled the founding of Mission San Francisco, Father Francisco Palóu wrote that "the gentiles of the villages adjoining this site visited frequently," but "in the last visits that they made at the beginning of December they became shameless, now in thefts, now by firing an arrow at the corporal of the guard, now in wanting to kiss the wife of a soldier, as well as the indication of wanting to fire an arrow at a neophyte from the mission of Carmelo who was at this mission."[50] According to Palóu's account, the Spanish soldiers only punished the last offense directly, and that, it seems, only because the Indian who made the threat happened to turn up at the mission while the sergeant was present. The sergeant ordered two soldiers to arrest and flog the offender. Two Indians came to the man's defense, firing arrows at the Spanish soldiers, and fled when the soldiers fired back with guns.

The following day, the sergeant led a group of soldiers to the beach to seize the two would-be rescuers and flog them as well. While two soldiers pursued the two men, the rest of the Spanish soldiers came under fire from the men's companions, who were armed with bows and arrows. The Spanish returned fire with their guns, killing one Indian and wounding another. The two Indians who had fled were eventually caught and duly flogged.

Given the low regard in which Spanish soldiers generally held the California Indians, it is unlikely that they would have gone to such trouble to punish a mere threat made by one Indian against another, as Palóu's account implied. This apparently exaggerated response suggests that the punishment inflicted on this band of Indians represented the sergeant's response not just to the last infraction that Palóu mentioned—the threat to shoot another Indian with an arrow—but also to all of the offenses listed as well as the subsequent attempts to resist punishment. It also suggests that the sergeant was responding not just to the infractions but also to the violation of Spanish colonial order—the challenge to Spanish control—that the infractions represented.

From the Hispanic colonists' perspective, all of the offenses that Palóu listed included an element of defiance toward the Spanish soldiers' authority as it was expressed in the civil order they were charged with maintaining. Within colonial Spanish gender codes, this defiance implicitly threatened the Spanish soldiers' honor and masculinity by challenging their ability to control those whom the Spanish soldiers regarded as social inferiors. The desire of one Indian to kiss a soldier's wife, however, went beyond an implicit threat, openly challenging that soldier's ability to protect the sexual purity of a woman in his family and to maintain his exclusive sexual rights to his wife.

The Indians' threat of physical violence, as well as actual attempts to inflict bodily harm on the Spanish soldiers, also threatened the colonists' masculinity. Historian Steve J. Stern writes that "in the masculine popular culture of late colonial Morelos, certain types of extreme aggressions by men not only justified serious and even homicidal assaults. They virtually demanded it." The same held true in the masculine popular cultures of other late colonial Mexican regions. These aggressions included challenges "that explicitly violated one's manhood, personal reputation, or protection of family" and required "retribution, an effort to destroy or punish the transgressor and thereby redeem the masculinity of the avenger. Failure to respond aggressively to extreme challenges such as these had an emasculatory effect on the man who lost his nerve."[51] While firing an arrow at the corporal of the guard without hitting him might not seem to be an act of "extreme aggression" by the Bay Area Indian who took the shot, the Spanish military was hyperaware of threats of violence from the California Indians. A large-scale Indian revolt at Mission San Diego in 1775 had sent shock waves through the Hispanic population in Alta California, encouraging the military to respond to any hint of violence as if it was, in fact, an act of extreme aggression. When the soldiers at San Francisco, who were greatly outnumbered by the Indians in the area, came under renewed arrow fire the next day as they pursued the archer and his companions, their suspicions that the Indians wished to harm them were confirmed. By responding with gunfire, the Spanish soldiers turned the tables, emasculating the Indians who could neither respond in kind nor effectively defend themselves against such weaponry. The Spanish soldiers thus reasserted their control and redeemed their own masculinity.

In their attempts to protect California Indians from the soldiers' violence, the missionaries came into direct competition with Spanish soldiers for masculine honor. Echoing Junípero Serra's contention, Fermín Francisco de Lasuén reasserted the missionaries' right to discipline the Indians in 1801. "It is but natural in the circumstances that we should have the authority, the right, and the opportunity to correct and discipline [the baptized Indians] for their own good," he wrote. "In case there should be someone who would deny us this right," he continued, undoubtedly thinking of the military, "on May 6, 1773, the Council of War and Royal Treasury at a meeting in Mexico in regard to these missions thus declared: 'The management, control, punishment, and education of baptized Indians pertain exclusively to the missionary Fathers.'"[52] The missionaries' honor—and their sense of success in their mission—was directly related to their ability to prevent the abuse of those Indians they saw as members of their households, the missions.

︎

The honor-shame complex that informed the priests' efforts to protect Indians from soldiers also structured their treatment of Indian women in the missions. In order to protect the sexual "purity" of Indian women in the mission, the priests at Mission San Francisco separated adolescent girls, unmarried women, and widows from the rest of the mission population and housed them in the monjerío. This was the building in which Pismote, Sappím, and other women without ecclesiastically sanctioned husbands lived once they accepted baptism. Missionaries prioritized the construction of monjeríos: along with temporary chapels and missionary residences, these were usually among the first buildings constructed at a new mission.[53] According to naturalist Georg H. von Langsdorff, who visited Mission San Francisco in 1806, the dormitory there was arranged around three sides of a courtyard. Access to the courtyard could only be gained by passing through the priests' quarters, which made up the fourth side of the square.54 This arrangement made it easy for the Franciscans to monitor activities in the women's dormitory.

Langsdorff and other observers reported that contact between monjerío residents and other Indians at the mission took place primarily during the Mass and times of religious instruction. At other times, Langsdorff wrote, "All the girls and widows are closely guarded in separate houses, as though under lock and key, and kept at work. They are but seldom permitted to go out in the day, and never at night."55 According to Langsdorff, these women were "under the immediate supervision of the padres," though there may also have been a female supervisor.56 The priests taught the girls and women in the monjerío "useful occupations, such as cleaning and combing wool, spinning, weaving, etc.," wrote Langsdorff. "Their principal business is the manufacture of a woolen cloth and blankets for the Indians' own use."57 However, he noted, the women's training in these skills, as well as the quality of their production, was impeded by the missionaries' own lack of familiarity with the tasks they were teaching.

Assessing the impact of the monjerío on the transmission of knowledge from older to younger women at Mission San Francisco is difficult. Separated from their mothers and other older female relatives, the adolescent girls in the monjerío learned some of the skills the missionaries deemed useful for Hispanic women, but they missed opportunities to acquire the skills and knowledge women had accumulated over centuries of life in the San Francisco Bay Area. The physical separation imposed by the monjerío may have made it impossible for mothers and other older women to teach their younger female relations traditional ways of understanding and managing menstruation, sex, childbirth, and childrearing or to perform important rituals to mark the onset of puberty. Before the Hispanic colonists arrived, Indian women had conveyed much of this information during ceremonies—especially girls' initiation ceremonies. By disallowing indigenous ceremonial activities, the priests interrupted another conduit for the transmission of traditional knowledge.58 Kept busy learning to spin and weave, girls also had less time in which to learn traditional basket-weaving skills and the botanical knowledge that would help them find and use plants as their mothers had.

By physically separating girls from their older female relatives and keeping them busy at the mission, the missionaries made it more difficult for the women to pass on the "Old peoples' tales" of which Ramón Abella complained.⁵⁹ However, the separation was not absolute: the presence of older unmarried and widowed women in the dormitory may have allowed the transmission of some of this knowledge despite the Indian girls' separation from their own female relatives. Lonsom, an aged woman whom the priests described as "the grandmother of many of the new Christians," accepted baptism in 1780.⁶⁰ Lonsom did not marry after her baptism, so she was housed in the monjerío with other unmarried women. There, Lonsom may have told stories, sung songs, and taught skills to younger women like Quéyeme, who would later marry the Mission San Francisco alcalde Huetlícs.⁶¹

Whereas unbaptized Bay Area Indians lived and worked in lineage groups, the structures of space, time, and resource distribution at Mission San Francisco encouraged Indians who accepted baptism to identify themselves primarily as members of nuclear families. The priests broke extended lineages into nuclear families in the mission, using these smaller groups to organize residential arrangements and resource distribution. Married couples like Puyeles and Au-luté each received an "apartment" of their own in the Indian village next to the mission, which they shared with their children until the children were old enough to move to sex-segregated dormitories. The priests established the nuclear family as normative by removing from the mission's Indian village all those who did not belong: single men and women, widows and widowers, and even married women whose husbands were away from the mission temporarily. The missionaries placed these people in the men's and women's dormitories where they were subject to additional supervision.

The priests reinforced the nuclear family unit through such mundane activities as daily food distribution. "At mealtimes," which occurred three times a day, wrote Langsdorff, "a big bell is rung, and each family sends a vessel to the kitchen, and is served as many measures as there are members."⁶² Three times a day, then, baptized Indians were reminded of their membership in a nuclear family group (or their lack of it). As they collected the food and distributed it among family members, Indians were forced to acknowledge this new way of reckoning kinship and belonging: there was not enough food to feed the entire lineage group, nor even the baptized members of the lineage. There was only enough for parents and children, the nuclear family. Thus, the nuclear family became the organizing unit of the mission population.

The Franciscans' policies regarding marriage among baptized Indians also reinforced the nuclear family unit. When a polygynous man like Keqecég accepted baptism, the priests required that he choose one of his wives with whom to solemnize his marriage. According to a Catholic policy that had been in place since the sixteenth century, Keqecég was required to marry the first woman with whom he had sexual contact. However, if he was unable to remember which woman that was, he was free to marry whichever wife he chose. This policy originated in the Catholic Church's definition of marriage as a permanent union constituted by mutual consent, usually expressed in sexual contact, and its recognition of the existence and legitimacy of marriage among non-Catholic and non-Christian peoples.[63]

Keqecég, like many polygynous men, solemnized his marriage with his junior wife, Attiom. He may have based his decision to marry Attiom partly on her youthful good looks—she was about thirty years younger than he was. However, Keqecég's choice probably had more to do with practical considerations. Sappím, Keqecég's senior wife, had chosen not to accept baptism, while Attiom had been baptized two days before Keqecég. Sappím was well beyond her childbearing years, while Attiom was still nursing her first child and was likely to bear several more. Finally, Sappím was Keqecég's age and would probably be less able to take care of him in his old age than Attiom would. After their marriage, Keqecég and Attiom lived with their baby in one of the apartments next to the mission, spatially separated from the rest of Keqecég's lineage—both those children and grandchildren who had accepted baptism and those who had not.

According to the Franciscans, only Keqecég's sacramental marriage to Attiom was valid: his marriages to other women dissolved when he took his marriage vows. However, Keqecég and Sappím may have continued to consider themselves married. Baptized Indians who lived at the mission frequently left on trips that the missionaries termed paseos. The ostensible purpose of these journeys was usually food gathering or recruitment. The name given to the trips, though—paseo—translates to something like "promenade," hinting at the priests' understanding that an element of recreation was involved as well. These trips seem to have been a time for Indians to relax and visit friends and family, renewing social and familial bonds. For many polygynous, or formerly polygynous, men like Keqecég, these journeys probably included visits with "former" wives like Sappím. Thus, the alliance between the Ssalson and Puichon Indians that had been created by Keqecég's marriage to Sappím may have continued even after Keqecég and Attiom accepted baptism.[64]

Forming Families

There is no way to be certain whether Sappím and Keqecég still considered their marriage valid when she accepted baptism about a year after Keqecég had made the same choice. At some point, however, their marriage reached a definite end. Since the priests saw her as an unmarried woman, Sappím would have been housed in the monjerío immediately after her baptism, just as Pismote and every other baptized, unmarried woman was. The only way for women to leave the monjerío, other than flight or death, was by marrying a baptized man. Sappím exercised this option some six months after her baptism, marrying a man from her own tribal community.[65] This marriage provided her with a way out of the dormitory and made her a part of a nuclear family, even as it definitively ended her membership in Keqecég's lineage and weakened the alliance between the Puichons and Ssalsons that her marriage with Keqecég had reinforced.

By requiring that Indians participate in a Catholic wedding ceremony, and by reserving for themselves the right to approve or disapprove of baptized Indians' marriage partners, the missionaries greatly increased their control over marriage in the missions. While the Franciscans apparently did seek Indian parents' approval on occasion, they did not require it.[66] For centuries the Catholic Church's policies had favored children's desires over parental objections to marriage partners, but that had begun to change in late eighteenth-century Mexico. By the time Mission San Francisco was founded in 1776, Spanish civil and ecclesiastical laws required parental consent for most marriages.[67] In the Franciscan missions, however, the priests held both ecclesiastical and parental authority. Thus, the role that Indian parents could play in selecting marriage partners for their children diminished when their children accepted baptism. Keqecég and his wives, for example, must have taken an active role in negotiating his daughters' marriages to Jaluntis, the head of another important lineage in his village. When both of those daughters accepted baptism after Jaluntis's death, however, their parents likely had little say in their choice of partners for remarriage. Even if Keqecég did choose men for his daughters to marry at the mission, those choices were circumscribed by Catholic rules about appropriate marriage partners and ultimately subject to the missionaries' approval.

Some marriage partners that Keqecég and his wives would have considered ideal for their children were prohibited by Catholic kinship rules. Bay Area Indians routinely contracted marriages with affinal kin (persons related by marriage), in part because these marriages could strengthen existing alliances. However, both consanguineal kin and affinal kin were off-limits as marriage partners in the Catholic Church. "They do not know in their marriages the relationship of affinity, but rather this incites them to receive as their own wives their sisters-in-law and even the mothers-in-law, and the custom they observe is that he who gets one woman has as his all of her sisters," wrote Francisco Palóu in 1787.[68] Contrary to Palóu's claim, California Indians did recognize the affinal relationship; they simply did not see it as a bar to marriage. Some Bay Area Indians continued to consider affinal kin attractive marriage partners near the end of the Spanish colonial period.

The Mission San Francisco marriage registers record three marriages between 1816 and 1818 in which the officiating priest granted a dispensation allowing the partners to marry despite their being first- or second-degree affinal kin.[69] One of these marriages was between Sutay and Lalle.[70] The couple had been married before their baptism and already had at least three children together.[71] When Sutay was baptized, though, he solemnized his marriage with his senior wife, Uiumpi,[72] leaving Lalle "free," in the priests' terminology. Women like Lalle usually married other men after their baptisms, but this case was different. Uiumpi died a few months after accepting baptism, leaving Sutay widowed. Two months later Sutay and Lalle presented themselves to the missionaries to be married. Father Ramón Abella wrote that Sutay and Lalle were "[r]elatives in the first degree of Affinity because [Sutay] was married to Lugarda," Uiumpi's baptismal name. Abella's brief explanation and the prevalence of sororal polygyny in the Bay Area strongly suggest that Uiumpi and Lalle were sisters, making Sutay and Lalle siblings-in-law. In another marriage between affinal kin, the affinal relationship was more distant. When Clara and Tolepa married in 1818, Ramón Abella noted that Clara was a widow, having been married previously to Huyunjaquisto—known to the priests by his baptismal name, Pedro Crisólogo.[73] "This Pedro," wrote Abella, "was first cousin of Senen," the man also known as Tolepa who became Clara's second husband.

The priests attempted to prevent marriages that violated Catholic kinship rules: "I married the following [couples] . . . after having made some simple inquiries about whether they were Relatives or not," Abella wrote on another occasion. "The previous days while they were catechumens they talked to me."[74] Still, sometimes the battle was not worth fighting. "The principal cause that moved me to grant them a dispensation is the lack of respect that they have for the [relationship of] affinity,"[75] recorded Abella in the record of Clara and Tolepa's marriage, echoing Fermin Francisco Palóu's complaint. Prohibiting such marriages came with a cost: "They run away sometimes, and this moved me to grant a dispensation," Abella wrote in another case.[76]

In addition to trying to prohibit marriages between consanguineal or affinal kin, the priests also required that baptized Indians marry only other baptized people. Determining how successful they were in imposing this restriction is more difficult, because while the priests could refuse to perform a Catholic marriage ceremony to join a baptized person to an unbaptized one, we cannot know how often Bay Area Indians decided to forgo the Catholic ceremony and marry according to traditional customs outside the mission. In some cases, couples appear to have married according to Indian customs first and only later undergone the Catholic ceremony. Tubssúpa, for example, was a Ssalson man who accepted baptism at Mission San Francisco in 1784 when he was approximately twenty years old. He married Jaiguete, a Ssalson woman, at Mission San Francisco one month after her baptism in 1789. Their first child was born fewer than twenty-four weeks later. While premature births were common among Californian Indian women because of the prevalence of venereal disease, this child lived eight days, far longer than such a premature child could be expected to survive without advanced medical care.[77] If Tubssúpa was indeed the child's biological father, then he and Jaiguete conceived the child much earlier, indicating that they had probably married according to Indian custom after Tubssúpa's baptism, but long before Jaiguete underwent the ceremony. Only later, shortly before their child's birth, did the couple decide to participate in a Catholic wedding ceremony as well.[78]

Unlike Tubssúpa, many Indians who entered Mission San Francisco were married before they accepted baptism. The priests' requirement that baptized Indians marry other baptized people forced these Indians to separate from their spouses. While the priests recognized the validity of Indian marriage under natural law, according to Catholic doctrine these unions were not sacramental and therefore could be dissolved.[79] Some Indians who accepted baptism waited for their spouses to do the same, and then solemnized their already-existing marriages, making the unions official in the priests' eyes by going through the Catholic ceremony. Over the course of the Spanish colonial period, nearly nine hundred Indian couples accepted baptism and then solemnized their marriages. In only eighty of these were the husband and wife baptized on different days. In forty-nine cases, the husband was baptized first, while in thirty-one cases, the wife was baptized first. Most Indians had to wait only a short time for their spouses to be baptized: twenty-one of the eighty couples separated by baptism solemnized their marriages within thirty days of the first partner's baptism, and another eighteen couples did so before two months elapsed. The Huchiun woman Lulume, for example, accepted baptism on 20 September 1792. Her husband Punacche, however, waited almost a month after that before he was baptized on 17 October 1792. Immediately after Punacche's baptism, the couple presented themselves to Father Antonio Danti to be married.[80]

Other Indians waited longer to be reunited with a spouse, though men did so far more frequently than women. Of the thirty-one women baptized before their husbands, only nine—less than a third—waited more than two months for their husbands to be baptized. In contrast, of the forty-nine men baptized before their wives, thirty-two—about two-thirds—waited more than two months for their wives to accept baptism. Thirteen of these waited more than a year, while only two women did the same. Sumay, for example, was baptized in March 1801. He waited nearly two years for his wife, Ssagnemaien, to be baptized: she finally went through the ceremony in November 1802. The couple was married about three weeks later.[81] Men like Sumay may have opted to wait for a spouse more frequently because unmarried men enjoyed better living conditions and greater freedom of movement in the mission than unmarried women. Because the Franciscan missionaries supervised men's movements far less than women's, these men may have been able to visit unbaptized wives, and therefore continue their marital relationships, far more easily than women could visit unbaptized husbands.

Some Bay Area Indians—particularly women—may have used the requirement that baptized Indians marry other baptized people as a means of ending unsatisfactory marriages. Nayomi, who was baptized in 1782, seems to have used her baptism in this way. Nayomi, her older sister Au-luté, and her younger sister Pismote were all married to Puyeles. Nayomi was the first to be baptized, preceding Puyeles and her sisters by over four months. According to her baptismal entry, Nayomi told the officiating priest that "she had left [her husband] with the goal of getting baptized and marrying a Christian."[82] We cannot know how much the priest embellished Nayomi's statement, but her actions do indicate some discontent with her marriage. Five days after her baptism, Nayomi married Yapis, a man whose consistent recorded participation in mission activities seems to indicate his importance among the Indians in the mission.[83] By accepting baptism while a husband refused it, like Nayomi did, or by refusing baptism while a husband accepted it, like Keqecég's wife Sappím did, a Bay Area woman could effectively end a marriage.

Baptism was not the only way to end a marriage in Bay Area California: Costanoan and other Bay Area Indian societies permitted divorce, and unlike Catholicism, they allowed both men and women to remarry after separation from a partner. Gualson, for example, was a junior wife of the Oljon man Chiguilete. Together they had one child, Ferenbe. Within a couple years of Ferenbe's birth, however, Gualson had a child with another man, Chasinte, a good indication that her marriage to Chiguilete was over.[84] It is impossible to know whether Gualson decided to leave Chiguilete, or if Chiguilete sent Gualson away. Because Costanoan societies were both patrilineal and patrilocal, women were displaced in both marriage and divorce. Gualson had moved to Chiguilete's village when she married him, leaving her lineage behind. When they separated, Gualson moved back to her lineage. Her family may have had to return the gifts it received when Gualson and Chiguilete were married. Gualson may also have brought Ferenbe with her: though Costanoan groups were patrilineal and patrilocal, Ramón Abella and Juan Sainz de Lucio stated in 1814 that in the case of divorce among Bay Area Indians, "normally the children follow the Mother."[85] Gualson's reappearance at the family home, therefore, may have provoked mixed feelings among the members of her patrilineage. Her return, possibly with Ferenbe, meant one or two more mouths to feed, but it also brought one or two more people to contribute to the lineage's work. In addition, the possibility existed that Gualson might make a better match in her next marriage, bringing greater benefit to the lineage.[86]

For Bay Area Indian women whose return to their patrilineages would have created too great a burden for the family, Mission San Francisco may have provided an alternative destination in the event of divorce. In exchange for baptism, the missionaries provided women with a place to live and a means of sustenance without the negative consequences that might have come with a return to the patrilineage. Randall Milliken has suggested that once they entered the mission community by accepting baptism, many women may have used marriage as a way of gaining additional security.[87] The rapidity with which many single women married after accepting baptism at Mission San Francisco supports this idea. Of those Indians who were baptized at age eighteen or older by the Franciscans' estimation and who were single or *libre* (the term priests applied to former co-wives released from their polygynous marriages) at their baptisms, 520 eventually married at Mission San Francisco.[88] Women in this group married more than twice as quickly as men. The 365 single and libre women baptized at age eighteen or older who married at Mission San Francisco averaged about nine months between their baptisms and their first marriages at the mission. More than one hundred of these—over a quarter—married within a month of their baptisms. In contrast, the 155 single men aged eighteen or over at baptism who married at Mission San Francisco did so for the first time an average of slightly more than twenty-three months after their baptisms. Only thirteen of these men—less than a tenth—married within a month of their baptisms. These figures raise the possibility that many women accepted baptism *in order to* marry, though they may not have had a specific man in mind as a husband. Baptism allowed these women access to a pool of men that was otherwise unavailable. Threatened with diseases that had decimated their communities, faced with a rapidly changing natural and social environment, and possibly confronted with factionalism that tore communities apart, many unmarried women may have seen in Mission San Francisco the promise of a more stable, secure future.

By replacing indigenous Californian kinship rules with Catholic ones, requiring that baptized Indians marry other baptized people, and reserving for themselves the right to approve of Indians' marriage partners, the Franciscan priests at Mission San Francisco significantly altered the structures of many families in the Bay Area. The restrictions the priests imposed complicated the creation and maintenance of alliances between lineages, villages, and tribal communities through marriage. The requirement that both marriage partners be baptized contributed to the dissolution of many Indian marriages and may have made baptism a means of divorce in the Bay Area. The priests enforced these restrictions as best they could through the imposition of their authority in the mission, a paternal authority that weakened Indian parents' own authority over their children.

Keqecég may have believed that by accepting baptism at Mission San Francisco along with the other members of his lineage, he would create an alliance with the Spanish newcomers that would enhance his political stature on the San Francisco peninsula. While his association with the mission may have won Keqecég some advantages, it also made maintaining previous alliances, as well as creating new alliances, far more difficult. The priests' assertion of their spiritual fatherhood of all of the baptized

Indians significantly reduced Keqecég's authority over baptized members of his lineage. The missionaries separated Keqecég's extended family, which had lived and worked together before baptism, into nuclear family units. Keqecég therefore lived with his junior wife Attiom and their infant child, rather than with all of his wives, children, and other relatives. The women of Keqecég's lineage whom the priests considered unmarried—adolescent daughters, adult daughters whose husbands were not baptized, and former co-wives—were housed in the women's dormitory after their baptisms until they married men whom the missionaries deemed acceptable partners. This spatial separation physically removed these women from the supervision of their lineage, placing them under priestly surveillance instead.

The marriage of Sappím, Keqecég's senior wife, to another man weakened and may have dissolved the alliance that had existed between the Ssalson and Puichon Indians because of Sappím's marriage to Keqecég. Keqecég's intravillage alliance with Jaluntis, another powerful man in Uturpe, effectively ended with Jaluntis's death and Keqecég's daughters' subsequent baptisms. Though Keqecég would normally have negotiated the terms of his widowed daughters' new marriages in order to bring maximum political, social, and economic benefit to his patrilineage, the new rules the Franciscans introduced circumscribing the pool of acceptable marriage partners, as well as the missionaries' insistence that baptized Indians marry other baptized people and their ability to veto any match they deemed unacceptable, meant that Keqecég likely had little influence on these remarriages. Thus, by restructuring Indian families through the imposition of a Catholic kinship system and priestly authority, the Franciscans at Mission San Francisco had a significant effect on the economic, political, and social networks that bound people to one another throughout the San Francisco Bay Area.

4

Love and Marriage

∽ Mission San Francisco marked the middle of a war zone. What precipitated the hostilities is impossible to say, but the fact remained that the Yelamu Indians, in whose territory the mission was located, and the Ssalson Indians, twelve miles to the south, were at war when the mission began in 1776. As Father Francisco Palóu remembered,

> [t]he heathen of the village near this place [the Yelamu] made frequent visits, and were apparently pleased with our arrival, although, through lack of interpreters and our ignorance of their language, we could not tell them the purpose of our coming. They went on in this way until the 12th of August, when the heathen of San Mateo [the Ssalsons], who are their enemies, fell upon them at a large town about a league from this lagoon, burned it and had a fight, in which there were many wounded and dead on both sides. Apparently the Indians of this vicinity were defeated, and so fearful were they of the others that they made tule rafts and all moved to the shore opposite the presidio, or to the mountains on the east side of the bay.[1]

Six weeks after the Spanish arrival, members of Keqecég's Ssalson village and their allies had apparently driven off the missionaries' potential converts.[2] The Yelamus returned only slowly, and it was almost a year after the mission's founding before the first Indian, a Yelamu man named Chamis, was baptized, on 24 June 1777.

Chamis's sister Liloté followed him early the next month. Four years later, Liloté helped end the long and sometimes frightening war between the Yelamu and Ssalson Indians by marrying Letchentis, a Ssalson man who had accepted baptism a few days before the wedding. Fathers Francisco Palóu and Pedro Benito Cambón reported that "from [the Ssalson] villages, it has been accomplished that some, now that they are baptized, live in the mission and have married with those of this site [the Yelamus] . . . and with these conversions the continual warfare in which they lived has ceased, with which both nations show themselves pleased."[3] While Palóu and Cambón ascribed the cessation of hostilities to the Ssalson conversions in 1781, far more likely is that peace was achieved through intermarriages between the Yelamus and the Ssalsons, including the marriage between Liloté and Letchentis.

The far-reaching effects of this and other weddings in Mission San Francisco highlight the importance of marriage in indigenous California for the creation and maintenance of social, economic, and political networks. The Franciscans' imposition of priestly authority and insistence on a nuclear family model contributed to the transformation of Indian family structures and significantly complicated the maintenance of interfamilial networks that bound people to one another in the San Francisco Bay Area. Nevertheless, Indians at Mission San Francisco continued to create and reinforce those networks, adopting and adapting the Catholic rituals of marriage and baptism in order to develop and maintain relationships between lineages, villages, and tribal communities.

The Franciscan missionaries taught Indians at Mission San Francisco, as well as the colonists to whom they ministered, that marriage was a sacrament, a way in which humans experienced divine grace. Heavily influenced by the theology of Thomas Aquinas, they and the Spanish theologians who informed their thought saw marriage as an earthly model of Christ's union with the church, a union that sanctified both spouses. As a sacrament, marriage was a permanent, indissoluble bond. Though marriages could be annulled under certain circumstances, a valid marriage ended only upon the death of one spouse. Adultery, according to Thomas

Aquinas, constituted the only grounds for divorce, but *divorce* in this case meant only the separation of the couple, not the dissolution of the marriage bond. Because marriage was a sacrament, it fell under the jurisdiction of ecclesiastical courts in Spain and Spanish America. Disputes over every aspect of marriage, from the selection of partners to the frequency of sexual intercourse between married couples, came before these courts for adjudication.[4]

The Catholic Church's doctrinal teachings on marriage as a way in which humans experienced divine grace contributed to a more general emphasis in the Church on the freedom of individual will. This emphasis found expression in the Church's insistence that both partners enter the marriage relationship of their own accord. The essential ingredient for a marriage between two eligible people, according to Catholic doctrine, was the freely given consent of both parties. At the Council of Trent (1545–63), the Church issued orders requiring that a priest officiate and two other people witness every marriage to ensure that both parties freely consented to the union. In strengthening its support of individual free will in this way, the Church placed itself in opposition to many parents—especially members of the elite—who wished to use their children's marriages to advance familial interests.

At the same council, however, the Church severely restricted clandestine marriages, which had been a common way of circumventing parental opposition and avoiding public scandal. Except in certain situations, the council declared these marriages invalid. By opposing clandestine marriages, the Church made it far more difficult for individuals to exercise their free will in the face of familial pressure.

In 1776 Spanish king Carlos III acted to strengthen parental control over children's marriages in legislation known as the *Real Pragmática*. Opponents of the Catholic Church's marriage policy charged that it "eroded parents' authority over their children and contributed to the moral collapse of society."[5] King Carlos III used the Real Pragmática to shift the balance of power over marriage to favor the state and, through the state, parental interests. Extended to all Spanish territories in 1778, and signed into law in California the following year, the Real Pragmática "prohibited the legitimation of unequal unions"[6] and required parental consent for the marriage of anyone under age twenty-five. That the legislation was concerned primarily with the maintenance of social and economic hierarchies that could be upset by an egalitarian marriage policy is evident in the exceptions to the Real Pragmática's directives: Parental consent was not required for the "marriage of Negros, mulattoes, coyotes, and other such individuals with each other, except for those who serve in an official capacity or otherwise distinguish themselves by their reputation."[7]

The idea that parents would choose marriage partners for their children, and that social status would be a primary consideration in that choice, was thus a familiar one to the Spanish missionaries and a time-honored one in Hispanic culture. Ramón Gutiérrez remarks in his study of marriage in colonial New Mexico that "New Mexico's Spanish colonists believed that there should be *igualdad de calidad* (equality in social status) between marriage partners."[8] The 1776 Real Pragmática wrote this expectation into law. Another Real Pragmática, issued in 1803, allowed parents "to prevent the marriages of their sons under the age of twenty-five and their daughters under twenty-three without having to state their reasons, whether social, racial, or economic inequality, resentment, a grudge, or greed."[9] Historian Patricia Seed has found that two-thirds of parents in late eighteenth- and early nineteenth-century New Spain who objected to their children's marriage choices did so for reasons of "differences of wealth, income, or social status."[10]

Using marriage as a means to create interfamilial alliances and protect social prestige was a longstanding tradition in Europe, and Europeans continued to use the strategy in the New World. On his 1806 journey to California, for instance, Russian count Nikolai Rezanov fell in love with Concepción Arguello, the daughter of José Darío Arguello, the commander of the San Francisco Presidio. Georg H. von Langsdorff, the German naturalist who accompanied Rezanov, wrote that "[t]he bright sparkling eyes of Doña Concepción had made upon him a deep impression, and pierced his inmost soul." Rezanov's intentions were not purely romantic, however: the potential union had political and economic possibilities. "He conceived the idea," continued Langsdorff,

> that through a marriage with the daughter of the comandante of the Presidio de San Francisco a close bond would be formed for future business intercourse between the Russian American Company and the provincia of Nueva California. He had therefore decided to sacrifice himself, by wedding Doña Concepción, to the welfare of his country, and to bind in friendly alliance both Spain and Russia.[11]

The Count was right that his marriage to Doña Concepción might facilitate trade between the Spanish and the Russians in California, but Governor Arrillaga did not share Rezanov's optimism that the marriage would be influential enough to "bind in friendly alliance both Spain and Russia." He objected to the marriage, citing "the difference between the religions of the parties" as well as "the critical political situation in Europe, and the well-known suspicious nature of the Spanish government" for which Arguello worked.[12] Neither man doubted, however, that the marriage would have international political consequences.

While personal attraction and political advantage coincided for Rezanov in his quest to marry Doña Concepción, individuals did not always find themselves in love with a person their parents deemed an acceptable marriage partner. Scholars disagree about the role romantic love played by the end of the eighteenth century. Historian Ramón Gutiérrez argues that by 1800, the verb *amar* (to love) had taken on the romantic connotations that we associate with it today, and that romantic love had become a socially acceptable reason for marriage.[13] In fact, the acceptance of romantic love as a justification for marriage had its roots in the Spanish Catholic turn to Thomist theology, which emphasized individual will. In this view, romantic love was an expression of individual freedom.[14] This expression, however, could run deeply contrary to the interests of an individual's family, and as the Spanish government moved to shore up the authority of the patriarchal family at the end of the eighteenth century, a growing emphasis on economic and social status rendered romantic love a less persuasive justification for marriage.[15]

Emotional attachment remained an important factor in the Franciscans' understanding of the marriage relationship, despite government and Church officials' general tendency to back parents in their opposition to children's love matches by the end of the eighteenth century. In 1791 an anonymous Franciscan published a work of moral theology entitled *Brief Instruction to Married Christians and Useful Warnings to Those Who Intend to Be Such* in which he emphasized the need for love in a marriage. "Love makes chores soft and sweet," he wrote, "and as in the conjugal life there are so many, and such large chores, if love is lacking between the spouses, the chores become intolerable—but love makes them easier."[16] Here, love was not based on duty, nor was it demonstrated through practical action on behalf of the beloved. Rather, in this context, love was an emotional bond between the spouses. That bond, in the equation laid out by the Franciscan author, directly affected the happiness of the married couple. The terms on both sides of the equation, love and happiness, illustrate the Thomist emphasis on individual will in the Franciscan author's thinking.

For families of means, the path to marriage officially began with a formal proposal, usually involving the families of both the bride and groom.[17] If the bride accepted the proposal, a formal betrothal took place. This was the occasion for the exchange of gifts between the two families whose children would be married: the bride gave the groom a small gift such as a rosary or medallion of the Virgin Mary to symbolize her virginity; he responded by presenting her with a chest containing her wedding trousseau. This substantial gift included the bride-to-be's wedding gown and other clothing; jewelry; household goods; and sometimes money. In some cases, the father of the bride then presented the groom's family with the bride's dowry, a gift that represented the bride's inheritance and might consist of any kind of wealth, though livestock was a common form of dotal property. Though the husband would control this property during his wife's lifetime, it remained her property and passed to her children upon her death. If the groom was a wealthy man, he would conclude the gift exchange by presenting the bride with another gift of moveable property such as livestock. This gift became the bride's property and, like her dowry, passed to her heirs when she died.

Few Hispanic colonists in California possessed the means to fund a complete exchange of wedding gifts. Lacking title to land or other significant property that would be affected by children's marriages, most families in Alta California probably exhibited less concern with regard to their children's choices of marriage partners. Historian Antonia Castañeda suggests, as well, that these families "found little reason to enter into a sacramental Christian marriage. . . . [L]andless peasants, *genízaros*, and wage earners were more apt to enter into consensual unions and relationships based on personal desire or love."[18] This disregard for sacramental marriage may have held sway in the civilian settlement of San José, founded in 1777. Colonists living under military supervision at the San Francisco Presidio, however, may have felt more pressure to follow the dictates of the Catholic Church.

If an engaged couple intended to marry in the eyes of the Church, the local priest completed a matrimonial investigation to ensure that each partner was eligible to marry the other. Certain factors, termed "diriment impediments," could render a marriage invalid, even if they were discovered after the union had been consummated and children had been born.

Numerous conditions might result in a diriment impediment. For example, if one or both partners was below the legal age for marriage, if the groom was impotent, if either partner was already validly married to another person, or if the bride and groom had a consanguineous or affinal relationship with one another, the marriage would be invalid.[19] If, in the investigation, the priest discovered a diriment impediment, the Church permanently forbade the proposed marriage.[20]

Once the investigation was completed, the banns were read. These announcements, mandated by the Council of Trent, informed the local Catholic community of the couple's intention to marry. They were read at Mass on three successive Sundays or holy days of obligation (days on which Catholics are required to attend Mass). If one or both of the partners was from a different parish, the banns were also read at his or her home church. Like the investigation, the banns aided in uncovering any possible impediments to the marriage, since parishioners were encouraged to inform the local priest of any reason why one or both of the betrothed could not validly marry.

The marriage ceremony itself took place in the local church, presided over by the priest. It might be performed in the context of a Mass, but this was not necessary. After the Council of Trent, at least two people besides the priest were required to witness the ceremony and to verify the free consent of both contracting parties. If the marriage was performed during a Mass, the entire congregation filled the role of the witnesses, though at Mission San Francisco the priest usually also recorded the name of at least one specific person as a witness.

After the marriage ceremony, the couple was veiled and received the nuptial blessing. This ceremony, which did take place during a Mass, might happen immediately after the wedding ceremony or it might be postponed for days, weeks, or even months. The couple lay prone in front of the altar while a veil was held over them and the priest pronounced the nuptial benediction. This ceremony was performed only for persons who had not been married in the Church previously; widows and widowers who remarried, for example, were not veiled again.[21]

⸎

The elaborate ceremonies that marked Hispanic marriages were, in the Franciscans' eyes, conspicuously lacking among Bay Area Indians. One item on the questionnaire about California Indians and mission life to which the Mission San Francisco priests responded in 1814 asked about marriage among the local Indians: "What pacts or conditions do they celebrate for matrimonial contracts? What type of service do suitors provide to the fathers of the bride and for how long?" Taking the term "matrimonial contracts" to refer, as it did in Catholicism, to a permanent bond between a man and a woman, marked by a formal ceremony presided over by a religious specialist, Father Ramón Abella answered simply: "None, it seems to me."[22]

Though Abella asserted that the local Indians did not enter into formal matrimonial contracts, he went on to describe the very rituals that anthropologists agree symbolized a formal marriage contract among California Indian tribes. "The most liberal suitor might give the bride some abalones, which are perforated shells or some little pieces of marble, also carved; and she will break them in the first quarrel that they have. To the parents of the bride they do not provide any service, because these are content that the daughter is [content]."[23] These gifts, though they seemed insignificant to Abella, were actually valuable trade goods among Bay Area Californians, objects obtained from far away through trading networks.[24] Gift giving created an economic bond between the families represented by bride and groom that would last as long as the marriage did. In some societies, if the marriage ended in divorce, the gifts exchanged on the wedding day (or their equivalents) were returned, formally dissolving the economic bonds created by the marriage. It is possible that the breaking of the shells during a quarrel that Abella mentioned was another way of dissolving these bonds through the destruction of property. Because of the economic impact divorce could have, families might place great pressure on the couple to stay married.[25] Often more important than the economic bond, however, was the kinship relationship that it represented. Because California Indian societies were organized around kinship, a marriage between people from two different lineages, villages, or tribal communities represented far more than a relationship between two people. Marriage could turn enemies into kin, making it an effective way of ending wars. Thus, when Ssalson man Letchentis and Yelamu woman Liloté married at Mission San Francisco in 1781, they helped create a bond between the Ssalsons and Yelamus strong enough to end the war between their two tribal communities.

As in Hispanic culture, marriage was a primary way of regulating sexual behavior within Californian Indian societies. However, many practices that the Catholics classified as, and associated with, sexual "sin," such as transgendered behavior, homosexuality, and polygyny, were commonly accepted in indigenous California. When a priest at Mission San Antonio found two men engaged "in an unspeakably sinful act," recalled Father Francisco Palóu, he responded by punishing the men and trying "to present to them the enormity of their deed." To the priest's consternation, one of the men replied that the other "was his wife."[26]

This person was not the only third-gendered individual with whom the Spanish tangled in Alta California. Recalling the founding of Mission Santa Clara, Father Francisco Palóu described one person who, "by the clothing that she wore, modestly dressed, and according to the gentile adornments she bore and the manner of working, sitting, etcetera, seemed to be a woman; but according to the aspect of the face and without breasts, even though old enough," caught the Spanish priests' attention. When the missionaries asked about the individual, some newly baptized Indians informed them "that it was a man, and that he went about as a woman and always went with the women and not with the men."[27] Failing to recognize the person in question as third-gendered, the Spanish instead assumed a man was cross-dressing to gain sexual access to the women with whom he spent his time. Spanish soldiers confronted the individual, stripped him of his clothing, and kept him locked up for three days. "After they had expressed to him that it was not good to go about in that dress and even less to surround himself with the women, with whom it was presumed he would be sinning, they gave him his liberty and he left," recounted Palóu. The person fled, and continued dressing and acting as a woman in another village.[28]

The existence of a third and perhaps a fourth gender category in Native Californian societies has been well documented, though scholars have only recently begun to understand individuals of these genders as inhabiting categories other than homosexual or transsexual.[29] In fact, productive activity and specialization was a far more important indicator of gender identity than sexual activity in Native North America generally:[30] as Palóu indicated, the cross-dressing male confronted at Mission Santa Clara apparently took on feminine labor activities, thereby appearing to Palóu to be a woman. Further south in California, among the Chumash Indians and their neighbors the Yokuts and Western Mono, third-gender or "two-spirit" people were identified with their specialization as undertakers.[31]

That the Franciscans misunderstood the behavior of the third-gendered individual at Mission Santa Clara as a devious ploy to gain sexual access to multiple women, rather than as a socially accepted manifestation of an alternative gender identity, was due at least in part to their Aristotelian view of human society and the California Indians' place in it. According to Aristotle, men were at the top of the human hierarchy, above both women and children, because men possessed both reason and authority. Women, like men, were classified as rational beings, but did not possess authority, whereas children were only partially rational, having not yet fully developed their rational faculties. In Aristotle's hierarchy, then, women and children were distinguished from men in part by a lack of self-control, because they did not have the rational capacity to govern their passions.[32] Relegating the California Indians to the status of children, the Franciscans expected Indians to behave in ways that demonstrated a lack of self-control.

As the priests saw it, polygyny was a way for Indian men to indulge their uncontrolled sexual appetite. Polygyny was an accepted practice among the Bay Area Indians, though it was limited to high-status men such as village headmen and shamans. Sororal polygyny, which was common among the Costanoan Indians who comprised the majority of Mission San Francisco's population, helped reinforce interlineage alliances and ensured that those alliances would not wane in the event of divorce or the death of one wife. As I discussed in chapter 3, sororal polygyny may also have been a preferred form of polygyny among co-wives, because it may have been easier to share a husband, and household duties, with one's sisters than with perfect strangers. As Francisco Palóu recalled, "the custom that they observe is that he who gets one woman has as his all of her sisters, having many women, without there being among them the slightest jealousy, the second or third wife looking at the children of her sisters with the same love as at her own children, [and] all of them living together in the same house."[33]

The missionaries' descriptions of Indian marriage tended to focus on the ways it differed from Hispanic norms: the acceptance of polygamy, the apparent lack of a formal contract, and the absence of a ceremony presided over by a religious specialist all stood out to Hispanic observers. However, some broad similarities between Native Californian and Hispanic customs were likely the key to the persistence of some traditional Indian marriage practices in Mission San Francisco. For example, the practice of gift exchange between the families of the bride and groom continued in the missions alongside the newly added Catholic wedding ceremony. At nearby Mission Santa Clara, the missionaries wrote that baptized Indians "marry with all the solemnities of the Holy Church, without pacts or services on the part of the couple other than some presents before the celebration, to the Bride, or to her Parents, or closest Relatives,"[34] making clear that traditional Indian practices persisted alongside the Catholic marriage ritual.

Historian James Lockhart's concept of Double Mistaken Identity is helpful in understanding why both Catholic and Indian marriage practices could coexist at Mission San Francisco.[35] Indians—especially those who had accepted baptism as adults—likely presumed that gift exchange continued to be the act that formalized a marriage. Outside the mission, the gift exchange was the most recognizable way in which a marriage was symbolically concluded. It is only logical that the exchange of gifts would retain its significance among those who accepted baptism. For the missionaries, on the other hand, the exchange of gifts was peripheral to the marriage. Although it was a long-standing tradition in Hispanic culture, gift exchange was not a constitutive element of marriage as it was in California Indian cultures. The priests therefore tolerated the gift exchange, but continued to view it as an optional element. The Santa Clara missionaries' comment that the groom gave "some presents before the celebration to the Bride or to her Parents, or closest Relatives" shows clearly that the missionaries saw this exchange of gifts as separate from, and unnecessary to, marriage at the missions.[36] As long as baptized Indians participated in the Catholic ceremony, the priests did not object to the exchange of gifts. While the practice of gift exchange in the missions may have been reinforced by its acceptance in the Hispanic communities outside the missions, its roots remained firmly in traditional Californian practice.

Along with the ritual of gift exchange to seal a marriage contract, Indians in Mission San Francisco retained some important understandings of how marriage worked in society and what it entailed for both partners. The 1781 marriage between the Yelamu woman Liloté and the Ssalson man Letchentis, which helped end the war between their tribal communities, was not the only one of its kind. In fact, Letchentis's sister, a Ssalson woman, also entered Mission San Francisco and married a Yelamu man at approximately the same time, contributing to the stability of the peace between the two groups.[37] Other instances of intermarriage with political consequences also occurred in the mission, clearly indicating that the Indians who accepted baptism continued to see marriage as a way of creating alliances and extending kinship networks.

Liloté and Letchentis's marriage, along with the other Yelamu-Ssalson marriages, brought peace between the two communities even though the men and women who married did so at Mission San Francisco. The efficacy of these marriages clearly demonstrates that the web of political alliances that covered the Bay Area also extended into Mission San Francisco. Though Indians like Liloté accepted baptism, they retained their positions in the social and political networks that connected Bay Area societies, and they still had the ability to manipulate that web through their own actions—in this case, through their marriages.

The use of marriage as a diplomatic strategy continued in the nineteenth century, and evidence suggests that the missionaries may have consciously encouraged intermarriage as a means of achieving peace between various groups in the missions. Following his 1806 visit to nearby Mission San José, German naturalist Georg H. von Langsdorff reported that he had seen two groups of Indians: "These neighboring tribes formerly lived at great mutual enmity," he commented. "Although they are now united here by the bond of religion, yet the old hostility is so rooted in them that it is still apparent. As an instance of this, the misioneros cannot induce them to intermarry. They will unite themselves with only those of their own tribe, and it is an exception that they mingle or associate with members of any tribe other than their own."[38] While these tribal enmities were apparently too large to overcome at Mission San José, Indians at Mission San Francisco continued to form alliances between villages and tribal communities.

Early in 1792, for example, a recently baptized Huchiun Indian named Tolomucse married an Indian woman from the village of Urebure named María Soledad.[39] Two years after Tolomucse's death, María Soledad married another man from outside her village—only this time her husband was a Spanish soldier, Ygnacio Higuera.[40] María Soledad was not the only Native Californian to make such a marriage. In 1801 the president of the California mission system wrote of twenty-four marriages between Hispanic men and Indian women of which he was aware, extolling the cross-cultural cooperation and understanding that these marriages promoted.[41] (At the time, only eighteen missions had been established.) In 1814 Abella reported that three California Indian women were married to non-Indian men at Mission San Francisco.[42]

Marriage between the Hispanic colonists and the California Indians resembled other Indian intermarriages in that it catalyzed contact between different groups; but Spanish-Indian marriage was also very different. For Hispanic men like Ygnacio Higuera, marriage to Indian women was a logical response to the scarcity of available Hispanic women in Alta California. According to all accounts, the Hispanic population in Alta California was overwhelmingly male throughout the Spanish colonial period, despite governmental attempts to recruit women as marriage partners for Spanish soldiers.[43] With very few exceptions, those women who did move to California were already married to soldiers or other settlers. Yngacio Higuera's wife traveled with him from Mexico, but when she died, the most obvious place to look for a new partner was among the Indian women at Mission San Francisco. Though in earlier times and places in the Americas Spanish men had deliberately married the daughters of elite indigenous families, Hispanic men in Alta California selected their Indian partners without regard to status or wealth. Instead, physical attractiveness seems to have been their main criterion in choosing a wife. "The Indians of this Misión are indeed generally considered the handsomest in Nueva California," wrote Langsdorff of Mission San José, "and hence the Spanish soldiers, in the absence of Spanish women, often marry the Indian women of this Misión."[44]

For the colonial government and the missionaries, marriages between Hispanic men—especially soldiers—and Indian women were a way to control, or perhaps channel, what governmental officials, missionaries, and Indians all agreed was rampant sexual misbehavior on the soldiers' part. Missionaries and governmental officials hoped that by providing legitimate sexual partners to these soldiers, marriage to Indian women would decrease the frequency of soldiers' violence against Indian women and the Indian men who tried to protect them. The small number of intermarriages during the Spanish colonial period suggests the inadequacy of this remedy: at Mission San Francisco only a handful of soldiers married Indian women, and Alta California as a whole yielded similarly small numbers.[45]

The missions also stood to benefit from intermarriages between Hispanic colonists and Indian women. Both Junípero Serra and Francisco Palóu urged the Spanish government to encourage its soldiers stationed in Alta California, as well as other Spanish men, to marry Indian women. "I . . . beg your Excellency to determine some reward for those soldiers or those who are not soldiers who may marry new Christian daughters of that country [Alta California]," wrote Palóu to the viceroy of New Spain in 1775.

> I am of the opinion that one who marries in this way will remain at the mission of his consort, and will not go moving around to

others. Let him be given for the present a mule to go about on, if he has none, and after one year or somewhat more in the service of the mission in planting the land, let him be given from the herds of the king a couple of cows and a mule, or whatever may seem best to your Excellency. And in time we might assign to them a piece of ground, so that they may plant for themselves, since there is nothing else to give them.[46]

Hispanic husbands of Indian wives were worth much more to the missions than unattached soldiers, because husbands were bound to one location and might be persuaded to work for the mission.

While Hispanic men were looking for sexually desirable, and available, women, and Franciscan missionaries sought to create a stable workforce, women like María Soledad may well have intended their marriages with Spanish soldiers to perform the same function as intermarriages with men from other Bay Area villages and tribal communities. Since Bay Area Indians used marriage as a means of integrating new people into existing kinship networks, marriages like María Soledad's may have represented an attempt to neutralize the threat posed by the Hispanic newcomers by converting them into kinsmen. Fourteen intermarriages took place over the course of the Spanish colonial period at Mission San Francisco involving eleven Indian women baptized at the mission.[47] The mission registers yield no information regarding the families of three of these women. Of the remaining eight, however, at least four were the daughters of polygynous men.[48] The family trees of the four without obvious polygamous parentage contain other hints that these women came from families of some status: Ubiumis's mother married a polygynous man after Ubiumis's birth;[49] the brothers of the other three all married women from other villages or tribal communities.[50] This information strongly suggests that the women who married colonists did so not because they had no other options, but rather because they wanted to augment or perpetuate their families' social and economic status through their marriages.

Marriage was only the first step in weaving Hispanic men into the web of relationships that bound indigenous Californians to one another. Some evidence indicates that Hispanic men who married Indian women were more fully integrated into their wives' societies. The moiety system, which bound communities together by making Indians dependent on and obligated to members of the opposite moiety, was one way in which these groups absorbed "foreign" spouses. The adoption of spouses from outside a tribal community into local moieties was routine among Bay Area Californians. Moiety exogamy, which forced many Indians to look beyond the boundaries of their villages and tribal communities for spouses, necessitated this practice of adoption: foreigners simply joined the moiety to which their spouses did not belong.

Hispanic husbands were treated in the same way. Anthropologist Edward Gifford's work on Central Sierra Miwok moieties has made this moiety system the best understood of the California moiety systems. While it undoubtedly contained some features unique to the Central Sierra Miwok, it may stand generally as a model for the moiety systems in use around the San Francisco Bay. Gifford found that children "of Miwok mothers and white fathers are always considered as belonging to the moiety of which the mother is not a member."[51] By extension, the father (who normally passed his moiety identity to his children) also belonged to the moiety of which his wife was not a member. Hispanic husbands like Ygnacio Higuera were treated in the same way. By making foreign spouses like Higuera members of the moiety opposite that of their local partners, Bay Area Californians produced "proper," moiety-exogamic marriages. They also created bonds between the foreign spouse and the members of her or his adoptive moiety. In addition, Higuera, like other foreign spouses, gained rights and responsibilities in relation to the members of his wife's moiety, though he may not have been aware of them or called upon to perform them.

Intermarriage between Hispanic men and Indian women has long been interpreted as an exploitative relationship, and some marriages undoubtedly were. In this respect, marriages between Hispanic men and Indian women were no different than marriages between Hispanic men and Hispanic women.[52] However, Bay Area Indians routinely used intermarriage as a tool of diplomacy, ending or avoiding intertribal conflict by creating kinship relations between tribal communities. This practice continued in the missions and may have been encouraged, or even manipulated, by the missionaries. Given the continued diplomatic use of intermarriage between Indians at the missions and the evidence indicating that Hispanic men who married Indian women were integrated into tribal kinship networks, we must consider the possibility that Indians saw intermarriage with Hispanic colonists as a means of creating political alliances between societies.

Because they played a crucial role in the Catholic wedding ceremony, the Franciscans at Mission San Francisco exercised a great deal of control over marriage in the mission. The ways the priests exercised their power significantly complicated the creation and maintenance of familial, social, political, and economic alliances between lineages, villages, and tribal communities in the San Francisco Bay Area. Nevertheless, the marriage registers from Mission San Francisco show that Indians continued to create and maintain the networks of relationships that connected people to one another in the Bay Area.

Both the Franciscan priests and the Bay Area Indians saw marriage as a means of creating alliances between groups, and the missionaries may have encouraged Indians at the mission to use marriage as a tool of diplomacy. The diplomatic marriage between Liloté and Letchentis, which helped end the war between the Yelamu and Ssalson Indians in 1781, demonstrates that this process became more complicated once the priests were involved. Because of the restrictions the priests placed on baptized Indians, requiring that they marry other baptized Indians and that they participate in a Catholic wedding ceremony, Letchentis had to accept baptism in order to marry Liloté, and they had to marry each other in the church at Mission San Francisco.

The extant evidence does not reveal whether Liloté and Letchentis exchanged gifts when they married, as was customary among Bay Area Indians. If they did, it would not have been cause for comment among the priests at Mission San Francisco, since Hispanic men and women also commonly performed gift exchange rituals when they married. This commonality between Hispanic and Indian marriage rituals allowed the priests to overlook, or to remain ignorant of, the constitutive nature of gift exchange in traditional Bay Area Indian marriages. This Double Mistaken Identity may also have worked in reverse, enabling baptized Indians to adopt the Catholic wedding ceremony as an additional, but peripheral, marriage ritual while retaining the traditional gift exchange. Whether or not Liloté and Letchentis saw their Catholic vows as peripheral, their marriage was effective in ending the war between the Yelamus and Ssalsons. It thus demonstrates that their decisions to accept baptism did not diminish their influence within their tribal communities and that their participation in the Catholic wedding ceremony did not weaken the bond they created between their tribal communities. Though the priests had complicated the creation and maintenance of alliances between lineages, villages, and tribal communities in the San Francisco Bay Area, they did not make it an impossibility.

5

Ties That Bind

༳ When Liloté and Letchentis married, they created kinship ties that bound their tribal communities together. María Soledad and other Indian women used the same strategy to weave the Hispanic colonists into the kinship networks on the San Francisco peninsula. Marriage was not the only ritual that offered the possibility of creating and extending kinship networks, however. Far more frequent at Mission San Francisco was the creation of spiritual kinship ties through baptism. Webs of spiritual kinship connecting Indians and Hispanic colonists began to form with the very first Indian baptisms at the mission.

"On the twenty-fourth of June, 1777, in the Church of this mission of Our Seraphic Father Saint Francis, the Baptisms of the Gentiles were begun to the greater honor and Glory of God," Father Francisco Palóu wrote, hinting at the celebration that must have accompanied these first baptisms.[1] The solemnity of the occasion certainly helped Chamis, Pilmo, and Taulvo, the three baptismal candidates, experience their baptism as an important, meaningful transition into a new life as Catholics.[2] However, the Mass in which these baptisms were performed was also intended to impress other Indians enough that they would accept baptism as well. Catholic missionaries had long used the spectacle of the Mass and other rituals as a means of attracting recruits. Father Alonso de Molina, a Franciscan missionary to the Pueblo Indians in seventeenth-century New Mexico, wrote that details like incense, fine priestly vestments, candles, and music were necessary to the rituals missionaries performed. These items helped "uplift the souls of the Indians and move them toward the things of God ... because they are by nature lukewarm and forgetful of internal matters and must be helped by means of external displays."[3] Like Molina and his colleagues, Franciscans in California a century later paid careful attention to the details of their rituals and made them as impressive as possible.

The men who stood as godparents on this occasion heightened the pageantry: Lieutenant José Joaquin Moraga, the commander of the San Francisco Presidio and, as such, the most powerful of the Hispanic colonists in the area, stood as godfather to the first two of the three Indians baptized that day, Chamis and Pilmo. Another high-ranking official, Sergeant Juan Pablo Grijalva, sponsored Taulvo. By agreeing to be the godfathers of the three Indian men who accepted baptism that day, Moraga and Grijalva became part of a web of spiritual kinship ties that bound Hispanic colonists and Indians to one another. While marriage created kinship ties that could bind Liloté's and Letchentis's tribal communities together and offered the possibility of weaving Hispanic colonists into the kinship networks of the San Francisco Bay Area, baptism was a far more frequent ritual that offered similar possibilities. In the eighteenth and nineteenth centuries, and still today, godparenting created a relationship between the godparent and the godchild, known as godparenthood, as well as a relationship between the godparent and the godchild's biological parents, known as coparenthood. Lacking an English word that encompasses the entire godparenthood-coparenthood complex, scholars have combined the two Spanish terms, *padrinazgo* (godparenthood) and *compadrazgo* (coparenthood), creating the neologism *compadrinazgo* to refer to the phenomenon as a whole.[4]

On that June day in 1777, Father Francisco Palóu probably performed the entire baptismal ritual for Chamis, Pilmo, and Taulvo, down to the last detail. Theologian Alonso de la Peña Montenegro, whose work was widely read by Franciscans in New Spain, gave detailed instructions for baptism. If Palóu followed these instructions, the ritual was quite long. First, the Indians and their prospective godfathers stood outside the church. "Sons, have you come to make yourselves Christians, and do you firmly intend to do so?" the priest asked. The Indians responded affirmatively. Father

Palóu then questioned Chamis, Pilmo, and Taulvo about their knowledge of the Catholic faith, and after receiving satisfactory answers, he brought the baptismal candidates to the entrance of the church and exorcized them. He then told the Indians, "My sons, you are now free from the power of the devil, and so you may well enter into the church, which is the house of God," and recited a Latin formula inviting them to enter.

Inside the church, Chamis, Pilmo, and Taulvo stripped to the waist and lined up, with Lieutenant Moraga and Sergeant Grijalva, in front of the baptismal font. Here, Father Palóu again asked them if they wanted to be baptized and tested their knowledge of the faith. Once the candidates had answered satisfactorily, Palóu led them through an act of contrition for their past sins.

After invoking the Holy Spirit with a hymn, Palóu baptized Chamis, Pilmo, and Taulvo.[5] He led each man to the font by the hand and, intoning a Latin formula, Palóu made the sign of the cross on each baptismal candidate with water from the font.[6] After the baptism, Father Palóu anointed each newly baptized Indian with holy oil, symbolizing thanksgiving, and chrism, a mixture of consecrated oil and balsam that signified divine grace.[7] He signed their ears and noses with saliva and put salt, which stood for grace, wisdom, and preservation from sin, in the mouths of the three Indians.[8] Finally, he made the sign of the cross on each Indian's chest, symbolically marking them as belonging to the Christian god.

Once the ritual was completed, if Palóu continued to follow Montenegro's advice, he made a great show of affection for the newly baptized Indians. He gave them his stole to kiss as he quoted the gospel, and he invited the most important personages in the fledgling colony to embrace the newly baptized Indians.[9] That Lieutenant José Joaquin Moraga and Sergeant Juan Pablo Grijalva, two of the most important people in the colony, were also the godfathers to these Indians only added to the pageantry of this elaborate ritual. The baptismal names the priest bestowed on the baptismal candidates, Francisco Moraga, José Antonio, and Juan Bernardino, echoed portions of their godfathers' names, acknowledging the relationships that were created between the Indians and their high-ranking godfathers.

Unlike the ritual of baptism to which it is related, godparenthood began sometime after the apostolic period. Perhaps as early as the late second century CE, Christian communities began to require that adult converts have Christian sponsors who would vouch for both their sincerity and their comprehension of the religion. Around the same time, Christians in some areas also began baptizing infants regularly. While infants did not need anyone to attest to their sincerity, they did require an adult to speak and act on their behalf in the baptismal liturgy. In the first few centuries of Christianity, this sponsor was usually the child's parent. However, by the end of the fifth century, when infant baptism had become the norm throughout the Christian world, evidence indicates that many children were sponsored by adults other than their parents.[10] The practice of inviting nonparents to sponsor children gradually gained acceptance and in the eighth century the church officially forbade parents to sponsor their own children.

The idea that sponsors were spiritual parents of the children for whom they stood emerged in the fifth or sixth century.[11] In addition to speaking for the child during the baptismal liturgy, the sponsor received the godchild from the baptismal font, literally taking the child in her or his arms. Christians came to understand this act as constitutive of the spiritual relationship between sponsor and child so that even if it was performed unwittingly, a bond of spiritual kinship resulted. Godparents' obligations varied greatly once the baptismal ritual was completed, but by the late medieval period, godparents in Western Europe were generally given the responsibility of overseeing their godchildren's religious education. They might also be called upon to raise their godchildren, especially if the children were orphaned.

Godparenthood also created a special bond between the godparent and the godchild's biological parents, a tie of coparenthood that Catholics saw as "more sacred than ordinary kinship."[12] This spiritual kinship relationship found its Catholic doctrinal expression in prohibitions on sexual contact between coparents. As a social relationship, coparenthood gave godparents the right to turn to their coparents for assistance in social and economic matters unrelated to the godchild and the obligation to provide their coparents with the same sort of assistance.[13]

Viewed generationally, compadrinazgo creates both horizontal ties (of coparenthood) and vertical ties (of godparenthood). Compadrinazgo may also create either horizontal or vertical bonds in the arena of social class. In the first case, parents select their child's godparents from among their social peers, extending their social network horizontally. This strategy strengthens solidarity among members of a single social class. In the second case, parents select their child's godparents from among those who enjoy higher, or sometimes lower, social status. This strategy often functions as a means of integrating social classes.[14] At Mission San Francisco, this strategy created links between the Bay Area Indians and the newly arrived colonists, starting with the bonds of padrinazgo that tied Lieutenant Moraga and Sergeant Grijalva to their godsons.

In addition, the bonds of compadrinazgo may either intensify or extend kinship relationships. In the former instance, parents select their child's godparents from among their existing kin. For example, they might ask the father's sister to be the godmother. Thus, the sibling relationship between the child's father and paternal aunt is compounded by the new coparental relationship. The child's mother's relationship with her sister-in-law is also intensified, since they become comothers. When soldier Nicolas Berreyesa's daughter María de la Luz Ynes was baptized at Mission San Francisco, for example, he and his wife, Gertrudis Peralta, asked their siblings to sponsor the girl. Nicolas's sister Ysabel and Gertrudis's brother Pedro Regalado became the infant's godmother and godfather, intensifying their existing relationships with the child's biological parents.[15]

When compadrinazgo is used to extend kinship relationships, on the other hand, parents select their child's godparents from among nonkin. In this case, friendships or patronage relationships may be formalized by making the child's parents spiritual kin of the child's godparents. In 1779 María Gertrudis Rivas gave birth to a daughter, Francisca Saturnina, who was baptized at Mission San Francisco. María Gertrudis and her husband, Ygnacio Linares, turned to Ygnacio's commanding officer, Sergeant Juan Pablo Grijalva, and his wife, María Dolores Valencia, to be the girl's godparents.[16] Ygnacio and María Gertrudis may have seen this as a politically astute selection: presumably Grijalva would think twice before disciplining his cofather too harshly, and he might be able to secure favors for the family of his goddaughter. Whether Chamis, Pilmo, and Taulvo thought about their godfathers, Lieutenant Moraga and Sergeant Grijalva, in these terms is impossible to say, but they may have seen the creation of these relationships as a way of weaving the Hispanic colonists into local kinship networks.

༄

While many godparents at Mission San Francisco, like Moraga and Grijalva, came from among the Hispanic colonists, a significant minority of the godparents at Indians' baptisms—more than 41 percent—were other baptized Indians. Many Indian godparents sponsored only a few Indian baptismal candidates, suggesting that they stood as godparents by special request. Some of these godparents had biological or affinal kinship relationships with their godchildren. Likewise, in the cases of some Indian godparents who sponsored large numbers of Indian candidates from a single village or tribal community, there is evidence of a longstanding relationship between the godparent and the group represented by the godchildren. In these instances, the baptismal candidates themselves likely played the most prominent role in selecting their godparents. Nevertheless, though the priests may not have played a decisive role in selecting godparents in these baptisms, they at least agreed with, and often may have encouraged, these decisions.

In their godparental selections, Indians at Mission San Francisco used compadrinazgo ties to create and reinforce networks of social, political, and economic relationships as well as to strengthen bonds of kinship. Three basic strategies are evident: first, many Indians' selections suggest that the compadrinazgo bond created or reinforced an advantageous personal alliance. Second, groups of Indians from the same village or tribal community often shared one godparent or a few godparents. By sticking together, such groups could establish a corporate allegiance between the two villages or tribal communities represented by the godparents and godchildren. Third, Indians at Mission San Francisco often asked family members to stand as godparents. By doing so, they were able to use compadrinazgo to strengthen their family ties.

The high status of certain members of the mission community contributed to their desirability as godparents. Diego Olvera, for example, worked as a servant at Mission San Francisco from its founding in 1776 until his death in 1815. An Indian from Cadereyta, in Mexico's Sierra Gorda, Olvera occupied the bottom of the status hierarchy among the Hispanic colonists of San Francisco.[17] Olvera's access to mission resources, however, and his affiliation with the colonists likely raised his status in the eyes of Indian catechumens. Olvera's first wife at Mission San Francisco was Ubiumis, a Yelamu woman whose marriage outside her tribal community may indicate that she occupied an important position in Bay Area social and political networks.[18] Olvera stood as godfather to 463 Indians, more than any other person at Mission San Francisco. Ubiumis sponsored in excess of 300 baptismal candidates, sometimes alone and sometimes with her husband.

Interpreters, who controlled the flow of information between the Hispanic colonists and the Indians, also proved to be popular godfathers. The two interpreters who can be identified in the mission records, Jacinto and Jobocholá, godfathered 164 and 86 Indians, respectively.[19] In contrast, the average Indian godparent at Mission San Francisco had ten or eleven godchildren. Indians at Mission San Francisco may have chosen Diego Olvera, Ubiumis, Jacinto, Jobocholá, or another person who occupied a similar position in the mission community as a godparent in order to ensure access to mission goods or to gain influence within the mission power structure.

Other high-status individuals were not as popular as godparents. Indians who entered the missions did not relinquish their positions in the social and political networks that connected Bay Area Indians to one another. However, despite their status as the most powerful individuals in those networks, village headmen never acted as godfathers at Mission San Francisco. There are at least three possible explanations for the absence of village headmen from among the ranks of godfathers. First, the headmen may have returned to their villages after their baptisms, making themselves unavailable to stand as godfathers. Unfortunately, it is impossible to determine from the extant sources whether this was the case.

Second, it may have been customary for a headman to be among the last of his village to accept baptism, rendering him ineligible to godfather members of his own village. Determining the exact membership of any Bay Area village in order to test this hypothesis is impossible. However, the Ssalson village headman Keqecég was the last member of his patrilineage to accept baptism. This pattern held true for most of the other village headmen who were baptized at Mission San Francisco. Though headmen from other villages might have been available, selecting them as godfathers might very well have created political problems. When Jotes, the son of Lamchin headman Sapache, accepted baptism in 1789, several headmen had been baptized and might have seemed attractive as godfathers because of their high status.[20] However, taking any of these men, all of whom led different villages and tribal communities, as godfather might have meant dividing the loyalty Jotes owed to his father and his patrilineage. Jotes appears to have been Sapache's eldest son, and therefore he might very well have been in line to inherit the headmanship of his village.[21] To place himself in what may have seemed like a submissive relationship to another headman, then, might have been political suicide.

A third explanation for why headmen never acted as godfathers is that the priests may have prevented the headmen from being godparents in a deliberate attempt to weaken headmen's authority. Other ways in which the priests apparently tried to diminish village headmen's influence suggest that this may have been the case. As I discussed in chapter 2, Franciscan priests at Mission San Francisco may have tried to exclude village headmen from the mission's political hierarchy by not selecting them as alcaldes. Likewise, although all of the identified village headmen baptized at Mission San Francisco had colonists as godfathers, none of those colonists enjoyed significant social or political influence in the local Hispanic community. The headmen were thus unable to form advantageous alliances with high-status colonists in their own baptisms. The Franciscans also may have deliberately weakened headmen's leadership by preventing village headmen from godfathering other Indians.

Alcaldes at Mission San Francisco acted as godfathers only slightly more frequently than village headmen. Of the five alcaldes identifiable from the Mission San Francisco registers and other documents, only three ever acted as godfathers at Mission San Francisco. Two of these men godfathered well under the average for Indian godparents: the first, Tacsinte, had only one goddaughter, Oyumain.[22] He probably stood as Oyumain's godfather because he happened to be available: she was baptized *in periculo mortis* (in imminent danger of death, a condition that exempted the baptismal candidate from catechetical requirements) and died the following day.

The second alcalde, Uilmoxsi, had two godchildren, Toróz and Lolue'pig.[23] In contrast to Oyumain, who probably had little control over who sponsored her, Toróz probably chose Uilmoxsi as his godfather. Perhaps Toróz selected Uilmoxsi because of the alcalde's status within the mission, or perhaps the selection reflected a preexisting relationship of kinship, friendship, or patronage between the two men. Six months after Toróz's baptism, his wife Lolue'pig also took Uilmoxsi as her godfather. Lolue'pig's choice was almost certainly a matter of following her husband's earlier decision. Toróz and Lolue'pig renewed their marriage the day after Lolue'pig's baptism, with Uilmoxsi as a witness. Toróz and Lolue'pig's consistency in turning to Uilmoxsi, first as a godfather and then as a witness of their marriage, clearly indicates their desire to cement an alliance with the alcalde.

The third alcalde, Huetlícs, sponsored forty-three people in baptism at Mission San Francisco.[24] The reasons for Huetlícs's popularity as a godfather probably had little to do with his position as alcalde. His first thirty godchildren, more than two-thirds of his total godchildren, were baptized about a decade before he appears in mission records as an alcalde. Huetlícs's family background and his position in Bay Area social networks may offer some clue to his frequent selection as a godfather. He was the son of Liquiique, an important man from the independent village of Pruristac, and Huitpote, Liquiique's senior wife.[25] Huitpote was an important Yelamu woman herself and had been married previously. By her previous husband, Huitpote had two children, Chamis (the first Indian to be baptized at Mission San Francisco) and Liloté (the first female Indian to be baptized at Mission San Francisco).[26] In 1784 Huetlícs married Quéyeme, the daughter of an influential Yelamu man.[27] Thus, Huetlícs had important connections in the social and political networks that covered the Bay Area, and he occupied an important position in those networks. This social capital probably made him a very attractive godfather, just as it would later make him a logical candidate to be one of the mission's alcaldes.

While selecting godparents often seems to have created or reinforced a personal alliance between the godparent and the godchild, or between the godparent and the biological parents, in other cases selecting godparents appears to have conformed to a logic of corporate relations in which the godparents and godchildren represented their villages or tribal communities. In this way, compadrinazgo may have worked like intermarriage to create alliances between villages and tribal communities. For large numbers of Indians from the same tribal community to be baptized on the same day was not unusual at Mission San Francisco. The presence of these large, homogeneous baptismal groups in the mission registers indicates that entire villages or tribal communities decided to join the mission system together. Often, one person or a small group of people stood as godparents for the entire group of baptismal candidates.

The limited number of godparents was easier for the officiating priest to manage, but these godparents were not always chosen purely for convenience. In March 1786, for example, sixteen Ssalson adults accepted baptism, joining their children who had been baptized the previous month.[28] Mission servant Diego Olvera and his Yelamu wife Ubiumis stood as godparents to the group. As I discussed earlier, Olvera and Ubiumis may have been desirable godparents because of their status within the mission. However, the ties of compadrinazgo formed at these Ssalson baptisms also reinforced the political alliance created in 1781, when Yelamu and Ssalson men and

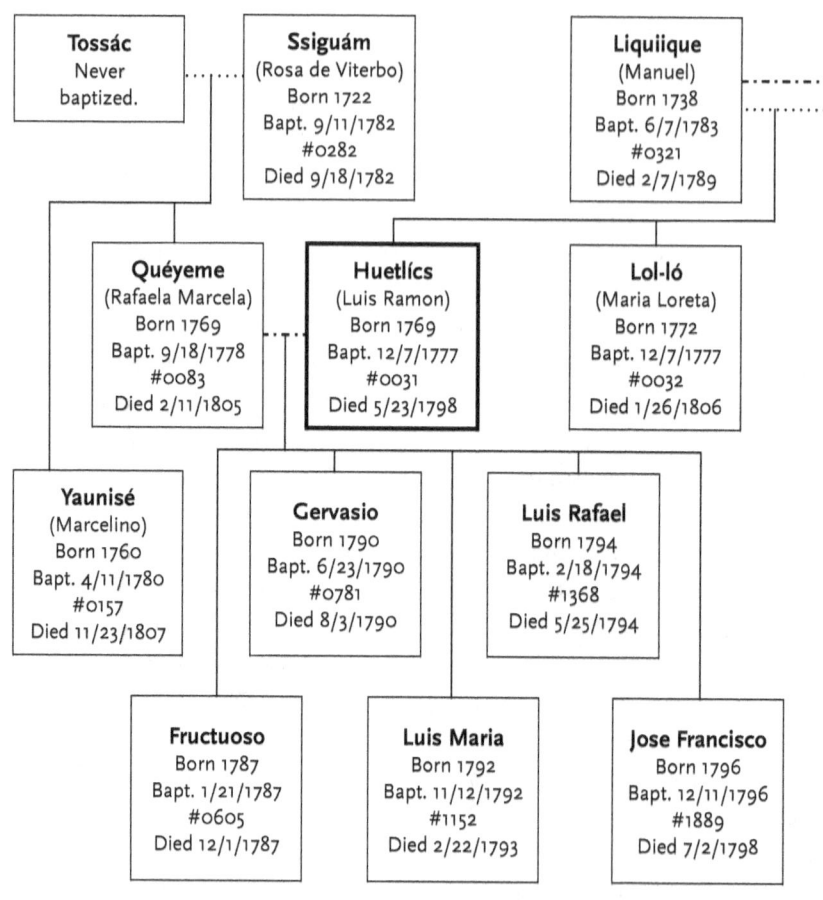

FIGURE 3. Huetlícs's family. The son of important parents, Huetlícs probably owed his popularity as a godfather to his familial connections rather than to his position as an alcalde at Mission San Francisco.

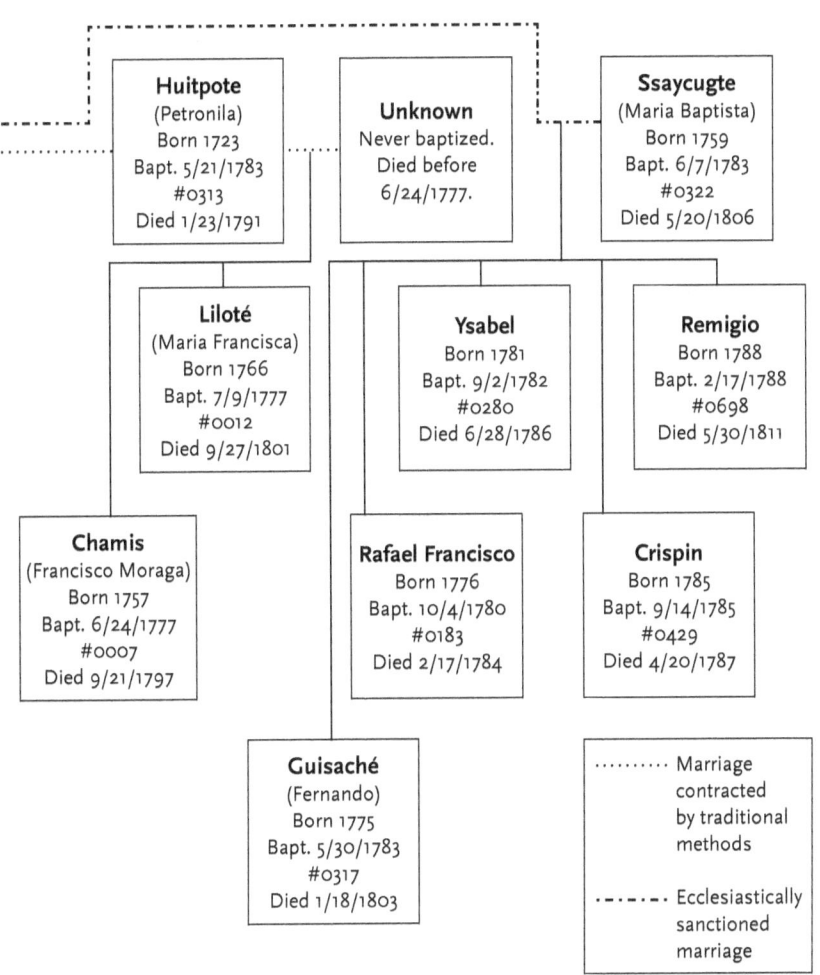

Ties That Bind

women formed several intermarriages in order to end a war between their two tribal communities. By taking an important Yelamu woman and her husband as their godparents, these Ssalson Indians strengthened the bonds between the two tribal communities that Liloté and Letchentis's marriage, along with other intermarriages, had created some five years earlier. By accepting baptism as a group, these Ssalson Indians also reinforced social bonds between village members, emphasizing the solidarity of the village group as its members joined the diverse mission society. Sharing the same godparents may have increased this sense of group unity even as it committed the Ssalsons to continued peaceful relations with members of other tribal communities in the mission.

Bay Area Indians continued to use compadrinazgo to create or express corporate allegiances throughout the Spanish colonial period. On 19 June 1821 missionaries at San Francisco baptized 165 Indians, probably all from the same tribal community. The missionaries recorded their tribal identity as "Canicaymo," a term that actually encompassed several Wappo-speaking tribal communities. Most of the Indians identified in the Mission San Francisco register were members of the Caymu tribal community.[29] Of those baptized Indians, 130 had a Huchiun man named Tolecsse as godfather.[30] No apparent previous links exist between Tolecsse and the Canicaymos or any other Wappo speakers. Nevertheless, the selection was clearly deliberate. About a month after their baptisms, 126 of Tolecsse's 130 Canicaymo godchildren renewed their marriages, with Tolecsse as one of their two official witnesses.

Tolecsse's participation in the baptisms and subsequent marriages of these Canicaymo Indians might be taken as a simple indication that he was in or near the San Francisco Mission church regularly. However, other facts argue against his being a "convenient" godfather: Tolecsse sponsored only six other Indians throughout the Spanish colonial period, and he was not named as a witness to a marriage for nearly three months before the Canicaymo marriages. Tolecsse's presence at the baptisms and marriages of these Canicaymo people, then, was not coincidental; it was a deliberate choice on his part and on the part of his godchildren. Later events indicate that Tolecsse and the Canicaymos continued to seek ways to strengthen their alliance: Saqueninispi, a Canicaymo woman, married Tolecsse two years later.[31]

As a linguistic minority within the San Francisco mission, the Canicaymos may have decided to use their baptisms as a way of allying themselves with one of the dominant linguistic groups in the mission through Tolecsse.[32] Tolecsse was a Huchiun Indian, and therefore a Costanoan speaker. He also seems to have held a position of some social importance, as the widower of a Huchiun headman's daughter.[33] The combination of Tolecsse's social and political standing in the mission and the Canicaymos' need for some security in this new situation, then, may have led the Canicaymos to choose Tolecsse as their collective godfather.

In numerous instances, Indians stood as godparents to their own relatives—nephews, nieces, cousins, and grandchildren. This strategy was a familiar one to the Franciscan missionaries, because it was common among Western European and Hispanic Catholics as well. In fact, the priests may have encouraged Indians to choose family members as godparents in order to strengthen the Catholic system of reckoning kinship bilaterally. However, the Bay Area Indians probably needed little encouragement. Many families in Mission San Francisco used godparenthood to reinforce kinship ties that might otherwise have withered. By asking relatives to stand as godparents to their children, Indian parents also ensured that in the likely event of their own premature deaths, their children would be cared for by kin. This family-centered strategy of godparent selection was undoubtedly more common at the mission than we can now know, because the priests failed to record many familial relationships in the baptismal registers, and so the affinal or biological relationships between godparents and godchildren are now lost. However, where family trees can be reconstructed, or where the priests recorded godparents' relationships to their godchildren, this strategy is often apparent.

For example, Guonis and her husband Alajuta had three children, all of whom had aunts for godmothers.[34] The first, Macario, became the godson of Guonis's sister Malany'eum.[35] By asking Malany'eum to be Macario's godmother, Guonis and Alajuta reproduced some of the kinship ties that the prohibition of polygyny in the mission had made more difficult. Through godparenthood, Malany'eum became a second mother for Macario, just as she would have been had she and Guonis both married Alajuta. Even as it circumvented the Catholic prohibition on polygyny and provided Macario with a second mother, godparenthood also reinforced the Catholic bilateral kinship system by strengthening Macario's ties to his mother's family.

Otchacaminimac, Alajuta's sister, stood as godmother for the couple's second and third children.[36] All three of Guonis and Alajuta's children died

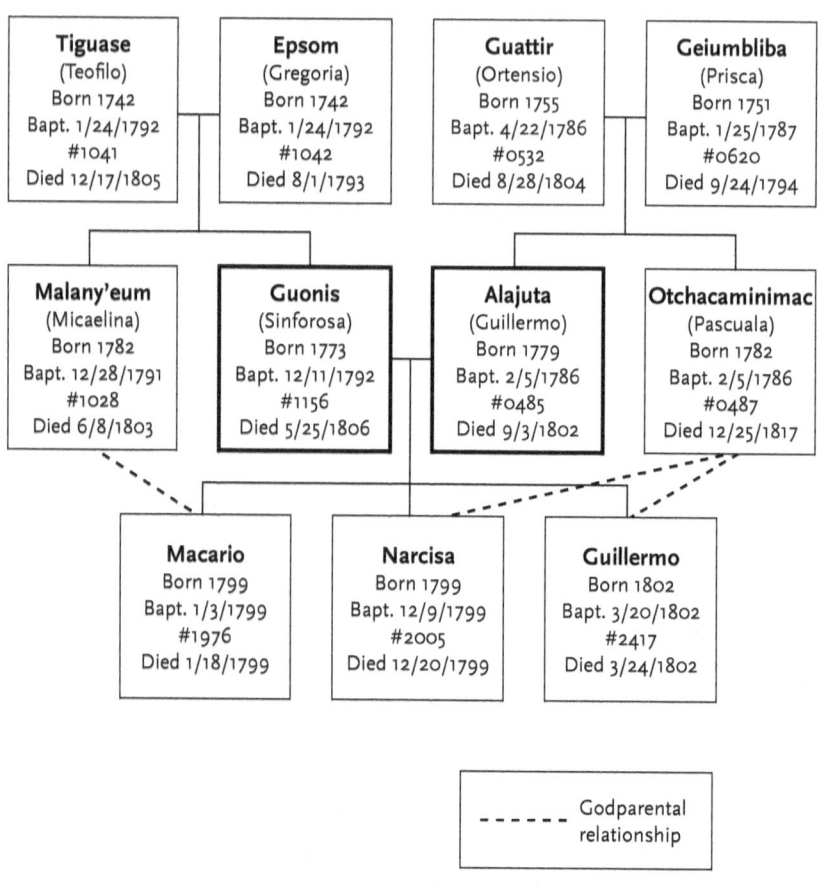

FIGURE 4. Guonis's and Alajuta's family, showing compadrinazgo relationships. Guonis and Alajuta used godparenting to strengthen relationships between their siblings and their children. In some situations, this strategy could be used to mimic the relationships that the prohibition of polygyny had made impossible.

shortly after baptism, ending Malany'eum's and Otchacaminimac's stints as godmothers. Nevertheless, though these godparental relationships did not last, their repetition indicates a strong push for family solidarity. By asking Malany'eum and Otchacaminimac to act as godmothers to their children, Guonis and Alajuta reinforced kinship bonds between their siblings and their children and ensured that in the case of their own deaths, their children would be cared for by their relatives.

With soaring death rates in the San Francisco Bay Area threatening to wipe out families, lineages, and even entire villages, compadrinazgo provided Bay Area Indians with a way of strengthening and consolidating kinship ties. The family of Uichase and his wife Ygnacia Barbara shows how Bay Area Indians used compadrinazgo to intensify kinship relationships.[37] Uichase was the son of a Lamchin village headman; Ygnacia Barbara's father Puyeles was a polygynous man from the independent village of Urebure, suggesting that he enjoyed a high social status. Uichase and Ygnacia Barbara married in March 1795. They had seven children over the course of the next ten years. Uichase's sister, Ugité, stood as the godmother for their second daughter (their fourth child), Micaela.[38] This relationship strengthened Ugité's ties to her own influential patrilineage. Even when she married and left her father's lineage to join that of her husband, Ugité would remain a coparent to Uichase and Ygnacia Barbara and a godmother to Micaela. In this way, she might retain a stronger connection to her natal patrilineage.

Ygnacia Barbara's brother, Chi-uéc, also godfathered two of the couple's sons. He stood as godfather first for Uichase and Ygnacia Barbara's second son (their third child), Santiago, who lived less than one month and died in October 1800.[39] When they had a third son (their fifth child), in 1803, Uichase and Ygnacia Barbara again chose Chi-uéc to be the godfather. This child lived only slightly longer than Chi-uéc's previous godson. Nevertheless, the repeated selection of Chi-uéc as godfather demonstrates that Uichase and Ygnacia Barbara strongly desired an intensification of their existing kinship relationship. By asking Chi-uéc to godfather their sons, Uichase and Ygnacia Barbara gave those children a stronger connection to Chi-uéc's patrilineage, the lineage to which Ygnacia Barbara had belonged until her marriage to Uichase. As a male, Chi-uéc would remain in the lineage even after his marriage. Thus, Uichase's sons— members of Uichase's patrilineage—also gained some claim to membership in Chi-uéc's lineage by becoming his godsons. In addition, by asking Chi-uéc to be her sons' godfather and her coparent, Ygnacia Barbara, like

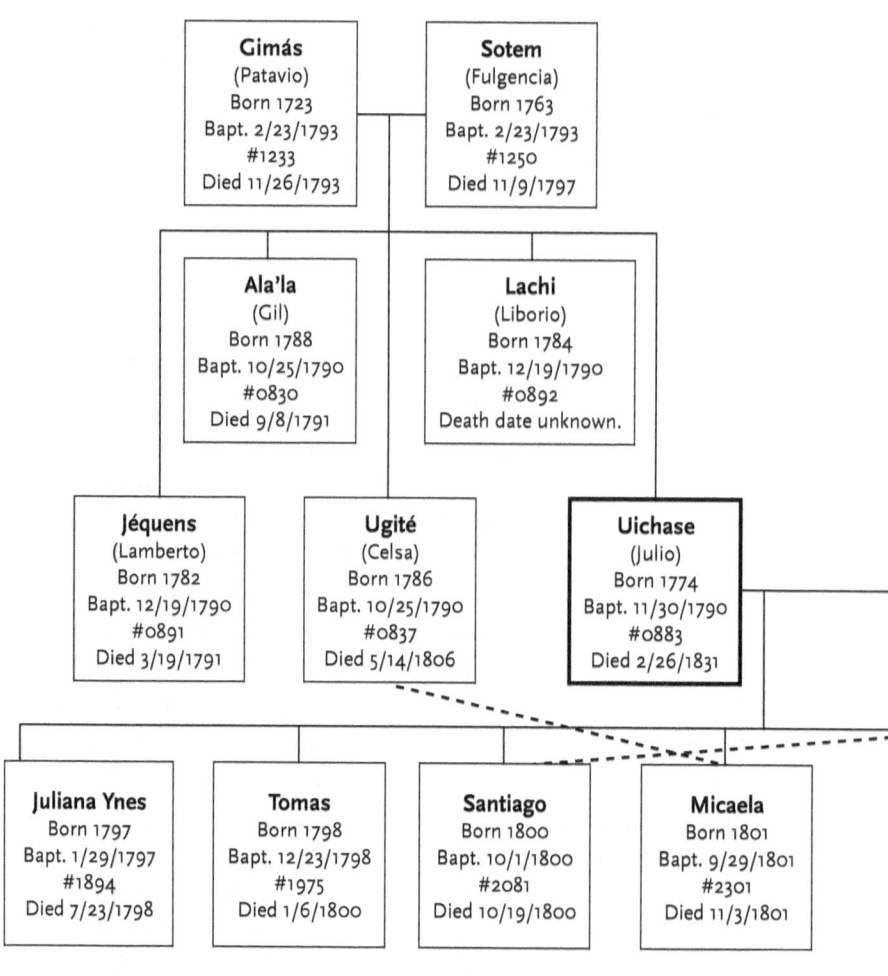

FIGURE 5. Uichase's and Ygnacia Barbara's family, showing compadrinazgo relationships. Uichase and Ygnacia Barbara appear to have selected godparents for their children with an eye to intensifying their existing kinship relationships.

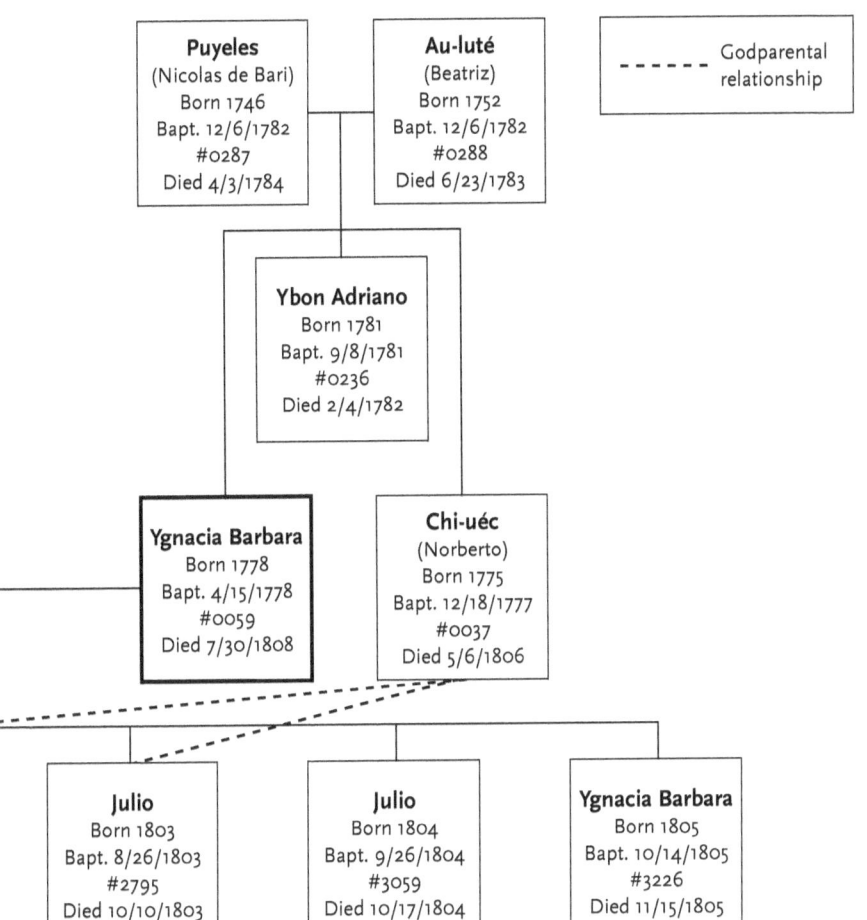

Ties That Bind

her comother Ugité, may also have regained some measure of membership in her father's lineage, giving her and her family additional resources on which to draw in times of need.

Aunts and uncles were not the only family members to act as godparents; Indian parents at Mission San Francisco also called on members of older and younger generations to stand as godparents to their children. Pascual and María del Carmen, for example, had only one child, Valentín.[40] Though María del Carmen had a brother who could have godfathered the child, the couple named their son after María's father and asked the older Valentín to be the child's godfather.[41] This tactic, though uncommon at Mission San Francisco, may have been an effective way to graft the boy onto his mother's patrilineage, to which he would have had no claim under the traditional system of kinship reckoning.

Compadrinazgo could also be an effective means of uniting children of multiple marriages and creating bonds among them that endured beyond their parents' deaths. For example, when Polehova and his second wife Masuete had a son in 1815, they asked Polehova's eldest living son from his previous marriage, Pispistole, to be the boy's godfather.[42] In this way the couple ensured that even if Polehova died, their new son, Manuel Encarnación, would remain a member of his father's patrilineage rather than reverting to his mother's patrilineage or, if she remarried, following her into the family of her new husband. This move benefitted Manuel Encarnación, but it also benefitted the patrilineage by ensuring that Polehova's death would not result in the loss of multiple members.

Half siblings, full siblings, and cousins made repeated appearances as godparents throughout the Spanish colonial period. Godparenting allowed these relatives to step into caretaking roles normally filled by members of older generations. When Oljon village headman Ysúu and his third wife, Etmén, had their first child, the boy's godmother was Teopista Josefa, a daughter from Ysúu's first marriage.[43] By standing as a godmother to her father's son, Teopista Josefa committed herself to acting as the child's second mother. Had Teopista Josefa's own mother still been alive, this role would have fallen to her. As the boy's godmother, then, Teopista Josefa filled some of the functions that a co-wife would have performed outside the mission. Compadrinazgo provided a way for members of younger generations, like Teopista Josefa, to fill multiple roles—sibling, half sibling, or cousin as well as godparent—in a formal manner recognized by both the priests and the baptized Indians.

Many Indians at Mission San Francisco used multiple strategies in selecting godparents. Tabasuse and Guecmaie, for example, were part of a large group of Saclan Indians baptized in January 1795.[44] When their first child, Baltasara, was born in 1801, Diego Olvera and his wife, Ubiumis, stood as godparents.[45] Tabasuse and Guecmaie thus became coparents with the mission servant and his influential Yelamu wife. When their second child was born, Tabasuse and Guecmaie turned to Toyleme, the girl's aunt.[46] By godmothering her niece, Toyleme intensified her existing relationships with Tabasuse and Guecmaie. The couple's third child, Manuel, was baptized during Holy Week, the seven days leading up to Easter.[47] As befitted the importance of the time, he was sponsored by Paula Arguello, a member of the most influential Hispanic family on the San Francisco peninsula. Although she was a woman, Paula Arguello was a high-status colonist, and her participation in Manuel's baptism heightened the pageantry of the occasion. Tabasuse and Guecmaie turned to Teute, another Saclan Indian, to godmother their next two children.[48] In addition to strengthening their ties to their tribal community by selecting a Saclan woman, Tabasuse and Guecmaie may also have gained some influence through Teute: she was married to Antonio de Padua Morante, the son of Raymundo Morante, a mission servant.[49] As they had more children, Tabasuse and Guecmaie continued to turn to relatives and influential nonkin as godparents.

In some cases parents combined strategies in the same baptism. For example, Monózse, one of the mission alcaldes, and his wife, Arpin, had three children.[50] When Juan, the first child, was born in 1786, they asked his aunt Puruem and her husband Raymundo Morante to be his godparents.[51] Puruem was probably Arpin's sister: she is identified in the baptismal register as the aunt of Monózse and Arpin's children, but there is no indication whether she is a maternal or paternal aunt. Monózse's siblings are enumerated elsewhere, however, and Puruem is not listed, suggesting she was related to Arpin. In the event of Arpin's death, Puruem would be able to step in as a second mother to her godchildren, mimicking the kinship relationships that resulted from sororal polygyny. By godmothering her sister's children, she also intensified the kinship bonds that linked her with Arpin and Monózse. Puruem's husband Raymundo Morante was an Indian from Baja California and a servant of the mission. By selecting him as Juan's godfather, Monózse and Arpin created a personal alliance that might prove advantageous: Morante might be able to provide them with increased access to the mission's resources. Juan died in April 1787, shortly before he reached four months old, and when Monózse and Arpin's next child was born a year later, they again turned to Puruem and Raymundo to act as godparents. That child died in May 1788. Monózse and Arpin renewed their compadrazgo relationship with Raymundo and Puruem once more, however, with the baptism of their third child in 1791.

While a great deal of information about relationships between Indians at Mission San Francisco can no longer be recovered, the compadrinazgo relationships recorded in baptismal records reveal that Indians selected godparents in order to create or reinforce personal alliances, corporate allegiances, and family ties. These spiritual kinships presumed lasting compadrinazgo relationships and reinforced and extended the familial, social, political, and economic networks that connected people in the San Francisco Bay Area.

The entries in Mission San Francisco's baptismal register record the missionaries' mindfulness of the spiritual kinship relationship that godparenting created. After recording the names and social positions of godparents in the register, the priests consistently wrote that the godparents had been "notified of the relationship and the obligation contracted."[52] The obligation of which the priests wrote, however, was probably quite minimal. The Franciscan missionaries had committed themselves to providing religious instruction to every baptized Indian, so godparents were not required to do so. The mission also provided for orphaned Indians, relieving godparents of any responsibility in the event of their coparents' deaths.

Perhaps because the obligations they incurred were so minimal, Hispanic colonists and other newcomers to the San Francisco Bay Area frequently stood as godparents for Indians who accepted baptism at Mission San Francisco. Except for the handful of Hispanic men who married Indian women, the newcomers had no kinship ties to Bay Area Indians. In most cases, the only possible relationship that could have preceded a compadrinazgo relationship between Hispanic colonists and Bay Area Indians was a labor relationship. While it is possible that colonists godparented their Indian employees and those employees' children, it is unlikely. In most labor relationships involving Indians baptized at Mission San Francisco, the priests acted as intermediaries between the employer and employees. Indian laborers were interchangeable in this system: they show up in account books of the time not as named individuals but as anonymous workers. Employers do not appear to have requested Indian workers by name, as they would have if they had formed lasting relationships with their employees. Likewise, labor relations between unbaptized Indians and colonists were most often negotiated by a village headman or tribal community chief, reducing the likelihood that individual Indians would form relationships with colonists who might then act as their godparents. Instead, Hispanic colonists probably knew the Franciscan priests best, and these priests likely were the ones who, in most cases, asked Hispanic colonists to stand as godparents for Indian baptismal candidates. Priests seem to have selected these godparents based on two very different considerations: they chose some godparents to heighten the pageantry of the baptism. Selecting Lieutenant José Joaquín Moraga and Sergeant Juan Pablo Grijalva as godfathers for the first three Indians baptized at Mission San Francisco is an example of this strategy. Other colonists seem to have been selected as godparents primarily because they were convenient.

Some people at Mission San Francisco seem to have served as "default" godparents, standing for baptismal candidates when nobody else was available. These people stood as godparents frequently, often to large groups of baptismal candidates with whom they had no apparent affiliation. While these groups were sometimes composed of people from a single tribal community or village, they more often included people from many villages and tribal communities, making it less likely that the baptismal group had deliberately chosen its godparent or godparents for political, economic, or social reasons. In these cases, it seems most probable that the officiating priest pressed the godparent into service because of her or his presence more than anything else. Diego Olvera is the most extreme example of this pattern. The most prolific godparent at Mission San Francisco, Olvera was probably a desirable godfather from the Indians' perspective because of his status in the mission community and his access to mission resources. The frequency with which Olvera stood as godfather to Indian baptismal candidates, however, suggests that his availability was also a decisive factor in his selection as godfather.

Soldiers posted at the mission to protect the missionaries from violent Indian uprisings were also convenient godparents because, like Olvera, these men were more readily available than other Hispanic colonists. The priests may also have believed that by creating compadrinazgo ties between the soldiers and the Indians at the mission, they could encourage positive relations between the two groups and reduce the threat of violence. Like marriage between Spanish soldiers and Indian women, but far more frequent, compadrinazgo relationships between soldiers and Indians might encourage cross-cultural interaction and understanding.

Other instances of Hispanics godparenting Indians involved colonists who were rarely at the mission. In many of these cases, the godparents were colonists who had come to the Mission San Francisco church for the baptism of a Hispanic child. For example, when Juana María Pacheco was baptized in 1795, her godparents, Apolinario Vernal and Apolonia Soberanes, also stood for two Indian children baptized at the same time.[53] After these three baptisms, Vernal stood as godfather twice more at Mission San Francisco, in 1796 and 1806; Soberanes never again stood as a godmother at the mission. In 1807, when his son José Ygnacio was baptized, José Reyes Berreyesa stood as godfather to an Indian baby baptized on the same day.[54] The infant, Bernardo, was the only Indian Berreyesa ever godfathered at Mission San Francisco, though he stood as godfather to a number of Hispanic infants baptized in the mission church over the course of his life on the San Francisco peninsula.[55] The godparenting records of these three colonists strongly suggest that they sponsored these Indian children only because they happened to be in the right place at the right time.

Like colonist godparents, many Bay Area Indian godparents may have been chosen as a matter of convenience. Certainly, if Diego Olvera was a convenient godfather because his position as mission servant meant that he was usually present, his Indian wife Ubiumis made a convenient godmother for the same reason, a factor that partly explains why she godmothered more than three hundred Indians at Mission San Francisco. The mission's interpreters also stood as godfathers far more frequently than most other baptized Native Americans. Jacinto, Jobocholá, and other interpreters whose identities are unknown may have been particularly easy to call upon as godfathers as they stood translating the baptismal ritual for Indians who understood little Spanish.

While interpreters frequently sponsored baptismal candidates, other Indians who appear to have been equally convenient did not. Indians trained as sacristans, acolytes, and other church helpers did not regularly godparent other Indians, though they must have been present at the baptismal rituals quite often. Three sacristans are named in mission records, but none of the three godfathered more than four other Indians at Mission San Francisco. Other church helpers cannot be identified from the mission records. Throughout the baptismal register, no godparent is ever identified as a sacristan, acolyte, or other church helper. Had the priests had frequent recourse to these people as godparents, however, they almost certainly would have noted their positions in the baptismal record at some point. This apparent anomaly may have occurred because acolytes and sacristans were busy performing their own duties during baptisms and could not simultaneously act as godparents. It might also suggest that interpreters enjoyed a higher status than acolytes or sacristans. If this was the case, then the interpreters' frequency of godparenting shows that selecting convenient godparents was still subject to negotiation between the Franciscans and the Indians. While the priests might be most concerned with finding a readily available sponsor, Indians preparing for baptism (or, in the case of children, their parents) might express a preference for a more prestigious godparent, such as an interpreter, over a lower-status one like a sacristan. In fact, although the priests often may have selected godparents for Indian baptismal candidates, the candidates' willingness to follow through with the ritual indicates that they probably agreed with the priests' selections in many cases.

Although both Indians and priests likely had a hand in them, these selection strategies—pageantry and convenience—show little concern for creating lasting compadrinazgo relationships. Though ties of compadrinazgo could have brought the Hispanic colonists and Bay Area Indians together by creating networks of spiritual kinship between the two groups, they do not appear to have done so at Mission San Francisco. On occasion, priests asked high-status colonists to be godparents in order to heighten the pageantry of certain Masses, hoping to create a deeper impression on those who attended the ceremony. However, most of the godparents who seem to have been priests' selections appear to have acted as sponsors not because their status would make the baptismal ritual more impressive, but because their presence made them convenient. As a result, people like mission servant Diego Olvera, his wife Ubiumis, and Indian interpreters Jacinto and Jobocholá were some of the most prolific godparents at Mission San Francisco. In addition to their ubiquitous presence, these individuals occupied relatively high-status positions at the mission, possibly making them attractive godparents to both the priests and the Indians involved.

It is impossible to know, from the sources that survive, what came of the compadrinazgo relationships created in Indian baptisms at Mission San Francisco. It may be that none of these spiritual kinship relationships created any long-term obligations for the godparents. This certainly seems to be the case for godparents who were selected because their status heightened the pageantry of a baptism or because they were convenient. The priests may have hoped that compadrinazgo, like intermarriage, would help weave together the Indian and Hispanic populations in the San Francisco Bay Area, but there is no evidence to suggest that it did so. In fact, some Hispanic sailors stood as godfathers at Mission San Francisco and then sailed away, never to return.[56]

Similarly, Hispanic godparents who lived in the Bay Area do not appear to have maintained any sort of relationship with their Indian godchildren. Though the social and economic functions of compadrinazgo in Latin America today suggest that godparenthood in Alta California could have been instrumental in forming patronage relationships between Hispanic colonists and Bay Area Indians, this does not appear to have been the case. Junípero Serra remarked in a 1774 letter that when the Monterey Presidio was flush with provisions, "from the presidio come big piles of tortillas from the godfathers for the godchildren" at Mission San Carlos, but no such connection is evident between godparents at the San Francisco Presidio and their godchildren at Mission San Francisco.[57] Baptized Indians who lived and worked at the San Francisco Presidio, for example, did so under the supervision of persons other than their godparents.[58] Because the missionaries shouldered the responsibilities of teaching baptized Indians the rudiments of Catholicism and providing for their physical needs, the obligations of godparenthood appear to have been minimal. While godparents with only a few godchildren might have been able to shoulder more responsibility for their godchildren's well-being, such a task would have been impossible for those who frequently stood as godparents at the mission, sponsoring hundreds of Indian baptismal candidates. It is probable, therefore, that those who agreed to sponsor large numbers of baptismal candidates saw compadrinazgo as a short-term obligation entailing little responsibility.

Who selected the godparents who sponsored Indians' baptisms at Mission San Francisco is impossible to tell. In most cases, both priests and Indians probably had some say in the matter. Even in the selection of Hispanic colonists, the godparents most likely to have been chosen by priests, Indians probably agreed to the priests' recommendations. They must have seen some advantage in doing so: perhaps Hispanic godparents, even if they never interacted with their godchildren, became a status symbol in the mission, or perhaps agreeing to a priest's recommendation seemed a good way to establish an amicable relationship with the missionaries. It may be that Indians, like Hispanics in the San Francisco Bay Area, saw compadrinazgo as a relationship entailing minimal obligations. We do not know what Indians expected of their godparents or what Indian godparents saw as their responsibilities. However, the patterns underlying the selection of Indian godparents suggest that spiritual kinship became a way of using the Catholic ritual of baptism to knit together a social fabric that had begun to fray under the stress of Spanish colonization.

The frequent use of kin as godparents at Mission San Francisco suggests not only a desire on the part of Bay Area Indians to intensify kinship relationships but also a need to shore up family ties weakened by widespread death and possibly by disagreements over how best to deal with the invasion of Hispanic colonists in the San Francisco Bay Area. By overlaying their patrilineal kinship system with the Catholic system of spiritual kinship, and by using grandparents, aunts, uncles, and cousins as godparents, Indians were able to create closer kinship relationships, strengthening bonds of loyalty and reinforcing mutual obligations of assistance. Because children so frequently died in the first few years of life, these godparenting relationships required constant renewal, leading some Indians to act as godparents to several of their kin over the space of only a few years.[59]

Compadrinazgo also provided a means of creating kinship relationships with other baptized Indians and of filling in the holes that widespread death left in kinship networks. In addition, like marriage, compadrinazgo provided a method of creating and reinforcing social, political, and economic alliances between families, villages, and tribal communities. Since the use of compadrinazgo for alliance building was common among Hispanic Catholics, the Franciscan priests were probably aware of, and may have encouraged, this strategy at Mission San Francisco.

As Bay Area Indians accepted baptism in increasing numbers, certain strategies for creating alliances were no longer available to them. The Franciscan missionaries attempted to transform Bay Area patrilineal kin groups into Hispanic nuclear families. By imposing Catholic kinship rules, they severely limited customary means of creating alliances through marriage, such as polygyny. Faced with the continuing necessity of creating and maintaining familial, social, political, and economic alliances, baptized Indians may have turned to the Catholic concept of spiritual kinship, using compadrinazgo to create and reinforce alliances with other baptized Indians. Thus, for Bay Area Indians at the mission, baptism became a way of mending the holes that Spanish colonization had ripped in the social fabric of the Bay Area, using the thread of spiritual kinship.

6

The Varieties of Religious Experience at Mission San Francisco

◦∽ Ynocencio's parents were both baptized at Mission San Francisco before he was born in 1811. Ynocencio himself, as his Spanish name implies, was also baptized by a Catholic priest, also at Mission San Francisco.[1] Yet the beginning and ending of Ynocencio's life occurred outside Mission San Francisco. On both occasions, his parents were on paseo. The location of Ynocencio's birth, given in his baptismal record as "the other shore of the port," suggests that his parents were visiting their home village, located across the bay from the mission. They may have taken Ynocencio to the same place to die, when he fell ill shortly after his second birthday.

As Ynocencio's story reveals, baptized Bay Area Indians' responses to the Catholicism the Franciscan missionaries preached were far from uniform. While some Indians appear to have conformed their lives thoroughly to the priests' religion, the actions of others—like Ynocencio's parents— expressed a great deal of ambivalence. Like Ynocencio's parents, many Indians chose to situate important life events, including birth and death, outside the confines of Mission San Francisco. At least 19 percent of the just over six thousand Bay Area Indians listed in Mission San Francisco's book of baptisms during the Spanish colonial period were born outside the mission to previously baptized parents or died outside the mission.[2] Of the more than six hundred Bay Area Indians baptized at Mission San Francisco who died outside the mission by the end of 1821, about one-fifth did so at another Catholic mission—usually San José, San Francisco Solano, or San Rafael—where they had been *empadronados*, or incorporated into the mission population. More than twice that—just over 50 percent—died outside any mission or other colonial institution. While some of these Indians died while on mission errands, many died "in their lands," as the priests frequently wrote in the death records.

Less frequently, but still with some regularity, baptized Indians gave birth to children outside the mission. At least 4 percent of the Bay Area Indians baptized at Mission San Francisco were born to baptized parents who were away from the mission. Many of these parents, like Ynocencio's parents, were on paseo. Others had left the mission without a priest's permission and were designated as *huidos*, or runaways, in the mission registers. Most frequently, however, the priests recorded no explanation for why the births occurred elsewhere. The stories of these births and deaths suggest that Bay Area Indians' responses to Catholicism varied widely. Rather than a space in which Indians found their lives forced into the Catholic mold that the Franciscans promoted, Mission San Francisco was a place in which Indians and priests expressed and accommodated a range of positions regarding the reach and authority of Catholicism in the San Francisco Bay Area.

For Indians baptized at Mission San Francisco, birth and death could often be anticipated: except those that resulted in premature births or spontaneous abortions, pregnancies followed a known timetable. Likewise, disease and old age often provided ample time to prepare for death. Therefore, Indians often had the ability to choose where they wanted to situate both events, and evidence from Mission San Francisco's baptismal and death registers indicates that in many cases, they had the wherewithal to act on those choices. Indians' decisions about where to situate both events, and which rituals to use to mark each occasion, are telling. Those decisions, as they are reflected in the baptismal and death registers from Mission San Francisco, demonstrate a wide range of investment in Catholicism and mission life on the part of Indians baptized there. While the choices of some Indians demonstrate a heavy investment in the religion the priests advocated, the choices other Indians made illustrate a partial, and sometimes a complete, rejection of Catholicism and mission life.

Outside Mission San Francisco, Bay Area Indians observed multiple taboos before and after the birth of a child. When the Yelamu girl Juuim was born in about 1760, for example, her parents both avoided meat and salt during the pregnancy and for some weeks after her birth.[3] To avoid inciting malignant spiritual powers against them or their new baby, Juuim's parents behaved with extreme courtesy toward people and animals. They also refrained from sexual relations, ideally until she stopped nursing at about two years old. Expectant mothers and fathers like Juuim's parents also observed gender-specific taboos: women tried not to use awls, lest the baby be blinded; refrained from scratching themselves; and avoided the sight of owls and shooting stars. Men hunted rarely and avoided the use of tobacco. These taboos ensured that the child would be born healthy and become an upstanding member of society. When Juuim was born, an older female relative—one of her aunts, or perhaps her grandmother—burned the umbilical cord and afterbirth and disposed of the ashes. Her mother, Yssam, took Juuim to the ocean or a nearby stream to wash. Then both mother and child rested for several days on a mattress of herbs built in a pit lined with heated stones. Following this rest, Juuim's ears were pierced. She did not receive her name until eight to ten months later; until that time, the family simply called her "Baby."[4] While the specific taboos and the exact timing of ceremonies varied among tribal communities and linguistic groups, standard practice among Bay Area Indians was to take basic precautions to ensure the health of both child and mother and to ward off malign spiritual powers, and to perform rituals to make children like Juuim part of the local community.

The extant sources are silent on the priests' views regarding these rituals, perhaps because Indians did not perform them at Mission San Francisco. Observing all of the dietary and behavioral restrictions normally imposed on expectant couples and new parents would have been very difficult. Because families were separated in the mission, it may also have been more difficult for older female relatives to attend and assist in the birth. Work requirements and restrictions on women's movements at the mission may have precluded new mothers from completing traditional bathing and resting rituals as well. Alternatively, the priests may not have discussed these rituals in their writings because they were unaware that the Indians continued to perform them covertly. It is unlikely that priests would have noticed a man's failure to go hunting or a woman's refusal to look at the night sky for fear of spotting an owl or a shooting star. Avoiding meat and salt might have been more difficult, given the communal distribution of food at the mission, but it would not necessarily have been impossible.

Nevertheless, Indians at Mission San Francisco may have blamed parents' inability to observe the proper behavioral and dietary taboos or to complete the requisite rituals upon the births of their children for the high infant mortality rate at the mission. Children born at the mission rarely survived past their second birthday.[5] We do not know the life expectancy for children born outside the mission, but it was almost certainly higher. Several factors contributed to the high death rates among both children and adults at the mission. Scholars have noted that disease spread rapidly in the missions in part because the Indians who lived there spent a great deal of time crowded into enclosed, often unsanitary spaces like the women's dormitory.[6] Mission residents' diet was less varied, which may have weakened their immune systems;[7] and, some scholars have argued, mission residents were under greater psychological stress than Indians who lived elsewhere because of the mental effort required to cope with the unfamiliar way of life they had to follow in the mission.[8]

Like birth, death was a highly ritualized event in California Indian societies. Bay Area Indians differed in their burial and mourning ceremonies: some tribal communities preferred to cremate their dead and bury the ashes, while others reserved cremation for high-status individuals and merely buried the bodies of most of their deceased.[9] In both cases, however, disposal of the body was accompanied by loud and prolonged wailing by friends and family members. Mourners destroyed or buried the dead person's belongings, including houses, along with the body so that the ghost of the deceased would have no reason to return. Widows, and sometimes other female kin, cut their hair or singed it off and blackened their faces with pitch and ashes.[10]

In the California missions, Franciscan priests discouraged, and may even have prohibited, these practices. Writing in 1813 and 1814 about the funerary customs of the California Indians at their missions, priests throughout Alta California insisted that, as the Franciscans at Mission Santa Barbara put it, "[a]t the interment [at the mission] there is no ceremonial whatever but we give them all a Christian burial as laid down by the norms of Holy Mother, the Church." However, many also acknowledged that traditional customs continued. The missionaries at San Carlos, near Monterey, admitted, "[N]evertheless, in secret they cling to their pagan practice," and went on to detail many of the customs also observed by

Indians in the San Francisco Bay Area, including mourners cutting their hair and blackening their faces with pitch and ashes. That these practices continued "in secret," or, as the missionaries at San Luis Rey wrote, "when the missionary fathers are not looking," clearly indicates that the priests at least discouraged these practices, if they did not prohibit them altogether.[11] Though Fathers Ramón Abella and Juan Sainz de Lucio did not remark on funerary practices at Mission San Francisco, it is reasonable to believe that they, like their counterparts at other missions, frowned upon the continuation of traditional burial and mourning customs among the baptized Indians.

It is possible that the priests at Mission San Francisco actively discouraged traditional mourning practices among baptized Indians. Two men, Obmusa and Sumipocsé, reported in 1797 that they had left Mission San Francisco because they had been whipped because they were crying for relatives who had died.[12] Since Hispanic colonists saw crying as "a sign of grief and affection for the departed,"[13] and therefore an appropriate response to the deaths of family members, these punishments seem at first glance disproportionate and possibly entirely inexplicable. Archaeologist Richard Ambro, however, suggests that the men's crying was actually the traditional wailing associated with Bay Area mourning.[14] If Ambro is correct, the whippings that Obmusa and Sumipocsé received were part of the priests' larger effort to Hispanicize the Bay Area Indians. Obmusa and Sumipocsé may have left the mission so that they could mourn their dead appropriately, without fear of further punishment.

⁓

While Obmusa, Sumipocsé, and many other Indians may have attempted to carry on the traditional rituals that normally accompanied deaths and births in the San Francisco Bay Area, some Indians clearly invested themselves in Catholicism, or at least in mission life. They demonstrated their devotion in various ways that set them apart from other baptized Indians. That these Indians were able to opt for a higher level of commitment to the priests' religion demonstrates one way in which Bay Area Indians were able to exercise control over their own lives, even after accepting baptism at Mission San Francisco.

The devotion of some Indians was registered in the names by which they were known to the priests. Death records for 30 girls between the approximate ages of nine and nineteen who died at the mission in the years 1806, 1808, 1814, 1815, and 1816 indicate that they were commonly called *monjas*, or nuns.[15] Priests recorded the deaths of 72 other girls and young women in the same age range during those years, but did not describe these others as monjas. Of all 102 girls whose deaths the priests recorded, 24 were married. Four were widows; the remaining 74, including all of the monjas, were single. The monjas and other single and widowed women were prime candidates for housing in the monjerío, the dormitory for single women at the mission, and evidence from another mission indicates that the "monja" category may have been a reference to these girls' residence in that building. At Mission San Carlos, Fermín Francisco de Lasuén wrote in 1801 about "the girls and spinsters (wrongly known as *nuns*) [who] retire at night to an apartment."[16] Twenty years later, Father Vicente Francisco de Sarría noted in a death record at the same mission that the woman whose burial he had just completed had been healthy when she "entered with the rest of the girls into the so-called Nuns' room."[17] These references suggest that people throughout the Alta California mission system referred to the monjerío residents as monjas.

That the Mission San Francisco priests saw fit to record the nickname when registering the deaths of these thirty girls indicates that the other forty-eight girls of the same age and marital status may *not* have lived in the monjerío. If that is the case, then more than 60 percent of the eligible population lived outside the monjerío, away from the priests' supervision. These girls and women may have remained with their extended families and come into the mission every so often to attend Mass, receive religious instruction, and work. The small proportion of girls designated as monjas, combined with the priests' general preoccupation with controlling the behavior of their female charges, suggests that at Mission San Francisco the term *monja* may have had a more specialized meaning, relating perhaps to the behavior of those to whom it was applied.

Even if the monja designation simply denoted residence in the monjerío, it may also have signaled something about the girl's devotion. The family situations of the thirty monjas may have made the monjerío a more attractive option for them than for their single or widowed peers. Single women's status depended in large part on their families and especially, in the patriarchal, patrilocal San Francisco Bay Area, on their fathers. Eighteen of the monjas—60 percent—had lost their fathers by the time of their own deaths. Of the forty-eight unmarried girls not designated monjas, only twenty—about 42 percent—were fatherless by the time of their own deaths.[18] For many of the girls known as monjas, then, the lack of a father may have made the monjerío the most convenient housing available.

Still, fewer than half of the thirty-eight fatherless girls between the ages of nine and nineteen who died in the years 1806, 1808, 1814, 1815, and 1816 were known as monjas; twenty girls in the same circumstances did not receive that designation. If the term *monja* designated monjerío residents, the difference between the monjas and their non-monja peers emphasizes the choices individuals made about monjerío residence. Many of the monjas could have left the mission altogether or called on living kin—brothers, sisters, cousins, or stepparents—for assistance. The choice to stay at the monjerío may have resulted from the vagaries of individual circumstances: disagreements between a young woman and her living relatives, inability or lack of desire to make the journey back to a home village, or other factors could have prevented young women from making use of family resources. For many of the monjas, the monjerío may have been the only viable option. Nevertheless, by living in the monjerío and not scandalizing the priests through rebellious behavior, these young women also earned their monja status. To a greater degree than their peers, perhaps, they demonstrated their commitment—or acquiescence—to the belief system that the missionaries taught, or at least to the behavioral code the Franciscans advocated.

Other Indians at Mission San Francisco expressed similar commitments in different ways. The death records indicate that during the Spanish colonial period, three Indians were buried at Mission San Francisco wearing the *santo hábito*, or holy habit—the apparel normally worn by the Franciscan missionaries themselves.[19] This honor may have indicated that during their lives, these three Indians were Third Order Secular Franciscans, lay people who committed themselves to following the example of Saint Francis of Assisi in their everyday lives. Unlike other orders of Franciscans, Third Order Secular Franciscans may be married or single, male or female. They are distinguished from other orders of Franciscans in that they neither live in religious communities nor take the religious vows of poverty, chastity, and obedience. Becoming a Third Order Secular Franciscan does, however, represent a commitment to heightened religious observance and carries with it such rewards as burial in the Franciscan habit at death.[20] Fragmentary evidence suggests the presence of the Third Order Secular Franciscans in the Alta California mission system: the reredos in the Mission San Miguel Arcángel church, for example, included the seal of the Third Order Secular Franciscans.[21]

All three of the Indians buried in the Franciscan habit at Mission San Francisco died in 1814, suggesting that if it existed, the institution of the Third Order Secular Franciscans was a short-lived experiment there. Three times as many people—five California Indians and four Hispanic colonists—were buried in the habit at Mission San Buenaventura between 1819 and 1822. The more extensive information in these death records suggests that priests buried people in the habit as a way of recognizing the exemplary piety of the deceased. In the death record of María Ysabel, for example, Father José Señán wrote that "for many years she occupied herself indefatigably, and with admirable surrender, not only in cutting and sewing, with her companions, the clothing of the neophytes, but also in caring for the white and colored clothing of the Church, cutting and working on all sorts of ornaments with considerable skill for a poor neophyte woman." María Ysabel's spiritual devotion complemented her work for the mission and its church. "In the last days of her life," Señán continued, "accompanied by a friend of hers who attended her . . . she passed the day and part of the night in praying the Rosary of the Most Holy Virgin. In partial reward for her many and useful services," Señán concluded, "a solemn Mass was sung for her, and I buried her with the habit of Our Father Saint Francis, and in a coffin."[22] Similarly, Pío was buried in the habit in 1820. According to Señán's comments in his burial record, Pío was "a long time prayer leader of the mission, and he exercised [this office] with much perfection . . . because of the clarity of his voice."[23] Burial in the Franciscan habit was thus a way for priests at Mission San Buenaventura, and probably also at Mission San Francisco, to reward Indians who conformed their lives to the religion the Franciscans preached.

In many ways burial in the habit was an empty reward: by definition, the deceased could not enjoy the social recognition it represented. Nevertheless, these burials were also an opportunity to educate the living and inspire greater devotion among survivors. Indians in the Bay Area had long used clothing as a marker of authority: village headmen wore "extravagant" garments, distinguishing them from ordinary men, who generally wore little or no clothing.[24] Likewise, in the mission clothing distinguished those with authority from those without. When they accepted baptism, Indians received a set of clothing, usually sewn from cloth woven at the mission. Alcaldes like Huetlícs and Monózse received distinctive clothing

ILLUSTRATION 6. This 1934 photo of the Mission San Miguel Arcángel reredos shows the seal of the Third Order Secular Franciscans on the left side. Photo by Roger Sturtevant. Library of Congress, Prints and Photographs Division, Historic American Buildings Survey, HABS CAL, 40-SANMI. V, 1–7.

that set them apart from the rest of the baptized Indians and served as a visible reminder of their position.[25] The Franciscan missionaries, too, were distinguished by their clothing. Although the Franciscan habit was meant as a conscious rejection of sartorial vanity, in the Alta California missions it was inextricably linked with the priests' authority and spiritual power. By dressing Huitanac, Froylan, and Geél in the Franciscan habit for burial, Father Ramón Abella literally clothed them in the authority and power that he and his fellow missionaries wielded.

Some Indians at Mission San Francisco apparently distinguished themselves simply through their pious behavior. Otchacaminimac, a Huimen woman, died in 1817, having been baptized for more than thirty years. During her lifetime, Otchacaminimac had stood as godmother to 131 children and adults. Upon her death, she received the most effusive entry in the entire Mission San Francisco death register. "Throughout her illness, which was long," wrote Father Ramón Abella, "she had great conformity with the will of God, and greatly edified me; she died the day of the Nativity of Our Lord Jesus Christ, which is what she wished for, according to what she told me that morning."[26] If Abella is to be believed, Otchacaminimac had demonstrated an extraordinary level of commitment to Catholicism, and her life conformed in great measure to the ideals the missionaries espoused. Otchacaminimac may have maintained a concurrent allegiance to the Huimen Indian community to which she belonged before her baptism, or to the religious beliefs and practices of the people there, but the extant record of her actions betrays no hint of any such loyalty. In Abella's eyes, Otchacaminimac demonstrated the degree to which Indians at Mission San Francisco might devote themselves to Catholicism throughout their lives at the mission.

The monjas, those buried in the Franciscan habit, and pious Indians like Otchacaminimac went beyond the dictates of the priests at Mission San Francisco, actively extending the reach and authority of Catholicism in their lives. These Indians chose more priestly supervision, greater Catholic spiritual discipline, and more frequent sacramental participation. Why these Indians elected to embrace Catholicism to a greater degree than their peers is impossible to know. Perhaps they simply felt a desire to live a more fully Catholic life; perhaps they anticipated gaining the priests' favor through their participation, acquiring greater spiritual power, boosting their own status in the mission community, or some other reward. In the end, each individual Indian probably had several reasons for seeking a more Catholic life.

The Indians who pursued a more extensive Catholic experience were probably a small minority at Mission San Francisco. Most Indians seem to have been satisfied with a lower level of piety. Among these were many who sought ways to accommodate their ambivalence about, or rejection of, Catholicism and mission life. In their deaths, as well as in the births and deaths of their children, many Indians rejected an exclusively Catholic experience. Instead, they sought some combination of Indian and Catholic rituals or chose to eschew Catholic rites altogether.

Throughout the Spanish colonial period, some baptized Indians deliberately gave birth outside the walls of Mission San Francisco. We know about these births because some of them are explicitly acknowledged in Mission San Francisco's baptismal register, with notes such as "she was born while her mother was huida" explaining the delay between the child's birth and baptism.[27] The baptism records for these children indicate that they survived at least long enough to make the journey back to Mission San Francisco. In most cases, there was a delay of at least several days, if not weeks or months, between the birth of a child outside the mission and that child's baptism. That the mothers of these children gave birth early is highly unlikely: without modern medical care, severely premature babies would not have survived long enough to return to the mission.[28] Instead, mothers most likely carried these children to term, and parents timed their absences from Mission San Francisco to coincide with their children's births.

The particular locations of children's births outside the mission lends credence to the conclusion that parents planned the circumstances of these births. Usually, these children were delivered in parents' home villages. Elena, for example, was born in 1802. According to her baptismal record, "she was born among the Huimens when her parents were on paseo."[29] Elena's father was a Huimen Indian himself, and her mother was a member of the Habasto tribal community that lived directly north of the Huimens.[30] If the priests understood correctly, Elena's parents were visiting among her father's community, where relatives would have assisted Elena's mother during childbirth and conducted the necessary rituals to make Elena a member of the family and the local Huimen community.

In some cases, Indian children were clearly born among their mothers' extended families. María Egipciaca, for example, was born in 1819 "on the other shore of the tideland in the land of the Suisuns, [where] her parents were on paseo."³¹ Her mother, Omobala, came from the Suisun tribal community, which lived across the bay to the northeast of Mission San Francisco. María's father, on the other hand, was from the Achistaca tribal community, located south of the mission.³² It may be that the family of María's father had died or been scattered, while her mother's family remained in their tribal community's territory, able to receive the couple and aid with María's birth.

In most cases, the baptized mothers and fathers of children born outside the mission hailed from the same group or from neighboring groups, so it is neither possible, nor necessary, to determine precisely which relatives they were visiting at the time of the birth. Examples like María's parents notwithstanding, the patrilineal and patrilocal system that held sway in the Bay Area before the Spanish colonists' arrival suggests that in most cases Indians who left the mission to give birth sought out the father's family. These extended kin groups helped mothers in childbirth and initiated children into local Indian communities.

When Juuim was ready to give birth to her son Pedro de Alcantara, she and her husband Simmón went to visit Simmón's family.³³ Pedro was born in the Cotegen village of Ssalayme, where Simmón's mother, sisters, and sisters-in-law were able to help Juuim with the birth, just as Juuim's own mother had received help from her husband's female kin when Juuim was born.³⁴ One of these women took the umbilical cord and afterbirth and burnt it, perhaps while Juuim went to wash herself and her baby boy in the ocean or a nearby stream. Thus, Pedro was born among his extended patrilineage, and Simmón's family must have celebrated the addition to their lineage, piercing his ears and performing other rituals to mark him as one of their own. A month after Pedro's birth, released from the food taboos that prevented them from consuming meat and salt, Juuim and Simmón returned to Mission San Francisco to have Pedro baptized. By giving birth outside the mission, parents like Juuim and Simmón were able to provide their children with a sort of dual citizenship, making them members of Bay Area Indian society through rituals like ear piercing, and then of the local Catholic society through baptism. They also renewed their own places in both communities by participating in the rituals surrounding childbirth.

During the Spanish colonial period, approximately 11 percent of the more than six thousand Indians baptized at Mission San Francisco died away from the mission. According to the priests' records, about 13 percent of the Indians in this group died accidentally or even violently on paseos or other errands into the countryside, the result of conflicts with unbaptized or runaway Indians, encounters with bears, drownings in stormy seas, and other unfortunate occurrences. Most, if not all, of the rest died from illness. Unlike accidents and violence, illness often provided Bay Area Indians with the opportunity to choose the location and other circumstances of their deaths. Evidence from the Mission San Francisco death register indicates that about a third—more than two hundred—of the baptized Indians who died outside the mission during the Spanish colonial period seized that opportunity and elected to die among family and friends.

By going to their home villages to die, Indians baptized at Mission San Francisco created the possibility that traditional mourning rituals would be performed openly for them. María de la Asumpción was one person who apparently decided that she wanted these rituals to mark her death. A Yelamu woman, María de la Asumpción was baptized at Mission San Francisco in 1782 when she was twelve days old.[35] By the time she died in 1799, she had outlived her first husband and most of the baptized members of her family. Her father, Canoe, her older brother Coynis, and possibly her younger brother Aniceto, were alive; her mother and five other siblings had died.[36]

In January 1799, María remarried, taking as her husband the widower Chi-uéc, from the independent village of Urebure, which was located immediately south of the Yelamu territory along the bay side of the San Francisco peninsula.[37] Sometime early that summer, María became ill. According to the missionaries, she went on paseo "to convalesce at the Beach."[38] This journey probably took her to the homes of family and friends in the Yelamu and possibly Urebure villages, both of which were located along the coast. The priests may very well have seen María's paseo as an attempt to recover her health, as their comments indicated. However, María made her confession before leaving, an ominous step at the mission. Indians, like most Catholics, usually only confessed once a year, during Lent, unless death appeared imminent. In the latter case, confession functioned as a way of preparing one's soul for death.[39] María's decision to confess before leaving the mission therefore suggests that she was preparing to die. By arranging a visit to her home village, María assured herself that she would be able to die among family and friends, people who could perform the traditional burial and mourning rituals for her that the priests discouraged, or may even have prohibited, at the Mission. By confessing before leaving the Mission, however, María also ensured that she would die in the good graces of the Catholic god as well.

María was not the only one to draw on the resources of both Catholicism and traditional Bay Area religions in preparing for death. Other Indians went further: Tolemele, an Omiomi man, died in 1816. Ramón Abella wrote in his death record that Tolemele "received penitence and extreme unction before leaving, he went without my realizing it."[40] Tolemele died while on paseo on the north side of the San Francisco Bay, "in the direction of the Huimens," whence other baptized Indians brought back the news of his death. He was probably on his way to his home village, if he had not already reached it by the time of his death; the Omiomis lived to the north of the Huimen Indians. Even more than María de la Asumpción, Tolemele prepared for his death by receiving every applicable Catholic sacrament and making the journey to his home territory. By receiving the sacraments at Mission San Francisco, Indians like Tolemele and María de la Asumpción expressed their allegiance to the Catholic religion advocated by the missionaries. By leaving the mission to die, however, they added a final statement about the continuing importance of traditional Bay Area rituals associated with death and their allegiance to Indian communities outside the mission walls. Though Tolemele, María de la Asumpción, and other Indians had accepted baptism, thereby becoming members of the Catholic community centered at Mission San Francisco, their decisions to die elsewhere clearly demonstrate that they had not renounced their positions in the Indian communities from which they came.

Other Indians rejected Catholicism more emphatically than either Tolemele or María de la Asumpción, leaving the mission to die without receiving any sacraments. Mochechi, for example, died in 1817, when she was approximately eighteen years old. The priest who recorded her death wrote that "she died on the other shore, they [other Indians] took her there already gravely ill."[41] She had not confessed or received the sacrament of extreme unction. Mochechi had been baptized for fourteen years by the time she died and had long since reached the age of reason, so she was certainly eligible for the sacraments. Nevertheless, she chose not to receive them, perhaps demonstrating her disillusionment with or distrust of the missionaries' religion, or evincing a lack of confidence in the rituals themselves.

Mochechi was far from unique. Often, word of Indians' deaths reached the priests months or even years after their occurrences. These deaths were recorded in the death register in clusters, usually under a heading such as "It has been found out that the following neophytes have died in the countryside" or "The gentile Indians have brought news of the deaths of the following neophytes." Few of the Indians whose deaths were reported in this manner had received the sacraments of penitence or extreme unction before leaving the mission. Some died while on paseo; others died as runaways. Like Mochechi, many of these Indians may have decided to die in their home communities, preferring to make the passage from life to death under the guidance of members of their own villages rather than the Catholic priests.

Even when they died at the mission, baptized Indians were still able to express their ambivalence about or lack of confidence in Catholicism by refusing to receive the sacraments of penitence and extreme unction. Father Gerónimo Boscana, a Franciscan stationed at the Southern California mission of San Juan Capistrano, recounted his experience with one dying Indian there. On the verge of death, the man was asked by an onlooker why he would not confess. "In a tone of fury," reported Boscana, the man answered "Because I do not want to; having lived deceived, I do not want to die deceived."[42]

There are no extant records of Indians at Mission San Francisco explicitly refusing the sacraments associated with death like the man at San Juan Capistrano did. However, Indians embedded an implicit rejection of those sacraments in their frequent failures to inform the priests of their impending deaths. The twenty-seven-year-old man Otaya, for example, died at Mission San Francisco. Father Ramón Abella wrote Otaya's death record with a hint of surprise: "he died the previous day without receiving any sacrament because the [first] news of his illness was the request for a hoe to make the grave."[43] Others, similarly, kept the priests uninformed of their physical condition. In the death record for Saquenjeiun, a fifty-four-year-old Omiomi woman, Abella explained that she had not received the sacraments because "they told me when she was already deceased, I did not know she was ill, and she was old, and blind, and she was baptized that way."[44] In some cases, certainly, baptized Indians fell ill and died suddenly, or their illnesses unexpectedly worsened, causing them to die without opportunity to confess or receive extreme unction. In many cases, however, Indians' failure to receive these sacraments must be seen as a conscious decision to forgo Catholic rituals at the hour of death, combined with the complicity of the Indians who attended those deaths.

The Varieties of Religious Experience at Mission San Francisco

Children did not receive the sacraments of penitence and extreme unction before death because the priests judged them too young to understand the significance of the rituals. Nevertheless, the deaths of children shed some light on their parents' attitudes toward Catholicism and mission life. Like children born to baptized Indians outside the mission, most baptized children who died outside the mission did so because they accompanied parents who had left the mission with or without the priests' permission. Some children may have fallen ill outside the mission while traveling with their parents. Others were already ill when their parents took them out of Mission San Francisco.

Parents who removed ill children from Mission San Francisco may have gone in search of traditional cures to stave off their children's illnesses. According to Fathers Ramón Abella and Juan Sainz de Lucio, the Indians used both herbal and surgical remedies. "What they use most is Yerba Buena," Abella and Sainz de Lucio wrote in 1814.

> They do not use bleeding. Only when they have some inflammation, whether it is at the point of suppuration or not, like a headache or an interior pain, they use a Flint and Suck the Blood, and most of the time it does them more harm than good because they give themselves many cuts and they Irritate their body parts; but they give it up with difficulty, because some people heal. They do not use Purges nor Emetics. They do not know the Hot Springs.[45]

According to European observers, the priests' medical techniques were no more effective, and may have been worse. La Pérouse remarked that in California "several children die from hernias that the slightest skill could cure, and our surgeons were fortunate enough to help a few of them and teach them to use bandages."[46] Georg H. von Langsdorff observed a similarly bleak medical situation in 1806. "With the exception of some simple emetics and cathartics which they keep for their own use," he wrote, "the misioneros are unprovided with medicaments."[47] Adelbert von Chamisso was more caustic a decade later. "There is no medical assistance here, except for bleeding, which is said to have been taught them by a ship's surgeon," he wrote of Mission San Francisco. "This remedy being since applied on every occasion," he continued, "is more fatal than advantageous."[48] While Chamisso probably overstated the case, the remedies available to the Franciscan priests were of little help in reducing mortality at Mission San Francisco and probably inspired little confidence in the baptized Indians.

Indian parents' removal of their ill children also constituted an implicit rejection of the Catholic rituals associated with death. Some parents, having reconciled themselves to the inevitability of their children's deaths, may have taken their children to their home villages to ensure that they would have company in mourning the children's deaths. When their child Puqueccoime became seriously ill, for example, Tamal Indians Talmucse and Pispisooboj took him on paseo to the other side of the bay, back to the land where he had been born. One of the priests at Mission San Francisco later recorded that Puqueccoime's "parents buried him on the other side of the Bay, where they were on paseo; he went, already gravely ill, to change climate."[49] While the climate to the north of the mission was reputed among the priests to be less damp than that of the San Francisco peninsula, and thus more beneficial to human health, Talmucse and Pispisooboj also probably sought aid for their son from traditional healers and, later, help in burying his body and mourning his death.

Occasionally, the priests at Mission San Francisco recorded the death of a child who had been baptized but who lived outside the mission. Only a few of these children are identified in the San Francisco mission registers. Their number may be small because most children remained at Mission San Francisco after their baptisms. However, it may also be that those children survived to adulthood more often and, when they died as adults, priests did not record the circumstances of their childhoods in the burial register. Children born at the mission rarely survived past their second birthday. Over the entire existence of the mission, the mean life expectancy for children born at the mission averaged 4.2 years, and from 1793 to 1821, it never exceeded 2.0 years.[50] In contrast, Henry A. Gemery has estimated the life expectancy at birth for children born in East Haven, Connecticut, in roughly the same time period—1773 to 1822—at 45 to 50 years.[51] Before the arrival of Europeans, historical demographers believe that life expectancy at birth for children born in the Western Hemisphere ranged from the twenties to low thirties.[52] California Indian parents, observing the frequent deaths of children at Mission San Francisco, may have left their children to grow up with relatives in hopes of increasing the children's chances of survival into adulthood. Although the data does not exist to calculate life expectancy for children who grew up outside the mission during the Spanish colonial period, the lower density and greater mobility of the population suggests that it may have been higher: these factors inhibited the spread of infectious diseases that claimed many lives at the California missions.[53]

Those baptized Indian children living outside the mission who did not survive to adulthood appear in Mission San Francisco's death register. Teodorico, for example, was about five months old when he died. "A gentile from Las Pulgas brought the news of the death in his village (where he was being raised) of Teodorico," wrote Father Pedro Benito Cambón when he recorded the death in August 1788. "He was born the first of March of this year . . . the legitimate son of the Neophytes Alexos, and Madrona, deceased."[54] Oloyuig and Tacque'te, or, as the priests knew them, Alexos and Madrona, were both from the area south of the mission.[55] "Las Pulgas" was the Spanish name that had been given to Oloyuig's village, Cachagnigtac.[56] So Teodorico was being raised in his father's village, almost certainly by members of his father's family. The death of Tacque'te, Teodorico's mother, may have prompted Oloyuig to take the child to Cachagnigtac in search of kin to help care for the child. Whether Oloyuig remained at Cachagnigtac with Teodorico is impossible to tell. If he did, later evidence indicates that he eventually returned; he remarried at Mission San Francisco in May 1789.[57] That an unbaptized Indian brought the news of Teodorico's death may mean that Oloyuig remained at the village to perform the appropriate mourning rituals and to dispose of his son's body, or it may indicate that he was, in fact, at the mission all along.

In contrast to Teodorico, Saquenjelapi was raised by members of her mother's family. The daughter of Guequecse and Louete, Saquenjelapi died in 1816. All three members of this tiny family were baptized at Mission San Francisco, but Guequecse was baptized in 1811, three years before Saquenjelapi and her mother Louete. Before Louete accepted baptism, Guequecse married another woman. As a result, Louete probably returned to her own patrilineage, taking Saquenjelapi with her. When Louete died shortly after baptism, her mother and sisters apparently took responsibility for raising the child, just as they would have had Louete and Saquenjelapi remained unbaptized. When Saquenjelapi died some two years later, Father Ramón Abella wrote that she had died "in her land," and that the girl's maternal grandmother had assured him of the child's death.[58]

Saquenjelapi and Teodorico died long before they could accept or reject the Catholicism the missionaries preached. Their lives and deaths, though, reflect something of their parents' decisions about Catholicism and mission life. It may be that the parents of Teodorico, Saquenjelapi, and other children raised outside the mission made a simple calculation of the risks and benefits of living at the mission and decided that their children stood a better chance of survival if they lived elsewhere. However, the decision was probably far more complicated. Growing up outside the mission conferred benefits beyond sheer survival: living with extended kin groups, children had opportunities to learn the traditional skills and knowledge that priests tried to suppress at Mission San Francisco. Had he lived longer, Teodorico would have heard stories of Coyote and other mythological figures, and he would have learned from his grandfather or his uncles how to hunt deer, snare ducks, and provide for himself and his family. Saquenjelapi, had she survived, would have undergone traditional puberty rituals at her first menses. Her grandmother and aunts would have passed on a wealth of knowledge about local plants and animals, taught her the best ways to weave baskets, and counseled her about how to manage menstruation, sex, and pregnancy. Returning to the mission periodically, Teodorico and Saquenjelapi would also learn the catechism that the missionaries taught and the Catholic rituals the priests believed were necessary for salvation. Living outside the mission thus offered a way to extend children's dual citizenship, keeping one of their feet in each community.

Children's residence with extended families outside the mission might also have been a way of strengthening kinship networks that the mission threatened to disrupt. Children like Saquenjelapi and Teodorico may have functioned as living links between their parents at the mission and relatives elsewhere, precious tokens of their parents' desire to remain attached to their extended families. In addition, by choosing to have their children raised outside the mission, the parents of Saquenjelapi, Teodorico, and children like them resisted the desires of the mission priests, who would have preferred that the children remain at the mission with their parents, under the missionaries' watchful eyes. It is impossible to know whether these parents' resistance was rooted in uncertainty about the religion the priests advocated, in dissatisfaction with mission life, or in some combination of these and possibly other factors. That these parents were able to, and did, choose where their children would be raised, however, highlights both the permeability of the mission boundaries and the range of baptized Indians' options as they sought and found ways to accommodate their ambivalence about the reach and authority of Catholicism in their, and their children's, lives.

For those Indians who found life at Mission San Francisco too drastic a change or too religiously demanding, San Pedro y San Pablo offered a less intense alternative. The Franciscans first applied the name "San Pedro y San Pablo" to the independent Indian village of Pruristac, located about thirteen miles south of Mission San Francisco.[59] In the mid-1780s they made the place a rancho, a site for agricultural work. The mission depended on San Pedro y San Pablo's produce. As early as 1782, Fathers Francisco Palóu and Pedro Benito Cambón reported that Mission San Francisco's "harvests are not sufficient to maintain all the Neophytes and it has been necessary to get help from Mission Santa Clara; and as the Gentiles of the Rancherías near the Mission are converted, it will be indispensable to sow in the spot more than four leagues from the mission, which has already been found very suitable with good land, and enough water free of the winds."[60] San Pedro y San Pablo soon became more than a rancho, however. In 1787 the priests began to baptize Indians in the newly built church at San Pedro y San Pablo and to bury them in the church. A short time later the missionaries consecrated a cemetery at the site and moved burials outside the church. San Pedro y San Pablo thus became a satellite mission, a smaller version of Mission San Francisco. Priests from Mission San Francisco visited San Pedro y San Pablo to say Mass and to perform baptisms, marriages and burials, though it is difficult to say how often they made the trip between the two places. Among its growing collection of buildings, the outstation included quarters for the missionaries to facilitate lengthier stays there.[61]

Most of the Indians who participated in sacraments performed at San Pedro y San Pablo were from tribal communities whose territories lay to the south of Mission San Francisco. The Franciscans used San Pedro y San Pablo as a site for performing baptisms on a regular basis from mid-1787 through the end of the eighteenth century. During that time, the priests performed 160 baptisms at San Pedro y San Pablo, just over a tenth of the 1,285 total Indian baptisms they performed during the period. The priests began burying Indians at San Pedro y San Pablo earlier, in May 1786, and all but discontinued the practice in May 1793. During that time they buried 134 Indians at San Pedro y San Pablo. These burials constituted more than one-third of the 358 total burials of baptized Indians recorded for that seven-year period. Sixty-seven people were both baptized and buried at San Pedro y San Pablo. In addition, priests performed at least thirty-five marriages at San Pedro y San Pablo, most of them involving at least one partner who was baptized or later buried in the same place. Some people were married multiple times at San Pedro y San Pablo. San Pedro y San Pablo may

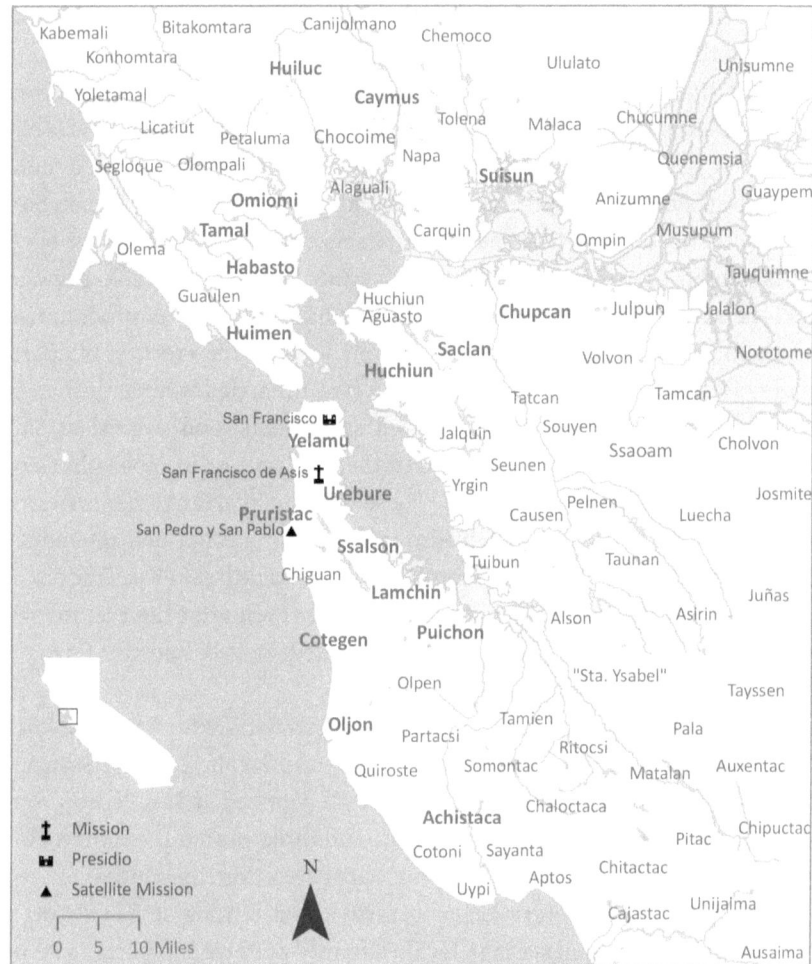

MAP 3. Tribal communities and villages of the San Francisco Bay Area, with Mission San Francisco, the San Francisco Presidio, and San Pedro y San Pablo (the mission's outstation). Tribal communities and villages mentioned in the text are in bold. Locations of all tribal communities and villages follow Randall Milliken, *A Time of Little Choice* (Menlo Park, CA: Ballena Press, 1995), 228–29. Wyoming Geographic Information Science Center, 2009.

have been the preferred location for these people because it was somewhat closer to their home territories.

The Indians who went to San Pedro y San Pablo may have preferred that location for a variety of other reasons as well: it was probably overseen by one or two of the mission servants, who may have been more lenient regarding behavioral requirements that the priests imposed at Mission San Francisco. In addition, San Pedro y San Pablo does not appear to have been a residential site: though the complex at San Pedro y San Pablo grew to include several adobe buildings, including quarters for the missionaries and a kitchen, construction ended in 1789 without the erection of apartments for Indian families or dormitories for unmarried women or men.[62] Thus, those who heard Mass, received sacraments, and worked at San Pedro y San Pablo continued to live in their villages or in other places of their choosing near the outstation. These residential arrangements meant that accepting baptism at San Pedro y San Pablo did not disrupt Indian families to the same degree as accepting baptism at Mission San Francisco: extended families could live and work together even after their baptisms, continuing patterns that had been established long before the Spanish arrival on the peninsula.

Indeed, many families seem to have chosen San Pedro y San Pablo as "their" mission for as long as it was in existence. Tacalú, his wife Ssatcón, and their five children, for example, were all baptized at San Pedro y San Pablo between January and May of 1791. The three youngest children also died and were buried at San Pedro y San Pablo over the course of 1791 and 1792.[63] This concentration of baptisms and burials at San Pedro y San Pablo clearly suggests that Tacalú's family preferred to participate in Catholic rituals at the satellite mission rather than at the main mission further north, just as other families concentrated their participation at Mission San Francisco. San Pedro y San Pablo was far closer than Mission San Francisco to the Cotegen village where Tacalú and Ssatcón were raised and was therefore probably far more accessible for their family.

Other families were even more thoroughly tied to San Pedro y San Pablo. Oljon headman Lachi was baptized in 1791 at San Pedro y San Pablo along with three of his wives and six of their children. Another wife and child had been baptized at the satellite mission two years earlier, and three daughters had accepted baptism at Mission San Francisco before the San Pedro y San Pablo church was built. After his baptism, Lachi renewed his marriage vows with one of his wives, Ssujan, in the San Pedro y San Pablo church. In the following years, at least ten members of Lachi's patrilineage died and were buried at San Pedro y San Pablo.[64] The outstation was closer to Lachi's territory, but many Oljon Indians were baptized, like his daughters, at Mission San Francisco during the Spanish colonial period. Perhaps Lachi found San Pedro y San Pablo preferable to Mission San Francisco because he was able to wield greater political power in that location, where he was one of very few baptized village headmen, or perhaps staying at San Pedro y San Pablo allowed him to avoid rival headmen who had taken up residence at Mission San Francisco.

We know even less about daily life at San Pedro y San Pablo than we do about daily life at Mission San Francisco. However, it is evident that family connections influenced where people were born and died, where they accepted baptism, and where their bodies were buried. That certain families seem to have preferred San Pedro y San Pablo as a site for receiving the Catholic sacraments while others preferred Mission San Francisco may indicate that extended families collectively decided which mission to patronize. Those who lived close to the San Pedro y San Pablo site may have remained in their villages and visited the satellite mission to hear Mass, attend religious instruction, or participate in one of the sacraments; others, who lived further away, may have moved to San Pedro y San Pablo or its environs, yet been able to maintain traditional residential and work patterns in that new place.

The locations and other circumstances of Indians' births and deaths, recorded in the Mission San Francisco registers, show that Bay Area Indians responded in a wide variety of ways to the Catholicism the Franciscans preached and the lifestyle they advocated. Some Indians, like the monjas, the Indians buried in the Franciscan habit, and pious people like Otchacaminimac sought to extend the reach and authority of Catholicism in their lives by accepting greater priestly supervision, more rigorous spiritual discipline, and greater involvement in the sacramental life of the mission. These Indians' extra investment in Catholicism could be read as a manifestation of false consciousness, a mistaken belief that the Indians' best interests lay in a complete adoption of the religion the priests advocated. Certainly, this may have been true in some cases. However, to write off these Indians as deluded is to deny the sincerity of their religious

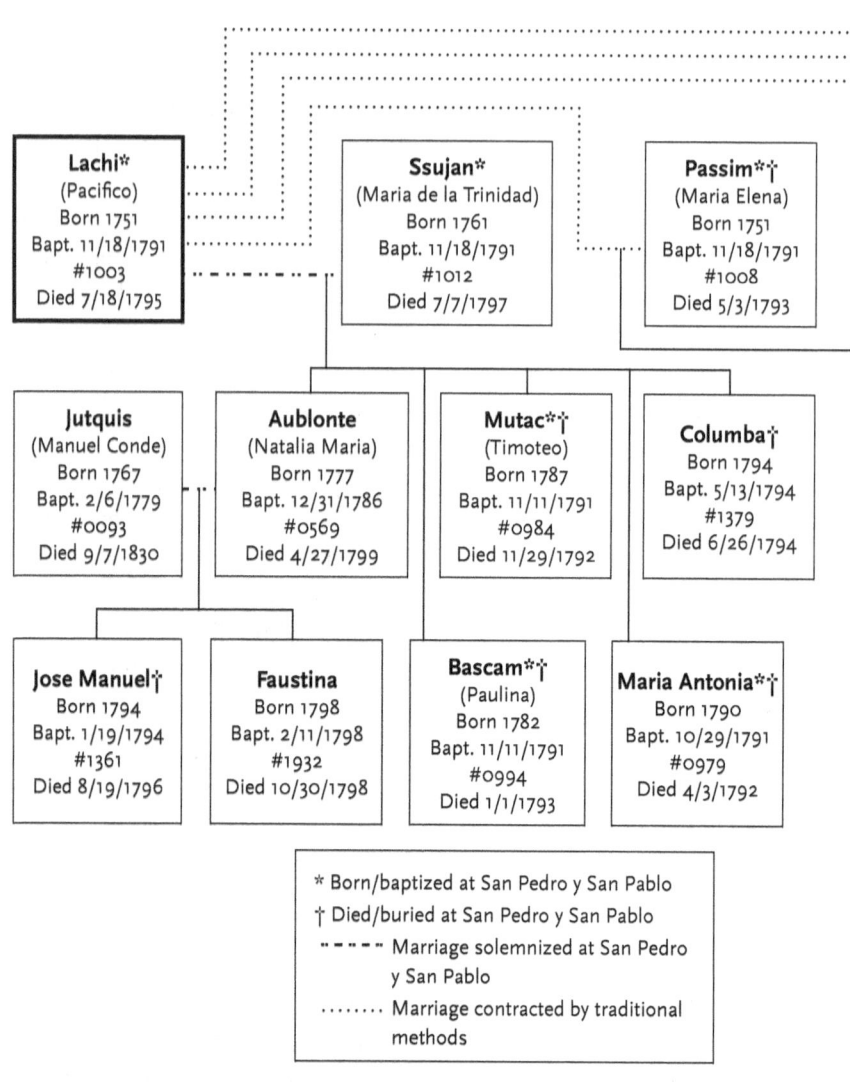

FIGURE 6. Lachi's family. When they had a choice, Lachi and his family seem to have preferred the chapel at San Pedro y San Pablo to the church at Mission San Francisco de Asís.

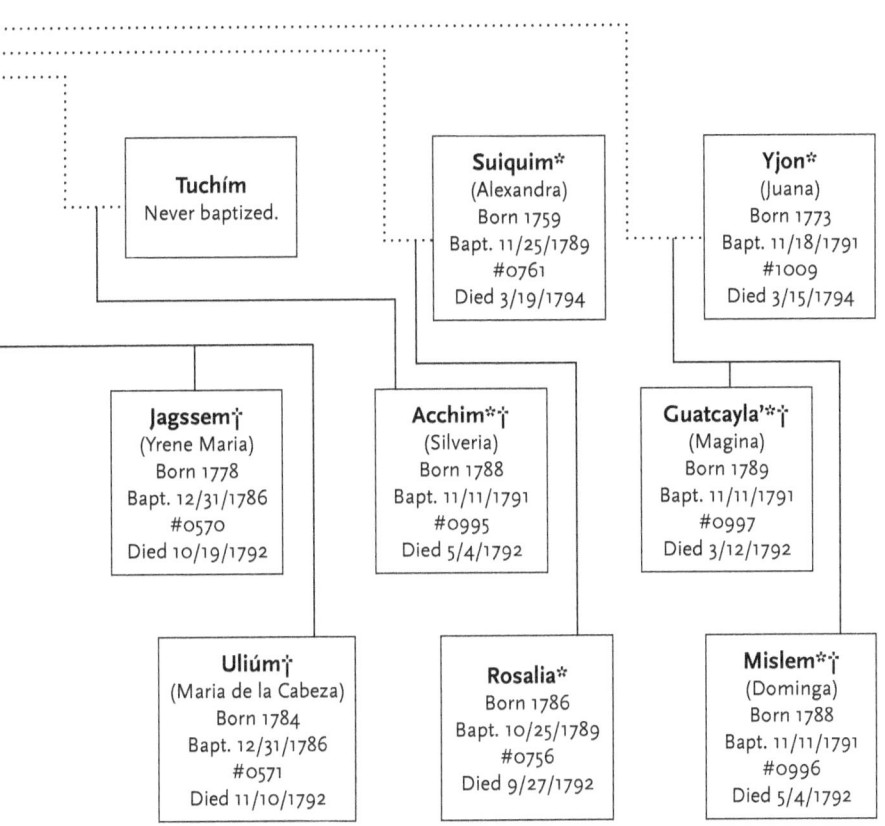

The Varieties of Religious Experience at Mission San Francisco

convictions and, ultimately, to paint them as passive victims of European oppression. It is also possible that these Indians put up a false front of devotion to gain some more worldly benefit. Again, this interpretation may hold true in some cases, but it also depends on a judgment of the Indians' Catholicism as insincere. In the end, we cannot know why some Indians sought ways to deepen their involvement in the religion the Franciscans taught. That they did, however, illustrates one way in which Indians shaped their own religious experiences at Mission San Francisco.

The choices these Indians made, however, represent only one way in which Indians responded to the Catholicism that the Franciscans preached. Other Indians sought, and found, ways to express continuing attachment to traditional Bay Area rituals and to their home villages in the circumstances surrounding their births and deaths. By choosing to give birth or die outside the mission, to leave baptized children to grow up with relatives in home villages, and to accept or reject the Catholic sacraments of penitence and extreme unction at the hour of death, Indians baptized at Mission San Francisco found ways to expand the range of religious possibilities available at the mission.

San Pedro y San Pablo offered another way for Bay Area Indians to accommodate their ambivalence about Catholicism and mission life. By baptizing, marrying, and burying Bay Area Indians at San Pedro y San Pablo, the Franciscans offered many Indians an opportunity to participate in Catholicism on slightly different terms than were available at Mission San Francisco. Indians who chose San Pedro y San Pablo as their mission likely did so for a variety of reasons, but the outstation appears to have allowed many people to stay closer to their home villages and make fewer changes to their ways of life while still taking part in Catholicism.

The Franciscan priests saw Indians' acceptance of baptism as a commitment to Catholicism. However, once Bay Area Indians accepted baptism, they made a range of choices in which they expressed the variegated nature of that commitment. While the priests at Mission San Francisco would have preferred that all of the Indians they baptized behave as piously as Otchacaminimac, the mission registers record a much wider range of responses, evident in the circumstances of Indians' births and deaths. The variety of these responses highlights the ability baptized Indians had to make choices regarding the most significant moments of their lives, and the wherewithal they had to act on those choices.

Conclusion
Uichase's Story

⁓ Uichase, the son of a Lamchin village headman, was born in 1774, two years before the founding of Mission San Francisco. He accepted baptism in 1790, along with several of his siblings; his parents followed a little more than a year later. Uichase lived through the entire Spanish colonial period at Mission San Francisco: he married four times and fathered ten children at the mission before his death in 1831.[1] The story of Uichase and his family exemplifies many of the themes discussed in this book and illustrates the partial, contingent, and variegated nature of Bay Area Indians' responses to the Catholicism that Franciscan missionaries tried to instill at Mission San Francisco de Asís.

For Uichase and many Indians at Mission San Francisco, as well as at the other Alta California missions, baptism was the starting point of conversion rather than its culmination.[2] The road that began at baptism, though, was far from direct. It meandered, twisting and turning with no clear destination. Some Indians, like Otchacaminimac and the Indians who were buried in the Franciscan habit, finally arrived in a place the priests recognized as thoroughly Catholic. Others traveled a circular path, learning the Catholic rituals but ultimately rejecting them at the hour of death. The majority,

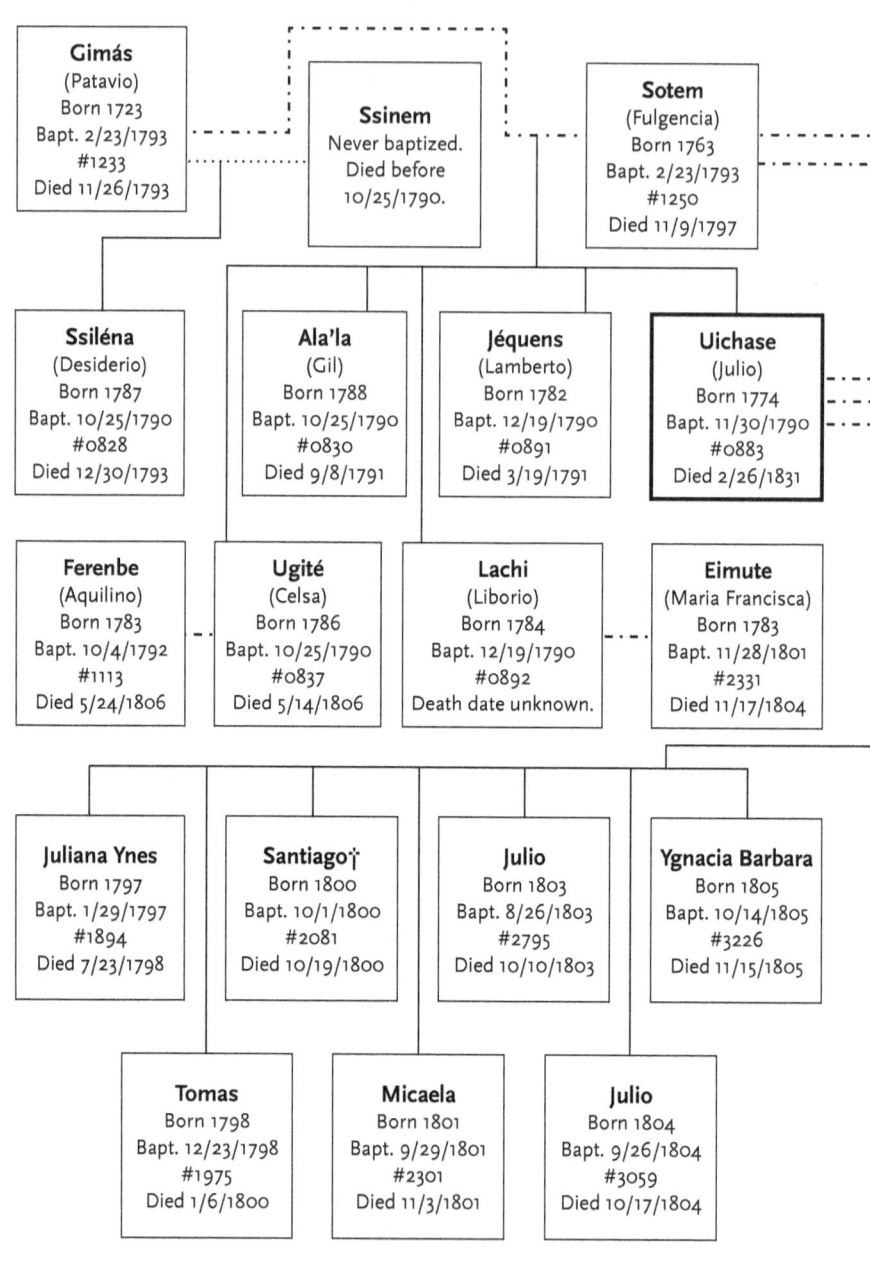

FIGURE 7. Uichase's family. Uichase was born two years before Mission San Francisco de Asís was founded and lived another ten years after the Spanish lost control of Alta California. He outlived four wives and all ten of his children.

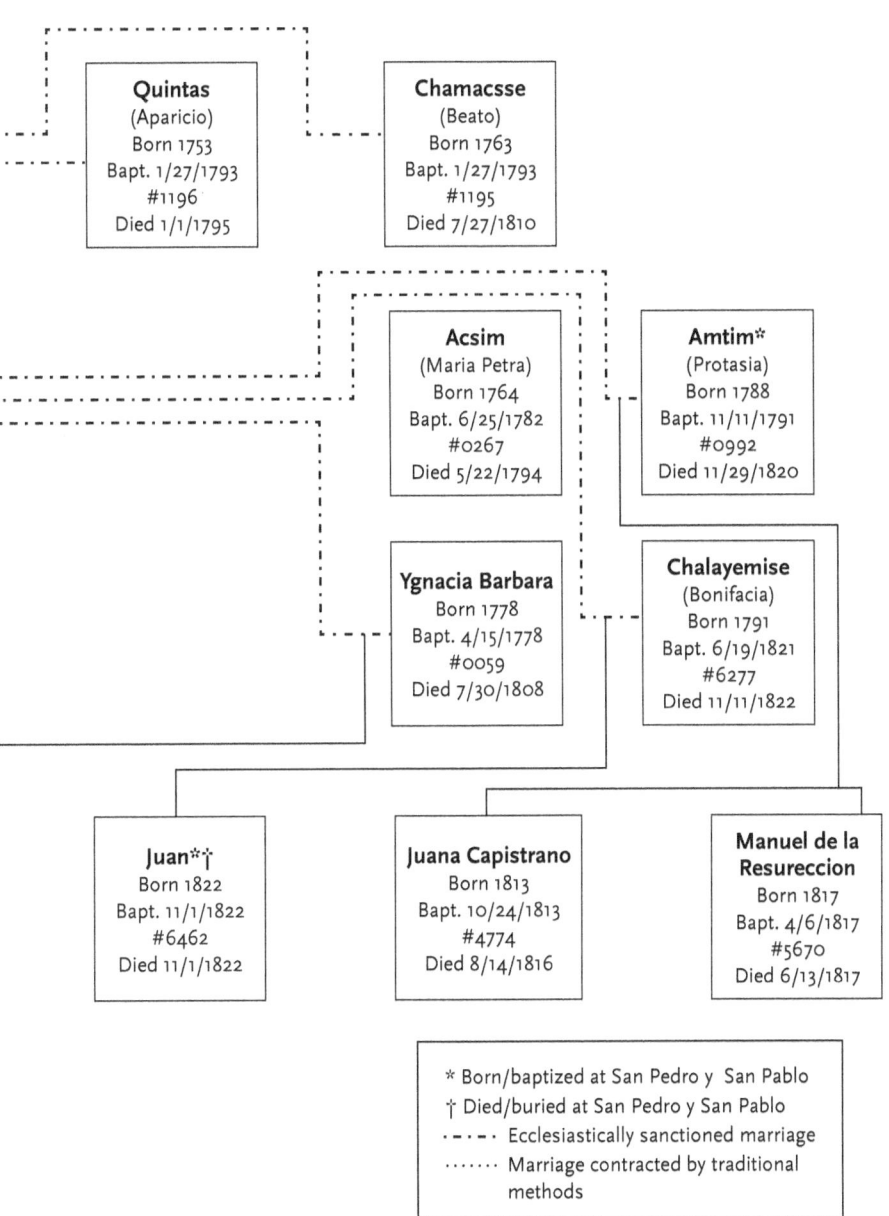

including Uichase and many others, proceeded slowly down the road, doubling back in times of crisis in order to avail themselves of tried and true rituals to accompany childbirth or alleviate sickness. In 1793 Uichase's father Gimas died outside the mission. The death record noted that Gimas was away from the mission without a license and that he was killed by a bear. At first glance, these details suggest that Gimas had left the mission to hunt.[3] However, about a month later Gimas's young son Ssiléna—the child of his deceased junior wife—was also reported dead outside the mission.[4] Ssiléna's death, and the significance of the bear as a spiritually powerful creature in Bay Area Indian cosmology, raise the possibility that Gimas had left the mission with his son in the hope of curing Ssiléna using traditional methods. If so, that quest was unsuccessful. Gimas and Ssiléna might have taken solace, though, in dying outside the mission where traditional mourning rituals could be performed for them. Like Gimas appears to have done, Uichase and most baptized Indians probably combined Catholicism with what they already knew, taking what seemed most useful and leaving what appeared inapplicable to their lives. As a result, religion at Mission San Francisco was messy, neither completely Catholic nor completely non-Catholic.

Even as they attended Mass, the central ritual of Catholicism, Uichase and the other baptized Indians at Mission San Francisco did not necessarily imbibe Catholicism as the Franciscans intended to impart it. Looking around the church, Uichase and his family learned, along with the other Indians, of a violent world, one in which a daily sacrifice to appease the deity might have made sense. However, they also saw designs like the ones on the baskets Uichase's mother Sotem made—designs that may have carried connotations of indigenous religious ideas.[5] Even if the iconography of the church did not communicate native religious concepts, Uichase, his family, and other Bay Area Indians filtered the priests' words and actions through their own experiences and the lessons of ceremonies, songs, and stories passed down from generation to generation.

Performing and teaching those rituals at Mission San Francisco was more difficult because of the restrictions the priests imposed. When Uichase's sister Ugité reached about age nine, for example, the priests separated her from the rest of her family.[6] From that time until she married, Ugité would live in the monjerío with other unmarried and widowed women. Though this separation from her older female relatives made it difficult for Ugité to learn the songs and stories that taught women how to be in the world, it was not impossible: shortly after Ugité moved to the monjerío, her mother Sotem joined her. Recently widowed by Gimas's run-in with a bear, Sotem may have taken advantage of her residence in the monjerío to teach her daughter some of this traditional knowledge. Perhaps other older women in the monjerío picked up where Sotem left off when she remarried five months later.[7]

Historians know that eighteenth- and nineteenth-century European Catholics drew on a variety of folk beliefs and practices.[8] Most American Indian religious systems were even more inclusive. It is logical, then, that the California missions were sites of religious combination, despite the priests' efforts to create orthodox Catholic communities. The question of orthodoxy, of whether Indians' conversions were "real," was one that worried the Catholic missionaries in Alta California. Their doubt about the authenticity of Indians' conversions and, indeed, about their own ability to translate Catholic concepts into native terms adequately, led to the Franciscans' reluctance to administer the Eucharist to baptized Indians.

The question of authenticity, however, was probably not of great concern to the Bay Area Indians themselves.[9] Rather than whether a conversion was "true," the baptized Indians and those around them were more likely to ask whether it *worked*: did it bring the baptized person new spiritual power? Did it offer the possibility of creating social harmony, ensuring food supplies, or healing the sick?[10] Like people elsewhere in Native North America, Bay Area Indians saw spiritual power as a force to be acquired, managed, and used for the good of the community, and the techniques for harnessing spiritual power—what colonists called "religion"—were not, in Indians' understanding, mutually exclusive. It may be that this view of spiritual power motivated Uichase's baptism. As the oldest son of a Lamchin headman, Uichase had grown up learning how to be a leader and acquiring the skills necessary to protect his people. The Franciscan missionaries, whose apparently potent spiritual powers were manifested in extraordinary technological capabilities, may have appeared to Uichase and his father Gimas as appropriate tutors for the boy as he learned to manage spiritual power. Accepting baptism and participating in other sacraments at Mission San Francisco, then, was one way of acquiring and deploying spiritual power, but it was not the only way. Indians who left Mission San Francisco to give birth and then brought their children to the mission for baptism, as well as Indians who confessed and received extreme unction before leaving Mission San Francisco to die, vividly illustrate this inclusive approach to the supernatural.

In contrast to this inclusivist stance, the Franciscan missionaries held an exclusivist understanding of truth, which they attempted to instill in the baptized Indians at Mission San Francisco. Although they were certainly part of the Spanish colonial project and shared, at least to some extent, in the ideology of that enterprise, the Franciscans were also motivated by a profound conviction that they were acting for the good of Indians' eternal souls. As the baptized Indians' legal guardians according to Spanish law, and as their spiritual fathers according to Catholic doctrine, the Franciscans saw themselves as heads of a large spiritual family centered at the mission. Viewing the mission as a metaphorical household, and themselves as the *padres de familias* at the household's head, the priests acted to control every aspect of their spiritual sons' and daughters' lives. This paternalistic impulse led the priests into conflict with the military as they sought to protect Bay Area Indians from sexual and economic exploitation by the military and individual colonists. Some Indians, however, eschewed that protection and chose to work at the San Francisco Presidio. The decision of some baptized Indians, like Tujulalis, to become "Presidio Indians" illustrates, in one way, the success of the missionaries' quest to Hispanicize the Bay Area Indians and integrate them into the lowest levels of the colonial economy. However, it also demonstrates the priests' incomplete control over the mission community.

A closer look at labor at Mission San Francisco reveals other gaps in priestly control. The mission depended on Indian labor for its success, which put the priests in a bind: they could not be too picky about how or when that labor was accomplished. Baptized Indians at Mission San Francisco, therefore, were able to combine Hispanic and indigenous techniques and aesthetics in food selection and preparation and in building design and construction. When Uichase married for the first time in 1792, he and his wife lived in a thatch house in the mission ranchería.[11] This home closely resembled the houses both Uichase and Acsim, Uichase's wife, had always known: it was designed and constructed in the same way. Acsim placed her cooking fire in the center of the dwelling, just as her own mother had done.[12] Uichase may have been a member of the work crews that began constructing adobe apartments the following year, and when Gimas and Sotem accepted baptism, they may have moved into one of these newly constructed apartments. Nevertheless, despite the rectangular floor plan and the lack of a smoke hole in the ceiling, Sotem probably still located her cooking fire in the center of the room.

Baptized Indians were also able to prioritize traditional food gathering tasks such as hunting and acorn harvesting over the work of the mission. When Uichase married for the second time, his bride was Ygnacia Barbara.¹³ Her father Puyeles had died years earlier while away from the mission hunting ducks.¹⁴ The records do not reflect whether Uichase ever took part in such a hunting expedition after his baptism, but the communal nature of Bay Area hunting makes it likely that he did. In addition, he almost certainly accompanied Acsim, Ygnacia Barbara, and his later wives on their annual acorn-harvesting trips.

At San Pedro y San Pablo, Indians were probably able to sustain their traditional ways of living and working to an even greater degree than at Mission San Francisco, and many Indians may have deliberately chosen to patronize this satellite mission for that reason. Uichase's third wife, a widow named Amtim, was baptized at San Pedro y San Pablo when she was a child.¹⁵ Since San Pedro y San Pablo's buildings included no women's dormitory, nor any other housing for baptized Indians, it is most likely that Amtim lived with her parents—who never accepted baptism—throughout her youth until she married her first husband.¹⁶ Uichase appears to have moved back and forth between Mission San Francisco and San Pedro y San Pablo: though most of his children were born and baptized at Mission San Francisco, one son, Santiago, died at San Pedro y San Pablo.¹⁷ More than two decades later, Uichase's last child, Juan, was born, baptized, and buried at San Pedro y San Pablo.¹⁸ While Uichase and his family probably helped with the mission's agricultural work at San Pedro y San Pablo, they may also have welcomed the respite from priestly supervision and Hispanic residential forms that they found at the satellite station.

The Franciscan missionaries asserted their paternal control over Bay Area Indians at Mission San Francisco most noticeably in the area of family structures. The Franciscans broke up patrilineages, dissolved polygynous marriages, and limited the pool of potential marriage partners for baptized Indians by imposing Catholic kinship rules and prohibiting baptized Indians from marrying unbaptized people. In addition, they used the structures of space and resource distribution at the mission to make the nuclear family normative. By segregating unmarried women and men and by allowing married couples to live with their young children in apartments or houses in the mission ranchería, the Franciscans imposed a nuclear family model on Indians who had previously lived in extended kin groups. Uichase had grown up in a household filled with his extended family, including his father Gimas; Gimas's two wives, Sotem and Ssinem; Gimas's children, Uichase's brothers and sisters; and possibly other kin whose existence was not recorded.[19] Had Uichase married outside the mission, his wife and eventual children might have joined that group, at least until Uichase established his own household. They certainly would have been considered members of Gimas's patrilineage. At Mission San Francisco, in contrast, Uichase lived in the men's dormitory until his marriage. Uichase's other surviving siblings, Ugité and Lachi, also eventually moved to the women's and men's dormitories when the priests deemed them old enough.[20] When Uichase's parents accepted baptism in 1793, they lived in an apartment or thatch house in the mission ranchería. The spatial separation meant that Gimas and Sotem had less contact with, and less influence over, their children. Although they would normally have arranged marriages for their children, Gimas and Sotem probably had little say in whom Uichase, Ugité, and Lachi married at Mission San Francisco. Instead, the Franciscan missionaries stepped in to fill the parental role.

Even as they attempted to destroy indigenous Bay Area social structures, however, the priests provided tools with which to repair the damage. Through marriage and godparenting, Uichase and other Bay Area Indians created alliances between villages and tribal communities and resolved conflicts that threatened the social harmony of the region. Uichase began to use this strategy shortly after accepting baptism. Acsim, his first wife, was the daughter of another Lamchin headman. By marrying her, Uichase promoted the solidarity of the Lamchin tribal community by uniting two of its leading families. He also consolidated his own position, poising himself to become a Lamchin leader. The father of Uichase's second wife, Ygnacia Barbara, was an influential man from the independent village of Urebure. This marriage created an alliance between the Lamchin people and those of Urebure that might have been useful both inside and outside the mission.

Uichase and Ygnacia Barbara had seven children together, and they used the baptisms of these children to create compadrinazgo relationships that both intensified and extended their kinship networks. Chi-uéc and Ugité, Ygnacia Barbara's brother and Uichase's sister, both godparented children for the couple; Raymundo Morante, a mission servant, godfathered their first child (and later Uichase's first child with his third wife); and other baptized Indians, as well as one colonist, also sponsored children for the couple.[21] Through compadrinazgo, Uichase and Ygnacia Barbara were able to strengthen existing kinship bonds and incorporate new people into their kinship network, reinforcing ties that the imposition of Catholic family structures had threatened to dissolve.

Baptized Bay Area Indians tried to extend the logic of marriage as a diplomatic tool to create alliances with the Hispanic colonists. Uichase's coparent Servate—the godmother of the second child he had with Ygnacia Barbara—was a Lamchin woman married to a man from Urebure. Her sister-in-law, María Soledad, was one of eleven women baptized at Mission San Francisco who married Hispanic colonists.[22] María Soledad was married four times at Mission San Francisco and, except for her first, all of her husbands were Spanish soldiers.[23] All of these men were widowed, just as María Soledad was. The shortage of Hispanic women in the San Francisco Bay Area made it logical for them to look to the baptized Indian population for replacements for their de razón wives. The Franciscan missionaries encouraged soldiers to marry baptized Indian women on the theory that men who did so would then have a legitimate outlet for their sexual urges and would therefore be less likely to prey upon other baptized and unbaptized Indian women. Soldiers who married Indian women, the priests believed, would also be more likely to settle down near the missions, adding stability to the population and contributing to the labor needs of the mission. It is unlikely that María Soledad considered these factors. Instead, marrying Hispanic soldiers was a way to connect her kinship network, and therefore her village, to the networks the soldiers represented. Through María Soledad's marriages, alliances were created.

Bay Area Indians also may have seen baptism itself as a way of creating an alliance with the Franciscans and possibly with the Hispanic colonists more generally. Since it was impossible to marry the Franciscans, baptism may have seemed to be the next-best diplomatic strategy. Just as it is possible that Uichase accepted baptism in order to learn the priests' techniques for acquiring and deploying spiritual power, it is also possible that he joined the Catholic community at Mission San Francisco to create an allegiance with these powerful newcomers. As he anticipated assuming a leadership role in his tribal community, Uichase may have considered it important to establish cordial relations with the Hispanic colonists.

The Indians' desire to create alliances with the Spanish by weaving them into local kinship networks made sense in the Bay Area, where villages and tribal communities controlled relatively small territories and depended on their neighbors for trade, joined them in festivals, and looked to them for marriage partners. Bay Area Indians' attempts to create alliances with the colonists using traditional means suggests that they saw the Spanish as yet another tribal community. While the colonists' material goods and technological expertise made them attractive trading partners, their unauthorized occupation of Yelamu lands and their thoughtless destruction of indigenous food sources made them a tempting target for attacks. Bay Area villages and tribal communities therefore pursued a variety of policies toward the newly arrived Hispanic tribal community. Some, like the Lamchins that Gimas led, watched their new neighbors warily and eventually decided to seek an alliance. Others, like the Yelamu Indians in whose lands the colonists built Mission San Francisco and the San Francisco Presidio, acted more rapidly to establish favorable relations with the newcomers. Still others, especially groups located further from the mission, avoided contact altogether. As Gimas's eventual decision to join the mission illustrates, each community's strategy changed over time. Chalayemise, Uichase's fourth wife, was probably either a Caymu or Huiluc Indian.[24] Both tribal communities stayed away from Mission San Francisco until 1820, forty-four years after the mission had been founded.

Bay Area Indians' treatment of the Hispanic colonists as yet another tribal community was one factor that helped the Spanish colonization effort succeed to the degree it did. The Spanish enjoyed superior firepower and they were backed by the resources of the Spanish government. In addition, although they did not understand it, the Spanish were aided by the germs they introduced, which decimated Indian populations and weakened survivors without affecting the Hispanic colonists substantially. However, the Spanish were vastly outnumbered in the Bay Area. In San Diego, the year before San Francisco's founding, Chumash Indians had mounted a successful rebellion, killing one priest and several soldiers and effectively closing two missions.[25] Spanish control of the Bay Area was anything but inevitable; in fact, it was somewhat surprising, given the outpost's distance from centers of Spanish military strength and the small number of colonists. Had the Indians immediately mounted a unified attack on the colonists, the likelihood that the Spanish would have been driven out seems high. Instead, however, Bay Area Indians behaved toward the Spanish in the same way that they behaved toward other Indians, allowing the colonists to gain a toehold and eventually establish a dominant presence in the region.

While Gimas and other Bay Area Indians treated the Spanish as one more tribal community among many, the Hispanic colonists viewed the

Bay Area Indians, like all California Indians, as a single, subordinate group. The Franciscan missionaries communicated their understanding of human hierarchy at Mission San Francisco. Only two distinctions mattered in the Mass: gender and racial identity. The priests reinforced a patriarchal social structure and a binary gender division in the Mass by emphasizing the difference between men and women spatially, placing men on the privileged Gospel side of the church and women on the less important Epistle side. They also privileged men's voices, so that women's voices were never heard distinctly during the Mass. While individual Indian men like Uichase might play the roles of sacristan, prayer leader, or musician, the voices of Uichase's wives and other Indian women were always subsumed in the collective voice of the congregation.

Even as they subordinated women to men in the Mass, the priests also enacted a racialized hierarchy that placed Hispanic, de razón people above Indians. The priests themselves, representing the Catholic Church and the Spanish government, were the only ones able to perform the sacrifice of the Mass. The Indians who watched the priests' performance were unnecessary to the efficacy of the ritual. In the Mass, Indians learned to act as one undifferentiated group: they stood and knelt together and responded in one voice to the priests' cues. In the Mass, Uichase, the son of a Lamchin headman, was no different than the orphaned son of a Yelamu commoner. The unity that the Mass imposed on baptized Indians may have contributed to a growing racialized understanding of Bay Area society that disregarded tribal community and village affiliations in favor of a strong distinction between Hispanic colonists and Indians.

Despite this racialized flattening of identity in the mission, Indians who accepted baptism were as diverse in their motivations as they were in their tribal community and village affiliations. Some Indians, like Otchacaminimac, appear to have accepted baptism and stuck with mission life because they were convinced of the truth of Catholicism. Others found their niche at the mission. For women like Nayomi, the mission offered a way of leaving a husband without suffering the consequences that would normally come with such a move. For the monjas, the mission offered security and sustenance when family structures crumbled. For still others, entering the mission community was a political move: some, like Letchentis, accepted baptism in order to marry and thereby resolve a conflict between villages and tribal communities. Others, like Keqecég and Uichase, may have seen baptism as a means of creating an alliance with the Hispanic tribal community. Still others may have accepted baptism in order to gain access to the priests' material goods, technological expertise, or spiritual power. For the majority of those who accepted baptism at Mission San Francisco, the decision was probably a collective, rather than an individual, one. Families, villages, and tribal communities valued the collectivity over the individual before the Spanish arrived, and the appearance of large groups in the baptismal register suggests that this inclination to prioritize the group over the single person persisted during the Spanish colonial period. Most Indians probably accepted baptism for a combination of these reasons, and perhaps others. Accepting baptism was rarely, if ever, capitulation to Spanish superiority. Instead, it was another strategic move in Indians' ongoing management of the social, political, and economic situations that shaped life in the San Francisco Bay Area.

Just as they differed in their reasons for accepting baptism, Bay Area Indians varied in the ways they treated the Franciscans' religion once they had been baptized. Although one scholar has argued that "the decision to reject mission life could be made a thousand times, but the decision to join a mission community could be made only once," baptized Indians still exhibited a range of attitudes toward the Catholicism the Franciscans preached at Mission San Francisco.[26] Indians at Mission San Francisco did not simply accommodate Catholicism or simply resist it. Instead, some adopted it, some adapted it, and some rejected it—and many did all three in different ways and at different times according to their needs. This religious heterogeneity highlights the resourcefulness of Bay Area Indians in the face of a potentially disastrous colonial situation.

Uichase's story is in many ways a tragic one: when he was born, Gimas and Sotem might reasonably have expected the baby boy to grow up into a respected leader of the Lamchin people, to marry multiple women from several influential families, to father numerous children, and to grow old surrounded by friends and family. The Spanish arrival, with the alterations it caused in the environment, the diseases the colonists introduced, and the political and social changes the Hispanics instigated, made that vision of the future impossible. Having accepted baptism, Uichase did marry multiple women, at least two of whom were from influential families. Instead of marrying them concurrently, however, he married them in succession, the death of each wife occasioning marriage to a new woman. In all, Uichase buried four wives. He also fathered ten children, none of whom lived to see their third birthday. The disease environment that wiped out the next generation of Uichase's family also affected his own generation: of Uichase's four brothers and one sister whose existence is recorded in the Mission San Francisco registers, only one brother might have been alive to mourn Uichase's death. The others had all died at least a quarter-century before him.[27]

In the face of this tragedy, however, Uichase and his family continued to adapt to the Spanish colonial presence in the San Francisco Bay Area and put the resources of Catholicism to work in mitigating the damage the Hispanic colonists caused. Uichase used both marriage and baptism to shore up weakening social and political networks. He and his family moved in and out of the mission to avail themselves of both Catholic and indigenous rituals, food supplies, and other resources. Although the Spanish colonization irrevocably changed the texture of indigenous life in the San Francisco Bay Area, Uichase and his family did not stand idly by. Instead, they, like other Bay Area Indians, used the resources of both traditional cultures and Hispanic Catholicism to make the new world the Spanish introduced into a livable one.

NOTES

INTRODUCTION

1. San Francisco de Asís Mission, *Libro de Casamientos*, vol. 3 of *Libros de Misión* (Berkeley: Library Photographic Service, University of California, 1980), microfilm, marriage entry 117. Unless otherwise noted, all marriage information is drawn from this volume. This and all other translations from Spanish texts are my own, unless otherwise noted.

2. San Francisco de Asís Mission, *Libro de Bautismos*, vol. 1 of *Libros de Misión*, baptismal entry 1967. All baptismal information is drawn from this volume and volume 2 of the same series, unless otherwise noted. Hereafter, baptismal entries will be noted simply as "bapt." with a four-digit entry number.

3. San Francisco de Asís Mission, *Libro de Difuntos*, vol. 5 of *Libros de Misión*, death entry 3396. All death information is drawn from this volume and volume 4 of the same series, unless otherwise noted.

4. For cautionary notes on the use of mission registers, see John R. Johnson, "Mission Registers as Anthropological Questionnaires: Understanding the Limitations of the Data," *American Indian Culture and Research Journal* 12, no. 2 (1988): 9–30.

5. Zephyrin Engelhardt, *San Francisco or Mission Dolores*, The Missions and Missionaries of California (Chicago: Franciscan Herald Press, 1924), 67.

6. One page appears to have been removed from the baptismal register because it held the signature of Father Junípero Serra, the founder and first president of the Alta California missions. As the Catholic Church has taken steps toward canonizing Serra (he was beatified in 1988), his signature has become an increasingly valuable artifact. For one historian's consideration of Serra as a potential saint, see James A. Sandos, "Junípero Serra's Canonization and the Historical Record," *American Historical Review* 93, no. 5 (Dec. 1988): 1253–69.

7. See, for example, Sherburne F. Cook, *The Conflict Between the California Indian and White Civilization* (Berkeley: University of California Press, 1976); Robert H. Jackson, *Indian Population Decline: The Missions of Northwestern New Spain, 1687–1840* (Albuquerque: University of New Mexico Press, 1994).

8. See, especially, Randall Milliken, *A Time of Little Choice: The Disintegration of Tribal Culture in the San Francisco Bay Area, 1769–1810*, Ballena Press Anthropological Papers, no. 43 (Menlo Park, CA: Ballena Press, 1995);

and Steven W. Hackel, *Children of Coyote, Missionaries of Saint Francis: Indian-Spanish Relations in Colonial California, 1769–1850* (Chapel Hill: University of North Carolina Press for the Omohundro Institute of Early American History and Culture, 2005).

9. Randall Milliken and Steven W. Hackel have both used a technique called family reconstitution to make the information scattered throughout the mission registers usable by scholars. For information on family reconstitution, see Milliken, *Time of Little Choice*, 8–9; Hackel, *Children of Coyote*, 453–55. I have used two different databases in my analysis. Randall Milliken generously provided me with a copy of the relevant portions of his database, which I verified and augmented using the Mission San Francisco registers. More recently, the Huntington Library's Early California Population Project database has become publicly available online. This massive project, spearheaded by Hackel, includes information from all the extant mission registers in a searchable format. See the Huntington Library, Early California Population Project Database, 2006, http://www.huntington.org/Information/ECPPlogin.htm (accessed April 2009).

10. Jobócate (Yndalecia), bapt. 2068. Her sister, Geronima, bapt. 2069, was baptized on the same day. Their parents were baptized about five years earlier, at which time the priest who recorded the baptism sounded out their Indian names slightly differently. See Huniacsse (Demetrio), bapt. 1808, and Huihmate (Atanasia), bapt. 1810.

11. Liloté (Maria Francisca), bapt. 0012.

12. Herbert Eugene Bolton, "The Mission as a Frontier Institution in the Spanish-American Colonies," *American Historical Review* 22 (1917): 42–61.

13. This policy was referred to as *reducción* and was common to Spanish, French, and English missionary efforts in the Americas. The French and English manifestations have been treated at length by James Axtell in *The Invasion Within: The Contest of Cultures in Colonial North America*, The Cultural Origins of North America (New York: Oxford University Press, 1985).

14. Maynard J. Geiger, *Franciscan Missionaries in Hispanic California, 1769–1848: A Biographical Dictionary* (San Marino, CA: The Huntington Library, 1969), 239–45.

15. For a development of this theme, see especially James A. Sandos, *Converting California: Indians and Franciscans in the Missions*, Western Americana Series (New Haven, CT: Yale University Press, 2004), 33–54, 69–82.

16. John Leddy Phelan, *The Millennial Kingdom of the Franciscans in the New World*, 2nd ed. (Berkeley: University of California Press, 1970), especially 23–28, 53–68, 86–91.

17. Ibid., 59–68; Sandos, *Converting California*, 36–49.

18. Engelhardt, *San Francisco*, 33; Sandos, *Converting California*, 129.

19. Geiger, *Franciscan Missionaries*, 174–80, 136–42.

20. Engelhardt, *San Francisco*, 39, 46–49.

21. Bolton, "The Mission as a Frontier Institution," 47, 53. While Bolton sees the missions as existing in order to "convert," "civilize," and "exploit" the native populations of the Americas (43), they also served to Christianize the Spanish soldiers and other colonists sponsored by the Spanish government.
22. Jackson, *Indian Population Decline*, 100–101.
23. The exception was Father Lorenzo Morelo, who was apparently born in Haiti. He served at Mission San Francisco from mid-August 1799 until October 1800. Geiger, *Franciscan Missionaries*, 155.
24. Gloria E. Miranda, "Racial and Cultural Dimensions of Gente de Razón Status in Spanish and Mexican California," *Southern California Quarterly* 70, no. 3 (1988): 265.
25. Sandos, *Converting California*, 13.
26. Ibid., 11–12; Engelhardt, *San Francisco*, 136.
27. James J. Rawls, *Indians of California: The Changing Image* (Norman: University of Oklahoma Press, 1984), 67–133, 171–201.
28. Ibid., 175–76. See also Albert L. Hurtado, *Indian Survival on the California Frontier*, Western Americana Series, no. 35 (New Haven, CT: Yale University Press, 1988), 212.
29. Rawls, *Indians of California*, 205.
30. David J. Weber, *The Spanish Frontier in North America*, Western Americana Series (New Haven, CT: Yale University Press, 1992), 263.
31. Milliken, *Time of Little Choice*, 13, 19–20.
32. Alfred L. Kroeber, "The Patwin and Their Neighbors," *University of California Publications in Archaeology and Ethnology* 29, no. 4 (1932): 258.
33. Linda E. Dick-Bissonnette, "Gender and Authority among the Yokoch, Mono, and Miwok of Central California," *Journal of Anthropological Research* 54, no. 1 (Spring 1998): 67; Barbara Voss, personal communication, 19 September 2008. For an account of one Ohlone group's struggle for recognition in the face of Alfred Kroeber's declaration that the Ohlone Indians were "extinct," see Les Field, Alan Leventhal, Dolores Sanchez, and Rosemary Cambra, "A Contemporary Ohlone Tribal Revitalization Movement: A Perspective from the Muwekma Costanoan/Ohlone Indians of the San Francisco Bay Area," *California History* 71, no. 3 (1992): 412–32.
34. Milliken, *Time of Little Choice*, 21, 23–24.
35. Ibid., 28.
36. Ibid., 27.
37. Lowell John Bean and Sylvia Brakke Vane, "California Religious Systems and Their Transformations," in *California Indian Shamanism*, ed. Lowell John Bean, Ballena Press Anthropological Papers, ed. Sylvia Brakke Vane, no. 39 (Menlo Park, CA: Ballena Press, 1992), 34.
38. Milliken, *Time of Little Choice*, 27.
39. On shamans in California, see Bean, *California Indian Shamanism*.

40. Anna H. Gayton, "Yokuts-Mono Chiefs and Shamans," in *Native Californians: A Theoretical Retrospective*, ed. Lowell J. Bean and Thomas C. Blackburn (Ramona, Calif.: Ballena Press, 1976), 196, 222.
41. Bean and Vane, "California Religious Systems and Their Transformations," 39.
42. Ibid., 39, 43.
43. Milliken, *Time of Little Choice*, 28.
44. Ibid., 13–14.
45. Ibid., 179.
46. Ibid., 249.
47. Alan K. Brown has traced the history of both of these terms. See his essay "The European Contact of 1772 and Some Later Documentation," in *The Ohlone Past and Present: Native Americans of the San Francisco Bay Region*, comp. and ed. by Lowell John Bean, Ballena Press Anthropological Papers, no. 42 (Menlo Park, CA: Ballena Press, 1994), 29–31.
48. Minna Hewes and Gordon Hewes, trans. and eds., "Indian Life and Customs at Mission San Luis Rey: A Record of California Mission Life Written by Pablo Tac, an Indian Neophyte (Rome, *ca.* 1835)," *The Americas* 9 (July 1952): 87–106.
49. For Asisara's accounts, see Edward D. Castillo, trans. and ed., "An Indian Account of the Decline and Collapse of Mexico's Hegemony over the Missionized Indians of California," *American Indian Quarterly* 13, no. 4 (Fall 1989): 391–406; Edward D. Castillo, trans. and ed., "The Assassination of Padre Andrés Quintana by the Indians of Mission Santa Cruz in 1812: The Narrative of Lorenzo Asisara," *California History* 68, no. 3 (Fall 1989): 116–25, 150–52; E. L. Williams, "Narrative of a Mission Indian, etc.," in Edward S. Harrison, *History of Santa Cruz County* (San Francisco: Pacific Press, 1892), 45–48. For Librado's account, see Fernando Librado, *Breath of the Sun* (Banning, CA: Malki Museum Press, 1979).
50. Sandos, *Converting California*, 157–58; see also James C. Scott, *Domination and the Arts of Resistance: Hidden Transcripts* (New Haven, CT: Yale University Press, 1990).
51. James A. Sandos, "Christianization among the Chumash: An Ethnohistoric Perspective," *American Indian Quarterly* 15, no. 1 (1991): 75.
52. Drawing on the work of Edouard Glissant, Walter D. Mignolo notes that "imperial expansion ... allowed imperial agencies to inscribe the idea that people without writing were people without history and that people without history were inferior human beings." Mignolo, *The Darker Side of the Renaissance: Literacy, Territoriality, and Colonization* (Ann Arbor: University of Michigan Press, 1995), 127. See also Eric R. Wolf, *Europe and the People Without History* (Berkeley: University of California Press, 1982).
53. Jackson, *Indian Population Decline*, 100–102, 108–16, 172.
54. There is no good English translation for this word. I have seen *en paseo* rendered by scholars as "on pass"; "on vacation"; and once as "on walkabout." The last comes closest to the Spanish meaning, but would confuse most American readers. I have therefore chosen to leave it in Spanish.

CHAPTER 1

1. Pismote (Ysabel María), bapt. 0292.
2. Puyeles (Nicolas de Bari), bapt. 0287, marriage 0055; Au-luté (Beatriz), bapt. 0288.
3. Nayomi (Ana Francisca), bapt. 0272.
4. Fermín Francisco de Lasuén, "Refutation of Charges," Mission of San Carlos of Monterey, 19 June 1801, in *Writings of Fermín Francisco de Lasuén*, trans. and ed. Finbar Kenneally (Washington, DC: Academy of American Franciscan History, 1965), 2:200.
5. Geiger, *Franciscan Missionaries*, 38–40, 174–80. By my count, the pair had been working as missionaries for at least thirty-four years.
6. Herbert Eugene Bolton, trans. and ed., *Font's Complete Diary: A Chronicle of the Founding of San Francisco*. (Berkeley: University of California Press, 1933), 181. Font wrote that the California missionaries used the catechism of "Father Castañi," whom Bolton identified as Bartolomé Castaño.
7. Bartolomé Castaño, *Catecismo breve de lo que precisamente debe saber el cristiano* (Mexico: Imprenta del C. Alejandro Valdés, 1833), Ygnacio del Valle Family Collection, Department of Archives and Special Collections, Charles von der Ahe Library, Loyola Marymount University, Los Angeles, California.
8. Ramón Abella and Juan Sainz de Lucio to Ciriaco Gonzalez Carbajal, Mission San Francisco de Asís, 11 November 1814, question 3, *Preguntas y Respuestas*, Santa Barbara Mission Archive-Library, Santa Barbara, CA (hereafter SBMAL).
9. The missionaries regularly commented that older converts had far less facility with Spanish than did younger ones. See, for example, Abella and Sainz de Lucio to Carbajal, question 3, *Preguntas y Respuestas*.
10. Law 18, Title 1, Book 6, folio 190 of *Recopilación de Leyes de los Reynos de las Indias, Tomo Segundo* (Madrid, 1681), quoted in Maynard J. Geiger and Clement W. Meighan, trans. and eds., *As the Padres Saw Them: California Indian Life and Customs as Reported by the Franciscan Missionaries, 1813–1815*, The Santa Barbara Bicentennial Historical Series, vol. 1 (Santa Barbara, CA: Santa Barbara Mission Archive Library, 1976), 166 n. 49.
11. Abella and Sainz de Lucio to Carbajal, question 11, *Preguntas y Respuestas*.
12. August C. Mahr, ed. and trans., "Extract from Kotzebue's Report," in *The Visit of the "Rurik" to San Francisco in 1816*, Stanford University Publications University Series: History, Economics, and Political Science, vol. 2, no. 2 (Stanford, CA: Stanford University Press, 1932), 59.
13. August C. Mahr, ed. and trans., "Chamisso's Observations," in *Visit of the "Rurik,"* 79.
14. Frederick W. Beechey, *Narrative of a Voyage to the Pacific and Beering's Strait, to Co-operate with the Polar Expeditions* (London: Henry Colburn and Richard Bentley, 1831), microfilm, 359. Zephyrin Engelhardt, a sympathetic historian of the California missions, does not dispute Kotzebue's and Beechey's assertions that the missionaries did not speak the local languages.

See Engelhardt, *The Missions and Missionaries of California*, vol. 2, *Upper California* (San Francisco: James H. Barry, 1912), 156, 190.

15. Alonso de la Peña Montenegro, *Itinerario para parochos de indios* (Madrid: Ioseph Fernandez de Buendia, 1668), 122–23, Bernard J. Flatow Collection of Latin American Cronistas, Wilson Library, University of North Carolina, Chapel Hill.

16. Whether the priests at Mission San Francisco also used interpreters in the confessional is unknown. Priests at other missions prepared booklets for themselves known as *confesionarios*. The confesionarios usually contained the standard confessional questions and a variety of possible answers, as well as selected prayers, in both Spanish and the local indigenous language. For published examples of confesionarios, see Madison S. Beeler, ed. and trans., *The Ventureño Confesionario of José Señán, O.F.M.*, University of California Publications in Linguistics, vol. 47 (Berkeley: University of California Press, 1967) and Harry Kelsey, *The Doctrina and Confesionario of Juan Cortés* (Altadena, CA: Howling Coyote Press, 1979). No confesionario from Mission San Francisco has survived and, given the multiplicity of languages represented at the mission (and the priests' complaints about that linguistic diversity), the possibility that any of the priests might have prepared one seems somewhat remote. Franciscans elsewhere in Spain's North American colonies used interpreters in confessions; see David J. Weber, *The Spanish Frontier in North America*, 110.

17. Abella and Sainz de Lucio to Carbajal, question 35, *Preguntas y Respuestas*.

18. Many religions place little emphasis on the afterlife, so this characteristic should not be taken as an indication that Bay Area religions were somehow "inferior." Theorists of religion suggest that in most cases it is less important for religions to provide definitive answers to questions like "What happens after death?" than to provide assurance that answers to such questions exist or to provide the tools to think through such questions. See Clifford Geertz, "Religion as a Cultural System," in Geertz, *The Interpretation of Cultures* (New York: Basic Books, 1973), 108; Peter Berger, *The Sacred Canopy: Elements of a Sociological Theory of Religion* (New York: Anchor Books, 1967), 26–27; Jonathan Z. Smith, "Map Is Not Territory," in Smith, *Map Is Not Territory* (Chicago: University of Chicago Press, 1993), 289–309. See also Talal Asad's critique of Geertz and others in "The Construction of Religion as an Anthropological Category" in Asad, *Genealogies of Religion: Discipline and Reasons of Power in Christianity and Islam* (Baltimore: Johns Hopkins University Press, 1993), 27–54.

19. Louise M. Burkhart, *The Slippery Earth: Nahua-Christian Moral Dialogue in Sixteenth-Century Mexico* (Tucson: University of Arizona Press, 1989), 39.

20. Francisco Palóu and Pedro Benito Cambón, "Ynforme de la Mis[ió]n de N.S.P. S[a]n Fran[cis]co del Puerto del proprio Nombre, é Ynbentarios formados a ultimos de Diziembre del año 1782," Mission San Francisco de Asís, 31 December 1782, Colección de Documentos para la Historia de México (hereafter Historia), vol. 7, fol. 54v, Archivo General de la Nación, Mexico City (hereafter AGN). Palóu wrote that the monjerío was eight *varas* high. The length of a vara varied from place to place and time to time, but in

California during the Spanish colonial period, it was 32.99 inches. Manuel Carrera Stampa, "The Evolution of Weights and Measures in New Spain," *The Hispanic American Historical Review* 29, no. 1 (1949): 10. I have used this figure to convert all measurements from varas to feet and inches.

21. Diego García and Faustino de Solá, "Ynforme dela Mision de N.S.P.S. Fran[cis]co en el Puerto de su nombre, segun el estado en q[u]e se halla desde el dia prim[er]o de Enero de 1789, hasta el ultimo dia de Diciembre del mismo Año," Mission San Francisco de Asís, 31 December 1789, Historia, vol. 7, fol. 210r, AGN.

22. Chi-uéc (Norberto), bapt. 0037.

23. Ygnacia Barbara, bapt. 0059. Puyeles and Au-luté had at least one other child, Ybon Adriano, bapt. 0236, who had died by the time of their baptisms.

24. Francisco Palóu and Pedro Benito Cambón, "Ynforme . . . año 1782," vol. 7, fol. 54v.

25. Archibald Menzies, "Menzies' California Journal," *California Historical Society Quarterly* 2, no. 4 (1924): 273.

26. Antonio Danti and Martín de Landaeta, "Ynforme del estado dela Mision de N. P[adr]e S[a]n Fran[cis]co en 31 de Diciembre del año de 1793," Mission San Francisco de Asís, 31 December 1793, Historia, vol. 7, fol. 273r, AGN.

27. Martín de Landaeta and José de la Cruz, "Ynforme annual del estado de esta Mision de N.P.S. Francisco en 31 de Dici[embr]e de 1797," Mission San Francisco de Asís, 31 December 1797, Misiones, vol. 2, expediente 6, fol. 102r, AGN.

28. Francisco Palóu, copy of Francisco Palóu and Pedro Benito Cambón, "Ynforme de la Mision de N[uest]ro Ser[áfic]o P[adr]e San Fran[cis]co del Puerto del proprio Nombre, segun el estado en que se halla hoy ultimo de Dizi[embr]e del 1784," Mission San Francisco de Asís, 31 December 1784, copy made 7 January 1784 [*sic*], Historia, vol. 7, fol. 99r, AGN.

29. George Vancouver, *A Voyage of Discovery to the North Pacific Ocean and Round the World, 1791–1795*, ed. W. Kaye Lamb, Works Issued by the Hakluyt Society, Second Series, no. 164 (London: The Hakluyt Society, 1984), 2:712.

30. See, for example, Vancouver, *Voyage of Discovery*, 2:712; Mahr, "Extract from Kotzebue's Report," 61.

31. Palóu and Cambón, "Ynforme . . . año 1782," Historia, vol. 7, fol. 54v.

32. Gerhard Dohrn-van Rossum, *History of the Hour: Clocks and Modern Temporal Orders*, trans. Thomas Dunlap (Chicago: University of Chicago Press, 1996), 209.

33. Dohrn-van Rossum, *History of the Hour*, 198.

34. Palóu and Cambón, "Ynforme . . . año 1782," Historia, vol. 7, fol. 54v. See also, for example, Pedro Benito Cambón and Miguel Giribet, "Ynforme semestre dela Mi[si]on de N.S.P. S[a]n Fran[cis]co en el Puerto de su n[omb]re, seg[ú]n el est[ad]o en q[u]e se halla el dia ultimo de Junio de este pres[en]te año de 1787," Mission San Francisco de Asís, 30 June 1787, Historia, vol. 7, fo1. 133v. Dohrn-van Rossum calls attention to this expression in *History of the Hour*, 198.

35. Anthony Aveni, *Empires of Time: Calendars, Clocks, and Cultures* (New York: Basic Books, 1989), 92. See also Dorhn-van Rossum, *History of the Hour*, 29–43.
36. Abella and Sainz de Lucio to Carbajal, question 16, *Preguntas y Respuestas*.
37. This reference to natural cycles as a means of telling time continued elsewhere in Alta California as well. Linda E. Dick-Bissonnette notes that two different anthropologists found in the first half of the twentieth century that Miwok Indians continued to base their sense of the passage of the year on the growth and harvest of acorns. See Dick-Bissonnette, "Foothill Yokoch, Mono, and Miwok Women: An Anthropological Perspective" (PhD Dissertation, University of California, Santa Barbara, 1997), 98–99, citing B. W. Aginsky, "Culture Element Distributions: XXIV, Central Sierra," *University of California Anthropological Records* 8, no. 4 (1939): 460 and Anna H. Gayton "Yokuts and Western Mono Ethnography," *Anthropological Records* 10, nos. 1–2 (1948): 267.
38. "Memorias de los utensilios que ha dado el Rey para la fundación de las misiones de Monterrey," n.p., n.d., Archivo Histórico de Hacienda (hereafter AHH), vol. 283, expediente 67, AGN. Richard Steven Street claims that one of these bells would have been the work bell, tolling the beginning and ending of work hours. It is entirely possible that one of Mission San Francisco's bells was used in this way, but the priests never made any distinction in function between the two bells. See Street, *Beasts of the Field: A Narrative History of California Farmworkers, 1769–1913* (Stanford, CA: Stanford University Press, 2004), 40.
39. *The Catholic Encyclopedia* (1913; New Advent, 1997), s.v. "Genuflexion," http://www.newadvent.org/cathen/index.html (accessed June 2004).
40. Alfred Robinson reports the segregation of Indians by gender at Mission San Luis Rey in 1829 in *Life in California during a Residence of Several Years in that Territory, Comprising a Description of the Country and the Missionary Establishments* (1846; Reprint, New York: Da Capo Press, 1969), 26. James L. Nolan reports arrangement according to age, but does not document his assertion, in "Anglo-American Myopia and California Mission Art," *Southern California Quarterly* 58, no. 3 (1976): 288. On this point, see also Sandos, *Converting California*, 45. Combining information from the baptismal and death registers yields a total of 105 women and 88 men alive at the end of 1782. Of the women, twenty-five were eighteen years old or older; eighty were younger than eighteen years. (Of the men, twenty-seven were eighteen years or older, while sixty-one were younger than eighteen years.)
41. Kurt Baer suggests that most, if not all, mission churches did have windows, usually set high on the side walls of the buildings. See Baer, *Architecture of the California Missions* (Berkeley: University of California Press, 1958), 51–52. We do not know whether the church Pismote would have entered on 24 December 1782 had any windows, but the Mission San Francisco church built in 1791 still survives and does have windows set high on the side walls, just as Baer describes.
42. Palóu and Cambón, "Ynforme . . . año 1782," Historia, vol. 7, fol. 52v.

43. This description of typical images of St. Francis comes from Norman Neuerburg, *Saints of the California Missions* (Santa Barbara, CA: Bellerophon Books, 2001), n.p.
44. Palóu and Cambón, "Ynforme ... año 1782," Historia, vol. 7, fol. 52v.
45. Junípero Serra to Don Antonio Maria Bucareli y Ursúa, Mexico City, 21 May 1773, in Antonine Tibesar, ed. and trans., *Writings of Junípero Serra*, Publications of the Academy of American Franciscan History Documentary Series, vol. 4 (Washington, D.C.: Academy of American Franciscan History, 1955), 1:358. Although Tibesar translated all of the documents in this four-volume series, he also included the Spanish texts. In this book, all translations from the *Writings of Junípero Serra* are my own.
46. Edward D. Castillo, "Gender Status Decline, Resistance, and Accommodation among Female Neophytes in the Missions of California: A San Gabriel Case Study," *American Indian Culture and Research Journal* 18, no. 1 (1994): 69–70.
47. Edith Wallace, "Sexual Status and Role Differences," in *Handbook of North American Indians*, vol. 8, *California*, ed. Robert F. Heizer (Washington, DC: Smithsonian Institution, 1978), 687.
48. Women appear to have had less autonomy in the missions than outside them, but this may not have been readily apparent on the ground.
49. If all baptismal candidates above age nine are counted as adults, Indian men accepting baptism outnumbered Indian women doing the same in only six years during the Spanish colonial period at Mission San Francisco. Over the entire period under study, nearly 57 percent of adult Indians baptized were women.
50. Palóu and Cambón, "Ynforme ... año 1782," Historia, vol. 7, fol. 52v.
51. James L. Nolan designates St. Michael a "cross-santo" whose proper placement, according to the church design formula that Nolan deduced, would have been on the left-hand side of the church (as one is facing the main altar). While St. Michael's presence in a side altar at all seems to upset Nolan's scheme (which, in the case of a church dedicated to a "cross-santo" like St. Francis, calls for both side altars to be dedicated to "birth-santos"), Palóu also lists St. Michael before Our Lady of Remedies. If Palóu was "reading" the church decorations from left to right, this order would support the placement of St. Michael's altar on the left (Gospel) side of the church. See Nolan, "Anglo-American Myopia," especially 311, 313; Palóu and Cambón, "Ynforme ... año 1782," Historia, vol. 7, fol. 52v.
52. See Neuerburg, *Saints of the California Missions*, n.p.
53. For a more extensive argument about the encoding of gender norms in altarpieces, and the Indians' absorption of those ideas, see Nolan, "Anglo-American Myopia," 18–19, 163, 170–72.
54. Norman Neuerburg, *The Decoration of the California Missions* (Santa Barbara, CA: Bellerophon Books, 1987), 52. The beams of the church have been repainted in this design, using red, ochre, gray, and white. Decoration of the side walls may still be seen in some parts of the church.
55. On the basketry of the San Francisco Bay Area, see Christopher L. Moser, with Craig Bates and Eva Slater, *Native American Basketry of Central*

California (Riverside, CA: Riverside Museum Press, 1986), 69–100; Ralph Shanks, *Indian Baskets of Central California: Art, Culture, and History; Native American Basketry from San Francisco Bay and Monterey Bay North to Mendocino and East to the Sierras*, ed. Lisa Woo Shanks, Indian Baskets of California and Oregon Series, vol. 1 (Novato, CA: Costaño Books in association with Miwok Archaeological Preserve of Marin, 2006), 1–101.

56. Francisco Palóu, "Ynforme del estado de esta Mis[ió]n de N.S.P. S[a]n Fran[cis]co del Puerto del mismo nombre, y de los augmentos que ha tenido desde el 10. de enero hasta el ultimo de Diziembre de 1778," Mission San Francisco de Asís, 31 December 1778, Historia, vol. 7, fol. 42r, AGN.

57. Neuerburg, *Saints of the California Missions*, n.p.

58. Ibid.

59. Au-luté (Beatriz), death 0083.

60. Luis Resines, ed., *Catecismos de Astete y Ripalda* (Madrid: Biblioteca de Autores Cristianos, de La Editorial Católica, 1987), 321. I judge the popularity by the fact that it was the only catechism requested in the annual order of goods from the San Francisco Presidio, and it was requested repeatedly. See, for example, Jose de Arizde, "San Fran[cis]co: Factura de 30 Tercias, Caxones, y Barriles, cuio contenido por menor se expresa en esta que por Decreto del Exc[elentísi]mo señor Virrey de 2 de Junio ultimo remito, a cargo del conductor D[o]n Antonio José Barron, al Abilitado del R[ea]l Presidio de San Fran[cis]co en Californias D[o]n José Arguello, o el que lo fuere, marcados, y numerados como al Margen," Mexico, 25 January 1789, Californias, vol. 27, expediente 14, fol. 191v, AGN, which lists "30 Catechisms of Father Ripalda"; Gervasio Arguello, "Memoria de los Generos y Efectos q[u]e el Cadete D[o]n Gervasio Arguello como Habilitado del referido Presidio [de San Francisco] Considera nesesarios p[ar]a el Surtimiento de su comp[añi]a e Ymbalidos, y Solisita del Ex[celentísi]mo S[eñ]or Virrey de N[ueva] E[spaña] por conduto [al?] inmediato Gefe el S[eñ]or Gov[ernad]or de esta Provincia; y que su remicion sea p[o]r Havilitado G[ene]ral: Capitan D[o]n Manuel Rodriques: para el subcequente [año] de 1811," San Francisco, 30 January 1810, Californias, vol. 53, expediente 19, fol. 301v, AGN, which requests "2 dozen catechisms of Father Ripalda."

61. Malcolm Margolin, *The Ohlone Way: Indian Life in the San Francisco–Monterey Bay Area* (Berkeley, CA: Heyday Books, 1978), 142.

62. Palóu and Cambón, "Ynforme ... año 1782," Historia, vol. 7, fol. 52r.

63. Mission San Francisco was apparently quite well supplied with vestments of various colors. The 1782 inventory lists more than twenty chasubles of various colors. Stoles, when listed in the inventory, are listed along with chasubles. See Palóu and Cambón, "Ynforme ... año 1782," Historia, vol. 7, fol. 52r.

64. *Catholic Encyclopedia*, s.v. "Liturgical colours."

65. The "Spiritual Results" the priests reported are compiled in Engelhardt, *San Francisco*, 270–71.

66. 1 Cor 11:29; Hackel, *Children of Coyote*, 157.

67. Engelhardt, *San Francisco*, 270–71.

68. Hackel, *Children of Coyote*, 157, 161 n. 60.
69. Ibid., 161.
70. Maynard Geiger, "New Data on the Buildings of Mission San Francisco," *California Historical Society Quarterly* 46, no. 3 (1967): 197.
71. By the end of 1783, there were 218 living baptized Indians on Mission San Francisco's rolls, a slight increase over the previous year.
72. Pismote married Ssuíle (Crisanto), bapt. 0315, on 27 May 1784, marriage 0085.
73. Francisco Palóu and Pedro Benito Cambón, "Ynforme del estado de la Mision de N.S.P. S[a]n Francisco del Puerto del proprio Nombre del año 1783," Mission San Francisco de Asís, 31 December 1783, Historia, vol. 7, fol. 55r, AGN.
74. Palóu and Cambón, "Ynforme . . . año 1783," Historia, vol. 7, fol. 55r.
75. Huequés (María de los Remedios), bapt. 0454.
76. Palóu, copy of Palóu and Cambón, "Ynforme . . . 1784," Historia, vol. 7, fol. 98r.
77. Sofía, bapt. 0531.
78. Palóu, copy of Palóu and Cambón, "Ynforme . . . 1784," Historia, vol. 7, fol. 98r.
79. Miranda, "Racial and Cultural Dimensions," 266.
80. Sandos, *Converting California*, 181.
81. Art historian Norman Neuerburg dates this set of paintings to sometime in the 1820s. See Neuerburg, "The Indian Via Crucis from Mission San Fernando: An Historical Exposition," in *Mission San Fernando, Rey de España, 1797–1997: A Bicentennial Tribute*, ed. Doyce B. Nunis Jr. (Los Angeles: Historical Society of Southern California, 1997), 353. The stations are reproduced in this article as well, on 339–46.
82. George Harwood Phillips, "Indian Paintings from Mission San Fernando: An Historical Interpretation," *Journal of California Anthropology* 3 (1976): 98–99.
83. Telempis (Reginaldo), bapt. 0528; Mequeig (Braulio), bapt. 0529; Sofía, bapt. 0531; Heytém (Otilia), bapt. 0530.
84. Malcolm Margolin suggests that women could become leaders of villages and shamans. See Margolin, *Ohlone Way*, 105.
85. The six that are identified in the registers as interpreters are Jacinto, bapt. 0769; Cauanuse (Domiciano), bapt. 1817; Chalietti (Justino), bapt. 2493; Jumle (Geronimo), bapt. 3506; Gilac (Hipolito), bapt. 4439; and Cocos (Alvino José), bapt. 4740. Of these, Jumle is the only one to have been baptized as an adult; he was born in approximately 1784 and baptized in 1808. Many of these men worked as interpreters at missions other than Mission San Francisco: Chalietti and Jumle were interpreters at San Rafael, Gilac at San Francisco Solano, and Cocos at San José.
86. Abella and Sainz de Lucio to Carbajal, question 33, *Preguntas y Respuestas*.
87. Mahr, "Extract from Kotzebue's Report," 59.

88. August C. Mahr, ed. and trans., "Choris' Description of San Francisco," in *Visit of the "Rurik,"* 95, 97.
89. Sandos, *Converting California*, 141.
90. Edith Wallace, "Sexual Status and Role Differences," 688.
91. U.S. Naval Observatory Astronomical Applications Department, "Complete Sun and Moon Data for One Day," http://aa.usno.navy.mil/data/docs/RS_OneDay.php (accessed June 2006).
92. Lasuén, "Refutation of Charges," in *Writings of Lasuén*, 2:200.
93. Martín de Landaeta to Jose Viñals, Mission San Francisco, 28 May 1807, AHH, vol. 281, expediente 13, AGN.
94. Mahr, "Choris' Description of San Francisco," 97.
95. Jean-François de Galaup de la Pérouse, *The Journal of Jean-François de Galaup de la Pérouse, 1785–1788*, vol. 1, trans. and ed. John Dunmore, Works Issued by the Hakluyt Society, Second Series, no. 179 (London: The Hakluyt Society, 1994), 184.
96. Mahr, "Extract from Kotzebue's Report," 61. Choris described the same game: see Mahr, "Choris' Description of San Francisco," 97.

CHAPTER 2

1. Robert M. Denhardt, "The Horse in New Spain and the Borderlands," *Agricultural History* 25, no. 4 (1951): 148–49.
2. Fermín Francisco de Lasuén to Don Pedro Fages, San Carlos Mission, 21 August 1787, in *Writings of Lasuén*, 1:150.
3. Fermín Francisco de Lasuén to Sr. Brigadier Don Jacobo Ugarte y Loyola, San Carlos de Monterey, 20 October 1787, copy of letter made for the Colegio of San Fernando, 30 October 1787, Historia, vol. 6, fol. 330v, AGN.
4. Pedro Benito Cambón and Diego García, "Ynforme de la Mision de N.S.P.S[a]n Fran[cis]co en el Puerto de su n[omb]re seg[ú]n el estado en q[u]e se halla el dia 31 de Dic[iemb]re del año de 1787," Mission San Francisco de Asís, 31 December 1787, Historia, vol. 7, fol. 144r, AGN.
5. Massea (Salvador de Horta), bapt. 0014; Josef Arguello, Report on Indians' reasons for fleeing Mission San Francisco, San Francisco Presidio, 12 August 1797, Californias, vol. 65, expediente 2, fol. 108v, AGN.
6. Gualamuc (Eladio), bapt. 4215; death 4643.
7. Hackel, *Children of Coyote*, 288–96.
8. See, for example, Raymundo Carillo, Monterey, 17 July 1801, Californias, vol. 53, expediente 18, fol. 270r, AGN.
9. Abella and Sainz de Lucio to Carbajal, question 32, *Preguntas y Respuestas*.
10. Abella and Sainz de Lucio to Carbajal, question 26, *Preguntas y Respuestas*.
11. Michael A. Mullett, "Catholic and Quaker Attitudes to Work, Rest, and Play in Seventeenth- and Eighteenth-Century England," in *The Use and Abuse of Time in Christian History*, ed. R. N. Swanson (Suffolk, UK: Boydell Press for The Ecclesiastical History Society, 2002), 198.

12. Louis Bourdaloue, *Chefs-d'oeuvre oratoires de Bourdaloue* (Paris: Garnier Frères, Libraires-Éditeurs, 1910), 393. This and all subsequent translations of Bourdaloue's sermons are my own.
13. Castaño, *Catecismo breve*, 7.
14. Pedro de Calatayud y Florencia, *Tres doctrinas prácticas* (Madrid: Gráficas F. Martinez, 1951), 201.
15. William J. Callahan, *Honor, Commerce and Industry in Eighteenth-Century Spain*, Kress Library of Business and Economics, eds. James P. Baughman and Kenneth E. Carpenter, pub. no. 22 (Soldiers Field, Boston: Baker Library, Harvard Graduate School of Business Administration, 1972), 57–58.
16. Callahan, *Honor, Commerce and Industry*, 56–57.
17. Lorenzo Normante y Carcavilla, *Espíritu del Señor Melon en su ensayo político sobre el comercio* (Zaragoza, 1786), 32, translated and quoted in Callahan, *Honor, Commerce and Industry*, 58.
18. Nicolas de Arriquibar, *Recreacion politica. Reflexiones sobre el amigo de los hombres en su tratado de poblacion, considerado con respecto á nuestros intereses* (Vitoria, Spain: Tomas de Robles y Navarro, 1779), microfilm, 1:46. See also Callahan, *Honor, Commerce and Industry*, 59.
19. Fermín Francisco de Lasuén to José Gasol, Mission Santa Clara, 16 June 1802, California Mission Documents, Document 532, SBMAL.
20. Abella and Sainz de Lucio to Carbajal, question 26, *Preguntas y Respuestas*.
21. Lasuén to Ugarte y Loyola, 20 October 1787, copy, 30 October 1787, Historia, vol. 6, fol. 328r.
22. Carole M. Counihan, *The Anthropology of Food and Body: Gender, Meaning, and Power* (New York: Routledge, 1999), 6–24. I thank my colleague Nora Rubel for her guidance in the literature on foodways.
23. Georg H. von Langsdorff, *Langsdorff's Narrative of the Rezanov Voyage to Nueva California in 1806*, trans. Thomas C. Russell ([1927]; reprint, Fairfield, WA: Ye Galleon Press, 1988), 58.
24. La Pérouse, *Journal*, 183.
25. Shanks, *Indian Baskets of Central California*, 10.
26. La Pérouse, *Journal*, 182.
27. Heizer concludes that "compared to corn meal and wheat flour, acorn meal is in no way inferior as a food." According to his figures, acorn meal is 25.31% fat, 4.5% protein, and 62.0% carbohydrate; corn meal is 1.9% fat, 9.2% protein, and 74.4% carbohydrate; and wheat flour is 1.0% fat, 11.4% protein, and 75.4% carbohydrate. Robert F. Heizer, "Prehistoric Central California: A Problem in Historical-Developmental Classification," *Reports of the University of California Archaeological Survey* 41, no. 66 (1958): 20–21.
28. Rebecca Allen, *Native Americans at Mission Santa Cruz, 1791–1834: Interpreting the Archaeological Record*, Perspectives in California Archaeology, vol. 5 (Los Angeles: Institute of Archaeology, University of California, Los Angeles, 1998), 57.
29. Paul E. Langenwalter and Larry W. McKee, "Vertebrate Faunal Remains from the Neophyte Dormitory," in *Excavations at Mission San Antonio, 1976–1978,*

ed. Robert L. Hoover and Julia G. Costello, monograph 26 (Los Angeles: Institute of Archaeology, University of California, Los Angeles, 1985), 111.

30. Margolin, *Ohlone Way*, 29–32.
31. Richard D. Ambro, *They Danced in the Plaza: The Historical Archaeology of Notre Dame Plaza, Mission San Francisco de Asís (Dolores), 347 Dolores Street, San Francisco, California* (San Francisco: Holman and Associates, 2003), 120.
32. Puyeles (Nicolas de Bari), bapt. 0287, death 0099.
33. Mahr, "Chamisso's Observations," 81.
34. Abella and Sainz de Lucio to Carbajal, question 31, *Preguntas y Respuestas*.
35. Margolin, *Ohlone Way*, 35; see also 89.
36. Pispipuquel (Alejandra), bapt. 4094, death 3069.
37. Se'pente (Priscilla), bapt. 0550, death 0230.
38. Nopete (Deogracias), bapt. 0500, death 4809; Tuglum (Casimira), bapt. 1016.
39. Hackel, *Children of Coyote*, 286. The volume of a fanega varied widely in colonial Mexico, with different sources providing estimates ranging from 1.4 to 7.8 bushels. J. N. Bowman, after reviewing all the evidence, determined that in Alta California "the practical fanega measure" was approximately 1.6 bushels, "with the understanding that there were fluctuations at times from this unit." Bowman, "Weights and Measures of Provincial California," *California Historical Society Quarterly* 30, no. 4 (1951): 318–23.
40. Hackel, *Children of Coyote*, 287.
41. José Arguello to Diego de Borica, San Francisco, 11 December 1798, California Mission Documents, Document 409e, SBMAL.
42. Indian laborers at Mission San Francisco thus resembled workers elsewhere in Bourbon Mexico. Susan Deans-Smith, analyzing workers in tobacco manufactories, writes that "the workers retained some control over the disposal of their time, which enabled them to use their positions in the manufactories to their best advantage." Deans-Smith, *Bureaucrats, Planters, and Workers: The Making of the Tobacco Monopoly in Bourbon Mexico* (Austin: University of Texas Press, 1992), 208.
43. In his posthumously published book *The Lettered City*, Angel Rama discusses the deep concern with order in the Spanish colonization of the Americas and its manifestation in urban planning. See Angel Rama, *The Lettered City*, trans. and ed. John Charles Chasteen (Durham, NC: Duke University Press, 1996), 1–15.
44. Pedro Benito Cambón and Diego García, "Ynforme de lo mas particular acaecido en esta Mi[si]on de N.S.P. S[a]n Fran[cis]co en su Puerto de la Calif[orni]a septentrional desde 10. de Enero del año de 1788 hasta el dia ultimo de Junio de d[ic]ho año," Mission San Francisco de Asís, 1 July 1788, Historia, vol. 7, fol. 176r, AGN.
45. Cambón and García, "Ynforme . . . desde 10. de Enero del año de 1788 hasta el dia ultimo de Junio de d[ic]ho año," 1 July 1788, Historia, vol. 7, fol. 176v.
46. Vancouver, *Voyage of Discovery*, 714.
47. James Early, *Presidio, Mission, and Pueblo: Spanish Architecture and Urbanism*

in the United States (Dallas, TX: Southern Methodist University Press in cooperation with the William P. Clements Center for Southwest Studies, 2004), 8.

48. Barbara Lois Voss, "The Archaeology of El Presidio de San Francisco: Culture Contact, Gender, and Ethnicity in a Spanish-Colonial Military Community" (PhD Dissertation, University of California, Berkeley, 2002), 223.
49. La Pérouse, *Journal*, 179.
50. Geiger, "New Data," 197. On the timing of apartment construction, see 201–2.
51. Antonio Danti and Martín de Landaeta, "Ynforme . . . 1793," Historia, vol. 7, fol. 273r.
52. Landaeta and Cruz, "Ynforme annual . . . 1797," Misiones, vol. 2, expediente 6, fol. 102r.
53. Martín de Landaeta to Tomás de la Peña, Mission San Francisco, 30 October 1801, AHH, vol. 281, expediente 13, AGN.
54. Rama, *The Lettered City*, 5. See also J. H. Parry, *The Cities of the Conquistadores*, Canning House Eighth Annual Lecture, 11 May 1961 (n.p.: Hispanic and Luso-Brazilian Councils, 1961), 4; José Luis Romero, *Latinoamérica: Las ciudades y las ideas*, 3rd ed. (Mexico City: Siglo veintiuno editores, 1984), 56; Early, *Presidio, Mission, and Pueblo*, 8.
55. Allen, *Native Americans at Mission Santa Cruz*, 53.
56. Lasuén, "Refutation of Charges," in *Writings of Lasuén*, 2:206.
57. Allen, *Native Americans at Mission Santa Cruz*, 53.
58. W. B. Sawyer, "Excavation Procedures," in *Excavations at Mission San Antonio, 1976–1978*, ed. Robert L. Hoover and Julia G. Costello, 17, 19.
59. La Pérouse, *Journal*, 178.
60. The church roof was finally tiled in 1795. Martín de Landaeta, "Ynforme del estado de esta Mision de N.P.S. Fran[cis]co en 31 de Diciembre del año de 1795," Mission San Francisco, 20 January 1795, Historia, vol. 7, fol. 306r, AGN.
61. Robert Jütte, *Poverty and Deviance in Early Modern Europe* (Cambridge: University of Cambridge Press, 1994), 68.
62. James Lockhart, *Of Things of the Indies: Essays Old and New in Early Latin American History* (Stanford, CA: Stanford University Press, 1999), 99.
63. Neuerburg, *Decoration of the California Missions*, 27.
64. Mission Dolores Docent Paula Zimmerman stated unequivocally, during a tour of the mission on 16 February 2007, that these designs were exclusively "Ohlonean," that is, that they came from Bay Area Indian aesthetic traditions and had no roots in European decorative traditions.
65. Shanks, *Indian Baskets of Central California*, 6; Edith Wallace, "Sexual Status and Role Differences," 683, 688; James A. Bennyhoff, *Ethnogeography of the Plains Miwok*, Center for Archaeological Research at Davis Publication no. 5 (Davis: University of California, Davis, 1977), 13.
66. Margolin, *Ohlone Way*, 117–18.

67. Bennyhoff, *Ethnogeography of the Plains Miwok*, 13.
68. Ibid., 49.
69. Even if the decorations on the walls were not feminine, it is likely that they were strongly gendered: Linda E. Dick-Bissonnette, citing the work of several other anthropologists, notes that the designs woven into baby baskets differed based on the sex of the child. Dick-Bissonnette, "Foothill Yokoch, Mono, and Miwok Women," 200, 201. Barbara Voss pointed out to me that some basketry designs were associated specifically with women. Barbara Voss, personal communication, 17 February 2007.
70. This fusion might also be seen as a form of protective ingratiation, as discussed by James Sandos. See Sandos, *Converting California*, 6–7.
71. Street, *Beasts of the Field*, 51.
72. La Pérouse, *Journal*, 180.
73. Arguello to Borica, 11 December 1798, California Mission Documents, Doc. 409e.
74. Pedro Benito Cambón and Diego García, "Ynforme dela Mision de N.S.P. S[a]n Fran[cis]co en el Puerto de su Nombre segun el estado en que se halla desde ultimo de Junio de 1788 hasta ultimo de Diciembre del mismo Año," Mission San Francisco de Asís, 31 December 1788, Historia, vol. 7, fol. 171v, AGN.
75. Dick-Bissonnette, "Foothill Yokoch, Mono, and Miwok Women," 34–41.
76. Vancouver, *Voyage of Discovery*, 2:712.
77. On the subject of *recogimiento*, or enclosure, see especially Nancy E. van Deusen's excellent study *Between the Sacred and the Worldly: The Institutional and Cultural Practice of Recogimiento in Colonial Lima* (Stanford, CA: Stanford University Press, 2001).
78. Bennyhoff, *Ethnogeography of the Plains Miwok*, 13.
79. Junípero Serra to Fermín Francisco de Lasuén, Monterey, 12 January 1780, *Writings of Junípero Serra*, 3:420.
80. Arguello, Report on Indians' reasons for fleeing Mission San Francisco, 12 August 1797, Californias, vol. 65, expediente 2, fol. 108v, AGN.
81. Litel (Leonardo), bapt. 4213, death 4966, 16 April 1822.
82. Mission San Francisco de Asís, *Libro de Cuentas* fols. 16r, 22r; on Mission Dolores, *Manuscripts at Mission Dolores*, vol. 1, CD-ROM (2003).
83. Cullniq (Juan Capistrano), bapt. 0045, identified as page in marriage 0683.
84. Jacinto, bapt. 0769, identified as page in marriage 0683. Others identified as pages are Lilac (Alexos), bapt. 6049; Huiubnu (Ciro), bapt. 1694; Cochapuque (Silvestre), bapt. 4599; Guattir (Ortensio), bapt. 0532; Ssapsam (Valentín), bapt. 1290; Regulo, bapt. 3401; Marcos, whose exact identity cannot be discerned from the mission registers; Yuelusia (Macario), bapt. 4210; Pedro Juan, bapt. 3397; and Pispicse (Ysidro), bapt. 2400.
85. On fiscales, see Steven W. Hackel, "The Staff of Leadership: Indian Authority in the Missions of Alta California," *The William and Mary Quarterly*, 3rd ser., 54, no. 2 (1997): 354.
86. Hackel, "Staff of Leadership," 352.

87. Ibid., 360.
88. Antonine Tibesar, ed., in Serra, *Writings of Junípero Serra*, 3:462, n. 258.
89. Hackel, "Staff of Leadership," 354.
90. Antonine Tibesar, ed., in Serra, *Writings of Junípero Serra*, 3:462, n. 258.
91. Hermenegildo Sal to Diego de Borica, San Francisco Presidio, 30 March 1796, Californias, vol. 65, expediente 7, fols. 310v-311r, AGN.
92. Hackel, "Staff of Leadership," 357; Fermín Francisco de Lasuén to Felipe de Neve, San Diego Mission, 25 January 1779, in *Writings of Lasuén*, 1:76.
93. In Spain many municipal governments refused to allow artisans to hold office until 1783. Callahan, *Honor, Commerce and Industry*, 49–50, 52. Steven Hackel discusses the Franciscans' strategies for resisting the election of alcaldes and controlling the outcomes of elections in "The Staff of Leadership," 355–59.
94. Hackel, "Staff of Leadership," 359.
95. Junípero Serra to Fermín Francisco Lasuén, Monterrey, 29 March 1779, *Writings of Junípero Serra*, 3:294.
96. Hackel, "Staff of Leadership," 368–73.
97. Ibid., 367–72.
98. Ibid., 368.
99. Ibid., 368–69, 373.
100. The five are Monózse (Rogerio), bapt. 0350; Uilmoxsi (Pascual Baylon), bapt. 0027; Jojuis (Jorge), bapt. 0298; Tacsinte (Valeriano), bapt. 0442; and Huetlícs (Luis Ramón), bapt. 0031. Although Hermenegildo Sal also identified an alcalde named Juan at Mission San Francisco in the 1790s, multiple Indian men had that baptismal name, so a particular individual is impossible to identify.
101. For this and all other comparisons between the alcaldes and their fellow village or tribal community members, I have relied on Randall Milliken's tribal identifications in his database of the Mission San Francisco registers.
102. Monózse, a Huchiun man, was 29 in 1795, the first year for which there is documentary evidence that he served as an alcalde. Diego de Borica to Marqués de Branciforte, Monterrey, 23 June 1795, Californias, vol. 65, expediente 2, fol. 81r, AGN. In that year the average age of living baptized Huchiun men was 21.5 years. Jojuis, from the independent village of Pruristac, was 39 in 1797, the first year documentary evidence shows that he served as an alcalde. In that year, the average age of living baptized men from Pruristac was 28.8.
103. Huetlícs was very young when he began serving as an Indian official: Hermenegildo Sal identified him as fiscal in 1796 and said that by that time he had served for five years. Sal to Borica, 30 March 1796, Californias, vol. 65, expediente 7, fols. 310v–311v. In 1797, the first year in which documentary evidence indicates that Huetlícs served as an alcalde, he was 26 years old. Arguello, Report on Indians' reasons for fleeing Mission San Francisco, 12 August 1797, Californias, vol. 65, expediente 2, fol. 108v. The average age of living, baptized, Yelamu men that year was 32.2.

104. Hackel, "Staff of Leadership," 369. Hackel notes that "In addition, many alcaldes were related by marriage to soldiers" (369). This was definitely not the case at Mission San Francisco, where marriages between Indian women and Spanish soldiers were decidedly infrequent.
105. Ssojorois (Claudio), bapt. 0463; Sumipocsé (Homobono), bapt. 0504; Guecusia (Timoteo), bapt. 1159; Llucal (Magin), bapt. 1484. Arguello, Report on Indians' reasons for fleeing Mission San Francisco, 12 August 1797, Californias, vol. 65, expediente 2, fols. 108r–108v. Indian names and baptismal numbers are from Milliken, *Time of Little Choice*, 299–303.
106. Hackel, "Staff of Leadership," 362–63.
107. Abella and Sainz de Lucio to Carbajal, question 31, *Preguntas y Respuestas*.
108. Hackel, *Children of Coyote*, 248, citing Julio César, "Recollections of My Youth at San Luis Rey Mission," trans. Nellie Van de Grift Sanchez, *Touring Topics* 23 (1930), 42–43, reprinted in *Native American Perspectives on the Hispanic Colonization of Alta California*, ed. Edward D. Castillo, Spanish Borderlands Sourcebooks, vol. 26 (New York: Garland, 1992).
109. Hackel, *Children of Coyote*, 284.
110. Lasuén, "Refutation of Charges," in *Writings of Lasuén* 2:207.
111. Ibid., 2:208
112. Tapuissé (Diego), bapt. 0034. Tapuissé is identified as a blacksmith in marriage 0237, in which he is named as a witness.
113. Lasuén, "Refutation of Charges," in *Writings of Lasuén* 2:207–8; Hackel, *Children of Coyote*, 284.
114. Miguel Costansó to the Señor Comandante de Artilleria, Mexico, 16 October 1794, Californias, vol. 9, expediente 3, fols. 107v–108r, AGN.
115. The master blacksmith, Pedro García, and the master carpenter, Ciriaco Cayetano, are both named in marriage record 0351.
116. The three carpenters are Mono (Ygnacio), bapt. 1472; Olela (Ligorio), bapt. 3270; and Alalile (Gudelio), bapt. 3695. They all went to Mission San Rafael. The two blacksmiths are Tapuissé (Diego), bapt. 0034; and Caguampais (Pablo), bapt. 3735. Caguampais went to Mission San Francisco Solano.
117. Martín de Landaeta to José Viñals, Mission San Francisco, 30 February 1807, California Mission Letters, 1806–1823, vol. 1, fols. 1r–v, Bancroft Library, University of California, Berkeley. Although Landaeta identifies the Indian in question as "Pablo," no individual in Mission San Francisco's sacramental registers matches both that name and the other identifying information Landaeta provides. "Pablo" may have been a nickname for an individual with a completely unrelated baptismal name.
118. For the equation of the mission labor system and chattel slavery see, for example, Rupert Costo and Jeannette Henry Costo, eds., *The Missions of California: A Legacy of Genocide* (N.p.: Indian Historian Press for the American Indian Historical Society, 1987), 3. Robert Archibald takes a less strident position in "Indian Labor at the California Missions: Slavery or Salvation?" *The Journal of San Diego History* 24, no. 2 (1978): 172–96, in which he concludes, in part, that "The missions were not agents of

intentional enslavement, [but]. . . . The result in many cases was slavery in fact although not in intent" (181).

119. Susan M. Deeds, "Rural Work in Nueva Vizcaya: Forms of Labor Coercion on the Periphery," *Hispanic American Historical Review* 69, no. 3 (1989): 426.

120. A massive historiography on the labor history of Latin America exists. For examples, see Deans-Smith, *Bureaucrats, Planters, and Workers*; Deeds, "Rural Work in Nueva Vizcaya" and "Land Tenure Patterns in Northern New Spain," *The Americas* 41, no. 4 (1985): 446–61; Magnus Mörner, "The Spanish-American Hacienda: A Survey of Recent Research and Debate," *Hispanic American Historical Review* 53, no. 2 (1973): 183–216; Alan Knight, "Mexican Peonage: What Was It and Why Was It?" *Journal of Latin American Studies* 18, no. 1 (1986): 41–74; James Lockhart, "Encomienda and Hacienda: The Evolution of the Great Estate in the Spanish Indies," *Hispanic American Historical Review* 49, no. 3 (1969): 411–29; Ricardo D. Salvatore, "Modes of Labor Control in Cattle-Ranching Economies: California, Southern Brazil, and Argentina, 1820–1860," *Journal of Economic History* 51, no. 2 (1991): 441–51.

121. Lockhart, "Encomienda and Hacienda," 411–29. However, see Sandos's argument that baptized Indians were "spiritual debt peons," *Converting California*, 108.

122. On estate owners' ideal of self-sufficiency, see Lockhart, "Encomienda and Hacienda," 424.

123. On the paternalism of estate owners, see Lockhart, "Encomienda and Hacienda," 422.

124. Abella and Sainz de Lucio to Carbajal, questions 26 and 32, *Preguntas y Respuestas*.

125. Bolton, "The Mission as a Frontier Institution," 47.

126. Miguel Lull to Don Estevan Velez Escalante, 27 February 1815, AHH, vol. 333, expediente 24, fol. 10r, AGN.

127. Baldomero Lopez to Lucas Alaman, Colegio Apostolico de San Fernando, 5 July 1825, AHH, vol. 333, expediente 26, fols. 17–18, AGN.

128. José Arguello, "Cuenta, y Relacion Jurada que Yo D[o]n Jose Arguello como Havilitado dela Compañia de d[ic]ho Presidio formo delos gastos causados en los retechos [de] Guardia, y Quartel, dos Almacenes, Avitaciones del Destacamento de Voluntarios, y quatro Casas de las familias dela Tropa de Cavalleria, verificados en . . . este año de 1801," San Francisco Presidio, 31 December 1801, Californias, vol. 59, expediente 9, fol. 130r, AGN; Sylvia L. Hilton, *La alta California española* (Madrid: MAPFRE, 1992), 281–82. Voss discusses locally produced ceramics found at a pre-1800 San Francisco Presidio archaeological site, though the producers and exact location of production of these artifacts cannot be determined. See Voss, "The Archaeology of El Presidio de San Francisco," 487.

129. The herd sizes that missionaries reported in San Francisco's annual reports are conveniently collected in Engelhardt, *San Francisco*, 283.

130. On legal and illegal trade between the missions, presidios, and ships arriving from outside California, see Robert Archibald, *The Economic Aspects of the*

California Missions (Washington, DC: Academy of American Franciscan History, 1978), 115–41.

131. Fermín Francisco de Lasuén to Pedro Fages, San Carlos Mission, 23 July 1787, in *Writings of Lasuén*, 1:149–50.

132. Ibid., 1:150. A real was worth one-eighth of a peso.

133. Cambón and Giribet, "Ynforme semestre . . . 1787," 30 June 1787, Historia, vol. 7, fol. 132r.

134. Cambón and García, "Ynforme . . . 31 de Diciembre del año de 1787," 31 December 1787, Historia, vol. 7, fol. 143v.

135. On account keeping at the missions and presidios in Alta California, see Archibald, *Economic Aspects of the California Missions*, 63–68.

136. Palóu, copy of Palóu and Cambón, "Ynforme . . . 1784," Historia, vol. 7, fol. 99r; Pedro Benito Cambón and Miguel Giribet, copy of Pedro Benito Cambón and Miguel Giribet, "Ynforme de la Mi[si]on de N.P.S. Fran[cis]co en el Puerto de su n[omb]re, segun el esta[do] en que se halla en ultimo de Dic[iemb]re del año 1786," Mission San Francisco de Asís, 31 December 1786, copy made 2 January 1787, Historia, vol. 7, fol. 117v, AGN.

137. Archibald, *Economic Aspects of the California Missions*, 59.

138. José Arguello, "Relacion Jurada, y Cuenta que Yo D[on] Jose Arguello como Havilitado dela Compañia de d[ic]ho Presidio formo de todas las Cantidades que ha suplido esta Havilitacion en virtud de Superior or[de]n del S[eñ]or Governador D[on] Diego de Borica, y por dispocicion del Yngeniero extrahordinario D[on] Alberto de Cordova, se franquearon desde 26 de Abril de 1797 hasta 31 de Diciembre el mismo para la renovacion dela explanada, y Merlones del Fuerte de San Joaquin, y nueva construccion dela Yerbabuena, segun manifiestan las Partidas siguientes," San Francisco Presidio, 31 December 1797, Californias, vol. 53, expediente 16, fol. 205v, AGN; Martín de Landaeta, Receipt, Mission San Francisco de Asís, 10 October 1797, Californias, vol. 53, expediente 16, fol. 212, AGN.

139. A quarter *almud*, the measure of wheat allotted per Indian per day, works out to about a quart. Bowman, "Weights and Measures of Provincial California," 315; Raymundo Carillo, "Relacion Jurado q[u]e Yo D[o]n Raymundo Carillo, Habilitado del Presidio de S[a]n Fran[cis]co formo delas cantidades q[u] e ha suplido esta Habilitacion en virtud de superior or[de]n del S[eñ] or Governador D[o]n Diego de Borica, y por disposicion del Yngeniero Extraordinario D[o]n Alberto de Cordova, he franqueado desde 26 de Abril hasta 31 de Agosto del precente año enlaforma q[u]e expresan las Partidas Siguientes," [San Francisco Presidio], [1797], Californias, vol. 53, expediente 16, fol. 207r, AGN.

140. Carillo, Monterrey, 17 July 1801, Californias, vol. 53, expediente 18, fol. 270r, AGN.

141. Arguello, "Cuenta, y Relacion Jurada . . . 1801," 31 December 1801, Californias, vol. 59, expediente 9, fols. 131r, 132r.

142. See, for example, entries for 14 August 1808; 30 October 1819; 2 November 1819; 6 November 1819; 15 November 1819; 3 December 1819 in Mission San

Francisco de Asís, *Libro de Cuentas,* on Mission Dolores, *Manuscripts at Mission Dolores.*

143. Mission San Francisco de Asís, *Libro de Cuentas,* fol. 1v, on Mission Dolores, *Manuscripts at Mission Dolores.*
144. Hilton, *La alta California española,* 266.
145. Hackel, *Children of Coyote,* 316.
146. Isidro Alonso Salazar, copy of Isidro Alonso Salazar to Marqués de Branciforte, Colegio de San Fernando de México, 11 May 1796, Historia, vol. 20, expediente 21, fol. 180r, AGN.
147. Josef Arguello, "Comp[añi]a del R[ea]l Presidio de S[a]n Fran[cis]co: Estado de la fuerza efectiba que tiene d[ic]ha compañia hoy dia de la f[ec]ha sus [illegible] existencias faltas y nobedades ocurridas en Sep[tiem]bre de 1799," San Francisco Presidio, 1 October 1799, Californias, vol. 9, expediente 12, fol. 477v, AGN.
148. Ruth Pike, *Penal Servitude in Early Modern Spain* (Madison: University of Wisconsin Press, 1983).
149. Fermín Francisco de Lasuén to Don Pedro Fages, San Carlos Mission, 6 September 1787, in *Writings of Lasuén,* 1:152.
150. Fermín Francisco de Lasuén to Jacobo Ugarte y Loyola, San Carlos Mission, 20 October 1787, in *Writings of Lasuén,* 1:168.
151. On baptized Indians working informally at presidios, see Hackel, *Children of Coyote,* 308–9.
152. Testimony of Raymundo Carillo, Investigation into Indians' reasons for fleeing Mission San Francisco, Presidio of San Francisco, 12 September 1796, Californias, vol. 65, expediente 2bis, fol. 114r, AGN.
153. Tujulalis (Aurelio), bapt. 0812.
154. "Causa Criminal formada contra Aurelio Yndio Neofito dela Micion [*sic*] de San Fran[cis]co por omicidio y Estrupo ejecutado contra niña Guadalupe Galindo de edad de ocho años enla mañana del 9 de Mayo de d[ic]ho Año," Californias, vol. 59, AGN.
155. "Causa Criminal," testimony of Aurelio, 9 May 1805, Californias, vol. 59, fol. 10v.
156. "Causa Criminal," testimony of Ramón Linares, 13 May 1806, Californias, vol. 59, fol. 24v.
157. "Causa Criminal," testimony of José Galindo, 14 May 1806, Californias, vol. 59, fol. 27r.
158. Juan Amoros to Pablo Vicente Sola, San Francisco, 9 September 1816, California Mission Documents, Document 1266, SBMAL.
159. Pedro Fages, "Resumen General que demuestra el Ventajoso Estado en que se hallan los Nuevos establecimientos de la California Septentrional, y expresa los Presidios, Misiones, y Pueblos de que se compone: El Numero de sus Avitantes de ambos sexos inclusos los Parbulos; Cabezas de toda espesie de Ganados que poseen, y fanegas de todos granos que ultimamente cosecharon; y por nota lo demas concerniente al caval conocimiento de

su estado hasta fin del Año de 1790," Monterey Presidio, 20 May 1791, Californias, vol. 46, expediente 10, fol. 180r, AGN.

160. George Harwood Phillips, "Indians in Los Angeles, 1781–1875: Economic Integration, Social Disintegration," *Pacific Historical Review* 49, no. 3 (1980): 437, 442–51.

CHAPTER 3

1. Keqecég (Marcial), bapt. 0517; Keqecég was married to Puichon woman Sappím (Berengaria), bapt. 0646, and Ssalson woman Attiom (Candida), bapt. 0515. Two of his daughters were married to Jaluntis: Guasnete (Servanda), bapt. 0647, and Najam (María Elena), bapt. 0483.
2. Florence Shipek, "California Indian Reactions to the Franciscans," *The Americas* 41, no. 4 (1985): 487–88.
3. Lowell John Bean, "Social Organization," in *Handbook of North American Indians*, vol. 8, *California*, ed. Heizer, 677.
4. Guasnete (Servanda), bapt. 0647; Najam (María Elena), bapt. 0483.
5. Samisi (Adriano Conde), bapt. 0173.
6. Richard L. Levy, "Costanoan," in *Handbook of North American Indians*, vol. 8, *California*, ed. Heizer, 488.
7. Keqecég's known wives were Sappím (Berengaria), bapt. 0646; Attiom (Cándida), bapt. 0515; and a Ssalson woman named Ulpite who was dead by the time Keqecég accepted baptism. The baptismal entry for one of Keqecég's sons (Tapius [Bernardino], bapt. 0181) indicates that Tapius's mother was dead, but does not give her name. This woman may have been Ulpite, or she may have been a different woman.
8. Edith Wallace, "Sexual Status and Role Differences," 684.
9. I thank Michael D. Green for this insight. On moieties in California, see Edward W. Gifford, "Miwok Moieties," *University of California Publications in American Archaeology and Ethnology* 12, no. 4 (1916): 139–94.
10. William J. Wallace, "Southern Valley Yokuts," in *Handbook of North American Indians*, vol. 8, *California*, ed. Heizer, 453. Gifford notes that the Central Sierra Miwok Indians did not follow moiety exogamy rules strictly. See Gifford, "Miwok Moieties," 141–42.
11. Olavú (Formerio), bapt. 3078; Esupame (Formeria), bapt. 3080; marriage number 0950.
12. Eyume (Erasma), bapt. 3067; Mayunucse (Sebastiana), bapt. 3068.
13. Richard L. Levy, "Eastern Miwok," in *Handbook of North American Indians*, vol. 8, *California*, ed. Heizer, 411.
14. Levy, "Costanoan," 487–88. Keqecég's sons were Tapius (Bernardino), bapt. 0181 and Tiglis (Gerardo), bapt. 0507. Keqecég may have had additional sons who did not accept baptism and who therefore were not recorded in the mission registers.
15. Victoria D. Patterson, "Evolving Gender Roles in Pomo Society," in *Women and Power in Native North America*, ed. Laura F. Klein and

Lillian A. Ackerman (Norman: University of Oklahoma Press, 1995), 133; Dick-Bissonnette, "Foothill Yokoch, Mono, and Miwok Women," 126–31.
16. Dick-Bissonnette, "Foothill Yokoch, Mono, and Miwok Women," 174–77, 188–89.
17. Patterson, "Evolving Gender Roles," 133–34.
18. Dick-Bissonnette, "Foothill Yokoch, Mono, and Miwok Women," 297.
19. Quoted in Ramón A. Gutiérrez, "Family Structures: The Spanish Borderlands," in *Encyclopedia of the North American Colonies*, ed. Jacob Ernest Cooke (New York: Charles Scibner's Sons, 1993), 2:673.
20. See Richard J. Boyer, *Lives of the Bigamists: Marriage, Family and Community in Colonial Mexico* (Albuquerque: University of New Mexico Press, 1995).
21. On honor and the shifting emphases on its various constituent elements, see Patricia Seed, *To Love, Honor, and Obey in Colonial Mexico: Conflicts over Marriage Choice, 1574–1821* (Stanford, CA: Stanford University Press, 1988), 61–74, 136–57.
22. For a general discussion of ascribed and achieved honor, see Ramón A. Gutiérrez, *When Jesus Came, the Corn Mothers Went Away: Marriage, Sexuality, and Power in New Mexico, 1500–1846* (Stanford, CA: Stanford University Press, 1991), 176–226; Seed, *To Love, Honor, and Obey*, 61–74.
23. See Asunción Lavrin, "In Search of the Colonial Woman in Mexico: The Seventeenth and Eighteenth Centuries," in *Latin American Women: Historical Perspectives*, ed. Asunción Lavrin (Westport, CT: Greenwood Press, 1978), 24–29. Note, however, that these gender ideals were not universally accepted. On the variation and contestation of gender codes in late colonial Mexico, see Steve J. Stern, *The Secret History of Gender: Women, Men, and Power in Late Colonial Mexico* (Chapel Hill: University of North Carolina Press, 1995).
24. Laura A. Lewis, "The 'Weakness' of Women and the Feminization of the Indian in Colonial Mexico," *Colonial Latin American Review* 5, no. 1 (1996): 76–77.
25. Van Deusen, *Between the Sacred and the Worldly*.
26. Lavrin, "In Search of the Colonial Woman in Mexico," 30.
27. Antonia I. Castañeda, "Engendering the History of Alta California, 1769–1848: Gender, Sexuality, and the Family," in *Contested Eden: California Before the Gold Rush*, ed. Ramón A. Gutiérrez and Richard J. Orsi (Berkeley: University of California Press, 1998), 232.
28. Ramón A. Gutiérrez, "Sexual Mores and Behavior: The Spanish Borderlands," in Cooke, *Encyclopedia of the North American Colonies*, 2:704, 705.
29. On gracias al sacar, see Ann Twinam, "Honor, Sexuality, and Illegitimacy in Colonial Spanish America," in *Sexuality and Marriage in Colonial Latin America*, ed. Asunción Lavrin (Lincoln: University of Nebraska Press, 1989), 118–55.
30. William Taylor, *Magistrates of the Sacred: Priests and Parishioners in 18th-Century Mexico* (Stanford, CA: Stanford University Press, 1996), 185.
31. Asisara made these accusations in an interview with Thomas Savage, a

historian working for Hubert Howe Bancroft. See Castillo, trans. and ed., "An Indian Account," 394–95, 399.

32. Castillo, "An Indian Account," 399.
33. Ibid.
34. Virginia Marie Bouvier, *Women and the Conquest of California, 1542–1840: Codes of Silence* (Tucson: University of Arizona Press, 2001), 135.
35. Taylor, *Magistrates of the Sacred*, 188. See also Sandos, *Converting California*, 12.
36. Francisco Palóu, "Palóu's Diary of the Expedition to San Francisco Bay, 1774," in *Anza's California Expeditions*, vol. 2, *Opening a Land Route to California: Diaries of Anza, Díaz, Garcés, and Palóu*, ed. and trans. Herbert Bolton (Berkeley: University of California Press, 1930), 418.
37. Taylor, *Magistrates of the Sacred*, 162, quoting *Concilios provinciales primero, y segundo, celebrados en la muy noble, y muy leal ciudad de México* ... (1769), 390. On priests as father figures, see Taylor, *Magistrates of the Sacred*, 151–79.
38. Abella and Sainz de Lucio to Carbajal, question 4, *Preguntas y Respuestas*.
39. Excerpts from the responses of missionaries at Missions San Miguel and San Antonio to an 1812 questionnaire sent to all of the missions, as translated and published in Geiger and Meighan, eds., *As the Padres Saw Them*, 25.
40. Abella and Sainz de Lucio to Carbajal, question 32, *Preguntas y Respuestas*.
41. Abella and Sainz de Lucio to Carbajal, question 7, *Preguntas y Respuestas*.
42. Bouvier, *Women and the Conquest of California*, 92. Bouvier asserts that "evangelization stratagems included capturing indigenous women and children in order to attract their parents or spouses" (90–91). Randall Milliken's demographic profile of Indians baptized at Mission San Francisco, however, gives lie to the notion that missionaries "captured" children to lure their parents into the mission. See Milliken, *Time of Little Choice*, 82.
43. Abella and Sainz de Lucio to Carbajal, question 13, *Preguntas y Respuestas*.
44. Abella and Sainz de Lucio to Carbajal, question 12, *Preguntas y Respuestas*.
45. Robert H. Jackson and Edward D. Castillo, *Indians, Franciscans, and Spanish Colonization: The Impact of the Mission System on California Indians* (Albuquerque: University of New Mexico Press, 1995), 90.
46. Ibid.
47. Junípero Serra to Don Antonio Maria Bucareli y Ursúa, Colegio Apostólico *de propaganda fide* de San Fernando, México, 11 June 1773, in *Writings of Junípero Serra*, 1:382.
48. Serra to Bucareli y Ursúa, Mexico City, 21 May 1773, in *Writings of Junípero Serra*, 1:362.
49. Antonia I. Castañeda, "Sexual Violence in the Politics and Policies of Conquest: Amerindian Women and the Spanish Conquest of Alta California," in *Building with Our Hands: New Directions in Chicana Studies*, ed. Adela de la Torre and Beatríz M. Pesquera (Berkeley: University of California Press, 1993), 25.
50. Francisco Palóu, *Noticias de la Nueva California* (San Francisco: Imprenta de Edouardo Bosqui y Cia., 1874), 322–23. Though Palóu's account was

first published, posthumously, in 1857 in Mexico's "Diario Oficial," I first ran across it in Francisco Palóu, "Palóu's Account of the Founding of San Francisco, 1776," translated by Herbert Eugene Bolton, in Bolton, ed., *Anza's California Expeditions*, vol. 3, *The San Francisco Colony* (New York: Russell and Russell, 1966), 402–3. Where the Spanish is ambiguous, I have followed Bolton's translation. I am also grateful to Professors Kevin Larsen and Carlos Mellizo, both of the University of Wyoming, for their assistance in some difficult translation questions.

51. Stern, *Secret History of Gender*, 184. For a general discussion of vengeance and masculinity, see Stern, *Secret History of Gender*, 184–87.
52. Lasuén, "Refutation of Charges," *Writings of Lasuén*, 2:216. Conflict between the Franciscans and the Spanish military over control of the Indians and their labor was hardly unusual. Such disputes had erupted repeatedly throughout the Spanish colonization of North America. See, for example, Weber, *Spanish Frontier in North America*, 129–33.
53. Jackson and Castillo, *Indians, Franciscans, and Spanish Colonization*, 48–49.
54. Langsdorff, *Langsdorff's Narrative*, 49.
55. Ibid., 50.
56. Ibid., 49. On female monjerío supervisors, see Bouvier, *Women and the Conquest of California*, 84. Though other California missions clearly employed women in this capacity, there is no evidence to indicate that Mission San Francisco did so.
57. Langsdorff, *Langsdorff's Narrative*, 49–50.
58. Bouvier, *Women and the Conquest of California*, 132–33; Florence Shipek, *Delfina Cuero: Her Autobiography, an Account of Her Last Years and Her Ethnobotanic Contributions* (Menlo Park, CA: Ballena Press, 1991), 43–44.
59. Abella and Sainz de Lucio to Carbajal, question 12, *Preguntas and Respuestas*.
60. Lonsom (Maria Coloma), bapt. 0200.
61. Quéyeme (Rafaela Marcela), bapt. 0083. Her marriage to Huetlícs (Luis Ramón), bapt. 0031, was her second. It is marriage number 0088.
62. Langsdorff, *Langsdorff's Narrative*, 51.
63. Gutiérrez, "Family Structures," 2:675, 676.
64. Sandos, "Christianization among the Chumash," 75.
65. Sappím married Asúlis (Juan Regis), bapt. 0610, on 10 October 1787, marriage 0166.
66. For Franciscans seeking parental approval, see marriage entries 1829–41.
67. See Seed, *To Love, Honor, and Obey in Colonial Mexico*, 200–204.
68. Francisco Palóu, *Evangelista del Mar Pacífico: Fray Junípero Serra, padre y fundador de la Alta California* (1787; reprint, Madrid: Impresiones Gráficas, 1944), 208.
69. See marriages 1646, 1762, and 1793.
70. Sutay (Lugardo), bapt. 5632; Lalle (Constantina), bapt. 5655; marriage 1762.

71. Ochacuela (Ybona), bapt. 5625; Ochacagoita (Antonia Abad), bapt. 5555; Putec (Rufino), bapt. 5551.
72. Uiumpi (Lugarda), bapt. 5643; marriage 1719.
73. Clara, bapt. 2268; Tolepa (Senen), bapt. 2788; their marriage is 1793. Huyunjaquisto (Pedro Crisólogo), bapt. 3778, had married Clara in marriage 1725.
74. See marriage entries 1568–69.
75. Ramón Abella, marriage entry 1793, 8 December 1818.
76. Ramón Abella, marriage entry 1646, 30 July 1816. See also Abella, marriage entry 1793, 8 December 1818.
77. Robert K. Creasy and Robert Resnik, eds., *Maternal-Fetal Medicine*, 4th ed. (Philadelphia: Saunders, 1999), 498–99, 1153–54.
78. Tubssúpa (Geminiano), bapt. 0399, and Jaiguete (Sebastiana), bapt. 0745, were married on 25 June 1789, in marriage 0194. Their daughter Braulia, bapt. 0766, was born on 6 December 1789 and died on 14 December 1789, death entry 0303.
79. Daisy Rípodas Ardanaz, *El matrimonio en Indias: Realidad social y regulación jurídica* (Buenos Aires: Fundación para la Educación, la Ciencia, y la Cultura, 1977), 196, 199.
80. Lulume (Monica), bapt. 1111; Punacche (Gervasio), bapt. 1149; marriage 0282.
81. Sumay (Amador), bapt. 2174; Ssagnemaien (Matea), bapt. 2498; marriage 0756.
82. Nayomi (Ana Francisca), bapt. 0272. Her sisters were Au-luté (Beatriz), bapt. 0288, and Pismote (Ysabel María), bapt. 0292; their husband was Puyeles (Nicolas de Bari), bapt. 0287.
83. Yapis (Raymundo), bapt. 0043; he was a witness in a large number of weddings. He married Nayomi in marriage 0049, 29 July 1782.
84. Bean, "Social Organization," 677.
85. Abella and Sainz de Lucio to Carbajal, question 4, *Preguntas y Respuestas*. Linda E. Dick-Bissonnette provides evidence that this custom was not limited to Bay Area Indians: a Wukchumni (Foothills Miwok) elder told her in 1994, "Before my grandparents' time, the couple would live with the wife's family for a year. . . . If any children were born (during that time) they'd go to the mother." This evidence raises the possibility that Bay Area Indians may not have been strictly patrilocal. Dick-Bissonnette, "Foothill Yokoch, Mono, and Miwok Women," 285.
86. Gualson (Salvia), bapt. 1280; Chiguilete (Leoncio), bapt. 1135; Ferenbe (Aquilino), bapt. 1113; Chasinte was not baptized, but had two children with Gualson, Tilicsse (Nicolas Factor), bapt. 1275, and Lauion (Salomea), bapt. 1277.
87. Milliken, *Time of Little Choice*, 178.
88. Eighteen is a somewhat arbitrary age floor for this analysis, but allows certainty that all the individuals in the sample were eligible for marriage.

CHAPTER 4

1. Herbert Eugene Bolton, trans. and ed., *Historical Memoirs of New California by Fray Francisco Palóu, O.F.M.*, vol. 4 (New York: Russell and Russell, 1966), 135. Milliken notes that the hostilities between the two groups may have been provoked by the missionaries' decision to locate the mission in Yelamu territory—the Ssalsons may have been trying to ensure their own unrestricted access to the newcomers or to help the Spanish secure their position in the area. Alternatively, the conflict may have been completely unrelated to the arrival of the colonists. It may also be that the arrival of Hispanic colonists inflamed an already-existing conflict between the Yelamu and Ssalson Indians. See Milliken, *Time of Little Choice*, 63.
2. Keqecég may or may not have been the village headman at this time; a decade later, when he accepted baptism at Mission San Francisco, his baptismal entry (number 0517) indicates that he was a *capitán* (headman).
3. Francisco Palóu and Pedro Benito Cambón, "Ynforme de la Mision de N.S. P[adr]e S[a]n Francisco del Puerto de el proprio nombre desde su Fundacion hasta el año de 1781 inclusive," Mission San Francisco de Asís, 30 December 1783, Historia, vol. 7, fol. 50r, AGN.
4. On Aquinas, see Sergio Ortega Noriega, "Un sueño totalitario y universalista: El discurso teológico de Santo Tomás de Aquino sobre el matrimonio, la familia y los compartamientos sexuales" in *El placer de pecar y el afán de normar*, by Seminario de Historia de las Mentalidades y Religión en México Colonial (Mexico City: Editorial Joaquín Mortiz, 1988); on divorce, see Asunción Lavrin, "Introduction: The Scenario, the Actors, and the Issues," in Lavrin, *Sexuality and Marriage in Colonial Latin America*, 43, n. 55.
5. Antonia I. Castañeda, "Marriage: The Spanish Borderlands," in Cooke, *Encyclopedia of the North American Colonies*, 2:736.
6. Ibid.
7. Real Pragmática, quoted in Castañeda, "Marriage: The Spanish Borderlands," 2:736.
8. Ramón A. Gutiérrez, *When Jesus Came, the Corn Mothers Went Away*, 233.
9. Seed, *To Love, Honor, and Obey in Colonial Mexico*, 223.
10. Ibid., 224.
11. Langsdorff, *Langsdorff's Narrative*, 85–86. Much has been written about the romance between Doña Concepción and Count Rezanov (though it never resulted in the marriage for which Rezanov had hoped). See, for example, Hubert Howe Bancroft, *History of California*, vol. 2, *1801–1824*, *The Works of Hubert Howe Bancroft*, vol. 19 (San Francisco: A. L. Bancroft and Company, 1885), 72–78; Robert Kirsch and William S. Murphy, *West of the West: The Story of California From the Conquistadores to the Great Earthquake as Described by the Men and Women Who Were There* (New York: E. P. Dutton and Co., 1967), 221–23.
12. Langsdorff, *Langsdorff's Narrative*, 86.
13. Ramón A. Gutiérrez, *When Jesus Came, the Corn Mothers Went Away*, 329–30.
14. Castañeda, "Marriage: The Spanish Borderlands," 2:731.

15. Seed, *To Love, Honor, and Obey in Colonial Mexico*, 134.
16. *Breve instrucción a los christianos casados y utiles advertencias a los que pretenden serlo*, 4th ed. (Mexico City: Herederos del Lic. Don Joseph de Jauregui, 1791), microfilm, 14.
17. The following description of the engagement and wedding process is based on Ramón A. Gutiérrez's work on New Mexico. It is logical to believe that the process in Alta California was substantially similar. See Gutiérrez, *When Jesus Came, the Corn Mothers Went Away*, 260–63.
18. Castañeda, "Marriage: The Spanish Borderlands," 2:735.
19. Seed, *To Love, Honor, and Obey in Colonial Mexico*, 84.
20. On impediments, see Seed, *To Love, Honor, and Obey in Colonial Mexico*, 84–91; Ramón A. Gutiérrez, *When Jesus Came, the Corn Mothers Went Away*, 243–48; and John P. Beal, James A. Coriden, and Thomas J. Green, *New Commentary on the Code of Canon Law* (New York: Paulist Press, 2000). Gutiérrez uses slightly different terminology; his "dire" impediments correspond to what I call "diriment" impediments, following Beal, Coriden and Green.
21. John A. Hardon, *Modern Catholic Dictionary* (Garden City, NY: Doubleday and Company, Inc., 1980), s.v. "Veil, Bridal"; *Catholic Encyclopedia*, s.v. "Marriage, ritual of." The most extensive discussion of veiling is in René Metz, *Le consécration des vierges dans l'église romaine* (Paris: Presses Universitaires de France, 1954). I am indebted to Rabia Gregory for bringing this source to my attention. Metz traces the history of veiling in the Catholic Church back to pre-Christian times, but he does not specifically discuss the practice of veiling in eighteenth- and nineteenth-century Spain or North America. In describing the ritual, he also omits the bridal couple's prostration before the altar. See Metz, *Le consécration des vierges*, 362–408.
22. Abella and Sainz de Lucio to Carbajal, question 14, *Preguntas y Respuestas*.
23. Ibid.
24. Robert F. Heizer, "Trade and Trails" in *Handbook of North American Indians*, vol. 8, *California*, ed. Heizer, 691–92.
25. Edith Wallace, "Sexual Status and Role Differences," 686.
26. Francisco Palóu, *Palóu's Life of Fray Junípero Serra*, trans. and ed. Maynard Geiger (Washington, DC: Academy of American Franciscan History, 1955), 199.
27. Palóu adds that these informants included a value judgment in their comments, saying that the behavior of the man in question was a "bad thing." Whether the speakers actually expressed that judgment, and if so whether they believed it, are open questions. See Palóu, *Evangelista del Mar Pacifico*, 211–12.
28. Ibid.
29. On third and fourth genders among Native Americans more generally, see Walter L. Williams, *The Spirit and the Flesh: Sexual Diversity in American Indian Culture* (Boston: Beacon Press, 1986).
30. Will Roscoe, "How to Become a Berdache: Toward a Unified Analysis of

Gender Diversity," in *Third Sex, Third Gender: Beyond Sexual Dimorphism in Culture and History*, ed. Gilbert Herdt (New York: Zone Books, 1994), 332.

31. Sandra E. Hollimon, "The Third Gender in Native California: Two-Spirit Undertakers Among the Chumash and Their Neighbors," in *Women in Prehistory: North America and Mesoamerica*, ed. Cheryl Claassen and Rosemary A. Joyce (Philadelphia: University of Pennsylvania Press, 1997).

32. Anthony Pagden, *The Fall of Natural Man: The American Indian and the Origins of Comparative Ethnology* (Cambridge: Cambridge University Press, 1982), 42, 44; Lewis, "The 'Weakness' of Women and the Feminization of the Indian in Colonial Mexico," 73–74.

33. Palóu, *Evangelista del Mar Pacifico*, 208.

34. Magín Catalá and José Viader, "Respuestas que los P[adre]s Min[is]tros de la M[isió]n de Sta. Clara de la Alta California dan al interrogatorio del Govierno, comunicado por el Yll[ustrísi]mo Sr. Obispo de Sonora, ÿ circulado por el R. P. Pre[sidente] de estas M[isione]s y Vicario Foraneo de este distrito Fr. Jose Señan," Mission Santa Clara, 4 November 1814, *Preguntas y Respuestas*, SBMAL.

35. Lockhart, *Of Things of the Indies*, 99.

36. Catalá and Viader, "Respuestas que los P[adre]s," 4 November 1814, *Preguntas y Respuestas*.

37. Letchentis's sister was Tanam (María de los Remedios), bapt. 0082; the Yelamu man she married was Momósa (Jacome de la Marca), bapt. 0065; marriage 0028.

38. Langsdorff, *Langsdorff's Narrative*, 104.

39. Tolomucse (Zacarias), bapt. 0962; María Soledad, bapt. 0102; marriage 0252.

40. Marriage 0508.

41. Lasuén, "Refutation of Charges," in *Writings of Lasuén*, 2:212.

42. Abella and Sainz de Lucio to Carbajal, question 2, *Preguntas y Respuestas*.

43. Bouvier, *Women and the Conquest of California*, 75–76.

44. Langsdorff, *Langsdorff's Narrative*, 104.

45. Castañeda, "Engendering the History of Alta California," 241. José Manuel Valencia, Ygnacio Higuera, José Antonio Aguilar, and Felipe Garcia, the grooms in marriages 0102, 0508, 1047, and 1506, were all soldiers. José Anacleto Barbosa, the groom in marriage 0999, was most likely a soldier as well.

46. Bolton, trans. and ed., *Historical Memoirs of New California*, 3:33–34.

47. The marriages were the following: 0014 (Diego Olvera and Ubiumis [Josefa María], bapt. 0063), 4 April 1779; 0015 (Raymundo Morante and Puruem [María Ynes], bapt. 0077), 9 April 1779; 0016 (Cipriano Agraz and Jojcóte [María Rosa Viterbo], bapt. 0061), 25 April 1779; 0017 (Joaquín Fabian and Ssoyóte [Ana María], bapt. 0022), 18 May 1779; 0048 (Joaquín Fabian and Uxsisté [Manuela María], bapt. 0055), 22 July 1782; 0065 (Joseph Ramos and Xilaite [Francisca Xaviera], bapt. 0095), 31 October 1783; 0075 (Joaquín Fabian and Acsim [María Petra], bapt. 0267), 18 April 1784; 0102 (José Manuel Valencia and Jojcóte [María Rosa Viterbo], bapt. 0061), 15 January 1786; 0327

(Raymundo Morante and Moquim [María Antonia], bapt. 1222), 1 April 1793; 0508 (Ygnacio Higuera and María Soledad, bapt. 0102), 28 June 1795; 0555 (Raymundo Morante and María Serafina, bapt. 0105), 18 April 1797; 0596 (Raymundo Morante and Tocsem [Luparia], bapt. 0880), 14 April 1799; 0999 (José Anacleto Barbosa and María Soledad, bapt. 0102), 6 November 1805; and 1047 (José Antonio Aguilar and María Soledad, bapt. 0102), 29 September 1806.

48. Ssoyóte (Ana María), bapt 0022; Jojcóte (María Rosa Viterbo), bapt. 0061; Xilaite (Francisca Xaviera), bapt. 0095; and Acsim (María Petra), bapt. 0267, all had polygynous fathers.

49. Ubiumis's mother was Tocióm (Feliciana), bapt. 0311; she was married to Chigué (Felix Cantalicio), bapt. 0310, with whom she had at least two children, including Jojcóte (María Rosa Viterbo), bapt. 0061.

50. The brother of Yelamu woman María Serafina, bapt. 0105, was Guatnaxsé (Bruno), bapt. 0030. He married Xilaite (Francisca Xaviera), bapt. 0095, an Aramai woman in marriage 0025. (She later went on to marry Joseph Ramos, marriage 0065.) Yelamu woman Uxsisté (Manuela María), bapt. 0055, had two brothers. The older one, Yapis (Raymundo), bapt. 0043, married twice: first to Nayomi (Ana Francisca), bapt. 0272, from Urebure, in marriage 0049; then to a woman from the Marin Peninsula, Motúpa (Jacinta), bapt. 0356, in marriage 0093. Uxsisté's younger brother Emptil (Sebastian), bapt. 0019, married four times. His second and fourth marriages were to non-Yelamu women: the first of these was to Lamchin woman Mermite (Josepha de Leonissa), bapt. 0268, marriage 0047; the second was to Abasto woman Jochaliba (Brigida), bapt. 2048, in marriage 0628. The brother of Urebure woman María Soledad, bapt. 0102, was Usscúltu (Cayetano), bapt. 0101. He married Oljon woman Yjon (Juana), bapt. 1009, in marriage 0256; Servate (Yluminata), bapt. 0879, a Lamchin woman, in marriage 0507; then Huchiun woman Ruruesmain (Luisa), bapt. 0201, in marriage 1759; and finally Suisun woman Culeli (Juana Valesia), bapt. 5026, in marriage 2020.

51. Gifford, "Miwok Moieties," 147–48.

52. Stern, *Secret History of Gender*, 59–66.

CHAPTER 5

1. Francisco Palóu, baptismal entry 0007, 24 June 1777.
2. Chamis (Francisco Moraga), bapt. 0007; Pilmo (José Antonio), bapt. 0008; and Taulvo (Juan Bernardino), bapt. 0009.
3. Alonso de Molina, quoted in Ramón A. Gutiérrez, *When Jesus Came, the Corn Mothers Went Away*, 81.
4. Donn V. Hart, *Compadrinazgo: Ritual Kinship in the Philippines* (De Kalb: Northern Illinois University Press, 1977), 1. Joseph H. Lynch complains that *compadrinazgo* "serves its purpose, but is of little use outside a Spanish-speaking context," but in this case the word is both appropriate and useful. See Joseph H. Lynch, *Godparents and Kinship in Early Medieval Europe* (Princeton, NJ: Princeton University Press, 1986), 7.

5. Alonso de la Peña Montenegro, *Itinerario para párrocos de indios*, 2 vols., ed. C. Baciero, M. Corrales, J. M. García Añoveros, and F. Maseda (Madrid: Consejo Superior de Investigaciones Científicas, 1995), 2:51.
6. Francisco de Lorra Baquio, *Manual Mexicano de la Administracion de los Santos Sacramentos conforme al Manual Toledano* (Mexico: Diego Gutierrez, 1634), fol. 11v, Peabody Library, Johns Hopkins University, Baltimore.
7. Hardon, *Modern Catholic Dictionary*, s.v. "Holy Chrism."
8. See Paul Kevin Meagher, Thomas C. O'Brien, and Consuelo Maria Aherne, eds., *Encyclopedic Dictionary of Religion*, vol. O–Z (Washington, DC: Corpus Publications, 1979), s.v. "Salt"; Hardon, *Modern Catholic Dictionary*, s.v. "Salt"; Pio Paschini et al., eds., *Enciclopedia Cattolica*, vol. 10 (Vatican City: Ente per l'enciclopedia cattolica e per il libro cattolico, 1953), s.v. "Sale (nella liturgia)."
9. Montenegro, *Itinerario para párrocos de indios*, 2:53.
10. Joseph H. Lynch, *Godparents and Kinship in Early Medieval Europe*, 83–140.
11. Ibid., 159–60.
12. Ibid., 192.
13. Ibid., 143–62.
14. See, for example, Hugo G. Nutini and Betty Bell, *Ritual Kinship: The Structure and Historical Development of the Compadrazgo System in Rural Tlaxcala*, vol. 1 (Princeton, NJ: Princeton University Press, 1980), 225–26; and Hugo G. Nutini, *Ritual Kinship: Ideological and Structural Integration of the Compadrazgo System in Rural Tlaxcala*, vol. 2 (Princeton, NJ: Princeton University Press, 1984), 343.
15. María de la Luz Ynes Berreyesa, bapt. 0294.
16. Francisca Saturnina Linares, bapt. 0139.
17. For Cadereyta's location and history, see Peter Gerhard, *A Guide to the Historical Geography of New Spain*, rev. ed. (Norman: University of Oklahoma Press, 1993), 62–63. San Pedro y San Pablo Cadereyta was a Franciscan parish until it was secularized in 1754; Franciscan missions remained strong in the area until much later.
18. Ubiumis (María Josefa), bapt. 0063.
19. Jacinto, bapt. 0769; Jobocholá (Rafael), bapt. 4518.
20. Jotes (Fructuoso), bapt. 0742; Sapache (Nicolas), bapt. 1176. The headmen who had been baptized and were still alive at the time of Jotes's baptism were Nopex-sé (Pio), bapt. 0346; Quimas (Romualdo), bapt. 0365; Keqecég (Marcial), bapt. 0517; and Ysúu (Juan de los Santos), bapt. 0734.
21. Jotes was certainly the oldest of Sapache's sons ever known to accept baptism at Mission San Francisco.
22. Tacsinte (Valeriano), bapt. 0442; Oyumain (Cristiana Maria), bapt. 1933.
23. Uilmoxsi (Pascual Baylon), bapt. 0027; Toróz (Nemesio), bapt. 0695; Lolue'pig (Praxedis Nicolasa), bapt. 0705.
24. Huetlícs (Luis Ramón), bapt. 0031. Approximately two-thirds of Huetlícs's godchildren were baptized in 1786 and 1787. Only one of the first thirty

godchildren was a member of Huetlícs's tribal community, but twenty-six others were Costanoan speakers like their godfather.

25. Liquiique (Manuel), bapt. 0321; Huitpote (Petronila), bapt. 0313.
26. Chamis (Francisco Moraga), bapt. 0007; Liloté (Maria Francisca), bapt. 0012.
27. Quéyeme (Rafaela Marcela), bapt. 0083; marriage 0088.
28. See baptismal entries 0498–0503, 0505, 0507, 0508, 0510–13, 0515–17.
29. Milliken, *Time of Little Choice*, 238.
30. Tolecsse (Celso), bapt. 1434; his godchildren were those in baptismal entries 6055–184. The other thirty-five, baptismal entries 6270–6303 and 6311, were godfathered by a Saclan man, Jo-ocsia (Crispo), bapt. 1538.
31. Saqueninispi (Petronila), bapt. 4805; she married Tolecsse in marriage 2001, on 22 June 1823.
32. Milliken, *Time of Little Choice*, 179.
33. The headman's daughter was Buenun (Dona), bapt. 1603.
34. Guonis (Sinforosa), bapt. 1156; Alajuta (Guillermo), bapt. 0485. Their children were Macario, bapt. 1976; Narcisa, bapt. 2005; and Guillermo, bapt. 2417.
35. Malany'eum (Micaelina), bapt. 1028. Interestingly, Malany'eum was the goddaughter of her paternal uncle's wife Arpin (Clara), bapt. 0016.
36. Otchacaminimac (Pascuala), bapt. 0487.
37. Uichase (Julio), bapt. 0883; Ygnacia Barbara, bapt. 0059.
38. Ugité (Celsa), bapt. 0837; Micaela, bapt. 2301. Micaela lived a little more than a month. Ugité married about thirteen months after Micaela's death, and never godmothered again.
39. Chi-uéc (Norberto), bapt. 0037; Santiago, bapt. 2081.
40. Pascual, bapt. 1854; María del Carmen, bapt. 2076B; Valentín, bapt. 5805.
41. The godfather, María del Carmen's father, was Ssapsam (Valentín), bapt. 1290.
42. Polehova (Yldefonso), bapt. 2201; Masuete (Arsenia), bapt. 3934; their son was Manuel Encarnación, bapt. 5041; Polehova's eldest surviving son was Pispistole (Juan Nepomuceno), bapt. 2135.
43. Ysúu (Juan de los Santos), bapt. 0734; Etmén (Quarta), bapt. 0919; their first child was also named Juan de los Santos, bapt. 2750; Ysúu's daughter was Teopista Josefa, bapt. 0729.
44. Tabasuse (Troyano), bapt. 1721; Guecmaie (Troyana), bapt. 1729.
45. Baltasara, bapt. 2128.
46. Troyana, bapt. 2878; Toyleme (Delfina), bapt. 1573. The mission registers do not contain enough information to determine whether Toyleme was the sister of Tabasuse or Guecmaie.
47. Manuel, bapt. 3490.
48. Teute (Prima), bapt. 1622; she sponsored Justo de Jesus, bapt. 4548, and Juan Francisco, bapt. 4762.
49. Antonio de Padua Morante, bapt. 0160; marriage 0920.

50. Monózse (Rogerio), bapt. 0350; Arpin (Clara), bapt. 0016. Their children were Juan, bapt. 0559; Pedro Benito, bapt. 0702; and María Juana, bapt. 0955.
51. Puruem (Ynés), bapt. 0077.
52. This example comes from the baptismal entry of Liloté (Maria Francisca), bapt. 0012, but it is typical of most baptismal entries in the Mission San Francisco *Libro de Bautismos*.
53. Juana María Apolonia Pacheco, bapt. 1761; her godparents Apolinario Vernal and Apolonia Soberanes also godparented the Indian children Elzeario, bapt. 1762, and Bonifacia, bapt. 1763, who were baptized the same day.
54. José Ygnacio Berreyesa, bapt. 3413; Bernardo, bapt. 3414.
55. José Reyes Berreyesa godfathered at least six Hispanic infants (baptisms 4043, 4111, 4117, 4899, 5724, and 5787).
56. See, for example, baptisms 0109, 0112–15.
57. Junípero Serra to the Father Guardian of San Fernando [Francisco Pangua], Monterey, 14 June 1774, in *Writings of Junípero Serra*, 2:70.
58. For example, death entry 4966 for Litel (Leonardo), bapt. 4213, indicates that he was raised as a servant in the house of Lieutenant Manuel Gomez. However, Litel's godfather was another Hispanic man, Ramón Laso de la Vega.
59. Jackson, *Indian Population Decline*, 101, 126, 132.

CHAPTER 6

1. Juniqueme (Onesimo), bapt. 4158; Guallec (Onesima), bapt. 4159; Ynocencio, bapt. 4409.
2. This figure does not include the Indians who were given emergency baptisms outside the mission.
3. Juuim (Restituta), bapt. 0535.
4. Margolin, *Ohlone Way*, 67, 70–71; Levy, "Costanoan," 490.
5. Jackson, *Indian Population Decline*, 100–102.
6. Cook, *The Conflict Between the California Indian and White Civilization*, 32.
7. Ibid., 33, 34.
8. See Milliken, *Time of Little Choice*, generally; Jackson, *Indian Population Decline*, 117–43.
9. Richard A. Gould, "Aboriginal California Burial and Cremation Practices," *Reports of the University of California Archaeological Survey* 60 (1963): 154, 167–68.
10. Margolin, *Ohlone Way*, 145–49; Levy, "Costanoan," 490–91.
11. Geiger and Meighan, *As the Padres Saw Them*, 98, 99, 119.
12. Obmusa (Tiburcio), bapt. 1108; Sumipocsé (Homobono), bapt. 0504. Arguello, Report on Indians' reasons for fleeing Mission San Francisco, 12 August 1797, Californias, vol. 65, expediente 2, fols. 108r–v. Indian names and baptismal numbers are from Milliken, *Time of Little Choice*, 299, 301.
13. Russell K. Skowronek, "Sifting the Evidence: Perceptions of Life at the

Ohlone (Costanoan) Missions of Alta California," *Ethnohistory* 45, no. 4 (1998): 685.
14. Ambro, *They Danced in the Plaza*, 287–88.
15. The girls were Ela (Adriana), bapt. 2808; Zecum (Lucilla), bapt. 1039; Eyumaen (Aurea), bapt. 2382; Motesipo (Fulgencia), bapt. 3348; Joubonpo (Fernanda), bapt. 2558; Joubocme (Pomponia), bapt. 2494; Uyum (Luisa Gonzaga), bapt. 3098; Collamis (Augusta), bapt. 3483; Tolenumaye (Eufemia), bapt. 2366; Chalamonese (Cirila), bapt. 4869; Suma (Melchora), bapt. 4533; Toluete (Angela de Fulgino), bapt. 4870; Geyumaie (Ricarda), bapt. 4450; Tabasume (Narcisa), bapt. 4055; Seupi (Telma), bapt. 4990; Gueyame (Silvana), bapt. 4452; Esiquesl (Claudia), bapt. 4067; Fructuosa, bapt. 2304; Lola (Ysidora), bapt. 3987; Uyumaye (Aparicia), bapt. 2910; Toletli (Ana María), bapt. 3485; Lulumaen (Jacinta María), bapt. 3614; Joluate (Nicolasa), bapt. 2426; Maura, bapt. 2155; Natalia, bapt. 2171; Uyumsu (Peregrina Espiritu Santo), bapt. 4544; Gipoe (Humiliana), bapt. 5326; Mepusio (Xista Margarita), bapt. 4147; Lobaya (Macedonia), bapt. 4221; Colla (Telesfora), bapt. 2504.
16. Lasuén, "Refutation of Charges," in *Writings of Lasuén*, 2:206.
17. Vicente Francisco de Sarría, San Carlos Borromeo burial record 2364, 24 June 1821, for María Josefa, San Carlos bapt. 2780, Huntington Library, *Early California Population Project Database*.
18. For both groups, the numbers of fathers who had died may be higher; only those deaths noted by the priests are counted in these figures. The priests did not record the deaths of the fathers of approximately 23 percent of these girls and young women. This percentage is very similar for both the monjas and those who were not designated monjas.
19. The three were Huitanac (Viridiana), bapt. 0366; Froylan, bapt. 0386; and Geél (Agaton), bapt. 0846.
20. For more on Third Order Secular Franciscans, see Willibrord-Christian Van Dijk, "The Franciscan Spirit Through the Ages," trans. Michael D. Meilach, in Anton Rotzetter, Willibrord-Christian Van Dijk, and Thaddée Matura, *Gospel Living: Francis of Assisi, Yesterday and Today* (St. Bonaventure, NY: The Franciscan Institute, St. Bonaventure University, 1994), 238–41.
21. Neuerberg, *Decoration of the California Missions*, 66.
22. María Ysabel, San Buenaventura bapt. 0076, death record 2326, 17 April 1820, Huntington Library, *Early California Population Project Database*.
23. Pío, San Buenaventura bapt. 0247, death record 2328, 2 May 1820, Huntington Library, *Early California*.
24. Lowell John Bean, "Social Organization in Native California," in Bean and Blackburn, *Native Californians*, 112.
25. Hackel, *Children of Coyote*, 248; Serra to Lasuén, Mission San Carlos, 29 March 1779, in *Writings of Junípero Serra*, 3:294.
26. Otchacaminimac (Pascuala), bapt. 0487.
27. This quotation comes from the baptism record of Micaela, bapt. 1997, 29 September 1799, written by Father Ramón Abella.

28. Creasy and Resnik, eds., *Maternal-Fetal Medicine*, 498–99, 1153–54.
29. Elena, bapt. 2459.
30. Elena's father was Cabachuliva (Elzeario), bapt. 2053; Elena's mother was Huiumutaca (Elena), bapt. 2058.
31. María Egipciaca, bapt. 5827.
32. Omobala (Susana), bapt. 4099; Ssapsam (Valentín), bapt. 1290.
33. Juuim (Restituta), bapt. 0535; Simmón (Gonzalo), bapt. 0534; Pedro de Alcantara, bapt. 0553.
34. Pedro de Alcantara's birthplace is identified in his baptismal record, 0553. Milliken identifies Ssalayme as a Cotegen town; see Milliken, *Time of Little Choice*, 242.
35. María de la Asumpción, bapt. 0264.
36. María's first husband was Uariucsé (Meliton), bapt. 0497. He died in 1798, burial 1222. María's surviving or possibly surviving family members were Canoe (Patricio), bapt. 0371; Coynis (Andrés), bapt. 0051; and Aniceto, bapt. 0518. María's mother Erajuimin (Geronima), bapt. 0372, died in 1794, burial 0623(B); her sister María Anastacia, bapt. 0090, died in 1779, burial 0016; her brother Francisco de Borja, bapt. 0187, died in 1780, burial 0030; her sister Ssoyóte (Ana María), bapt. 0022, died in 1781, burial 0039; her twin brother José Etonogenes, bapt. 0263, died in 1782, burial 0064; and her brother Justo, bapt. 0768, died in 1790, burial 0305.
37. Chi-uéc (Norberto), bapt. 0037.
38. José Espi, death entry 1259, 16 July 1799.
39. James A. Sandos, "Levantamiento! The 1824 Chumash Uprising Reconsidered," *Southern California Quarterly* 67, no. 2 (1985): 117.
40. Tolemele (Fernando), bapt. 4881, death 4202.
41. Mochechi (Nazaria), bapt. 2620, death 4453.
42. John P. Harrington, trans., *A New Original Version of Boscana's Historical Account of the San Juan Capistrano Indians of Southern California* (New York: Argonaut Press for University Microfilms, 1966), microfilm, 56.
43. Otaya (Cirilo), bapt. 1450, death 1628.
44. Saquenjeiun (Rogela), bapt. 4304, death 3610.
45. Abella and Sainz de Lucio to Carbajal, question 15, *Preguntas y Respuestas*.
46. La Pérouse, *Journal*, 187.
47. Langsdorff, *Langsdorff's Narrative*, 125.
48. Mahr, "Chamisso's Observations," 83.
49. Puqueccoime (Basilides), bapt. 3477, death 2884. Puqueccoime's father was Talmucse (Bonifacio), bapt. 3496; his mother was Pispisooboj (Bonifacia), bapt. 3497.
50. Jackson, *Indian Population Decline*, 101–2.
51. Henry A. Gemery, "The White Population of the Colonial United States, 1607–1790," in *A Population History of North America*, ed. Michael R. Haines and Richard H. Steckel (Cambridge: Cambridge University Press, 2000), 163.

52. Russell Thornton, "Population History of Native North Americans," in Haines and Steckel, *A Population History of North America*, 15.
53. Douglas H. Ubelaker, "Patterns of Disease in Early North American Populations," in Haines and Steckel, *A Population History of North America*, 80–83. See also Richard A. Easterlin, "Growth and Composition of the American Population in the Twentieth Century," in Haines and Steckel, *A Population History of North America*, 638–39.
54. Teodorico, bapt. 0701, death 0253.
55. Oloyuig (Alexos), bapt. 0548; Tacque'te (Madrona), bapt. 0549.
56. See, for example, San Francisco de Asís Mission, *Libro de Bautismos*, vol. 1, entry 0097 ("Cachagnitac, commonly known as Las Pulgas, near the arroyo of San Mateo") and entry 0218 ("Lamchin village, alias Las Pulgas").
57. Marriage 0191, 31 May 1789.
58. Saquenjelapi (Tranquilina), bapt. 4846, death 4173(A). Saquenjelapi's father was Guequecse (Hermenegildo), bapt. 4246. His first marriage at the mission is recorded in marriage entry 1502. Saquenjelapi's mother was Louete (Ramona), bapt. 4856, death 3539.
59. Milliken locates Pruristac, also known as San Pedro, on the Pacific coast, south and slightly west of the mission (Milliken, *Time of Little Choice*, 251). In contrast, Engelhardt states that San Pedro y San Pablo was five leagues southeast of the mission, which would put it on the bay side of the peninsula rather than the coast side (Engelhardt, *San Francisco*, 136). The weight of the evidence favors Milliken's location. According to Rose Marie Beebe and Robert M. Senkewicz, one league was equal to approximately 2.6 miles. See Rose Marie Beebe and Robert M. Senkewicz, introduction to *The History of Alta California*, by Antonio María Osio (Madison: University of Wisconsin Press, 1996), 258, n. 11.
60. Palóu and Cambón, "Ynforme . . . año 1782," Mission San Francisco de Asís, 31 December 1782, Historia, vol. 7, fol. 54r.
61. Quarters for the Franciscans were constructed first in 1787 of *palizada* (wattle and daub) and then replaced in 1789, presumably with more substantial adobe buildings. Jackson and Castillo, *Indians, Franciscans, and Spanish Colonization*, 152.
62. Ibid.
63. Tacalú (Juvenal), bapt. 0934; Ssatcón (Magna), bapt. 0938. Their children were Sancio, bapt. 0911; Manuela, bapt. 0916; Petronila, bapt. 0932(B); Magencia, bapt. 0940; and Antonino, bapt. 0949.
64. Lachi (Pacifico), bapt. 1003; Ssujan (Maria de la Trinidad), bapt. 1012. Others baptized in 1791 were wives Passim (Maria Elena), bapt. 1008, and Yjon (Juana), bapt. 1009; children María Antonia, bapt. 0979; Mutac (Timoteo), bapt. 0984; Bascam (Paulina), bapt. 0994; Acchim (Silveria), bapt. 0995; Mislem (Dominga), bapt. 0996; and Guatcayla' (Magina), bapt. 0997. The wife and child baptized in 1789 at San Pedro y San Pablo were Suiquim (Alexandra), bapt. 0761, and Rosalia, bapt. 0756, respectively. The three daughters baptized before the establishment of the San Pedro y San Pablo church were Aublonte (Natalia Maria), bapt. 0569; Jagssem (Yrene Maria),

bapt. 0570; and Ulium (Maria de la Cabeza), bapt. 0571, all baptized on 31 December 1786. Family members who died at San Pedro y San Pablo included Mislem, death 0426; Guatcayla', death 0411; Jagssem, death 0462; Ulium, death 0475; Passim, death 0537; Maria Antonia, death 0418; Mutac, death 0483; Bascam, death 0496; Acchim, death 0425(B); and Columba, bapt. 1379, death 0668.

CONCLUSION

1. Uichase (Julio), bapt. 0883, death 5150B.
2. Sandos, "Christianization among the Chumash," 72.
3. Gimas (Patavio), bapt. 1233, death 0586.
4. Ssiléna (Desiderio), bapt. 0828, death 0598.
5. Sotem (Fulgencia), bapt. 1250.
6. Ugité (Celsa), bapt. 0837.
7. Sotem married Quintas (Aparicio), bapt. 1196, in marriage 0363, 28 April 1794.
8. See, for example, William A. Christian Jr., *Local Religion in Sixteenth-Century Spain* (Princeton, NJ: Princeton University Press, 1981); Keith Thomas, *Religion and the Decline of Magic* (New York: Scribner, 1971).
9. R. David Edmunds made this point in a discussion about the authenticity of conversion to Methodism among American Indians at the Western History Association meeting, Oklahoma City, 4 October 2006.
10. William McLoughlin, "Native American Reactions to Christian Missions," in *The Cherokees and Christianity, 1794–1870: Essays on Acculturation and Cultural Persistence*, ed. Walter H. Conser Jr. (Athens: University of Georgia Press, 1994), 15.
11. Marriage 0253, 9 January 1792.
12. Acsim (María Petra), bapt. 0267.
13. Marriage 0490, 25 March 1795; Ygnacia Barbara, bapt. 0059.
14. Puyeles (Nicolás de Bari), bapt. 0287, death 0099, 3 April 1784.
15. Marriage 1409, 9 May 1812; Amtim (Protasia), bapt. 0992.
16. Marriage 0706, 31 January 1802, to Mequeig (Braulio), bapt. 0529. Mequeig died on 13 July 1806, death 2304.
17. Santiago, bapt. 2081, death 1365, 19 October 1800.
18. Juan, bapt. 6462, 1 November 1822. No death entry number was assigned.
19. Ssinem was the mother of Ssiléna; she was dead by the time Ssiléna was baptized on 25 October 1790.
20. Lachi (Liborio), bapt. 0892.
21. Chi-uéc (Norberto), bapt. 0037, godfathered Santiago, bapt. 2081, and Julio, bapt. 2795. Ugité godmothered Micaela, bapt. 2301. Raymundo Morante godfathered Juliana Ynes, bapt. 1894, as well as Juana Capistrano, bapt. 4774, the daughter of Uichase and Amtim. Servate (Yluminata), bapt. 0879, godmothered Tomas, bapt. 1975; Guippoy (Segismundo), bapt. 0580,

godfathered Julio, bapt. 3059; and colonist Petrona Gutiérrez godmothered Ygnacia Barbara, bapt. 3226.
22. María Soledad, bapt. 0102.
23. Marriages 0508, to Ygnacio Higuera, 28 June 1795; 0999, to Joseph Anacleto Barbosa, 6 November 1805; and 1047, to José Antonio Aguilar, 29 September 1806.
24. Marriage 1859, 17 July 1821; Chalayemise (Bonifacia), bapt. 6277. On Chalayemise's probable tribal affiliation, see Milliken, *Time of Little Choice*, 237–38, 244.
25. Sandos provides a gripping account of the rebellion in *Converting California*, 55–68.
26. Milliken, *Time of Little Choice*, 11.
27. Uichase's half brother Ssiléna (Desiderio), bapt. 0828, died 30 December 1793, death 0598. His brother Jéquens (Lamberto), bapt. 0891, died 19 March 1791, death 0361. His brother Ala'la (Gil), bapt. 0830, died 8 September 1791, death 0378. His sister Ugité (Celsa), bapt. 0837, died 14 May 1806, death 2170. No death record has been found for Uichase's brother Lachi (Liborio), bapt. 0892, leaving the possibility that Lachi was still alive when Uichase died in 1831.

BIBLIOGRAPHY

ARCHIVAL SOURCES

Archivo General de la Nación (AGN), Mexico City, Mexico.

Archivo Histórico de Hacienda (AHH). Bulas de la Santa Cruzada. Californias. Cárceles y Presidios. Colección de Documentos para la Historia de México (Historia). Cultos Religiosos. Marina. Misiones. Tierras. Tribunal de Cuentas.

Bancroft Library, University of California, Berkeley, California.

Archives of California. *Archivo del Arzobispado de San Francisco. Archivos de las Misiones.* California mission and church miscellany. California mission and church miscellany, 1773–1846. California mission letters, 1806–1823. Mission and church miscellany: additions. *Documentos para la historia de California.* Documents for the history of California. Junípero Serra Letters and Documents. San Francisco Presidio account books.

Charles von der Ahe Library, Department of Archives and Special Collections, Ygnacio del Valle Family Collection, Loyola Marymount University, Los Angeles, California.

Castaño, Bartolomé. *Catecismo breve de lo que precisamente debe saber el cristiano.* Mexico: Imprenta del C. Alejandro Valdés, 1833.

Peabody Library, Johns Hopkins University, Baltimore, Maryland.

Lorra Baquio, Francisco de. *Manual Mexicano de la Administración de los Santos Sacramentos conforme al Manual Toledano.* Mexico: Diego Gutierrez, 1634.

Perez, Manuel. *Farol indiano, y guia de curas de indios.* Mexico City: Francisco de Rivera Calderon, 1713.

Santa Barbara Mission Archive-Library (SBMAL), Santa Barbara, California.

California Mission Documents. Diary of Ramon Abella. *Informe Anual del Estado de la Mision de Nuestro Padre San Francisco. Preguntas y Respuestas.* San Francisco Biennial Reports. San Francisco Report on Spiritual Results.

Wilson Library, University of North Carolina, Chapel Hill, North Carolina.

Montenegro, Alonso de la Peña. *Itinerario para parochos de indios.* Madrid: Ioseph Fernandez de Buendia, 1668. Bernard J. Flatow Collection of Latin American Cronistas.

THESES, DISSERTATIONS, AND PUBLISHED SOURCES

Adelman, Jeremy, and Stephen Aron. "From Borderlands to Borders: Empires, Nation-States, and the Peoples in Between in North American History." *The American Historical Review* 104, no. 3 (June 1999): 814–41.

Aizpuru, Pilar Gonzalbo. *Familia y orden colonial.* Mexico City: El Colegio de México, 1998.

———, ed. *Familias novohispanas: Siglos XVI al XIX.* Mexico City: El Colegio de México, 1991.

Aizpuru, Pilar Gonzalbo, and Cecilia Rabell, eds. *La familia en el mundo iberoamericano.* Mexico City: Universidad Nacional Autónoma de México, 1994.

———, eds. *Familia y vida privada en la historia de Iberoamérica.* Mexico City: El Colegio de México and Universidad Nacional Autónoma de México, 1996.

Allen, Rebecca. *Native Americans at Mission Santa Cruz, 1791–1834: Interpreting the Archaeological Record.* Perspectives in California Archaeology, vol. 5. Los Angeles: Institute of Archaeology, University of California, Los Angeles, 1998.

Alonso, Ana María. *Thread of Blood: Colonialism, Revolution, and Gender on Mexico's Northern Frontier.* Hegemony and Experience: Critical Studies in Anthropology and History. Tucson: University of Arizona Press, 1995.

Ambro, Richard D. *They Danced in the Plaza: The Historical Archaeology of Notre Dame Plaza, Mission San Francisco de Asís (Dolores), 347 Dolores Street, San Francisco, California.* San Francisco: Holman and Associates, 2003.

Applegate, Richard. "Native California Concepts of the Afterlife." In *Flowers of the Wind: Papers on Ritual, Myth and Symbolism in California and the Southwest,* edited by Thomas C. Blackburn. Socorro, NM: Ballena Press, 1977.

Archibald, Robert. *The Economic Aspects of the California Missions.* Washington, DC: Academy of American Franciscan History, 1978.

———. "The Economy of the Alta California Mission, 1803–1821." *Southern California Quarterly* 58 (1976): 227–40.

———. "Indian Labor at the California Missions: Slavery or Salvation?" *The Journal of San Diego History* 24, no. 2 (1978): 172–96.

Arguello, Luis Antonio. *The Diary of Captain Luis Antonio Arguello: October 17–November 17, 1821; The Last Spanish Expedition in California.* Translated by Vivian C. Fisher. Berkeley, CA: The Friends of the Bancroft Library, 1992.

Ariès, Philippe, and André Béjin, eds. *Western Sexuality: Practice and Precept in Past and Present Times.* Translated by Anthony Forster. New York: Basil Blackwell, 1985.

Arkush, Brooke S. "Yokuts Trade Networks and Native Culture Change in Central and Eastern California." *Ethnohistory* 40, no. 4 (1993): 619–40.

Arriquibar, Nicolas de. *Recreacion politica. Reflexiones sobre el amigo de los hombres en su tratado de poblacion, considerado con respecto á nuestros intereses.* Vitoria, Spain: Tomas de Robles y Navarro, 1779. Microfilm.

Asad, Talal. *Genealogies of Religion: Discipline and Reasons of Power in Christianity and Islam*. Baltimore: Johns Hopkins University Press, 1993.

Aveni, Anthony. *Empires of Time: Calendars, Clocks, and Cultures*. New York: Basic Books, 1989.

Axtell, James. "Ethnohistory: An Historian's Viewpoint." *Ethnohistory* 26, no. 1 (1979): 1–13.

———. *The Invasion Within: The Contest of Cultures in Colonial North America*. The Cultural Origins of North America. New York: Oxford University Press, 1985.

———. "Some Thoughts on the Ethnohistory of Missions." *Ethnohistory* 29, no. 1 (1982): 35–41.

Baer, Kurt. *Architecture of the California Missions*. Berkeley: University of California Press, 1958.

———. "California Indian Art." *The Americas* 16 (1959): 23–44.

Ballantyne, Tony, and Antoinette Burton, eds. *Bodies in Contact: Rethinking Colonial Encounters in World History*. Durham, NC: Duke University Press, 2005.

Bancroft, Hubert Howe. *California Pastoral, 1769–1848*. Vol. 34 of *The Works of Hubert Howe Bancroft*. San Francisco: A. L. Bancroft, 1888.

———. *History of California*. 3 vols. Vols. 18–20 of *The Works of Hubert Howe Bancroft*. San Francisco: A. L. Bancroft, 1884–85.

Barker, Leo R., and Julia Costello, eds. *The Archaeology of Alta California*. Spanish Borderlands Sourcebooks 15. New York: Garland, 1991.

Barton, Bruce Walter. *The Tree at the Center of the World: A Story of the California Missions*. Santa Barbara, CA: Ross-Erikson, 1980.

Bates, Craig D. "Scholars and Collectors Among the Sierra Miwok, 1900–1920: What Did They Really Find?" *Museum Anthropology* 17, no. 2 (June 1993): 7–19.

Bauer, Arnold J. "Rural Workers in Spanish America: Problems of Peonage and Oppression." *Hispanic American Historical Review* 59, no. 1 (1979): 34–63.

Beal, John P., James A. Coriden, and Thomas J. Green. *New Commentary on the Code of Canon Law*. New York: Paulist Press, 2000.

Bean, Lowell John. "Social Organization." In Heizer, *California*, 673–82.

———, ed. *California Indian Shamanism*. Ballena Press Anthropological Papers, edited by Sylvia Brakke Vane, no. 39. Menlo Park, CA: Ballena Press, 1992.

———, comp. and ed. *The Ohlone, Past and Present: Native Americans of the San Francisco Bay Region*. Ballena Press Anthropological Papers, no. 42. Menlo Park, CA: Ballena Press, 1994.

Bean, Lowell John, and Thomas C. Blackburn, eds. *Native Californians: A Theoretical Retrospective*. Ramona, CA: Ballena Press, 1976.

Bean, Lowell John, and Sylvia Brakke Vane. "California Religious Systems and Their Transformations." In Bean, *California Indian Shamanism*, 33–51.

———, eds. *Ethnology of the Alta California Indians*. Spanish Borderlands Sourcebooks 3–4. New York: Garland, 1991.

Beebe, Rose Marie, and Robert M. Senkewicz. Introduction to *The History of Alta California: A Memoir of Mexican California*, by Antonio María Osio. Madison: University of Wisconsin Press, 1996.

Beechey, Frederick W. *Narrative of a Voyage to the Pacific and Beering's Strait, to Co-operate with the Polar Expeditions*. London: Henry Colburn and Richard Bentley, 1831. Microfilm.

———. *Narrative of a Voyage to the Pacific and Beering's Strait*. 2 vols. Bibliotheca Australiana 34. 1831. Reprint, New York: Da Capo Press, 1968.

Beeler, Madison S., ed. and trans. *The Ventureño Confesionario of José Señán, O.F.M*. University of California Publications in Linguistics, vol. 47. Berkeley: University of California Press, 1967.

Bell, Catherine. *Ritual Theory, Ritual Practice*. New York: Oxford University Press, 1992.

Benavides, Gustavo. "Syncretism and Legitimacy in Latin American Religion." In *Enigmatic Powers: Syncretism with African and Indigenous Peoples' Religions Among Latinos*, edited by Anthony M. Stevens-Arroyo and Andres I. Pérez y Mena. Program for the Analysis of Religion Among Latinos, vol. 3. New York: Bildner Center for Western Hemisphere Studies, 1995.

Bennyhoff, James A. "The Ethnogeography of the Plains Miwok." PhD diss., University of California, Berkeley, 1961.

———. *Ethnogeography of the Plains Miwok*. Center for Archaeological Research at Davis, publication no. 5. Davis: University of California, Davis, 1977.

Benoist, Howard, and María Carolina Flores, eds. *The Spanish Missionary Heritage of the United States: Selected Papers and Commentaries from the November 1990 Quincentenary Symposium*. San Antonio, TX: United States Department of the Interior/National Park Service and Los Compadres de San Antonio Missions National Historical Park, 1993.

Benton, Lisa M. *The Presidio: From Army Post to National Park*. N.p.: Northeastern University Press, 1988.

Berger, Peter. *The Sacred Canopy: Elements of a Sociological Theory of Religion*. New York: Anchor Books, 1967.

Berlin, Ira, and Philip D. Morgan. *Cultivation and Culture: Labor and the Shaping of Slave Life in the Americas*. Carter G. Woodson Institute Series in Black Studies, edited by Armstead L. Robinson. Charlottesville: University Press of Virginia, 1993.

Bhabha, Homi K. *The Location of Culture*. New York: Routledge, 1994.

Bolton, Herbert Eugene. "The Epic of Greater America." *The American Historical Review* 38, no. 3 (1933): 448–74.

———. "Expedition to San Francisco Bay in 1770: Diary of Pedro Fages." *Publications of the Academy of Pacific Coast History* 2, no. 3 (1911): 143–59.

———. "The Mission as a Frontier Institution in the Spanish-American Colonies." *American Historical Review* 22 (1917): 42–61.

———, trans. and ed. *Anza's California Expeditions*. 5 vols. Berkeley: University of California Press, 1930.

———, trans. and ed. *Anza's California Expeditions*. Vol. 3, *The San Francisco Colony*. New York: Russell and Russell, 1966.

———, trans. and ed. *Font's Complete Diary: A Chronicle of the Founding of San Francisco*. Berkeley: University of California Press, 1933.

———, trans. and ed. *Historical Memoirs of New California by Fray Francisco Palou, O.F.M.* 4 vols. Berkeley: University of California Press, 1926.

———, trans. and ed. *Historical Memoirs of New California by Fray Francisco Palóu, O.F.M.* Vol. 4. New York: Russell and Russell, 1966.

Boscana, Gerónimo. *Chinigchinich; A Historical Account of the Origin, Customs, and Traditions of the Indians at the Missionary Establishment of St. Juan Capistrano, Alta California; Called the Acagchemem Nation; Collected with the Greatest Care, from the Most Intelligent and Best Instructed in the Matter.* Translated by Alfred Robinson. In *Life in California: During a Residence of Several Years in That Territory, Comprising a Description of the Country and the Missionary Establishments, with Incidents, Observations, Etc., Etc.*, by Alfred Robinson. New York: Wiley and Putnam, 1846.

———. *Chinigchinich: A Revised and Annotated Version of Alfred Robinson's Translation of Father Gerónimo Boscana's Historical Account of the Belief, Usages, Customs and Extravagancies of the Indians of this Mission of San Juan Capistrano Called the Acagchemem Tribe.* Annotated by John P. Harrington. Classics in California Anthropology 3. Banning, CA: Malki Museum Press, 1978.

Bossy, John. "The Mass as a Social Institution, 1200–1700." *Past and Present* 100 (1983): 29–61.

Bourdaloue, Louis. *Chefs-d'oeuvre oratoires de Bourdaloue*. Paris: Garnier Frères, Libraires-Éditeurs, 1910.

Bouvier, Virginia Marie. *Women and the Conquest of California, 1542–1840: Codes of Silence*. Tucson: University of Arizona Press, 2001.

Bowman, J. N. "Weights and Measures of Provincial California." *California Historical Society Quarterly* 30, no. 4 (1951): 315–38.

Boyer, Richard J. *Lives of the Bigamists: Marriage, Family and Community in Colonial Mexico*. Albuquerque: University of New Mexico Press, 1995.

Brading, David A. "Tridentine Catholicism and Enlightened Despotism in Bourbon Mexico." *Journal of Latin American Studies* 15, no. 1 (1983): 1–22.

Breve instrucción a los christianos casados y utiles advertencias a los que pretenden serlo. 4th edition. Mexico City: Herederos del Lic. Don Joseph de Jauregui, 1791. Microfilm.

Brooks, James F. *Captives and Cousins: Slavery, Kinship, and Community in the Southwest Borderlands*. Chapel Hill: University of North Carolina Press for the Omohundro Institute of Early American History and Culture, 2002.

Brown, Alan K. "The European Contact of 1772 and Some Later Documentation." In Bean, *The Ohlone Past and Present*, 1–42.

Brown, Linda Keller, and Kay Mussell, eds. *Ethnic and Regional Foodways in the United States: The Performance of Group Identity*. Knoxville: University of Tennessee Press, 1984.

Buckley, Thomas. "Doing Your Thinking." In *I Become Part of It: Sacred Dimensions in Native American Life*, edited by D. M. Dooling and Paul Jordan-Smith. New York: Parabola Books, 1989.

———. "Native Authorship in Northwestern California." In *New Perspectives on Native North America: Cultures, Histories, and Representations*, edited by Sergei A. Kan and Pauline Turner Strong. Lincoln: University of Nebraska Press, 2006.

Burkhart, Louise M. *The Slippery Earth: Nahua-Christian Moral Dialogue in Sixteenth-Century Mexico*. Tucson: University of Arizona Press, 1989.

Calatayud y Florencia, Pedro de. *Tres doctrinas prácticas*. Madrid: Gráficas F. Martinez, 1951.

Callahan, William J. *Honor, Commerce and Industry in Eighteenth-Century Spain*. Kress Library of Business and Economics, edited by James P. Baughman and Kenneth E. Carpenter, publication no. 22. Soldiers Field, Boston: Baker Library, Harvard Graduate School of Business Administration, 1972.

———. "The Problem of Confinement: An Aspect of Poor Relief in Eighteenth-Century Spain." *Hispanic American Historical Review* 51, no. 1 (1971): 1–24.

Calvo, Thomas. "Familia y registro parroquial: El caso tapatío en el siglo XVIII." Translated by Pastora Rodríguez Aviñoá. *Relaciones: Estudios de historia y sociedad* 10 (1982): 53–67.

Campbell, Leon G. "The First Californios: Presidial Society in Spanish California, 1769–1822." *Journal of the West* 11, no. 4 (1972): 583–95.

———. "The Spanish Presidio in Alta California During the Mission Period 1769–1784." *Journal of the West* 16, no. 4 (1977): 63–77.

Carrera Stampa, Manuel. "The Evolution of Weights and Measures in New Spain." *The Hispanic American Historical Review* 29, no. 1 (1949): 2–24.

Castañeda, Antonia I. "Engendering the History of Alta California, 1769–1848: Gender, Sexuality, and the Family." In Gutiérrez and Orsi, *Contested Eden*, 230–59.

———. "Marriage: The Spanish Borderlands." In Cooke, *Encyclopedia of the North American Colonies*, 2:727–38.

———. "Presidarias y Pobladoras: Spanish-Mexican Women in Frontier Monterey, California, 1770–1821." PhD diss., Stanford University, 1990.

———. "Sexual Violence in the Politics and Policies of Conquest: Amerindian Women and the Spanish Conquest of Alta California." In Torre and Pesquera, *Building with Our Hands*, 15–33.

Castillo, Edward D. "Gender Status Decline, Resistance, and Accommodation among Female Neophytes in the Missions of California: A San Gabriel Case Study." *American Indian Culture and Research Journal* 18, no. 1 (1994): 67–93.

———, ed. *Native American Perspectives on the Hispanic Colonization of Alta California*. Spanish Borderlands Sourcebooks 26. New York: Garland, 1992.

———, trans. and ed. "The Assassination of Padre Andrés Quintana by the Indians of Mission Santa Cruz in 1812: The Narrative of Lorenzo Asisara." *California History* 68, no. 3 (Fall 1989): 116–25, 150–52.

———, trans. and ed. "An Indian Account of the Decline and Collapse of Mexico's

Hegemony over the Missionized Indians of California." *American Indian Quarterly* 13, no. 4 (Fall 1989): 391–406.

Certeau, Michel de. *The Practice of Everyday Life*. Translated by Steven Rendall. Berkeley: University of California Press, 1984.

Cevallos-Candau, Francisco Javier, and Jeffrey A. Cole, eds. *Coded Encounters: Writing, Gender, and Ethnicity in Colonial Latin America*. Amherst: University of Massachusetts Press, 1994.

Chartkoff, Joseph L., and Kerry Kona Chartkoff. *The Archaeology of California*. Stanford, CA: Stanford University Press, 1984.

Choris, Louis. *Voyage pittoresque autour du monde*. Paris: Imprimerie de Firmin Didot, 1822. Microfilm.

Christian, William A., Jr. *Local Religion in Sixteenth-Century Spain*. Princeton, NJ: Princeton University Press, 1981.

Colley, Charles C. "The Missionization of the Coast Miwok Indians of California." *California Historical Society Quarterly* 49, no. 2 (1970): 143–62.

Combs, Gary, and Fred Ploogh. "The Conversion of the Chumash Indians: An Ecological Perspective." *Human Ecology* 5 (1977): 309–28.

Cook, Sherburne F. "The Aboriginal Population of the San Joaquin Valley, California." *University of California Publications Anthropological Records* 16 (1955–61): 31–78.

———. "Colonial Expeditions to the Interior of California, Central Valley, 1800–1820." *University of California Publications Anthropological Records* 16 (1955–61): 239–92.

———. "Colonial Expeditions to the Interior of California, Central Valley, 1820–1840." *University of California Publications Anthropological Records* 20, no. 5 (1962): 151–213.

———. *The Conflict Between the California Indian and White Civilization*. Berkeley: University of California Press, 1976.

Cook, Sherburne F., and Woodrow Borah. *Essays in Population History*. Vol. 2, *Mexico and the Caribbean*. Berkeley: University of California Press, 1974.

———. "Mission Registers as Sources of Vital Statistics: Eight Missions of Northern California." In *Essays in Population History*. Vol. 3, *Mexico and California*. Berkeley: University of California Press, 1979.

Cooke, Jacob Ernest, ed. *Encyclopedia of the North American Colonies*. 3 vols. New York: Charles Scribner's Sons, 1993.

Costello, Julia G., ed. *Documentary Evidence for the Spanish Missions of Alta California*. Spanish Borderlands Sourcebooks 14. New York: Garland Publishing, 1991.

———. "Variability and Economic Change in the California Missions: An Historical and Archaeological Study." PhD diss., University of California, Santa Barbara, 1990.

Costo, Rupert, and Jeannette Henry Costo, eds. *The Missions of California: A Legacy of Genocide*. N.p.: Indian Historian Press for the American Indian Historical Society, 1987.

Counihan, Carole M. *The Anthropology of Food and Body: Gender, Meaning, and Power*. New York: Routledge, 1999.

Counihan, Carole, and Penny Van Esterik, eds. *Food and Culture: A Reader*. New York: Routledge, 1997.

Creasy, Robert K., and Robert Resnik, eds. *Maternal-Fetal Medicine*. 4th edition. Philadelphia: Saunders, 1999.

Daniels, Christine, and Michael V. Kennedy, eds. *Negotiated Empires: Centers and Peripheries in the Americas, 1500–1820*. New York: Routledge, 2002.

Dartt-Newton, Deana, and Jon M. Erlandson. "Little Choice for the Chumash: Colonialism, Cattle, and Coercion in Mission Period California." *American Indian Quarterly* 30, nos. 3 & 4 (Summer & Fall 2006): 416–30.

Da Silva, Owen, comp. and ed. *Mission Music of California: A Collection of Old California Mission Hymns and Masses*. Los Angeles: Warren F. Lewis, 1941.

Davis, David Brion. *Inhuman Bondage: The Rise and Fall of Slavery in the New World*. New York: Oxford University Press, 2006.

Davis, James T. "The Archaeology of the Fernandez Site, a San Francisco Bay Region Shell Mound." *Reports of the University of California Archaeological Survey* 49 (1960): 11–52.

———. "Trade Routes and Economic Exchange among the Indians of California." In *Aboriginal California: Three Studies in Culture History*, edited by Robert F. Heizer. Berkeley: University of California, Berkeley, for the University of California Archaeological Research Facility, 1966.

Deagan, Kathleen A. *Spanish St. Augustine: The Archaeology of a Colonial Creole Community*. New York: Academic Press, 1983.

Deans-Smith, Susan. *Bureaucrats, Planters, and Workers: The Making of the Tobacco Monopoly in Bourbon Mexico*. Austin: University of Texas Press, 1992.

———. "The Working Poor and the Eighteenth-Century Colonial State: Gender, Public Order, and Work Discipline." In *Rituals of Rule, Rituals of Resistance: Public Celebrations and Popular Culture in Mexico*, edited by William H. Beezley, Cheryl English Martin, and William E. French. Wilmington, DE: Scholarly Resources, 1994.

Deeds, Susan M. "Land Tenure Patterns in Northern New Spain." *The Americas* 41, no. 4 (1985): 446–61.

———. "Rural Work in Nueva Vizcaya: Forms of Labor Coercion on the Periphery." *Hispanic American Historical Review* 69, no. 3 (1989): 425–49.

Denhart, Robert M. "The Horse in New Spain and the Borderlands." *Agricultural History* 25, no. 4 (1951): 145–50.

Dias, Christine Marie. "San Juan Capistrano Mission Records: Juaneño Conversion and Risk Minimization, a Case Study." Master's thesis, California State University, Long Beach, 1996.

Dick-Bissonnette, Linda E. "Foothill Yokoch, Mono, and Miwok Women: An Anthropological Perspective." PhD diss., University of California, Santa Barbara, 1997.

———. "Gender and Authority among the Yokoch, Mono, and Miwok of Central California." *Journal of Anthropological Research* 54, no. 1 (Spring 1998): 49–72.

Dohrn-van Rossum, Gerhard. *History of the Hour: Clocks and Modern Temporal Order.* Translated by Thomas Dunlap. Chicago: University of Chicago Press, 1996.

Donkin, R. A. "The Contribution of the Franciscan Missions to the Settlement of Alta California Colonization 1769–1823." *Revista de historia de América* 52 (1961): 373–93.

Doty, William G. *Mythography: The Study of Myths and Rituals.* 2nd ed. Tuscaloosa: University of Alabama Press, 2000.

Durán, Narciso. "Letters of Narciso Durán." Translated by Francis Price. *California Historical Society Quarterly* 37 (1958): 97–128.

Early, James. *Presidio, Mission, and Pueblo: Spanish Architecture and Urbanism in the United States.* Dallas, TX: Southern Methodist University Press in cooperation with the William P. Clements Center for Southwest Studies, 2004.

Easterlin, Richard A. "Growth and Composition of the American Population in the Twentieth Century." In Haines and Steckel, *A Population History of North America*, 631–75.

Elsasser, Albert B. "Basketry." In Heizer, *California*, 626–41.

Eltis, David, Frank D. Lewis, and Kenneth L. Sokoloff, eds. *Slavery in the Development of the Americas.* New York: Cambridge University Press, 2004.

Engelhardt, Zephyrin. *The Holy Man of Santa Clara, or, Life, Virtues, and Miracles of Fr. Magín Catalá, O.F.M.* San Francisco: James H. Barry, 1909.

———. *The Missions and Missionaries of California.* Vol. 2, *Upper California.* San Francisco: James H. Barry, 1912.

———. *San Francisco or Mission Dolores.* The Missions and Missionaries of California. Chicago: Franciscan Herald Press, 1924.

———. *San Luis Rey Mission.* The Missions and Missionaries of California. San Francisco: James H. Barry, 1921.

Erickson, Bruce A. "Violence and Manhood: Military Culture on the Northern Frontier of Colonial New Spain." PhD diss., University of New Mexico, 2001.

Farnsworth, Paul. "The Economics of Acculturation in the California Missions: A Historical and Archaeological Study of Mission Nuestra Senora de la Soledad." PhD diss., University of California, Los Angeles, 1987.

Farriss, Nancy. *Crown and Clergy in Colonial Mexico, 1759–1821.* London: Oxford University Press, 1968.

Field, Les, Alan Leventhal, Dolores Sanchez, and Rosemary Cambra. "A Contemporary Ohlone Tribal Revitalization Movement: A Perspective from the Muwekma Costanoan/Ohlone Indians of the San Francisco Bay Area." *California History* 71, no. 3 (1992): 412–32.

Fiorenza, Francis Schüssler. "Religious Beliefs and Praxis: Reflections on Catholic Theological Views of Work." In *Work and Religion*, edited by Gregory Baum. New York: Seabury Press, 1980.

Forster, Robert and Orest Ranum, eds. *Family and Society: Selections from the Annales: Economies, Sociétés, Civilisations.* Translated by Elborg Forster and Patricia M. Ranum. Baltimore: Johns Hopkins University Press, 1976.

Fuentes Díaz, Vicente. *La clase obrera. Entre el anarquismo y la religión*. Mexico City: Universidad Nacional Autónoma de México, 1994.

Garr, Daniel. "Planning, Politics and Plunder: The Missions and Indian Pueblos of Hispanic California." *Southern California Quarterly* 54, no. 4 (1972): 291–312.

———. "A Rare and Desolate Land: Population and Race in Hispanic California." *Western Historical Quarterly* 6, no. 2 (1975): 133–48.

Gayton, Anna H. "Yokuts-Mono Chiefs and Shamans." In Bean and Blackburn, *Native Californians*, 175–223.

Geertz, Clifford. "Religion as a Cultural System." In *The Interpretation of Cultures*. New York: Basic Books, 1973.

Geiger, Maynard J. *Calendar of Documents in the Santa Barbara Mission Archives*. Washington, DC: Academy of American Franciscan History, 1947.

———. *Franciscan Missionaries in Hispanic California, 1769–1848: A Biographical Dictionary*. San Marino, CA: The Huntington Library, 1969.

———. *The Indians of Mission Santa Barbara in Paganism and Christianity*. Santa Barbara, CA: Franciscan Fathers, 1960.

———. "New Data on the Buildings of Mission San Francisco." *California Historical Society Quarterly* 46, no. 3 (1967): 195–205.

———, ed. "Questionnaire of the Spanish Government in 1812 Concerning the Native Culture of the California Mission Indians." *The Americas* 5, no. 4 (1949): 474–90.

———, ed. "Reply of Mission San Carlos Borromeo to the Questionnaire of the Spanish Government in 1812 Concerning the Native Culture of the California Mission Indians." *The Americas* 6, no. 4 (1950): 467–86.

Geiger, Maynard J., and Clement W. Meighan, trans. and eds. *As the Padres Saw Them: California Indian Life and Customs as Reported by the Franciscan Missionaries, 1813–1815*. The Santa Barbara Bicentennial Historical Series, vol. 1. Santa Barbara, CA: Santa Barbara Mission Archive Library, 1976.

Gemery, Henry A. "The White Population of the Colonial United States, 1607–1790." In Haines and Steckel, *A Population History of North America*, 143–90.

Gentilcore, R. Louis. "Missions and Mission Lands of Alta California." *Annals of the Association of American Geographers* 51, no. 1 (1961): 46–72.

Gerhard, Peter. *A Guide to the Historical Geography of New Spain*. Rev. ed. Norman: University of Oklahoma Press, 1993.

Gifford, Edward W. "Clans and Moieties in Southern California." *University of California Publications in American Archaeology and Ethnology* 14, no. 2 (1918): 155–219.

———. "Miwok Moieties." *University of California Publications in American Archaeology and Ethnology* 12, no. 4 (1916): 139–94.

Goldschmidt, Walter. "Social Organization in Native California and the Origin of Clans." *American Anthropologist*, n.s., 50, no. 3, part 1 (July–Sept. 1948): 444–56.

Gould, Richard A. "Aboriginal California Burial and Cremation Practices." *Reports of the University of California Archaeological Survey* 60 (1963): 149–68.

Grimes, Ronald L. *Symbol and Conquest: Public Ritual and Drama in Santa Fe, New Mexico.* Ithaca, NY: Cornell University Press, 1976.

Guest, Francis F. "Cultural Perspectives on California Mission Life." *Southern California Quarterly* 65, no. 1 (1983): 1–65.

———. "An Examination of the Thesis of S. F. Cook on the Forced Conversion of Indians in the California Missions." *Southern California Quarterly* 61, no. 1 (1979): 1–77.

———. "An Inquiry into the Role of the Discipline in California Mission Life." *Southern California Quarterly* 71, no. 1 (1989): 1–68.

Gustafson, Janie L. "Never to Turn Back: The Controversy between Junípero Serra, O.F.M., Fermín Francisco de Lasuén, O.F.M., and Commander Fernando de Rivera y Moncada and Its Effects on the Evangelization/Acculturation of the California Indians at Mission San Diego de Alcalá and San Carlos Borromeo de Carmelo in the Years 1774–1777." PhD diss., Graduate Theological Union, 1986.

Gutiérrez, Gabriel. "Bell Towers, Crucifixes, and Cañones Violentos: State and Identity Formation in Pre-Industrial Alta California." PhD diss., University of California, Santa Barbara, 1997.

Gutiérrez, Ramón A. "Family Structures: The Spanish Borderlands." In Cooke, *Encyclopedia of the North American Colonies*, 2:672–82.

———. "Sexual Mores and Behavior: The Spanish Borderlands." In Cooke, *Encyclopedia of the North American Colonies*, 2:700–710.

———. *When Jesus Came, the Corn Mothers Went Away: Marriage, Sexuality, and Power in New Mexico, 1500–1846.* Stanford, CA: Stanford University Press, 1991.

Gutiérrez, Ramón A., and Richard J. Orsi, eds. *Contested Eden: California Before the Gold Rush.* California History Sesquicentennial Series. Berkeley: University of California Press, 1998.

Haas, Lisbeth. *Conquests and Historical Identities in California, 1769–1936.* Berkeley: University of California Press, 1995.

Hackel, Steven W. *Children of Coyote, Missionaries of Saint Francis: Indian-Spanish Relations in Colonial California, 1769–1850.* Chapel Hill: University of North Carolina Press for the Omohundro Institute of Early American History and Culture, 2005.

———. "Indian-Spanish Relations in Alta California: Mission San Carlos Borromeo, 1770–1833." PhD diss., Cornell University, 1994.

———. "The Staff of Leadership: Indian Authority in the Missions of Alta California." *The William and Mary Quarterly*, 3rd ser., 54, no. 2 (1997): 347–76.

Haines, Michael R., and Richard H. Steckel, eds. *A Population History of North America.* Cambridge: Cambridge University Press, 2000.

Halpin, Joseph. "Musical Activities and Ceremonies at Mission Santa Clara de Asís." *California Historical Quarterly* 50, no. 1 (1971): 35–42.

Harrington, John P., trans. "A New Original Version of Boscana's Historical Account of the San Juan Capistrano Indians of Southern California." New York: Argonaut Press for University Microfilms, 1966.

Harrison, Edward S. *History of Santa Cruz County*. San Francisco: Pacific Press, 1892.

Hart, Donn V. *Compadrinazgo: Ritual Kinship in the Philippines*. De Kalb: Northern Illinois University Press, 1977.

Hassig, Ross. *Time, History, and Belief in Aztec and Colonial Mexico*. Austin: University of Texas Press, 2001.

Heizer, Robert F. "Impact of Colonization on the Native Californian Societies." *Journal of San Diego History* 24, no. 1 (1978): 121–39.

———. "Prehistoric Central California: A Problem in Historical-Developmental Classification." *Reports of the University of California Archaeological Survey* 41, no. 66 (1958): 19–26.

———. "Trade and Trails." In Heizer, *California*, 690–93.

———, ed. *California*. Vol. 8 of *Handbook of North American Indians*, edited by William C. Sturtevant. Washington, DC: Smithsonian Institution, 1978.

———, ed. *A Collection of Ethnographical Articles on the California Indians*. Ballena Press Publications in Archaeology, Ethnology and History, no. 7. Ramona, CA: Ballena Press, 1976.

———, ed. *The Costanoan Indians*. Local History Studies, vol. 18. Cupertino, CA: California History Center at DeAnza College, 1974.

———, ed. *The Indians of Los Angeles County: Hugo Reid's Letters of 1852*. Southwest Museum Papers, vol. 21. Highland Park, Los Angeles: Southwest Museum, 1968.

Heizer, Robert F., and M. A. Whipple. *The California Indians: A Source Book*. Berkeley: University of California Press, 1971.

Herdt, Gilbert, ed. *Third Sex, Third Gender: Beyond Sexual Dimorphism in Culture and History*. New York: Zone Books, 1994.

Hewes, Minna, and Gordon Hewes, trans. and eds. "Indian Life and Customs at Mission San Luis Rey: A Record of California Mission Life Written by Pablo Tac, an Indian Neophyte (Rome, ca. 1835)." *The Americas* 9 (1952): 87–106.

Hilton, Sylvia L. *La alta California española*. Madrid: MAPFRE, 1992.

Hinton, Leanne. *Flutes of Fire: Essays on California Indian Languages*. San Bernadino, CA: Borgo Press, 1994.

Hollimon, Sandra E. "The Third Gender in Native California: Two-Spirit Undertakers Among the Chumash and Their Neighbors." In *Women in Prehistory: North America and Mesoamerica*, edited by Cheryl Claassen and Rosemary A. Joyce. Regendering the Past. Philadelphia: University of Pennsylvania Press, 1997.

Holterman, Jack. "The Revolt of Estanislao." *The Indian Historian* 3, no. 1 (1970): 43–54.

Hoover, Robert L., and Julia G. Costello, eds. *Excavations at Mission San Antonio, 1976–1978.* Monograph 26. Los Angeles: Institute of Archaeology, University of California, Los Angeles, 1985.

Huntington Library. Early California Population Project Database, 2006. http://www.huntington.org/Information/ECPPlogin.htm (accessed April 2009).

Hurtado, Albert L. *Indian Survival on the California Frontier.* Western Americana Series, no. 35. New Haven, CT: Yale University Press, 1988.

———. *Intimate Frontiers: Sex, Gender, and Culture in Old California.* Histories of the American Frontier. Albuquerque: University of New Mexico Press, 1999.

Hutchinson, C. Alan. "The Mexican Government and the Mission Indians of Upper California, 1821–1835." *The Americas* 21, no. 4 (1965): 335–62.

Ivanhoe, Francis, and Philip W. Chu. "Cranioskeletal Size Variation in San Francisco Bay Prehistory: Relation to Calcium Deficit in the Reconstructed High-seafoods Diet and Demographic Stress." *International Journal of Ostearchaeology* 6, no. 4 (1996): 346–81.

Jackson, Robert H. "La colonización de la Alta California: Un análisis del desarrollo de dos comunidades misionales." *Historia mexicana* 41, no. 1 (1991): 83–110.

———. "La dinámica del desastre demográfico de la población india en las misiones de la Bahía de San Francisco, Alta California, 1776–1840." *Historia mexicana* 40, no. 2 (1990): 187–215.

———. "Gentile Recruitment and Population Movements in the San Francisco Bay Area Missions." *Journal of California and Great Basin Anthropology* 6, no. 2 (1984): 225–39.

———. *Indian Population Decline: The Missions of Northwestern New Spain, 1687–1840.* Albuquerque: University of New Mexico Press, 1994.

———. *Missions and the Frontiers of Spanish America: A Comparative Study of the Impact of Environmental, Economic, Political, and Socio-cultural Variations on the Missions in the Rio de la Plata Region and on the Northern Frontier of New Spain.* Scottsdale, AZ: Pentacle Press, 2005.

———. "Patterns of Demographic Change in the Missions of Central Alta California." *Journal of California and Great Basin Anthropology* 9, no. 2 (1987): 251–72.

———. *Race, Caste, and Status: Indians in Colonial Spanish America.* Albuquerque: University of New Mexico Press, 1999.

Jackson, Robert H., and Edward D. Castillo. *Indians, Franciscans, and Spanish Colonization: The Impact of the Mission System on California Indians.* Albuquerque: University of New Mexico Press, 1995.

Johnson, John R. "Mission Registers as Anthropological Questionnaires: Understanding the Limitations of the Data." *American Indian Culture and Research Journal* 12, no. 2 (1988): 9–30.

Jorgensen, Joseph G. *Western Indians: Comparative Environments, Languages, and Cultures of 172 Western American Indian Tribes.* San Francisco: W. H. Freeman, 1980.

Joyce, Patrick, ed. *The Historical Meanings of Work.* New York: Cambridge University Press, 1987.

Jussen, Bernhard. *Spiritual Kinship as Social Practice: Godparenthood and Adoption in the Early Middle Ages*. Translated by Pamela Selwyn. The Family in Interdisciplinary Perspective. Newark: University of Delaware Press and Associated University Presses, 2000.

Jütte, Robert. *Poverty and Deviance in Early Modern Europe*. Cambridge: Cambridge University Press, 1994.

Kapitzke, Robert L. *Religion, Power and Politics in Colonial St. Augustine*. Gainesville: University Press of Florida, 2001.

Kealhofer, Lisa. "Cultural Interaction During the Spanish Colonial Period: The Plaza Church Site, Los Angeles." PhD diss., University of Pennsylvania, 1991.

Keefe, Susan A. *Water and the Word: Baptism and the Education of the Clergy in the Carolingian Empire*. 2 vols. Publications in Medieval Studies. Notre Dame, IN: University of Notre Dame Press, 2002.

Kelsey, Harry. *The Doctrina and Confesionario of Juan Cortés*. Altadena, CA: Howling Coyote Press, 1979.

———. "European Impact on the California Indians, 1530–1830." *The Americas* 41, no. 4 (1985): 494–511.

Kennedy, Roger G. *Mission: The History and Architecture of the Missions of North America*. Edited and designed by David Larkin. Boston: Houghton Mifflin, Marc Jaffe, 1993.

Kirkby, Dianne. "Colonial Policy and Native Depopulation in California and New South Wales, 1770–1840." *Ethnohistory* 31, no. 1 (1984): 1–16.

Kirsch, Robert, and William S. Murphy. *West of the West: The Story of California From the Conquistadores to the Great Earthquake as Described by the Men and Women Who Were There*. New York: E. P. Dutton, 1967.

Knight, Alan. "Mexican Peonage: What Was It and Why Was It?" *Journal of Latin American Studies* 18, no. 1 (1986): 41–74.

Kroeber, Alfred L. "California Kinship Terms." *University of California Publications in American Archaeology and Ethnology* 12, no. 9 (1917): 339–96.

———. "The Patwin and Their Neighbors." *University of California Publications in American Archaeology and Ethnology* 29, no. 4 (1932): 253–423.

Kroeber, Alfred L., and Edward W. Gifford. *World Renewal: A Cult System of Native Northwest California*. Anthropological Records 13, no. 1. Berkeley: University of California Press, 1948.

Lake, Alison. *Colonial Rosary: The Spanish and Indian Missions of California*. Athens: Ohio University Press, Swallow Press, 2006.

Lamar, Howard. "From Bondage to Contract: Ethnic Labor in the American West, 1600–1890." In *The Countryside in the Age of Capitalist Transformation: Essays in the Social History of Rural America*, edited by Steven Hahn and Jonathan Prude. Chapel Hill: University of North Carolina Press, 1985.

Lang, Sabine. *Men as Women, Women as Men: Changing Gender in Native American Cultures*. Translated by John L. Vantine. Austin: University of Texas Press, 1998.

Langelier, John Phillip and Daniel Bernard Rosen. *El Presidio de San Francisco: A History under Spain and Mexico, 1776–1846*. Historic Resource Study.

Presidio of San Francisco, Golden Gate National Recreation Area, CA: United States Department of the Interior, National Park Service, Denver Service Center, 1992.

Langellier, John Phillip, and Katherine Meyers Peterson. "Lances and Leather Jackets: Presidial Forces in Spanish Alta California, 1769–1821." *Journal of the West* 20, no. 4 (1981): 3–11.

Langenwalter, Paul E. and Larry W. McKee. "Vertebrate Faunal Remains from the Neophyte Dormitory." In Hoover and Costello, *Excavations at Mission San Antonio, 1976–1978*, 94–121.

Langer, Erick D., and Robert H. Jackson. "Colonial and Republican Missions Compared: The Cases of Alta California and Southeastern Bolivia." *Comparative Studies in Society and History* 30, no. 2 (1988): 286–311.

———, eds. *The New Latin American Mission History*. Latin American Studies Series. Lincoln: University of Nebraska Press, 1995.

Langsdorff, Georg H. von. *Langsdorff's Narrative of the Rezanov Voyage to Nueva California in 1806*. Translated by Thomas C. Russell. 1927. Reprint, Fairfield, WA: Ye Galleon Press, 1988.

La Pérouse, Jean-François de Galaup de. *The Journal of Jean-François de Galaup de la Pérouse, 1785–1788*. Vol. 1. Translated and edited by John Dunmore. Works Issued by the Hakluyt Society, Second Series, no. 179. London: The Hakluyt Society, 1994.

———. *Life in a California Mission: Monterey in 1786*. Edited by Malcolm Margolin. Berkeley, CA: Heyday Books, 1989.

Laslett, Peter, ed. *Household and Family in Past Time: Comparative Studies in the Size and Structure of the Domestic Group over the Last Three Centuries in England, France, Serbia, Japan and Colonial North America, with Further Materials from Western Europe*. New York: Cambridge University Press, 1972.

Lasuén, Fermín Francisco de. *The Writings of Fermín Francisco de Lasuén*. 2 vols. Translated and edited by Finbar Kenneally. Washington, DC: Academy of American Franciscan History, 1965.

Lavrin, Asunción. "In Search of the Colonial Woman in Mexico: The Seventeenth and Eighteenth Centuries." In Lavrin, *Latin American Women: Historical Perspectives*, 23–59.

———. *Sexuality and Marriage in Colonial Latin America*. Latin American Studies Series. Lincoln: University of Nebraska Press, 1989.

———, ed. *Latin American Women: Historical Perspectives*. Westport, CT: Greenwood Press, 1978.

Leon Mujal, Carlos. "Out of the Apocalypse to Alta California: Franciscans in the New World (1524–1833)." PhD diss., University of California, Berkeley, 2002.

Levy, Richard L. "Costanoan." In Heizer, *California*, 485–95.

———. *Costanoan Internal Relationships*. Berkeley: Archaeological Research Facility, Department of Anthropology, University of California, Berkeley, 1976.

———. "Eastern Miwok." In Heizer, *California*, 398–415.

Lewis, Laura A. "The 'Weakness' of Women and the Feminization of the Indian in Colonial Mexico." *Colonial Latin American Review* 5, no. 1 (1996): 73–94.

Librado, Fernando. *Breath of the Sun*. Banning, CA: Malki Museum Press, 1979.

Lightfoot, Kent G. *Indians, Missionaries, and Merchants: The Legacy of Colonial Encounters on the California Frontiers*. Berkeley: University of California Press, 2005.

———. "Native Negotiations of Missionary Practices in Alta California." *Missionalia* 32, no. 3 (November 2004): 380–93.

Lockhart, James. "Encomienda and Hacienda: The Evolution of the Great Estate in the Spanish Indies." *Hispanic American Historical Review* 49, no. 3 (1969): 411–29.

———. *Of Things of the Indies: Essays Old and New in Early Latin American History*. Stanford, CA: Stanford University Press, 1999.

Lynch, Katherine A. *Individuals, Families, and Communities in Europe, 1200–1800: The Urban Foundations of Western Society*. Cambridge Studies in Population, Economy and Society in Past Time, vol. 37. New York: Cambridge University Press, 2003.

Lynch, Joseph H. *Godparents and Kinship in Early Medieval Europe*. Princeton, NJ: Princeton University Press, 1986.

Mahr, August C., ed. and trans. *The Visit of the "Rurik" to San Francisco in 1816*. Stanford University Publications Series: History, Economics, and Political Science, vol. 2, no. 2. Stanford, CA: Stanford University Press, 1932.

Margolin, Malcolm. *The Ohlone Way: Indian Life in the San Francisco—Monterey Bay Area*. Berkeley, CA: Heyday Books, 1978.

Martin, Norman F. "La desnudéz in la Nueva España del siglo XVIII." *Anuario de estudios americanos* 29 (1972): 261–94.

Mason, J. Alden. "The Mutsun Dialect of Costanoan Based on the Vocabulary of De La Cuesta." *University of California Publications in American Archaeology and Ethnology* 11, no. 7 (1916): 399–472.

Mason, William Marvin. *The Census of 1790: A Demographic History of Colonial California*. Ballena Press Anthropological Papers, edited by Sylvia Brakke Vane, no. 45. Menlo Park, CA: Ballena Press, 1998.

Mauss, Marcel. *The Gift: The Form and Reason for Exchange in Archaic Societies*. Translated by W. D. Halls. New York: W. W. Norton, 1990.

McCaa, Robert. "*Calidad, Clase*, and Marriage in Colonial Mexico: The Case of Parral, 1788–90." *Hispanic American Historical Review* 64, no. 3 (1984): 477–501.

McCormack, Brian T. "Marriage, Ethnic Identity, and the Politics of Conversion in Álta California, 1769–1834." PhD diss., University of California, San Diego, 2000.

McDonald, Dedra Shawn. "Negotiated Conquests: Domestic Servants and Gender in the Spanish and Mexican Borderlands, 1598–1860." PhD diss., University of New Mexico, 2000.

McGarry, Daniel D. "Educational Methods of the Franciscans in Spanish California." *The Americas* 6 (1950): 335–58.

McLoughlin, William. "Native American Reactions to Christian Missions." In *The Cherokees and Christianity, 1794–1870: Essays on Acculturation and Cultural Persistence*, edited by Walter H. Conser Jr. Athens: University of Georgia Press, 1994.

Meighan, Clement W. "Indians and California Missions." *Southern California Quarterly* 69, no. 3 (1987): 187–201.

Menzies, Archibald. "Menzies' California Journal." *California Historical Society Quarterly* 2, no. 4 (1924): 265–340.

Metz, René. *La consécration des vierges dans l'église romaine*. Étude d'histoire de la liturgie. Paris: Presses Universitaires de France, 1954.

Mignolo, Walter D. *The Darker Side of the Renaissance: Literacy, Territoriality, and Colonization*. Ann Arbor: University of Michigan Press, 1995.

Milliken, Randall. *A Time of Little Choice: The Disintegration of Tribal Culture in the San Francisco Bay Area, 1769–1810*. Ballena Press Anthropological Papers, no. 43. Menlo Park, CA: Ballena Press, 1995.

Mintz, Sidney and Eric R. Wolf. "An Analysis of Ritual Co-Parenthood (Compadrazgo)." *Southwestern Journal of Anthropology* 6, no. 4 (1950): 341–68.

Miranda, Gloria E. "Racial and Cultural Dimensions of *Gente de Razón* Status in Spanish and Mexican California." *Southern California Quarterly* 70, no. 3 (1988): 265–78.

Mission Dolores. *Manuscripts at Mission Dolores*. Vol. 1, *Libro de Cuentas, Libro de Ordenes*. CD-ROM. Mission Dolores, 2003.

Mitchell, Simon. *The Patterning of Compadrazgo Ties in Latin America*. Institute of Latin American Studies Occasional Papers, no. 24. Glasgow: University of Glasgow, 1978.

Montenegro, Alonso de la Peña. *Itinerario para párrocos de indios*. Edited by C. Baciero, M. Corrales, J. M. García Añoveros, and F. Maseda. 2 vols. Madrid: Consejo Superior de Investigaciones Científicas, 1995.

Mörner, Magnus. "The Spanish-American Hacienda: A Survey of Recent Research and Debate." *Hispanic American Historical Review* 53, no. 2 (1973): 183–216.

Moser, Christopher L., with Craig Bates and Eva Slater. *Native American Basketry of Central California*. Riverside, CA: Riverside Museum Press, 1986.

Mosk, Sanford A. "Subsidized Hemp Production in Spanish California." *Agricultural History* 13, no. 4 (1939): 171–75.

Mullett, Michael A. "Catholic and Quaker Attitudes to Work, Rest, and Play in Seventeenth- and Eighteenth-Century England." In *The Use and Abuse of Time in Christian History*, edited by R. N. Swanson. Suffolk, UK: Boydell Press for the Ecclesiastical History Society, 2002.

Neuerburg, Norman. *The Decoration of the California Missions*. Santa Barbara, CA: Bellerophon Books, 1987.

———. "The Function of Prints in the California Missions." *Southern California Quarterly* 67, no. 3 (1985): 263–80.

———. "Indian Pictographs at Mission San Juan Capistrano." *The Masterkey for Indian Lore and History* 56, no. 2 (1982): 55–58.

———. "The Indian Via Crucis from Mission San Fernando: An Historical Exposition." In *Mission San Fernando, Rey de España, 1797–1997: A Bicentennial Tribute*, edited by Doyce B. Nunis Jr. Los Angeles: Historical Society of Southern California, 1997.

———. "Indians as Artists in California Before and After Contact with the Europeans." In Vol. 2 of *Congrés Internacional D'Estudis Històrics "Les Illes Balears I Amèrica,"* edited by Román Piña Homs. Palma, Mallorca: Institut D'Estudis Baleàrics, 1992.

———. *Saints of the California Missions*. Santa Barbara, CA: Bellerophon Books, 2001.

Newcomb, Rexford. *The Franciscan Mission Architecture of Alta California*. New York: Dover Publications, 1973.

———. *The Old Mission Churches and Historic Houses of California: Their History, Architecture, Art and Lore*. Philadelphia: J. B. Lippincott, 1925.

———. *Spanish-Colonial Architecture in the United States*. New York: J. J. Augustin, 1937.

Newell, Quincy D. "Indian Marriage in the California Missions: An Ethnohistorical Study of Missions San Francisco, Santa Clara, and San José." Master's thesis, University of North Carolina at Chapel Hill, 2001.

———. "Transforming Mission: Catholic Rites of Passage and Changing Family Structures among Central California Indians at Mission San Francisco de Asís, 1776–1821." PhD diss., University of North Carolina at Chapel Hill, 2004.

Noel, Charles C. "Missionary Preachers in Spain." *American Historical Review* 90, no. 4 (1985): 866–92.

Nolan, James L. "Anglo-American Myopia and California Mission Art." Pts. 1–3. *Southern California Quarterly* 58, no. 1 (Spring 1976): 1–44; no. 2 (Summer 1976): 143–204; no. 3 (Fall 1976): 261–332.

Norton, Jack. "Songs of Continuance: Rhythm, Ritual and Ceremony in Native Northwestern California." In *Proceedings of the Ninth International Conference on the Study of Shamanism and Alternate Modes of Healing*. Berkeley, CA: Independent Scholars, 1992.

Nunis, Doyce B. Jr., and Edward D. Castillo. "California Mission Indians: Two Perspectives." *California History* 70, no. 2 (1991): 206–15, 236–38.

Nutini, Hugo G. *Ritual Kinship: Ideological and Structural Integration of the Compadrazgo System in Rural Tlaxcala*. Vol. 2. Princeton, NJ: Princeton University Press, 1984.

Nutini, Hugo G., and Betty Bell. *Ritual Kinship: The Structure and Historical Development of the Compadrazgo System in Rural Tlaxcala*. Vol. 1. Princeton, NJ: Princeton University Press, 1980.

O'Keefe, Timothy J., ed. *Columbus, Confrontation, Christianity: The European-American Encounter Revisited*. N.p.: Forbes Mill Press, 1994.

Ordaz, Blas. "La última exploración española en América." *Revista de Indias* 18, no. 72 (1958): 227–41.

Ortega, Sergio, ed. *De la santidad a la perversión: O de porqué no se cumplía la ley de Dios en la sociedad novohispana*. Mexico City: Editorial Grijalbo, 1985.

Ortega Noriega, Sergio. "Un sueño totalitario y universalista: El discurso teológico de Santo Tomás de Aquino sobre el matrimonio, la familia y los compartamientos sexuales." In Seminario de Historia de las Mentalidades y Religión en México Colonial, *El placer de pecar y el afán de normar*, 13–78.

Pagden, Anthony. *The Fall of Natural Man: The American Indian and the Origins of Comparative Ethnology*. Cambridge: Cambridge University Press, 1982.

Palóu, Francisco. *Evangelista del Mar Pacifico: Fray Junípero Serra, padre y fundador de la Alta California*. 1787. Reprint, Madrid: Impresiones Gráficas, 1944.

———. *Junípero Serra y las misiones de California*. 1787. Reprint, Madrid: Historia 16, 1988.

———. *Noticias de la Nueva California*. San Francisco: Imprenta de Edouardo Bosqui y Cia., 1874.

———. "Palóu's Diary of the Expedition to San Francisco Bay, 1774," in Bolton, *Anza's California Expeditions*, vol. 2, *Opening a Land Route to California: Diaries of Anza, Díaz, Garcés, and Palóu*, 2:393–456.

———. *Palóu's Life of Fray Junípero Serra*. Translated and edited by Maynard J. Geiger. Washington, DC: Academy of American Franciscan History, 1955.

Parise, Frank, ed. *The Book of Calendars*. New York: Facts on File, 1982.

Parry, J. H. *The Cities of the Conquistadores*. Canning House Eighth Annual Lecture, 11 May 1961. N.p.: Hispanic and Luso-Brazilian Councils, 1961.

Patterson, Victoria D. "Evolving Gender Roles in Pomo Society." In *Women and Power in Native North America*, edited by Laura F. Klein and Lillian A. Ackerman. Norman: University of Oklahoma Press, 1995.

Peterson-del Mar, David. "Intermarriage and Agency: A Chinookan Case Study." *Ethnohistory* 42, no. 1 (1995): 1–30.

Phelan, John Leddy. *The Millennial Kingdom of the Franciscans in the New World*. 2nd ed. Berkeley: University of California Press, 1970.

Phillips, George Harwood. "The Alcaldes: Indian Leadership in the Spanish Missions of California." In *The Struggle for Political Autonomy: Papers and Comments from the Second Newberry Library Conference on Themes in American Indian History*. N.p.: Newberry Library, 1989.

———. "Indian Paintings from Mission San Fernando: An Historical Interpretation." *Journal of California Anthropology* 3 (1976): 96–114.

———. *Indians and Intruders in Central California, 1769–1849*. The Civilization of the American Indian Series, vol. 207. Norman: University of Oklahoma Press, 1993.

———. "Indians and the Breakdown of the Spanish Mission System in California." *Ethnohistory* 21, no. 4 (1974): 291–302.

———. "Indians in Los Angeles, 1781–1875: Economic Integration, Social Disintegration." *Pacific Historical Review* 49, no. 3 (1980): 427–51.

Pierce, Richard A., ed. *Rezanov Reconnoiters California, 1806: A New Translation of Rezanov's Letter, Parts of Lieutenant Khvostov's Log of the Ship* Juno, *and*

Dr. Georg von Langsdorff Observations. San Francisco: The Book Club of California, 1972.

Pike, Ruth. *Penal Servitude in Early Modern Spain*. Madison: University of Wisconsin Press, 1983.

Pilcher, Jeffrey M. *Food in World History*. Themes in World History, edited by Peter N. Stearns. New York: Routledge, 2006.

———. *¡Que vivan los tamales! Food and the Making of Mexican Identity*. Diálogos, edited by Lyman L. Johnson. Albuquerque: University of New Mexico Press, 1998.

Pilling, Arnold R. "Northwest California Indian Gender Classes: 'Those who could not marry,' 'Those men who have never been near a woman,' and 'Women who do men's things.'" *Society of Lesbian and Gay Anthropologists Newsletter* 14, no. 2 (May 1992): 15–23.

Polanich, Judith K. "Ramona's Baskets: Romance and Reality." *American Indian Culture and Research Journal* 21, no. 3 (1997): 145–62.

Powell, Philip Wayne. "Genesis of the Frontier Presidio in North America." *Western Historical Quarterly* 13, no. 2 (1982): 125–41.

Powers, Karen Vieira. "Conquering Discourses of 'Sexual Conquest': Of Women, Language, and *Mestizaje*." *Colonial Latin American Review* 11, no. 1 (2002): 7–32.

Preston, William. "Serpent in Eden: Dispersal of Foreign Diseases into Pre-Mission California." *Journal of California and Great Basin Anthropology* 18, no. 1 (1996): 2–37.

Priestley, Herbert Ingram, trans. *A Historical, Political, and Natural Description of California by Pedro Fages, Soldier of Spain, Dutifully Made for the Viceroy in the Year 1775*. Berkeley: University of California Press, 1937.

Pubols, Helen Louise. "The de la Guerra Family: Patriarchy and the Political Economy of California, 1800–1850." PhD diss., University of Wisconsin, Madison, 2000.

Rabell, Cecilia. "El patrón de nupcialidad en una parroquia rural novohispana. San Luis de la Paz, siglo XVIII." In *Memorias de la I Reunion Nacional sobre la investigación demográfica en México*. Mexico City: Consejo Nacional de Ciencia y Tecnología, 1978.

Radding, Cynthia. *Wandering Peoples: Colonialism, Ethnic Spaces, and Ecological Frontiers in Northwestern Mexico, 1700–1850*. Durham, NC: Duke University Press, 1997.

Rama, Angel. *The Lettered City*. Translated and edited by John Charles Chasteen. Durham, NC: Duke University Press, 1996.

Rawls, James J. *Indians of California: The Changing Image*. Norman: University of Oklahoma Press, 1984.

Reid, Hugo. *The Indians of Los Angeles County*. Los Angeles: Privately printed, 1926.

Resines, Luis, ed. *Catecismos de Astete y Ripalda*. Madrid: Biblioteca de Autores Cristianos, de la Editorial Católica, 1987.

Ricard, Robert. *The Spiritual Conquest of Mexico: An Essay on the Apostolate and the Evangelizing Methods of the Mendicant Orders in New Spain: 1523–1572*.

Translated by Lesley Byrd Simpson. Berkeley: University of California Press, 1966.

Rípodas Ardanaz, Daisy. *El matrimonio en Indias: Realidad social y regulación jurídica*. Buenos Aires: Fundación para la Educación, la Ciencia y la Cultura, 1977.

Robinson, Alfred. *Life in California during a Residence of Several Years in That Territory, Comprising a Description of the Country and the Missionary Establishments*. 1846. Reprint, New York: Da Capo Press, 1969.

Rojas, Mary Virginia. "She Bathes in a Sacred Place: Rites of Reciprocity, Power, and Prestige in Alta California." *Wicazo Sa Review* 18, no. 1 (Spring 2003): 129–56.

Romero, José Luis. *Latinoamérica: Las ciudades y las ideas*. 3rd ed. Mexico City: Siglo veintiuno editores, 1984.

Salvatore, Ricardo D. "Modes of Labor Control in Cattle-Ranching Economies: California, Southern Brazil, and Argentina, 1820–1860." *Journal of Economic History* 51, no. 2 (1991): 441–51.

Sánchez, Joseph P. *Spanish Bluecoats: The Catalonian Volunteers in Northwestern New Spain, 1767–1810*. Albuquerque: University of New Mexico Press, 1990.

Sandos, James A. "Christianization among the Chumash: An Ethnohistoric Perspective." *American Indian Quarterly* 15, no. 1 (1991): 65–89.

———. *Converting California: Indians and Franciscans in the Missions*. Western Americana Series. New Haven, CT: Yale University Press, 2004.

———. "Junípero Serra's Canonization and the Historical Record." *American Historical Review* 93, no. 5 (December 1988): 1253–69.

———. "Levantamiento! The 1824 Chumash Uprising Reconsidered." *Southern California Quarterly* 67, no. 2 (1985): 109–33.

San Francisco de Asís Mission. *Libros de Misión*. 6 vols. Berkeley: Library Photographic Service, University of California, 1980. Microfilm.

Sawyer, W. B. "Excavation Procedures." In Hoover and Costello, *Excavations at Mission San Antonio, 1976–1978*, 11–17.

Schmidt, Robert A., and Barbara L. Voss, eds. *Archaeologies of Sexuality*. New York: Routledge, 2000.

Schuetz, Mardith Keithly. "The Indians of the San Antonio Missions, 1718–1821." PhD diss., University of Texas at Austin, 1980.

Schwaller, John F., ed. *The Church in Colonial Latin America*. Jaguar Books on Latin America, no. 21. Wilmington, DE: Scholarly Resources, 2000

———, ed. *Francis in the Americas: Essays on the Franciscan Family in North and South America*. Berkeley, CA: Academy of American Franciscan History, 2005.

Scott, James C. *Domination and the Arts of Resistance: Hidden Transcripts*. New Haven, CT.: Yale University Press, 1990.

Seed, Patricia. *American Pentimento: The Invention of Indians and the Pursuit of Riches*. Minneapolis: University of Minnesota Press, 2001.

———. *To Love, Honor, and Obey in Colonial Mexico: Conflicts over Marriage Choice, 1574–1821*. Stanford, CA: Stanford University Press, 1988.

Seminario de Historia de las Mentalidades y Religión en México Colonial. *Familia y sexualidad en Nueva España: Memoria del primer simposio de historia de las mentalidades: "Familia, matrimonio y sexualidad en Nueva España."* Mexico City: Fondo de Cultura Económica, 1982.

———. *El placer de pecar y el afán de normar*. Mexico City: Editorial Joaquín Mortiz, 1988.

Serra, Junípero. *Writings of Junípero Serra*. 4 vols. Edited and translated by Antonine Tibesar. Publications of the Academy of American Franciscan History Documentary Series, vols. 4–7. Washington, DC: Academy of American Franciscan History, 1955–66.

Shanks, Ralph. *Indian Baskets of Central California: Art, Culture, and History; Native American Basketry from San Francisco Bay and Monterey Bay North to Mendocino and East to the Sierras*. Edited by Lisa Woo Shanks. Indian Baskets of California and Oregon Series, vol. 1. Novato, CA: Costaño Books in association with Miwok Archaeological Preserve of Marin, 2006.

Shipek, Florence. "California Indian Reactions to the Franciscans." *The Americas* 41, no. 4 (1985): 480–92.

———. *Delfina Cuero: Her Autobiography, an Account of Her Last Years and Her Ethnobotanic Contributions*. Ballena Press Anthropological Papers, edited by Sylvia Brakke Vane, no. 38. Menlo Park, CA: Ballena Press, 1991.

Shoup, Laurence H., and Randall T. Milliken. *Inigo of Rancho Posolmi: The Life and Times of a Mission Indian*. Ballena Press Anthropological Papers, no. 47. Novato, CA: Ballena Press, 1999.

Silliman, Stephen W. "Colonial Worlds, Indigenous Practices: The Archaeology of Labor on a Nineteenth-Century California Rancho." PhD diss., University of California, Berkeley, 2000.

———. *Lost Laborers in Colonial California: Native Americans and the Archaeology of Rancho Petaluma*. Tucson: University of Arizona Press, 2004.

Skowronek, Russell K. "Sifting the Evidence: Perceptions of Life at the Ohlone (Costanoan) Missions of Alta California." *Ethnohistory* 45, no. 4 (1998): 675–708.

Smith, Jonathan Z. *Map Is Not Territory*. Chicago: University of Chicago Press, 1993.

Smith, Raymond T., ed. *Kinship Ideology and Practice in Latin America*. Chapel Hill: University of North Carolina Press, 1984.

Spickard, James V. "Environmental Variation and the Plausibility of Religion: A California Indian Example." *Journal for the Scientific Study of Religion* 26, no. 3 (1987): 327–39.

Stern, Steve J. "Paradigms of Conquest: History, Historiography, and Politics." *Journal of Latin American Studies* 24, Quincentenary Supplement: The Colonial and Post Colonial Experience. Five Centuries of Spanish and Portuguese America (1992): 1–34.

———. *The Secret History of Gender: Women, Men, and Power in Late Colonial Mexico*. Chapel Hill: University of North Carolina Press, 1995.

Stodder, Ann Lucy W. *Mechanisms and Trends in the Decline of the Costanoan Indian Population of Central California*. Archives of California Prehistory, no. 4. Salinas, CA: Coyote Press, 1986.

Street, Richard Steven. *Beasts of the Field: A Narrative History of California Farmworkers, 1769–1913*. Stanford, CA: Stanford University Press, 2004.

Taylor, William. *Magistrates of the Sacred: Priests and Parishioners in 18th-Century Mexico*. Stanford, CA: Stanford University Press, 1996.

Teixeira, Lauren S. *The Costanoan/Ohlone Indians of the San Francisco and Monterey Bay Area: A Research Guide*. Ballena Press Anthropological Papers, no. 46. Menlo Park, CA: Ballena Press, 1997.

Thomas, David Hurst, ed. *Columbian Consequences*. Vol. 1, *Archaeological and Historical Perspectives on the Spanish Borderlands West*. Washington, DC: Smithsonian Institution Press, 1989.

———, ed. *Columbian Consequences*. Vol. 3, *The Spanish Borderlands in Pan-American Perspective*. Washington, DC: Smithsonian Institution Press, 1991.

Thomas, Keith. *Religion and the Decline of Magic*. New York: Scribner, 1971.

Thornton, Russell. "Population History of Native North Americans." In Haines and Steckel, *A Population History of North America*, 9–50.

Torre, Adela de la, and Beatríz M. Pesquera, eds. *Building with Our Hands: New Directions in Chicana Studies*. Berkeley: University of California Press, 1993.

Toscano, Alejandra Moreno. "Algunas características de la población urbana: Ciudad de México, siglos XVIII y XIX." In *Memorias de la I Reunion Nacional sobre la investigación demográfica en México*. Mexico City: Consejo Nacional de Ciencia y Tecnología, 1978.

Trexler, Richard C. *Sex and Conquest: Gendered Violence, Political Order, and the European Conquest of the Americas*. Cambridge: Polity Press, 1995.

Turner, Victor. *The Ritual Process: Structure and Anti-Structure*. New York: Aldine de Gruyter, 1995.

Twinam, Ann. "Honor, Sexuality, and Illegitimacy in Colonial Spanish America." In Lavrin, *Sexuality and Marriage in Colonial Latin America*, 118–55.

Ubelaker, Douglas H. "Patterns of Disease in Early North American Populations." In Haines and Steckel, *A Population History of North America*, 51–97.

U.S. Naval Observatory Astronomical Applications Department. "Complete Sun and Moon Data for One Day," http://aa.usno.navy.mil/data/docs/RS_OneDay.php (accessed June 2006).

Vancouver, George. *A Voyage of Discovery to the North Pacific Ocean and Round the World, 1791–1795*. Edited by W. Kaye Lamb. 4 vols. Works Issued by the Hakluyt Society, Second Series, nos. 163–66. London: The Hakluyt Society, 1984.

Van Deusen, Nancy E. *Between the Sacred and the Worldly: The Institutional and Cultural Practice of Recogimiento in Colonial Lima*. Stanford, CA: Stanford University Press, 2001.

Van Dijk, Willibrord-Christian. "The Franciscan Spirit Through the Ages." Translated by Michael D. Meilach. In *Gospel Living: Francis of Assisi, Yesterday and Today*, by Anton Rotzetter, Willibrord-Christian Van Dijk, and Thaddée Matura. Franciscan Pathways. St. Bonaventure, NY: The Franciscan Institute, St. Bonaventure University, 1994.

Vecsey, Christopher. *On the Padres' Trail*. Notre Dame: University of Notre Dame Press, 1996.

Voght, Martha. "Shamans and Padres: The Religion of the Southern California Mission Indians." *Pacific Historical Review* 36, no. 4 (Nov. 1967): 363–73; reprinted in *Religions and Missionaries around the Pacific, 1500–1900*, edited by Tanya Storch. The Pacific World: Lands, Peoples, and History of the Pacific, 1500–1900, vol. 17. Burlington, VT: Ashgate Publishing, 2006.

Voss, Barbara Lois. "The Archaeology of El Presidio de San Francisco: Culture Contact, Gender, and Ethnicity in a Spanish-Colonial Military Community." PhD diss., University of California, Berkeley, 2002.

———. *The Archaeology of Ethnogenesis: Race and Sexuality in Colonial San Francisco*. Berkeley: University of California Press, 2008.

Wagner, Henry R. "The Last Spanish Exploration of the Northwest Coast and the Attempt to Colonize Bodega Bay." *Quarterly of the California Historical Society* 10, no. 4 (1931): 313–45.

Wallace, Edith. "Sexual Status and Role Differences." In Heizer, *California*, 683–89.

Wallace, William J. "Southern Valley Yokuts." In Heizer, *California*, 448–61.

Warner, W. Lloyd. *The Living and the Dead: A Study of the Symbolic Life of Americans*. Westport, CT: Greenwood Press, 1959.

Webb, Edith Buckland. *Indian Life at the Old Missions*. 1952. Reprint, with a foreword by Norman Neuerburg, Lincoln: University of Nebraska Press, 1982.

Weber, David J. *The Spanish Frontier in North America*. Western Americana Series. New Haven, CT: Yale University Press, 1992.

———, ed. *New Spain's Far Northern Frontier: Essays on Spain in the American West, 1540–1821*. Albuquerque: University of New Mexico Press, 1979.

Weber, Francis J. *A History of San Buenaventura Mission*. Hong Kong: Libra Press, 1977.

———. *Mission Dolores: A Documentary History of San Francisco Mission*. Hong Kong: Libra Press, 1979.

Williams, E. L. "Narrative of a Mission Indian, etc." In Harrison, *History of Santa Cruz County*, 45–48.

Williams, Walter L. *The Spirit and the Flesh: Sexual Diversity in American Indian Culture*. Boston: Beacon Press, 1986.

Wilson, Tamar Diana. "Reciprocity Networks in Anthropological Research." *Anthropology UCLA* 19, no. 1 (1992): 83–96.

Wolf, Eric R. *Europe and the People Without History*. Berkeley: University of California Press, 1982.

INDEX

Page numbers in boldface indicate maps, figures, and illustrations.

Abella, Ramón: on death and mourning among San Francisco Bay Area Indians, 155, 160, 164, 165, 168; on healing practices among San Francisco Bay Area Indians, 166; on Indians' labor at Mission San Francisco de Asís, 51, 71; on marriage and divorce among San Francisco Bay Area Indians, 103–4, 106, 116, 120; paternalistic attitude toward San Francisco Bay Area Indians, 73, 92–93; on San Francisco Bay Area Indians' religious beliefs, 25, 94; on San Francisco Bay Area Indians' traditional ways of measuring time, 30; on the traditional distribution of game by San Francisco Indians, 57; on training baptized Indians in European music, 45–46
Acchim (Silveria), bapt. 0995, 172–73, **174–75**
Acsim (María Petra), bapt. 0267, 122, **178–79**, 182, 183, 184, 219–20nn47–48
Alajuta (Guillermo), bapt. 0485, 2, 137–39, **138**
Ala'la (Gil), bapt. 0830, **140–41**, **178–79**, 228n27
Alalile (Gudelio), bapt. 3695, 208n116
Allen, Rebecca, 55, 61

almudes, 210n139
Amador, José Maria, 92
Ambro, Richard, 56, 155
Ambrosio Tomas, bapt. 2029, **84–85**
Amoros, Juan, 80
Amtim (Protasia), bapt. 0992, **178–79**, 183
Aniceto, bapt. 0518, 163, 225n36
Antonino, bapt. 0949, 172, 226n63
Arguello, Concepción, 112–13
Arguello, José, 65, 78
Arguello, Luis, 66, 112–13
Aristotle, on human hierarchy, 118
Arpin (Clara), bapt. 0016, 143–44, 222n35
Arriquibar, Nicolas de, 52
Asisara, Lorenzo, 91–92
Asúlis (Juan Regis), bapt. 0610, 102, 108, 215n65
Attiom (Candida), bapt. 0515, 1–2, **84–85**, 87–89, 101, 108
Aublonte (Natalia Maria), bapt. 0569, 172–73, **174–75**
Au-luté (Beatriz), bapt. 0288: death of, 37; family of, **22–23**, 27, 100, **140–41**, 197n23; marriage of, 21, 26, 105

Baltasara, bapt. 2128, 143
baptism: ceremonial procedure, 126–27; as a means of building alliances, 83, 129, 136, 185, 187–88;

as a means of divorce, 107, 187; at Mission San Francisco de Asís, 2, 4, 21, 33, 41, 42, 44; at San Pedro y San Pablo, 170, 183; as spectacle, 125–26; as a transition to Catholicism, 125; as a way of gaining access to marriage partners, 107; as a way of gaining spiritual power, 181

Bascam (Paulina), bapt. 0994, 172–73, **174–75**

Bay Miwok speakers. *See* linguistic groups of the San Francisco Bay Area

Beechey, Frederick, 24–25

bells, 28–30, 198n38

Bernardo, bapt. 3414, 146

birth: outside Mission San Francisco de Asís, 151–53, 161–62; San Francisco Bay Area Indian rituals surrounding, 162

Bolton, Herbert, 5, 74

Bonifacia, bapt. 1763, 146, 223n53

Borica, Diego de, 65

Boscana, Gerónimo, 165

Bourdaloue, Louis, 51

Bouvier, Virginia Marie, 92, 93

Branciforte, Marqués of, 77

Braulia, bapt. 0766, 104, 216n78

Bucareli y Ursúa, Antonio María, 95

Buenun (Dona), bapt. 1603, 137, 222n33

building construction: combination of San Francisco Bay Area and Hispanic aesthetics and techniques, 61; Hispanic aesthetics and techniques, 60–61; at Mission San Francisco de Asís, 26–27, 34, 40, 59, 60, 98, 182, 196n20, 205n60; at San Pedro y San Pablo, 170, 172, 226n61; traditional California Indian aesthetics and techniques, 27, 59–60

burial. *See under* death

Burkhart, Louise, 26

Cabachuliva (Elzeario), bapt. 2053, 161, 225n30

Caguampais (Pablo), bapt. 3735, 208n116

Cambón, Pedro Benito: on agricultural production at Mission San Francisco de Asís, 170; cofounder of Mission San Francisco de Asís, 7; experience as a priest, 21–24; on Indian labor at Mission San Francisco de Asís, 59, 65; records the death of a child outside Mission San Francisco de Asís, 168; reports on Mission San Francisco de Asís, 29–30, 50; on San Francisco Bay Area Indians' marriages, 1, 110

Canicaymo Indians, 136–37

Canoe (Patricio), bapt. 0371, 163, 225n36

Carillo, Raymundo, 76–77, 79

Carlos III (Spanish king), 111

Castañeda, Antonia, 96, 114

Castaño, Bartolomé, 24, 52, 195n6

Castillo, Edward, 33

catechism lessons and books, 24, 38, 52, 195n6, 200n60

Catholic doctrine: teaching of, 21–24, 46; translation of, 25–26

Cauanuse (Domiciano), bapt. 1817, 201n85

Cecilia, bapt. 0177, **84–85**

Chalamonese (Cirila), bapt. 4869, 155–56, 224n15

Chalayemise (Bonifacia), bapt. 6277, **178–79**, 186, 228n24

Chalietti (Justino), bapt. 2493, 201n85

Chamacsse (Beato), bapt. 1195, **178–79**

Chamis (Francisco Moraga), bapt. 0007, 110, 125–27, 129, 133, **134–35**

Chamisso, Adelbert von, 24, 56, 166

Chasinte, 106, 216n86

Chigué (Felix Cantalicio), bapt. 0310, 122, 220n49

Chiguilete (Leoncio), bapt. 1135, 106

children: deaths of (*see under* death); living outside Mission San Francisco de Asís, 167–69

Chi-uéc (Norberto), bapt. 0037: family, **22–23, 140–41**; as godfather, 139, **140–41**, 184; life at Mission San Francisco de Asís, 27, 45; marriage of, 163

Choris, Louis, 46, 47

Clara, bapt. 2268, 103–4

clothing: for baptized Indians at Mission San Francisco de Asís, 28, **29**, 66; Franciscans,' 16, 32, 39, 200n63; San Francisco Bay Area Indians' traditional, 66, 158; as status marker, 46, 158, 160

Cochapuque (Silvestre), bapt. 4599, 206n84

Cocos (Alvino José), bapt. 4740, 201n85

Colla (Telesfora), bapt. 2504, 155–56, 224n15

Collamis (Augusta), bapt. 3483, 155–56, 224n15

colonialism: colonizers' power to name and narrate, 14, 194n52; dependence on Indian labor, 50–51, 64, 72, 74, 81; economic aspects, 73, 81; effects on California Indians, 186, 192n13; success, 186

Columba, bapt. 1379, 172–73, **174–75**

communion. *See* eucharist

compadrinazgo: definition of, 126; Franciscans' perspectives on, 18, 130, 132, 137, 144–47; Hispanic colonists' perspectives on, 18, 144–45, 148; neologism, 126, 220n4; San Francisco Bay Area Indians' perspectives on, 18–19, 129, 130–44, 148–49; social functions of, 18–19, 125–27, 128–29, 136, 142, 143, 148, 184–85

confession, 163–65, 181, 196n16

coparenting, 126, 128, 129, 139. *See also* compadrinazgo

Costanoan speakers: in contemporary California, 193n33; "Costanoan" versus "Ohlone," 14, 194n47; social organization of, 83, 86, 106, 118. *See also* linguistic groups of the San Francisco Bay Area

Costansó, Miguel, 72

Coynis (Andrés), bapt. 0051, 163, 225n36

Crisanto, bapt. 1875, **22–23**

Crispin, bapt. 0429, **134–35**

Cruz, José de la, 27, 60

Culeli (Juana Valesia), bapt. 5026, 122, 220n50

Cullniq (Juan Capistrano), bapt. 0045, 67

death: burial in Franciscan habit, 19, 157–60; burial at San Pedro y San Pablo, 170; outside Mission San Francisco de Asís, 2, 151–52, 162–65, 168–69, 180; of San Francisco Bay Area Indian children, 166, 168–69; traditional Hispanic practices surrounding, 155; traditional San Francisco Bay Area Indian practices surrounding, 2, 87, 154–55, 163, 167, 168, 180

Dimas, bapt. 1172, **84–85**

Dionisia, bapt. 0103, **22–23**

divorce: in Catholic thought, 89, 111; occasioned by baptism of one partner, 107, 187; among San Francisco Bay Area Indians, 106, 116

Double Mistaken Identity, 62, 119, 124

economic activity in Alta California, 74–76, 81. *See also* labor

Eimute (Maria Francisca), bapt. 2331, **178–79**

Ela (Adriana), bapt. 2808, 155–56, 224n15

Elena, bapt. 2459, 161

Elzeario, bapt. 1762, 146, 223n53

Emptil (Sebastian), bapt. 0019, 122, 220n50
Epsom (Gregoria), bapt. 1042, **138**
Erajuimin (Geronima), bapt. 0372, 163, 225n36
Esiquesl (Claudia), bapt. 4067, 155–56, 224n15
Esupame (Formeria), bapt. 3080, 87
Etmén (Quarta), bapt. 0919, 142, 222n43
eucharist, 39–40
Europeans, religious beliefs and practices of, 181
Eyumaen (Aurea), bapt. 2382, 155–56, 224n15
Eyume (Erasma), bapt. 3067, 87

Fages, Pedro, 49, 68, 75–76, 78
families. *See* kinship
family reconstitution, 3–5, 192n9
fanegas, 204n39
Faustina, bapt. 1932, **174–75**
Ferenbe (Aquilino), bapt. 1113, 106, **178–79**
food: combination of Hispanic and San Francisco Bay Area Indian foodways, 54–56, 58, 64, 81, 182; in economic exchanges, 74, 75, 77; gathering, by San Francisco Bay Area Indians, 11, 44, 58, 88, 95, 183; at Mission San Francisco de Asís, 40, 53, 54, 57, 74, 95, 100; nutritional value, 54–55, 203n27; preparation techniques, 54–56; San Francisco Bay Area Indians' traditional diet, 10, 54, 55, 56–58, 88, 92–93, 169; spiritual aspects of, 38, 55–57, 153–54, 162, 181
Franciscans: legal guardians of California Indians, 94–95; and local languages, 3, 24–25, 46, 195n14, 196n16; and Marianism, 6, 43; and millennialism, 6; missionaries' biographical details, 193n23, 195n5; and missions, 5, 9, 16, 25, 182; paternalism of, 37, 73, 83, 92–95, 102, 182, 183, 184; relations with Spanish military, 95–96, 98, 182, 215n52; restrict traditional San Francisco Bay Area customs, 103–4, 107–8, 124, 153, 154–55, 163–64, 180, 183–84; sexual activity in California, 91–92; Third Order Secular, 157–58, **159**; views of California Indians, 2–3, 6, 37, 118, 40, 181, 182, 187; views of Hispanic colonists, 5–6. *See also individual Franciscans' names*
Francisco de Borja, bapt. 0187, 163, 225n36
Francisco de las Llagas, bapt. 0241, **22–23**
Froylan, bapt. 0386, 157–60
Fructuosa, bapt. 2304, 155–56, 224n15
Fructuoso, bapt. 0605, **134–35**

Galindo, José, 80
Galindo, María Guadalupe, 79
gambling, **29**, 48, 88
García, Diego, 27, 50, 59, 65
Geél (Agaton), bapt. 0846, 157–60
Geiumbliba (Prisca), bapt. 0620, **138**
Gemery, Henry A., 167
gender: balance, among Hispanic colonists in Alta California, 121, 185; balance, at Mission San Francisco de Asís, 198n40, 199n49; hierarchy, at Mission San Francisco de Asís, 43–44, 187; roles, among California Indians, 33, 88, 206n69; roles, among Hispanic colonists, 43–44, 66, 90, 96–98, 213n23; roles, among San Francisco Bay Area Indians, 33, 43–44, 46, 55–56, 62, 66, 87–89, 99, 153, 156, 201n84; roles, at Mission San Francisco de Asís, 28, 31, 33, 43–44, 46, 47–48, 54, 55–56, 66, 198n40; roles, in Alta California mission system, 199n48;

third gender, 118; treatment of women and men at Mission San Francisco de Asís, 26–27, 43–44, 45–46, 47–48, 98–100, 105, 108, 180, 215n56

gente de razón. *See* race

Geronima, bapt. 2069, 4, 192n10

Gervasio, bapt. 0781, **134–35**

Geyumaie (Ricarda), bapt. 4450, 155–56, 224n15

Gifford, Edward, 123

Gilac (Hipolito), bapt. 4439, 201n85

Gil y Taboada, Luis, 91–92

Gimas (Patavio), bapt. 1233: death of, 180, 181; family of, **140–41**, **178–79**, 184, 188; and Mission San Francisco de Asís, 181, 182, 184, 186

Gipoe (Humiliana), bapt. 5326, 155–56, 224n15

godparenting: godparental relationship, 18, 126, 128; history of, 127–28; selection of godparents, 130, 133, 136–39, 143, 145–47, 148–49. *See also* compadrinazgo

Grijalva, Juan Pablo, 126–27

Gualamuc (Eladio), bapt. 4215, 50

Guallec (Onesima), bapt. 4159, 2, 151

Gualson (Salvia), bapt. 1280, 106, 216n86

Guanúte (Micaela), bapt. 0253, **84–85**

Guasnete (Servanda), bapt. 0647, 83, **84–85**, 86–87

Guatcayla' (Magina), bapt. 0997, 172–73, **174–75**

Guatnaxsé (Bruno), bapt. 0030, 122, 220n50

Guattir (Ortensio), bapt. 0532, **138**, 206n84

Guecmaie (Troyana), bapt. 1729, 143, 222n44

Guecusia (Timoteo), bapt. 1159, 70–71

Guequecse (Hermenegildo), bapt. 4246, 168–69

Gueyame (Silvana), bapt. 4452, 155–56, 224n15

Guillelmina, bapt. 0759, **84–85**

Guillermo, bapt. 2417, 137–39, **138**, 222n34

Guippoy (Segismundo), bapt. 0580, 227n21

Guisaché (Fernando), bapt. 0317, **134–35**

Guonis (Sinforosa), bapt. 1156, 2, 137–39, **138**

Hackel, Steven W., 68–69, 192n9

headmen: families of, **84–85**, 172–73, 177, **174–75**, **178–79**, 181, 184, 188–89; as godfathers, 131–32; office of, 44, 88, 181; political strategies of, 82–83, 172–73, 181, 184, 185–86; privileges of, 57, 86, 118; responsibilities of, 95, 145; status of, 4, 137, 139, 158; treatment in California missions, 43, 69, 70, 187

healing practices, 12, 166–67, 180

Heizer, Robert, 54

Heytém (Otilia), bapt. 0530, 44

Hispanic colonists: ancestry of, 9; "Hispanic" versus "Spanish," 9; history of, 15; intermarriage with native Californians (*see under* intermarriage); kinship system (*see under* kinship); and labor, 73, 77–78, 79–81; relations with Mission San Francisco de Asís, 30–31, 95; religious beliefs and practices, 38, 112–14, 155; views of San Francisco Bay Area Indians, 14, 15, 42, 96–98, 121, 122, 186–87

homosexuality. *See* gender: third gender

honor-shame complex, 89–91; in colonist-Indian relations, 96–98; at Mission San Francisco de Asís, 98; priests' role, 91, 98. *See also* gender

horses, Indians riding, 49–50, 71

Huequés (María de los Remedios), bapt. 0454, **22–23**, 41–42

Huetlícs (Luis Ramón), bapt. 0031: alcalde, 70, 132–33, 158–60, 207n103; family of, 100, 133, **134–35**; as godfather, 132–33, 221n24

Huihmate (Atanasia), bapt. 1810, 4, 192n10

Huitanac (Viridiana), bapt. 0366, 157–60

Huitpote (Petronila), bapt. 0313, 4, 133, **134–35**

Huiubnu (Ciro), bapt. 1694, 206n84

Huiumutaca (Elena), bapt. 2058, 161, 225n30

Huniacsse (Demetrio), bapt. 1808, 4, 192n10

Huyunjaquisto (Pedro Crisólogo), bapt. 3778, 103, 216n73

Indian officials: alcaldes, 16, 67–71, 134–35, 158, 160, 207n93, 207–8nn100–104; characteristics of, 68–70; fiscales, 67; and godparenting, 132–33; relations with lower status Indians, 43, 45, 70–71; selection of, 67–68

Indians of California: historical sources, 15; legal status, 9, 94; population, 10; relations with Hispanic colonists, 10, 42; religious beliefs and practices, 11–12, 32–33; social organization, 10–11, 83, 216n85; time, measurement of, 198n37. *See also* Indians of the San Francisco Bay Area; linguistic groups of the San Francisco Bay Area; *names of individual tribal communities and villages*

Indians of North America, religious beliefs and practices, 181

Indians of the San Francisco Bay Area: arts and crafts of, 34, **35**, **36**, 62, **63**, **64**, 88; conflicts between, 109–10, 217n1; education of children, 92–93; kinship system of (*see under* kinship); recruitment of, 7, 125–26, 214n42; religious beliefs and practices of, 25, 38, 47, 62, 93–94, 99, 153, 162, 164, 180, 196n18; responses to missionization and colonization, 3, 5, 93–94, 182; social organization of, 26, 83, 216n85; views of Catholicism, 151–52, 157–58, 160, 161, 164–65, 166–67, 168–69, 173–76, 177, 180, 181, 187–88; views of Hispanic colonists, 185–86; villages and tribal communities, locations of, **171**. *See also* linguistic groups of the San Francisco Bay Area; *names of individual tribal communities and villages*

intermarriage: benefits to the missions, 121–22, 185; between Indians and Hispanic colonists, 18, 120–23, 185, 186, 208n104; among California Indians, 11; Franciscan encouragement of, 120, 124, 185; among San Francisco Bay Area Indians, 18, 82, **84–85**, 108, 110, 116, 119–20, 123, 124, 136, 163, 184, 185–86, 187; as a way of controlling soldiers' sexual activity, 121, 185

interpreters: characteristics of, 44, 45, 67, 201n85; employed at Mission San Francisco de Asís, 25, 26, 46, 196n16; as godfathers at Mission San Francisco de Asís, 131, 146–47

Jacinto, bapt. 0769, 67, 131, 146, 147

Jacome de la Marca, bapt. 1919, **84–85**

Jagssem (Yrene Maria), bapt. 0570, 172–73, **174–75**

Jaiguete (Sebastiana), bapt. 0745, 104

Jaitúm (Manuela), bapt. 0458, **84–85**

Jaluntis, 82, 83, **84–85**, 86–87, 102, 108

Jéquens (Lamberto), bapt. 0891, **140–41**, **178–79**, 228n27

Jobócate (Yndalecia), bapt. 2068, 4, 192n10

Jobocholá (Rafael), bapt. 4518, 131, 146, 147

Jochaliba (Brigida), bapt. 2048, 122, 220n50

Jojcóte (María Rosa Viterbo), bapt. 0061, 122, 219–20nn47–49

Jojuis (Jorge), bapt. 0298, 70, 207n102

Joluate (Nicolasa), bapt. 2426, 155–56, 224n15

Jo-ocsia (Crispo), bapt. 1538, 222n30

José Etonogenes, bapt. 0263, 163, 225n36

Jose Francisco, bapt. 1889, **134–35**

Jose Guido, bapt. 0260, **22–23**

Jose Manuel, bapt. 1361, **174–75**

Jotes (Fructuoso), bapt. 0742, 131, 221nn20–21

Joubocme (Pomponia), bapt. 2494, 155–56, 224n15

Joubonpo (Fernanda), bapt. 2558, 155–56, 224n15

Juan (alcalde at Mission San Francisco de Asís), 207n100

Juana Capistrano, bapt. 4774, **178–79**, 227n21

Juan, bapt. 0559, 143–44

Juan, bapt. 6462, **178–79**, 183

Juan de los Santos, bapt. 2750, 142, 222n43

Juliana Ynes, bapt. 1894, **140–41**, **178–79**, 227n21

Julio, bapt. 2795, 139–42, **140–41**, **178–79**, 227n21

Julio, bapt. 3059, **140–41**, **178–79**, 227n21

Jumle (Geronimo), bapt. 3506, 201n85

Juniqueme (Onesimo), bapt. 4158, 2, 151

Justo, bapt. 0768, 163, 225n36

Jutquis (Manuel Conde), bapt. 0093, **174–75**

Juuim (Restituta), bapt. 0535, 153, 162

Keqecég (Marcial), bapt. 0517: as father, 87–88, 212n14; lineage of, 83, **84–85**, 86–87, 102; marriages of, 1–2, 101–2, 212n1, 212n7; political activity, 82–83, 86–87, 102, 107–8, 187–88; status as headman, 86, 131, 217n2, 221n20

kinship: changing systems at Mission San Francisco de Asís, 1–2, 11, 17, 22, 83, 84, 95, 100–106, 107–8, 110, 118, 122, 124, 153, 180, 183–85, 187, 188–89; and child rearing, 167–69; and compadrinazgo, 18–19, 125–27, 128, 129, 130, 132, 137–44, **138**, **140–41**, 147, 149–50; deduced from mission registers, 3–4 (*see also* family reconstitution); Hispanic Catholic system, 17, 27, 89–91, 112–13; San Francisco Bay Area Indian systems, 18, 83–89, **84–85**, 100, 102–3, 106, 110, 116, 119, 123–24, 161–62, 172–73, **174–75**, **178–79**, 184–85, 188, 216n85; and status, 70, 82, 86, 122, 133, **134–35**. *See also* intermarriage; marriage; polygyny

Kotzebue, Otto von, 24, 46, 48

Kumi·vit Indians, 32–33

labor: by California Indians, for Euro-Americans, 7, 10, 74; by captives and convicts, 78; Catholic theology of, 51–52; and compadrinazgo, 144–45, 148; component of identity, 50, 66–67, 117; dependence of Mission San Francisco de Asís on, 16, 49–51, 53–54, 58, 59, 62–64, 74–75, 81, 182; Franciscan view of, 16, 52–53, 62–64; gender division, 44, 65–66, 87–89, 99; Hispanicizing effects on San Francisco Bay Area Indians, 16, 51, 53, 58, 62–64, 81, 182; hours, 30, 48, 65; Indian control of, 54, 58, 62–64, 81, 95, 182; by Indians at San Francisco Presidio, 16–17, 75–81; informal, 79; organization, 16, 46, 71, 73–74; and "Presidio Indians," 79–81; San Francisco Bay

Area Indians' traditional patterns of, 87–89, 100, 106, 108; skilled, 71–73; and Spanish policy, 52; system of, 73, 204n42, 208n118; by unbaptized Indians, 77–78
Lachi (Liborio), bapt. 0892, **140–41**, 178–79, 184, 228n27
Lachi (Pacifico), bapt. 1003, 172–73, **174–75**
Lalle (Constantina), bapt. 5655, 103
Landaeta, Martín de, 27, 46, 60–61, 72
Langenwalter, Paul E., 55
Langsdorff, Georg H. von: on Mission San Francisco de Asís, 98–99, 100, 166; on Nikolai Rezanov, 112–13; on San Francisco Bay Area Indians, **35**, 54, 99, 120, 121
La Pérouse, Jean-François de Galaup de, 48, 54, 60, 61–62, 65, 166
Lassímin (Emerenciana), bapt. 0457, **84–85**
Lasuén, Fermín Francisco de: on Indian labor in the Alta California missions, 49–50, 53, 71, 72, 75–76, 78; and the organization of Indian life in the Alta California missions, 61, 68, 98, 156; president of the Alta California mission system, 7
Lauion (Salomea), bapt. 1277, 216n86
Lilac (Alexos), bapt. 6049, 206n84
Liloté (Maria Francisca), bapt. 0012: baptism of, 4–5, 110; family of, 133, **134–35**; marriage of, 110, 116, 119–20, 124, 125, 126, 136
Linares, Ramón, 79–80
linguistic groups of the San Francisco Bay Area, 12, **13**; dominant linguistic groups at Mission San Francisco de Asís, 13–14, 137. *See also* Costanoan speakers
Liquiique (Manuel), bapt. 0321, 133, **134–35**
Litel (Leonardo), bapt. 4213, 66–67, 223n58

livestock, at Mission San Francisco de Asís, 50, 74, 95
Llucal (Magin), bapt. 1484, 70–71
Lobaya (Macedonia), bapt. 4221, 155–56, 224n15
Lockhart, James, 62, 73, 119
Lola (Ysidora), bapt. 3987, 155–56, 224n15
Lol-ló (Maria Loreta), bapt. 0032, **134–35**
Lolue'pig (Praxedis Nicolasa), bapt. 0705, 132
Lonsom (Maria Coloma), bapt. 0200, 100
Louete (Ramona), bapt. 4856, 168–69
Luis Maria, bapt. 1152, **134–35**
Luis Rafael, bapt. 1368, **134–35**
Lull, Miguel, 74
Lulumaen (Jacinta María), bapt. 3614, 155–56, 224n15
Lulume (Monica), bapt. 1111, 105

Macario, bapt. 1976, 2, 137–39, **138**
Magencia, bapt. 0940, 172, 226n63
Magin, bapt. 0943, **22–23**
Malany'eum (Micaelina), bapt. 1028, 2, 137–39, **138**, 222n35
Manuel, bapt. 3490, 143
Manuela, bapt. 0916, 172, 226n63
Manuel de la Resureccion, bapt. 5670, **178–79**
Manuel Encarnación, bapt. 5041, 142
Marcos (page at Mission San Francisco de Asís), 206n84
María Anastacia, bapt. 0090, 163, 225n36
Maria Antonia, bapt. 0979, 172–73, **174–75**
Maria Bernardina, bapt. 0239, **84–85**
María de la Asumpción, bapt. 0264, 163–64, 225n36
María del Carmen, bapt. 2076B, 142

María Egipciaca, bapt. 5827, 161–62
María Josefa, San Carlos Borromeo bapt. 2780, 156, 224n17
María Juana, bapt. 0955, 143, 144, 223n50
Marianism: in California, 32–33; and Franciscans, 6, 43
María Serafina, bapt. 0105, 219n47, 220n50
María Soledad, bapt. 0102, 120, 122, 125, 185, 219n47, 220n50
María Ysabel, San Buenaventura bapt. 0076, 158
marriage: of affinal kin, 102–3; of baptized Indians outside Mission San Francisco de Asís, 104–5; Catholic theology of, 110–11, 113–14; and compadrinazgo, 139–42; as diplomatic strategy, 82, **84–85**, 86, 108, 110, 112–13, 116, 119–20, 123, 124, 184, 185, 187, 188; Franciscans' control of, 17, 100–101, 102, 103–6, 107, 123–24, 183, 184; in Hispanic Catholic culture, 17, 89, 114–15, 218n17; Hispanic Catholic and San Francisco Bay Area Indian thought and practice compared, 17–18, 115–16, 118–19; as indication of status, 70, 86; and kinship relations, 83, 139, 184; and moiety system, 87, 123; partner selection, 84, 86–87, 89, 102, 111–12, 184; as practiced in the Alta California mission system, 1–2, 3–4, 21, **22–23**, 40, 44, 101, 103, 104–5, 106–7, 108, 118–19, 124, 188; and romantic love, 113–14; same-sex, in California Indian cultures, 117; in San Francisco Bay Area Indian culture, 17, 18, 83, 106, 116, 124, 184, 186, 188; at San Pedro y San Pablo, 170, 172–73, **174–75**, 176; and Spanish law, 111–12; witnesses, 69, 132, 136; for women at Mission San Francisco de Asís, 102, 106–7, 180, 181. *See also* divorce; intermarriage; polygyny

Mass: and marriage ceremonies, 115; music in, 45–46; as sacrifice, 38; San Francisco Bay Area Indians' experiences of, 16, 31, 33–34, 37–40, 48, 62, **64**, 180; and San Francisco Presidio residents, 30–31; at San Pedro y San Pablo, 170, 172, 173; and social status, 42–45, 46, 187; as spectacle, 16, 39–40, 48, 125–26, 147
Massea (Salvador de Horta), bapt. 0014, 50
Masuete (Arsenia), bapt. 3934, 142
Maura, bapt. 2155, 155–56, 224n15
Mayunucse (Sebastiana), bapt. 3068, 87
McKee, Larry W., 55
Menzies, Archibald, 27
Mepusio (Xista Margarita), bapt. 4147, 155–56, 224n15
Mequeig (Braulio), bapt. 0529, 44–45, 183, 227n16
Mermite (Josepha de Leonissa), bapt. 0268, 122, 220n50
Micaela, bapt. 2301, 139, **140–41**, **178–79**, 222n38, 227n21
millennialism, 6
Milliken, Randall, ix, 171, 188, 192n9
Mislem (Dominga), bapt. 0996, 172–73, **174–75**
Mission registers, 2, 3–5
Mission San Antonio de Padua, 55, 61
Mission San Buenaventura, 158
Mission San Carlos Borromeo: compadrinazgo at, 148; Indian labor at, 65, 66; Indian officials at, 68–70; persistence of traditional Indian practices at, 54, 58, 61, 154–55; women's lives at, 48, 156
Mission San Diego de Alcalá, 5, 68, 95–96, 97, 186
Mission San Fernando Rey de España, 42
Mission San Francisco de Asís: construction at (*see under* building construction); family structures at

INDEX 261

(*see under* kinship); founding, 6, 7, 83, 96; as frontier institution, 7, 74; known as Mission Dolores, 3; gender roles at (*see under* gender); and hide and tallow trade, 74–75; housing at, 26–27, 59, 100, 156–57, 180, 182, 183, 184; Indian clothing at (*see under* clothing); Indian labor at (*see under* labor); Indians' agency at, 3, 5, 20, 54, 58, 64, 152, 176, 188; languages spoken at, 24, 46, 196n16 (*see also* linguistic groups of the San Francisco Bay Area); layout, 17, 26–27, 40, 59–61, 98–99; location of, 7, **8**, **13**, **171**; marking of time at, 30; mortality of Indians at, 7–8, 19, 37, 154–55, 167, 169, 188; music at, 16, 45–46, 47, 48; population of, 8, 18, 31, 201n71 (*see also* gender: balance at Mission San Francisco de Asís); staffing of, 9, 21; social hierarchy at, 5, 16, 43–46, 66–67, 69–71; territory claimed by, 9. *See also* Mission San Francisco de Asís church

Mission San Francisco de Asís church: architecture of, 61–62, 198n41; construction of, 61–62; interior decoration and furnishings, 31–38, **36**, 39, 40, 41–42, 62, **64**, 180, 199n51, 199n54, 205n64, 206n69

Mission San Francisco Solano, 7, 72, 152

Mission San Gabriel Arcángel, 32

Mission San José, 65, 120, 121, 152

Mission San Juan Capistrano, 165

Mission San Luis Rey de Francia, 155

Mission San Miguel Arcángel, 158, **159**

Mission San Rafael Arcángel, 7, 72, 152

Mission Santa Barbara, 154

Mission Santa Clara, 65, 67–68, 75, 117, 118–19, 170

Mission Santa Cruz, 55, 61, 65, 67–68, 91

Mission Santa Inés, 7

Mission system (Alta California), 5–7, **8**, 9–10, 94, 193n21

Mochechi (Nazaria), bapt. 2620, 164–65

Modesto, bapt. 0551, **84–85**

moieties, 87, 122–23, 212n10

Molina, Alonso de, 126

Momósa (Jacome de la Marca), bapt. 0065, 119–20, 219n37

monjas, 19, 155–57, 187, 224n18

Mono (Ygnacio), bapt. 1472, 208n116

Monózse (Rogerio), bapt. 0350, 70, 143–44, 158–60, 207n102

Montenegro, Alonso de la Peña, 25, 126

Moquim (María Antonia), bapt. 1222, 122, 219n47

Moraga, José Joaquin, 126–27

Morante, Antonio de Padua, bapt. 0160, 143

Morante, Raymundo, 143, 184, 219n47

Motesipo (Fulgencia), bapt. 3348, 155–56, 224n15

Motúpa (Jacinta), bapt. 0356, **84–85**, 122, 220n50

Mutac (Timoteo), bapt. 0984, 172–73, **174–75**

Najam (María Elena), bapt. 0483, 83, **84–85**, 86–87

Narcisa, bapt. 2005, 137–39, **138**, 222n34

Natalia, bapt. 2171, 155–56, 224n15

Native Americans. *See* Indians of North America

Native Californians. *See* Indians of California

Nayomi (Ana Francisca), bapt. 0272, 21, **22–23**, 105–6, 187

Neuerburg, Norman, 62

Neve, Felipe de, 68

Ninfa Maria, bapt. 0719, **84–85**

Nopete (Deogracias), bapt. 0500, 57

Nopex-sé (Pio), bapt. 0346, 131, 221nn20–21
nuclear families. *See* kinship
Nuestra Señora la Reina de los Angeles (pueblo), **8**

Obmusa (Tiburcio), bapt. 1108, 155
Ochacagoita (Antonia Abad), bapt. 5555, 103, 216n71
Ochacuela (Ybona), bapt. 5625, 103, 216n71
Ohlone Indians, 14, 193n33
Olavú (Formerio), bapt. 3078, 87
Olela (Ligorio), bapt. 3270, 208n116
Oljon Indians, 14, 172–73
Oloyuig (Alexos), bapt. 0548, 168–69
Olvera, Diego: godfather, 130, 131, 133, 143, 145, 146, 147; marriage witness, 2
Omobala (Susana), bapt. 4099, 162
Otaya (Cirilo), bapt. 1450, 165
Otchacaminimac (Pascuala), bapt. 0487, 137–39, **138**, 160, 173–76, 177, 187
Oyumain (Cristiana Maria), bapt. 1933, 132

pages, 66–67, 206n84
Palóu, Francisco: and baptisms at Mission San Francisco de Asís, 4–5, 21, 125–27; biographical details, 6–7, 21–22; cofounder of Mission San Francisco de Asís, 7; encourages intermarriage between Hispanic colonists and California Indians, 121–22; on Indians of the San Francisco Bay upon the founding of Mission San Francisco de Asís, 96, 97, 109, 110; interim president of the Alta California mission system, 6, 7; on marriage and sexuality among California Indians, 103, 104, 117, 118, 218n27; paternalism toward California Indians, 92; records the death of Puyeles, 56; reports on Mission San Francisco de Asís, 26, 27, 28, 29–30, 33, 170
Pascual, bapt. 1854, 142
paseos: definition, 19, 101; for food gathering, 57–58; occasions of births and deaths, 151–52, 161–64, 166, 167, 176; an opportunity to continue polygynous marriages, 101; translation of, 101, 194n54
Passim (Maria Elena), bapt. 1008, 172–73, **174–75**
Patwin speakers. *See* linguistic groups of the San Francisco Bay Area
Paula Maria, bapt. 2305, **84–85**
Pedro Benito, bapt. 0702, 143, 144, 223n50
Pedro de Alcantara, bapt. 0553, 162, 225n34
Pedro Juan, bapt. 3397, 206n84
Peña, Tomás de la, 60
Petronila, bapt. 0932(B), 172, 226n63
Pilmo (José Antonio), bapt. 0008, 125–27, 129
Pío, San Buenaventura bapt. 0247, 158
Pismote (Ysabel María), bapt. 0292: baptism of, 21, 40; family of, **22–23**, 41, 44, 45, 105; life at Mission San Francisco de Asís, 21, 26–48, 98, 102, 198n41
Pispicse (Ysidro), bapt. 2400, 206n84
Pispís (Leon), bapt. 0472, **84–85**
Pispisooboj (Bonifacia), bapt. 3497, 167
Pispispuquel (Alejandra), bapt. 4094, 57
Pispistole (Juan Nepomuceno), bapt. 2135, 142
Plains Miwok speakers. *See* linguistic groups of the San Francisco Bay Area
Polehova (Yldefonso), bapt. 2201, 142, 222n42
polygyny: in California, 15, 86;

Catholic policy regarding, 89, 101, 117, 183; Franciscan views of, 118; by Hispanic Catholics, 89; mimicked by godparenthood, 137–39, 142, 143, 149–50; in San Francisco Bay Area, 1, 21, **22–23**, 101, 118, 122; and social status, 86, 118, 122, 139, 220n48; sororal, 22, **22–23**, 82, 83, 86, 103, 118. *See also* kinship; marriage

Pomo speakers. *See* linguistic groups of the San Francisco Bay Area

"Presidio Indians," 79–81, 182

presidios, **8**. *See also* San Francisco Presidio

protective ingratiation, 206n70

Punacche (Gervasio), bapt. 1149, 105

Puqueccoime (Basilides), bapt. 3477, 167

Puruem (María Ynes), bapt. 0077, 122, 143–44, 219n47

Putec (Rufino), bapt. 5551, 103, 216n71

Puyeles (Nicolas de Bari), bapt. 0287: baptism of, 21; death of, 56, 183; family of, **22–23**, 27, 37, 139, **140–41**, 197n23; marriages, 21, 26, 86, 100, 105; and Spanish language, 44, 46

Quéyeme (Rafaela Marcela), bapt. 0083, 100, 133, **134–35**

Quimas (Romualdo), bapt. 0365, 131, 221nn20–21

Quintas (Aparicio), bapt. 1196, **178–79**, 227n7

race, 9, 42–43, 187

Rafael Francisco, bapt. 0183, **134–35**

reales, 210n132

Real Pragmática. *See* marriage: and Spanish law

Regulo, bapt. 3401, 206n84

Remigio, bapt. 0698, **134–35**

Rezanov, Nikolai, 112–13

rituals, Catholic, as spectacle, 126

Rosalia, bapt. 0756, 172–73, **174–75**

Ruruesmain (Luisa), bapt. 0201, 122, 220n50

sacraments, 19, 164, 165, 170. *See also individual sacraments*; rituals, Catholic

sacristans, 28, 30, 44, 67, 146–47, 187

Saint Joseph, 34, 36–37, 41

Sainz de Lucio, Juan: and Indians' lives at Mission San Francisco de Asís, 2, 46, 51, 71, 155; paternalism toward Indians at Mission San Francisco de Asís, 73; on San Francisco Bay Area Indian cultures and languages, 24, 25, 30, 57, 106, 166

Sal, Hermenegildo, 67–68

Salazar, Isidro Alonso, 77–78, 80

Samisi (Adriano Conde), bapt. 0173, 83, **84–85**

Sancio, bapt. 0911, 172, 226n63

Sandos, James, 15

San Francisco Presidio: catechism used at, 200n60; founding, 7, 28–29; Indian labor at (*see under* labor); location of, **8**, **13**, **171**; marriage customs at, 114; and "Presidio Indians" (*see* "Presidio Indians"); relations with Mission San Francisco de Asís, 7, 30–31, 74–76, 148; skilled artisans at, 72

San José de Guadalupe (pueblo), **8**, 80–81, 114

Sanoas (Eleuterio), bapt. 0505, **84–85**

San Pedro y San Pablo (satellite mission), 41, 169–73, **171**, 183, 226n59, 226n61

Santiago, bapt. 2081, 139, **140–41**, **178–79**, 183

Santos, bapt. 1150, **84–85**

Sapache (Nicolas), bapt. 1176, 131, 221nn20–21

Sappím (Berengaria), bapt. 0646: marriage at Mission San Francisco de Asís, 102, 108; as mother, 87–88; senior wife of Keqecég (Marcial), bapt. 0517, 1–2, **84–85**, 101–2, 106; status in traditional San Francisco Bay Area Indian society, 88–89; as unmarried woman, 102

Saqueninispi (Petronila), bapt. 4805, 136

Saquenjeiun (Rogela), bapt. 4304, 165

Saquenjelapi (Tranquilina), bapt. 4846, 168–69

Sarría, Vicente Francisco de, 40, 156

Sauoyome (Paula Maria Belem), bapt. 0203, **84–85**

Scott, James, 15

Seed, Patricia, 112

Señán, José, 158

Se'pente (Priscella), bapt. 0550, 57

Serra, Junípero: advice on selecting Indian officials in missions, 68; asserts right to discipline baptized Indians, 95, 98; biography of, 6; canonization process for, 191n6; on devotion of Kumi·vit Indians to Mary, 32–33; first president of Alta California mission system, 6–7; on the Indians of Mission San Carlos Borromeo, 66, 148; on relations between Spanish soldiers and California Indians, 95–96

Servate (Yluminata), bapt. 0879, 122, 185, 220n50, 227n21

Seupi (Telma), bapt. 4990, 155–56, 224n15

Simmón (Gonzalo), bapt. 0534, 162

Sofía, bapt. 0531, **22–23**, 41, 44

Solá, Faustino de, 27

Solá, Pablo Vicente de, 80

soldiers, Spanish: ancestry, 9; and compadrinazgo, 18, 126–27, 129, 145–46, 147; Indian attempts to enlist, 72; intermarriage with California Indians (*see under* intermarriage); and labor, 50–51; relations with California Indians,

95–98, 117, 186; staff Mission San Francisco de Asís, 9, 37

Sotem (Fulgencia), bapt. 1250, **140–41**, **178–79**, 180–81, 182, 184, 188

spiritual kinship. *See* compadrinazgo

Ssagnemaien (Matea), bapt. 2498, 105

Ssalson Indians: baptisms of, 42, 82, 133–34; relations with Yelamu Indians, 109–10, 116, 119–20, 124, 133–34, 217n1. *See also* Indians of the San Francisco Bay Area

Ssapsam (Valentín), bapt. 1290, 206n84, 222n41

Ssatcón (Magna), bapt. 0938, 172

Ssaycugte (Maria Baptista), bapt. 0322, **134–35**

Ssiguám (Rosa de Viterbo), bapt. 0282, **134–35**

Ssiléna (Desiderio), bapt. 0828, **178–79**, 180, 227n19, 228n27

Ssinem, **178–79**, 183–84, 227n19

Ssojorois (Claudio), bapt. 0463, 70–71

Ssoyóte (Ana María), bapt. 0022, 122, 219–20nn47–48, 225n36

Ssuíle (Crisanto), bapt. 0315, **22–23**, 41, 44

Ssujan (Maria de la Trinidad), bapt. 1012, 172–73, **174–75**

Stern, Steve J., 97

Street, Richard, 65

Suiquim (Alexandra), bapt. 0761, 172–73, **174–75**

Suma (Melchora), bapt. 4533, 155–56, 224n15

Sumay (Amador), bapt. 2174, 105

Sumipocsé (Homobono), bapt. 0504, 70–71, 155

Sutay (Lugardo), bapt. 5632, 103

Tabasume (Narcisa), bapt. 4055, 155–56, 224n15

Tabasuse (Troyano), bapt. 1721, 143, 222n46

Tacalú (Juvenal), bapt. 0934, 172

Tacsinte (Valeriano), bapt. 0442, 70, 132

Tadeo, bapt. 0750, **84–85**

Talmucse (Bonifacio), bapt. 3496, 167

Tanam (María de los Remedios), bapt. 0082, 119–20

Tapius (Bernardino), bapt. 0181, **84–85**, 212n7, 212n14

Tapuissé (Diego), bapt. 0034, 71–72, 208n112, 208n116

Taque'te (Madrona), bapt. 0549, 168–69

Taulvo (Juan Bernardino), bapt. 0009, 125–27, 129

Taylor, William, 91, 92

Telempis (Reginaldo), bapt. 0528, 44–45

Teodorico, bapt. 0701, 168–69

Teopista Josefa, bapt. 0729, 142

Teute (Prima), bapt. 1622, 143, 222n48

Tiglis (Gerardo), bapt. 0507, **84–85**, 212n14

Tiguase (Teofilo), bapt. 1041, **138**

Tilicsse (Nicolas Factor), bapt. 1275, 216n86

Tocióm (Feliciana), bapt. 0311, 122, 220n49

Tocsem (Luparia), bapt. 0880, 122, 219n47

Tolecsse (Celso), bapt. 1434, 136–37, 222n30

Tolemele (Fernando), bapt. 4881, 164

Tolepa (Senen), bapt. 2788, 103–4

Toletli (Ana María), bapt. 3485, 155–56, 224n15

Tolomucse (Zacarias), bapt. 0962, 120

Toluete (Angela de Fulgino), bapt. 4870, 155–56, 224n15

Tomas, bapt. 1924, **84–85**

Tomas, bapt. 1975, **140–41, 178–79**, 227n21

Toróz (Nemesio), bapt. 0695, 132

Tossác, **134–35**

Toyleme (Delfina), bapt. 1573, 143, 222n46

Troyana, bapt. 2878, 143, 222n46

Tubssúpa (Geminiano), bapt. 0399, 104

Tuchím, **174–75**

Tuglum (Casimira), bapt. 1016, 57

Tujulalis (Aurelio), bapt. 0812, 79–81, 182

Uariucsé (Meliton), bapt. 0497, 163, 225n36

Ubiumis (Josefa María), bapt. 0063, 122, 130–31, 133, 143, 146–47, 219n47

Ugarte y Loyola, Jacobo, 49, 53, 78

Ugité (Celsa), bapt. 0837, 139–42, **140–41, 178–79**, 180–81, 184, 222n38

Uichase (Julio), bapt. 0883, 20, 139, **140–41**, 177–89, **178–79**, 228n27

Uilmoxsi (Pascual Baylon), bapt. 0027, 69, 132

Uilquis (Aduato), bapt. 0496, **22–23**

Uiumpi (Lugarda), bapt. 5643, 103

Ulium (María de la Cabeza), bapt. 0571, 172–73, **174–75**

Ulpite, **84–85**, 87–89, 212n7

Usscúltu (Cayetano), bapt. 0101, 122, 220n50

Uxsisté (Manuela María), bapt. 0055, 122, 219n47, 220n50

Uyum (Luisa Gonzaga), bapt. 3098, 155–56, 224n15

Uyumaye (Aparicia), bapt. 2910, 155–56, 224n15

Uyumsu (Peregrina Espiritu Santo), bapt. 4544, 155–56, 224n15

Vancouver, George, 28, 59–60, 65–66

varas, 196n20

Velez Escalante, Estevan, 74

Villa de Branciforte, **8**

Viñals, José, 72

Wappo Indians, **13**, 136. *See also* linguistic groups of the San Francisco Bay Area

Xilaite (Francisca Xaviera), bapt. 0095, 122, 219–20nn47–48, 220n50

Yapis (Raymundo), bapt. 0043, 105–6
Yaunisé (Marcelino), bapt. 0157, **134–35**
Ybon Adriano, bapt. 0236, **22–23**, **140–41**, 197n23
Yelamu Indians: control of Mission San Francisco de Asís's location, 186, 217n1; relations with Ssalson Indians (*see under* Ssalson Indians). *See also* Indians of the San Francisco Bay Area
Ygnacia Barbara, bapt. 0059: and compadrinazgo, 139–42, 184–85; family of, **22–23**, 139, **140–41**, 178–79, 183, 184; life at Mission San Francisco de Asís, 27, 45
Ygnacia Barbara, bapt. 3226, **140–41**, 178–79, 227–28n21
Yjon (Juana), bapt. 1009, 122, 172–73, **174–75**, 220n50, 226n64
Ynocencio, bapt. 4409, 2, 151
Yokuts speakers. *See* linguistic groups of the San Francisco Bay Area
Ysabel, bapt. 0280, **134–35**
Ysúu (Juan de los Santos), bapt. 0734, 131, 142, 221nn20–21, 222n43
Yuelusia (Macario), bapt. 4210, 206n84

Zecum (Lucilla), bapt. 1039, 155–56, 224n15

www.ingramcontent.com/pod-product-compliance
Lightning Source LLC
Chambersburg PA
CBHW021836220426
43663CB00005B/273